D0282506

DA

Folk Buddhist Religion

Harvard East Asian Series 83
The East Asian Research Center at Harvard University administers
research projects designed to further scholarly understanding of
China, Japan, Korea, Vietnam, Inner Asia, and adjacent areas.

Folk Buddhist Religion
Dissenting Sects in
Late Traditional China

Daniel L. Overmyer

Harvard University Press
Cambridge, Massachusetts, and London, England 1976

NORTH CENTRAL COLLEGE LIBRARY
NAPERVILLE, ILLINOIS 60540

Copyright © 1976 by the President and Fellows of Harvard College
All rights reserved
Preparation of this volume has been aided by a grant from the Ford
  Foundation.
Printed in the United States of America

Library of Congress Cataloging in Publication Data
Overmyer, Daniel L   1935-
    Folk Buddhist religion: dissenting sects in late traditional
    China.

    (Harvard East Asian series; 83)
    Bibliography: p.
    Includes index.
    1. Buddhism—China—History. 2. China—Religion—
History. I. Title. II. Series.
BQ628.09   1976   294.3'0951   75-23467
ISBN 0-674-30705-4

294.3
Ov2f

To Estella, Rebecca, and Mark

135503

Preface

In the fourth year of the [Yüan] Chih-yüan reign period
[1338] . . . Chou Tzu-wang, a disciple of the heretical monk
P'eng Ying-yü of Yüan-chou, rebelled [at the confluence of] the
yin year, month, day, and hour. The rebels had the character
fo (Buddha) written on their jackets, in the belief that this
would render them impervious to injury from weapons . . .
[Though Chou] had more than 5,000 followers, commandary
troops [soon] suppressed them, killing his sons, Born-of-
Heaven and Born-of-Earth, and his wife, Buddha-Mother.
[P'eng] Ying-yü himself fled [north] to Huai-hsi, where he hid
among the people. Ying-yü was originally from a village east
of the Compassionate Salvation monastery on Nan-ch'uan
mountain. In the monastery there was a monk named P'eng,
more than sixty years old, who was good at prognostication.
One night when it was snowing he saw a red light in the sky
about twenty li east of the monastery. The next day he ques-
tioned some village elders asking if there had been a fire during
the second watch, or if anything unusual had occurred. One of
the elders replied that the only thing that had happened
[during the night] was that his daughter-in-law had given birth

to a son. The monk joyously replied, "May he become my disciple?" and the elder consented . . .

The boy first entered the monastery when he was ten years old, and played happily with the other disciples. Before long [he began to tell fortunes] and his predictions of calamities or blessings all came true. When he was fifteen a spring suddenly appeared at the foot of the mountain, [the water of which] was very cold. Just at this time there was an epidemic among the people [of the area], and Ying-yü was able to heal all the sick with water from the spring. Because of this the people of Yüan-chou [began to] earnestly worship him as if he were a deity. [So it was] that when the rebellion was defeated, and he fled to Huai-hsi, his reputation had gone before him, and the people were eager to provide him shelter. Even though the officials searched diligently, they were never able to catch him.[1]

This account introduces the lively and ambiguous world of Chinese folk Buddhist sects, some of which staged uprisings like that of Chou Tzu-wang and P'eng Ying-yü, while others remained peaceful. There have been several treatments of such groups from the perspective of social and political history, but a more thorough understanding of their religious beliefs and rituals is needed. The intent of this book is toward that understanding.

Ch'üan Heng's description of P'eng Ying-yü introduces as well possibilities and problems in the sources available for the study of such groups, for while Ch'üan admits 'hat P'eng was a charismatic figure, his primary concern is with th ·prising itself, not with details of organization and belief. W⹁ ⹁ few exceptions this was the tenor of all reports on dissenting ɔvements made by officials and scholars. Most of these groups had scriptures and ritual texts, but they were usually destroyed when found. There is voluminous material about overt rebellions, but those interested in sectarian religion must to some extent work like archeologists, as Li Shih-yü has so aptly said,[2] trying to understand isolated data in relation to context, time, and similar phenomena elsewhere. Thus, for example, a study of P'eng Ying-yü's group is furthered by an understanding of the use of charms and healing in Chinese Buddhism and Taoism, and by the knowledge that nodal points in the cyclical time system were seen as the opportunity for cosmic and social renewal, a theme which had been used by popular movements since the Yellow Turbans in 184. Though the sources are scattered, there is enough material to reveal patterns of structure and myth, patterns that show better how sectarian activity might have looked from the inside, from the perspective of convinced participants.

The passage concerning the 1338 uprising in Kiangsi also introduces difficulties of interpretation that haunt the student of such associations. It seems clear that many people in the area sincerely believed in P'eng Ying-yü because of his ability as a fortune teller and healer. But what of P'eng and Chou themselves? Were they really convinced that they had a divine calling to bring about a new order, or was this merely clever propaganda by which they wished to gain support for more selfish ends? Or was their motivation perhaps a combination of both? There have been many varieties of interpretation; my own perspective is that for purposes of a coherent discussion of the content and development of sectarian beliefs it is first necessary to take them seriously as such. To be sure, we will never be able to grasp the real inner motivation of each leader, but statements of belief can be taken as statements of authentic intention for at least some of the people involved, if one remains aware of the ambiguity of this task and of the need for more explicitly social and historical interpretations.

Though the high point of sectarian religious activity was in the last decades of the Ming dynasty (1368-1644), I have felt it necessary to seek out their origins in earlier periods, so that they can be seen in the context of the history of Chinese religions. I have also sought to develop the beginnings, cross-cultural perspective from the point of view of similar phenomena in Europe and Japan. All this should be understood as supplementary to my main task, which is a discussion of patterns of belief and ritual.

I should like to thank Joseph Kitagawa and Philip Kuhn of the University of Chicago for encouraging me to undertake this study, Tai Hsüan-chih, now of Nan-yang University in Singapore, for helping me locate important sources in Taiwan, Ts'ai Mao-t'ang of the Interuniversity Program for Chinese Language Studies in Taipei for at the beginning assisting me with translation, and Susan

Naquin of the University of Pennsylvania for reading my book manuscript and making several helpful suggestions.

I owe a debt as well to those whose work on Chinese popular sects and rebellions opened in my mind the whole possibility of attempting this study, particularly J. J. M. DeGroot, C. K. Yang, Richard Chu, Shigematsu Shunshō, Tsukamoto Zenryū and Suzuki Chūsei. I am also grateful to Shui Yim Tse, Asian Studies Librarian at the University of British Columbia, for in some cases helping me find publication information and uncatalogued sources, and to Oberlin College and the Harvard East Asian Research Center for providing funds to prepare the manuscript. The support and suggestions of Research Center staff were also most helpful. Of course, without the understanding and support of my wife, Estella, the task would have been much more difficult. I am grateful for her patience and that of my children, Rebecca and Mark, for whom this book has meant many a postponement of times together.

Contents

1 Introduction: Issues and Perspectives   1

2 A Case in Point: The Ch'ang-sheng chiao   7

3 History of Interpretation: Rebels, Evangelists, or Both?   12

4 Cross-Cultural Perspectives   53

5 An Outline History of the White Lotus Tradition   73

6 Other Groups: An Introduction to the White Cloud and
     Lo Sects   109

7 Patterns of Folk Buddhist Religion: Beliefs and Myths   130

8 Patterns of Folk Buddhist Religion: Leadership, Scriptures,
     Ritual   162

9 Concluding Observations   193

Notes   207

Bibliography   261

Glossary   281

Index   293

1
Introduction
Issues and Perspectives

Popular religious sects proclaiming deliverance for all who respond have appeared in many cultures. They have usually been characterized by leaders claiming divine authority who initiate vernacular preaching, simplified rituals and scriptures, and systems of congregational organization. The best known of these movements are the Pure Land Buddhist in thirteenth century Japan, the Lutheran in sixteenth century Europe, and *bhakti* sects in medieval Hinduism. Similar groups developed in traditional China.

While some scholars have long recognized the existence of popular religious sects in China, there has been a tendency to confuse them with other forms of voluntary association such as secret societies and sporadic popular uprisings. There is a need for more precise typology of Chinese popular associations, a typology sensitive not only to political function but also to internal history and intention. Within such a classification distinctions should also be made between different forms of religious movements, based on origin, teaching, and practice. An important aspect of a discussion of sect origins is their relationship to the "Great Traditions" and to nonsectarian folk religion.

In China, Taoism, Buddhism, and Manichaeism all developed popularized sects, each borrowing from the other and influenced by Confucianism and folk tradition. My concern is to discuss those movements which appear to be most strongly influenced by Mahā-

1

yāna Buddhism, particularly its emphasis on universal deliverance through compassionate bodhisattvas. This choice is a matter of personal interest and the need for delimitation, not a denial of other traditions or their influence. Buddhist oriented associations separate from monasteries first appeared in the Northern Wei kingdom in the early fifth century led by what the sources call "rebel monks." From then on there are repeated references to such groups down through Chinese history into the twentieth century. I will devote most attention to the more influential of these movements, the Maitreya, White Lotus, White Cloud, and Lo or Wu-wei.[1] In all this I will attempt to discuss these groups as a structure in Chinese religious history, a structure closely related to social and political context, but for those involved representing as well an alternative solution to the problem of salvation.

Other than coming to an understanding of what the sects themselves believed and did, perhaps the most important issues are their relationship to the orthodox Buddhist sangha and their repeated association of piety with militant political activity. Both issues are too complex to admit dogmatic resolution. Concerning relationships with the sangha it must be stated at the outset that the sects were lay based, heterodox, and radically syncretic. While the White Lotus evidently came out of an orthodox Pure Land background, within a short time it developed such innovations as married clergy, new texts, and hereditary leadership. Within 200 years it absorbed folk Taoist images and ritual implements. By 1351 sects related to this tradition had a full-blown eschatology derived from Maitreyan Buddhism and Manichaeism, while by the late sixteenth century their chief deity was a mother goddess. The White Cloud and Wu-wei religions retained more of the substance of their popular Buddhist beginnings, but by the late nineteenth century the Mahāyānist impetus of most of these movements seems to have largely played itself out, cut off from monastic intellectual life, overwhelmed by indigenous folk tradition. While many Buddhist elements remain, it would not be accurate to call the twentieth century I-kuan tao (Way of Pervading Unity) a folk Buddhist sect. It is simply congregational folk religion.

What of the earlier groups then? Why associate them with Buddhism more than Taoism or Manichaeism? Have not others asserted the contrary, or denied that Chinese Buddhism ever produced independent sects? Detailed responses to these questions are developed below; my suggestion is simply that at the levels of origins, scriptures, and belief structure some Chinese sectarian movements were preponderantly Buddhist, despite the obvious importance of elements derived from other traditions. Furthermore, the structure of universal salvation through devotion to merciful bodhisattvas was not indigenous to China, and where this structure forms the foundation of sectarian thought it seems legitimate to claim Buddhist influence. The same might be said for the concept of messianic figures who appear at the end of world cycles. That there were Chinese prefigurations and analogs of these patterns should not obscure their essentially Buddhist origin and intention.

Folk sect association of piety with militant political activity has led many scholars to maintain that sects were rebel movements using religion to justify political ambitions. Perhaps the most common interpretation of the sects sees them as popular reactions to intolerable situations brought about by such factors as high taxes, corrupt officials, or natural disasters. In such situations shrewd leaders could take advantage of despair by proclaiming the imminent arrival of a new age in which all could participate if only they would join the movement. The combination of despair and hope led to an aggressive impatience easily channeled into attacks on gentry and officials.

While such manipulation undoubtedly took place, an interpretation which sees sectarian religion as nothing more than an ideological cover for rebellion cannot account for the continued vitality of these movements in times of peace, nor for the many groups which never rebelled at all. This approach tends to read too much sociological theory back into a traditional folk context in which the leaders were just as likely to be "religious" as anyone else, and perhaps more so, because of cultural expectations of the charismatic role.

It is of course true that many of the sectarian movements were involved in violent uprisings with political overtones; in the Chinese context such a development was quite natural. The sects confronted a state which claimed to represent cosmic order and thus all realms of authority, political and religious. The imperial government was intended to provide a complete centralized system for every aspect of life and thought. As such it could not abide competing centers of authority. Hence all independent voluntary gatherings were theoretically suspect, from Confucian academies to temple fairs. In this context a privately established folk sect existed only by official sufferance or neglect and might expect that any overt move toward more religious independence could arouse state opposition.

But this is not the whole story. Some of the sects were just as cosmically imperialistic as the government. Convinced that the future Buddha was about to arrive, they proceeded to try to install their own leader as a new, pious emperor who would prepare for the messiah's coming. Such a program of course led directly to civil war. In the White Lotus tradition this eschatological vision, always present after late Yüan times, provided the theoretical backdrop against which current events were viewed. If the signs seemed to indicate the collapse of an era, and the right leadership were present, a famine or an oppressive magistrate could provide the spark to ignite a new burst of messianic fervor. The situation is ambiguous. Surely there were charlatans and opportunists among sect leaders, as there were followers who were much more conscious of empty stomachs than of hope for Maitreya's paradise. Nevertheless, the religious intentions of the sectarian traditions themselves as recorded in their texts and in statements attributed to them in historical accounts need to be taken seriously.

Though it is the movements more prone to violence which have attracted most attention, many of the folk Buddhist sects existed continuously over long periods of time in peaceful obscurity, united over the generations by hereditary leadership, written scriptures, and ritual traditions. From the perspective of folk piety such nonviolent groups as the White Cloud, Ch'ang-sheng, and the Wu-wei met ordinary religious needs just as well as the White Lotus, but without its subversive associations. Some of these groups remind one of the Waldensians, or of the Anabaptists after the healing work of Menno Simons. This understanding makes it all the more imperative to distinguish them from other forms of popular movements.

If one grants that the associations in question were in fact religious sects oriented toward universal salvation, then their typological distinction from peasant rebellions and secret societies becomes relatively easy to state. It is, in short, that they were not peasant rebellions because they moved out of pre-existing cultic traditions, and they were not secret societies because they were not secret.

Throughout Chinese history there were all sorts of bandit gangs and popular resistance movements in varying permutations of size and combination. They ranged from local riots against intolerable conditions to full-scale rebellions openly ambitious to take over imperial power. In times of social and political chaos a great variety of violent movements could be operating at the same time and even in the same area, with frequent mutual contact and amalgamation. Whatever their origins, many of these groups performed religious rituals to gain assurance of divine support. Understandably, to a harassed county magistrate perhaps in imminent danger of losing his life, all such groups were simply rebels who must be destroyed. But for those of us at a safe distance it is possible to make distinctions at the level of fundamental intention. The distinction is essentially that only the sectarians operated out of organized congregational traditions, driven by an articulated eschatological vision.

As for secret societies, there were plenty of them in eighteenth and nineteenth century China, usually characterized by difficult initiation rituals, explicitly anti-Manchu political ambitions and elaborate secret codes involving both gestures and modified written characters. The best known of such groups is the T'ien-ti hui, the Heaven and Earth Society. It is true that there was some blending of T'ien-ti hui units with sectarian congregations in the mid-nineteenth century. For example, there were some White Lotus related groups which distributed sealed scriptures in secret characters, which could only be deciphered by use of a code book. But in the long run of folk Buddhist tradition such groups were not characteristic and the typological distinctions remain intact. The sects did not have initiation rituals but membership rituals of great simplicity, involving no more than inscribing one's name on a piece of paper and burning it as a memorial to the deity. They were not concerned to keep their doctrines secret but rather proclaimed their message openly whenever it was safe to do so. At most they went underground temporarily to avoid government attacks.

Introduction

C. K. Yang has written that in Chinese history:

The third form of institutional religion was that of the syncretic religious societies . . . Both the universal religions [Buddhism and Taoism] and the religious sects developed their theology, cults and organizational systems independent of the function and structure of the secular social institutions . . . Whatever its content, the salvational proposition was at the core of the popular religious movements . . . The basic claim of the sects was their ability to bring universal deliverance to tortured humanity.[2]

Much of the original impetus for my own study came from these passages in Mr. Yang's work. In what follows I will discuss the history, beliefs, and practices of some of the folk sects in an attempt to understand them on their own terms and in relationship to other forms of Chinese religious development.

2
A Case in Point:
The Ch'ang-sheng chiao

Before entering into more general and methodological discussion perhaps it would be useful to describe in detail a particular sect which manifests many characteristics of the phenomenon as a whole. I have chosen the Ch'ang-sheng chiao, a small, quiet group in Chekiang active in the mid-eighteenth century.

The Ch'ang-sheng sect is discussed at length in a memorial presented to the Ch'ien-lung Emperor in 1769 by Chüeh-lo Yung-te (d. 1784), the governor of Chekiang.[1] Following are relevant passages of this memorial.

Yung-te writes:

I, kneeling, humbly submit a case concerning a heterodox sect (*hsieh-chiao*) . . . which sect members apprehended in Kiangsu have confessed is active in Hsi-an county of Chekiang, where there is a Wang Ch'ang-sheng Vegetarian Hall (*chai-t'ang*). [Local officials] have uncovered their hymns, scriptures (*ching*), images, and record books and arrested several members [all the names are given] living in the temple . . . In Chia-hsing and Hsiu-shui counties they have also arrested [others] who [live in] an Amitābha temple, or worship at home (*tsai chia feng chiao*). They are all vegetarians who follow Buddhist ritual practices. I then redoubled my efforts to apprehend other members . . . and also arrested [several names] who live in the vegetarian hall of the Wang Cloister of Quietness (Wang ching an). This sect was founded in Hsi-an county by Wang Ch'ang-sheng, also called Wang P'u-shan, in the Wan-li period of the Ming

Dynasty [1573-1620]. Their temple was founded by Wang as a vegetarian hall; there he exhorted men to turn to a vegetarian diet and recite the Buddha's name, saying that by so doing one could avoid illness and lengthen life. Wang's female cousin . . . used the same approach to convert women. They named their religion the Ch'ang-sheng sect.[2]

. . . When Wang died he was buried at mount Wu-ying next to the temple. [Two of his] disciples and his cousin were also buried there, and their grave sites and inscriptions still exist.

Because of Wang's teaching the faith spread rapidly, the number of disciples increased, and a temple with several hundred rooms and units was built. The group also acquired fields and realized substantial farm income.

The memorial continues:

Even though they have done nothing illegal, they are still an heretical sect. [In fact] they were investigated and prohibited in the fifth year of the Yung-cheng period.[3]

At that time, those in the temple who were from elsewhere were sent home. Those from that same area were expelled from the temple, and the vegetarian hall itself was razed . . . Their land was confiscated . . . [but several remaining rooms] were given to Yü Sheng-kung, the tenant who tilled the confiscated fields. [However] he simply continued the old vegetarian hall tradition, and called the buildings by that name. [Eventually he was joined] by several homeless older men . . . who settled down nearby and continued the old ritual practices as before, [such as] vegetarianism and chanting sūtras. When Yü Sheng-kung died one [of the newcomers] took his place as a leader.

The memorial goes on to say that three years before the 1769 investigation, the revived temple accidentally burned down, and with it all the group's scriptures. One of the residents went to stay in the Amitābha temple mentioned above, while others stayed in the homes of fellow devotees. The members then got together to plan the rebuilding of their temple. Each contributed a substantial sum of money, while another member went all through the surrounding area seeking donations. By their combined efforts they succeeded in building a new center on the old site. One of the members contributed a porcelain image of Kuan-yin which was worshiped in the new edifice. At one side of the altar they placed an empty chair to represent the deceased founder. Members also brought texts and other images from their homes and placed them in the temple.

These members from northern Chekiang often went back to Hsi-an county to worship at Wang Ch'ang-sheng's tomb, as did other followers from Wu-chiang county of (southern) Kiangsu. Yung-te holds that the real reason for the resurgence of the sect was this worship at the tomb. His emphasis all through this section is on the fact that the members *ssu feng* (privately worshiped), that is, worshiped without official government authorization. He continues:

Their festival days are the first day of the first month [lunar calendar], third of the third, sixth of the sixth, ninth of the ninth, and seventeenth of the eleventh. On these five days they recite scriptures and perform Buddhist liturgy in the temple . . . The three gods worshiped in the temple are Kuan-yin, Maitreya and Wei-t'o.[4] The sūtras they read are the *Heart* and the *Diamond*, etc. . . . Every time they worship, each member contributes a pint of rice and twelve coppers, which are given [to the leaders] to buy equipment, incense, candles, and vegetables [after which] they all eat a vegetarian feast.

The investigator also mentions that when the older brother of a man named Wang Huai-te became ill, he turned to vegetarian food and reciting scriptures. Then several other villagers began coming to his home to chant the Buddha's name together. This resulted in the establishing of another Ch'ang-sheng vegetarian temple. The sick brother nonetheless died. Not long after, Wang Huai-te himself was stricken, but a sect leader continued to preach that illness could be cured by a vegetarian diet and recitation of Amitābha's name. Wang recovered, was converted, and became leader of the branch started by his older brother. The reporter holds that this was the beginning of worship in private homes, and of the practice of naming such homes the "Vegetarian Hall of the . . . family." Another home *chai-t'ang* later became a regular temple of the sect (the Wang ching an mentioned previously), directed by a monk named Li. After his death another member took over, and so on, from one generation to the next. In the Wang ching an the

9

deities worshiped were Kuan-yin, the Three Rulers (San Kuan—a Taoist Triad, originally Heaven, Earth and Water), and Kuan Ti.[5] There were always special services on the birthdays of these deities but no group recitation of scriptures.

After summing up corroborative evidence, Yung-te concludes:

> [In investigating this group] I was afraid that they would privately unite together to deceive the people and act as bandits . . . [Their scriptures and ritual objects] are "heretical implements of the left way" . . . [they] gather the people by burning incense, meet at night and disperse in the day, falsely claiming that they are carrying out religious and charitable activities.[6]

The governor continues:

> Even though the Ch'ang-sheng sect has no other [illegal] characteristics, yet it is a bandit group, and is really a heterodox association (*tso-tao i-tuan*) [which should be dealt with as such, that is] death by strangulation for the leaders, and 100 strokes of the bamboo cane for the followers.

His point in all this is not that the sect was acting in a rebellious manner at the time, but that it was continuing activities which had previously been prohibited, such as worshiping "heretical images" (*hsieh hsiang*). He says that those who worshiped in the house of Wang Huai-te and "repeatedly urged him to join the sect and read sūtras" should also be punished but asks for lesser sentences for those who worshiped and contributed money but did not actually live in the temples. He also recommends that:

> All the *chai-t'angs* should be razed, their land confiscated, the tombs [of the founders] leveled and tomb inscriptions destroyed— so that not the slightest trace remains, and [the sect] is cut off root and branch . . . all images, sūtras, and other books should be burned.

Other than the customary formal concluding phrases, the memorial ends with the statement that in searching one of the members' homes Yung-te found several sūtras, including two named *The Precious Sūtra of the Tathāgata of Universal Peace Who Oversees the Faith*, and the *Incarnation sūtra* (*Hsia sheng pao ching*).

The contents deal with such things as Śākyamuni descending to earth to be reborn, and [the means by which] people can escape the disasters and snares of life . . . Even though there are no rebellious words in these texts, nor illegal statements, they are nonetheless truly wild, exaggerated and uncanonical (*pu ching*). Therefore, after the investigation is concluded they should all be burned . . . Further, all local officials should be urged to search for such books and destroy them.

Thus, the Ch'ang-sheng sect was suppressed and to my knowledge never functioned again.[7]

This memorial has been quoted at length not only to give a picture of the life of a typical sect, but to give the reader something of the flavor of official reports dealing with popular religious organizations. While the text speaks for itself, perhaps a few additional comments are in order.

1. The Ch'ang-sheng chiao was a complete religious system, with founder, leader and defined membership. It had its own temples, ritual, liturgical calendar, and sacred texts. Its activities were supported by the members' voluntary contribution of their money, time, and possessions.

2. This group was not involved in any violent activities.

3. Though this sect is described as Buddhist, it employed Buddhist deities, rituals, and sūtras in a folk context which transformed vegetarian meals into a ritual means of attaining long life and was perfectly at ease in worshiping together deities originating in Buddhism, Taoism, and popular religion, along with the spirit of the founder-ancestor.

4. This association can by no stretch of the imagination be called a secret society; it built temples, worshiped, kept record books, and solicited funds, all in public. But this public was the common people, and clearly did not include literati and officials— in fact, the sect had been in open operation for forty-two years after first being proscribed before it was rediscovered by the investigator. In the government's eyes its crime was not secrecy but private, nonauthorized worship and temple construction, and the possession of unorthodox texts.

3
History of Interpretation: Rebels, Evangelists, or Both?

The phenomenologists have taught us that objects are manifested in consciousness, and that the primary structure of consciousness is intentionality. This means that while the object itself is not constituted by consciousness, its meaning is. "[The world] is essentially tied to consciousness by intentionality. In other words, the world gives itself to consciousness which confers on it its meaning."[1]

Whatever else they have accomplished, phenomenology, psychoanalysis, and the sociology of knowledge have all in their different ways revealed the inadequacy of naive realism by stressing the shaping role of the knower in the process of knowing. This means that in the study of a phenomenon one should be aware of its history of interpretation, so that one can understand more clearly the role played by methodological assumptions in the presentation of the data and thereby become more conscious of his own fundamental approach.

My primary methodological concern is to avoid reductionism as much as possible, that is, to meet the subject in question at every level on which it presents itself, without distortion. It is necessary to keep faith with the human beings who are the makers of history by seeking to understand their own purposes in relationship to the total context. This principle means to understand the relationship of historical situation to sectarian belief as a dialectical one, without seeking to give undue precedence to either. Such an approach is particularly important in dealing with folk movements deeply embedded in a holistic world view such as that of traditional China, a world view that did not allow for sharp distinctions between the divine and the human or the political and the religious. Though the sects were constituted by a delicate balance of intention and circumstance, many have tended to interpret them as simply pawns of unconscious social forces, as dominated by "latent functions" of which they were perhaps only dimly aware. What is needed is not an idealist over-reaction, but an approach which accepts the "thusness" of these complex movements in their own world. Perhaps through such an approach we can treat eschatology as seriously as famine and political chaos, rites of salvation as seriously as economic cooperation, and charismatic healing as seriously as military leadership.

There have been many scholarly interpretations of Chinese sectarian religion, ranging from sympathetic to hostile, for differing reasons, and with many variations. Awareness of this varied history of interpretation helps demonstrate that there is no completely necessary connection between any of these approaches and the data, and thus that each perspective, including that of this book, is to some extent arbitrary and should be maintained in dialectic with the others. For example, a supposedly more empathetic evaluation of the sects must understand as well the reasons for imperial Confucian antagonism and grant the Chinese elite the right to defend their own world view.

Some Recent Approaches to European Sectarian Movements

Many of the interpretive issues raised in modern discussion of the Chinese groups have of course been debated in treatments of their European counterparts. This debate provides a useful preliminary perspective. Though some recent studies of European folk sects have stressed the formative role of religious intention, these studies work against a background of sociological and Marxian interpretation.

Two of the earlier contemporary interpretations of European groups which stress class tensions and social functions are Norman

Cohn's *The Pursuit of the Millennium* (1957) and E. J. Hobsbawm's *Primitive Rebels* (1959). Cohn is interested in "revolutionary eschatology" as a forerunner of modern totalitarian ideology.
He stresses the relationship of millennial hopes to the poor and
oppressed classes. In the eleventh century it was conditions of rapid
social change which "incorporated the ancient eschatological myths
as dynamic social ideologies . . . [As peasants left the security of
their old way of life and sought upward mobility in the cities] . . .
there were many whose expectations were raised without fulfillment. It was this large group of marginal immigrants which was the
social seedbed for revolutionary movements . . . Salvationist religious groups were the most important outlet for the dispossessed."[2]
   Hobsbawm is also primarily interested in the origins of modern social revolution. To him an "element of class struggle" appears
with the disruption of the "social balance of the kinship society." In
this class struggle archaic movements are "pre-political phenomena"
which are destined to die out when the people gain political consciousness through peasant leagues and socialism.[3]
   Writing of Cohn, Hobsbawm, and others, Yonina Talmon emphasizes that they are not interested in millenarianism as such, but
"in the relation between religion and social change." To them millenarianism is the "religion of deprived groups," which appeals to
the socially isolated and politically powerless. Such movements are
either "an outlet for extreme anxiety and a delusion of despair"
(Cohn) or "a precursor of political awakening and a forerunner of
political organization" (Hobsbawm). In this context, eschatologically oriented beliefs help unify and organize masses of disaffected
people by giving them a common goal, with proofs of their invinci-
bility. Religious language is a means of establishing the authority of
leaders and communicating with traditionally oriented followers.
"In some cases the movement is started by . . . a politically minded
leader, but when its political ideology reaches the masses it is spon-
taneously interpreted in religious terms."[4] As we shall see, these
interpretations are often applied to Chinese movements.
   Byron R. Wilson applies this same type of sociological analysis
to modern sects in Britain. His approach is straightforwardly
stated:

Deviate social expression is to be understood only in terms of
the social structure in which it arises . . . [The Elim and Cristadel-
phian sects] perform important latent functions, namely, the recon-
ciliation of the disinherited to their social and economic status by
compensatory devices and transvaluation of social experience . . .
economic privation made the [Elim] . . . a very congenial atmos-
phere for those who were impoverished.

Wilson makes clear his reason for this interpretation:

This study accepts the hypothesis that religious movements, as
essentially social movements, can be expected to stand in specific
relation to social classes [and] to their prevailing economic and
social conditions . . . Sect adherence and religious adherence generally can be meaningfully understood only in terms of psychologi-
cal and sociological analysis . . . and in terms of the functions which
religious belief, affiliation and activity actually fulfil.[5]

Commenting on the above mode of interpretation, Yonina
Talmon, herself a sociologist, writes:

By and large, religion is treated here as an ideology which just
expresses concrete socio-economic issues rather than molds and
directs them . . . On the theoretical level, religion is denied any independent causal significance, and there is no adequate analysis of
internal, partly independent processes in the religious sphere.[6]

I agree. An analysis of social factors does much to explain the context, differentiation, and development of religious movements, but
it does not fully account for their existence per se. They can be perhaps more adequately dealt with by a method which gives full
play to the role of man's quest for sacred reality. As Joachim Wach
wrote of such sociological interpretations: "[They] should not be
pressed to the point of ignoring the genuine religious experiences
which more often than not supply the initial impulse."[7]

Mircea Eliade has also commented forcefully in his voluminous work on the need to respect the integrity of religious myth and
ritual if one is to come to a full understanding of the human dimension involved. The issue is not the belief or disbelief of the his-

torian, much less the "ultimate truth" of mythic language, but simply the methodological recognition that for some people religious belief has had a shaping power in its own right, though to be sure a power always conditioned by historical, social, and economic factors. This recognition is particularly difficult in the investigation of popular cult because the operative assumptions of such piety are usually so different from those of a modern scholar.[8]

In contrast to approaches which stress social function, some interpreters of European popular sects have given more attention to factors Wach would call specifically religious.[9] These writers include George H. Williams, Gordon Leff, and Jeffrey B. Russell.

Williams, in his book *The Radical Reformation*, is working with data long considered to be within the province of Christian church history, so he evidently does not feel compelled to respond to alternative methodologies. In his book doctrinal (that is, intentional) considerations are given primary emphasis as a matter of course. While such a treatment is as uncritical in its own way as the approach of Hobsbawm or Wilson, it does demonstrate that dissenting movements in Europe can be discussed as a part of religious history. The more specific value of Williams' work for my purposes is his emphasis on the unity and "inner coherence" of the "Radical Reformation," which was "at least as much an entity as . . . divided Protestantism itself."[10] The grasping of the Chinese folk Buddhist sects as part of a similarly coherent tradition is one of the concerns of my own work.

Leff's *Heresy in the Later Middle Ages* is also an essentially theological treatment, but one more sensitive to contemporary methodological debate. He gives full play to the intentional dimension of religious movements: "Heresy during the middle ages was an indigenous growth; its impulse was invariably the search for a fuller spiritual life." He describes the "growing sense of apocalypticism" in thirteenth century Europe as a key factor in the rise of heresy. We have noted that a similar sense of the end of the age was present also in the Chinese context. When dealing with common traits of heretical movements Leff discusses not social background but such factors as a sense of election, rejection of church authority, and the veneration of poverty and humility. In treating the po-

litically subversive phase of the Lollards, which began with their
persecution in 1382, he writes:

> Nor did the change to which [the conflict of Lollardy with the
> established authorities] led destroy its original characteristics, but
> rather overlaid them. Thus, if at one level Lollardy became increas-
> ingly identified with political subversion and plotting, it also re-
> mained true to its theological inspiration.[11]

The language is not what I would choose, but perhaps Leff's approach here is a needed corrective.

The most valuable recent study of European movements in
English is Jeffrey B. Russell's *Dissent and Reform in the Early Middle Ages*, which is written by a historian most conscious of his
methodological context. Not only does Russell give full weight to
theoretical and intentional factors, he also devotes eleven pages to
a detailed critique of commonly accepted sociological interpretations. He admits that the positive contributions of the "sociological
school" mean that "the eye of the historian can no longer skim
scornfully over circumstances to light upon the platonic essence . . .
even the historian who does not share the materialist interpretation
would not now deny the importance of correlating religious revolt
with economic and social circumstance." But nonetheless he maintains that his research shows "no clear connection between dissent
and any particular social group."

Russell then discusses one by one the main points raised by
sociologically oriented analysis. First, medieval dissent began with
Aldebert in the eighth century, long before the general social ferment of the eleventh century to which Cohn ascribes the origin of
European eschatological movements. Second, with only one or two
exceptions, there was no dissenting movement which "had anything
like a social or political program," despite the repeated insistence
by scholars that they were essentially concerned with social reform.
Rather, these groups usually "condemned the world," and looked
not to a future utopia but to a return to pure, apostolic Christianity. Third, though medieval people were of course concerned with
money, social position, and power, "They also frequently had a
concern just as deep if not deeper than these, holiness . . . The ulti-

mate concern of many medieval men was with the other world, not with this one." Fourth, the fact that the membership of many groups consisted primarily of peasants doesn't really prove anything, because from 70 to 80 percent of the population itself were peasants. In addition, many different social classes were involved, priests, nuns, and nobles included. Nor is the correlation of dissent with natural disasters conclusive, for there are such disasters recorded for almost every year. Further, "There is no significant correlation between commercial and industrial centers and dissent."[12]

With the exception of points one and two, all these considerations are relevant to the Chinese situation. The Chinese people were just as concerned with their relationship to the gods as medieval Europeans were with holiness; the ratio of peasants to the total population was even higher; and there are many accounts of Buddhist monks and nuns actively involved in the folk sects. Suzuki Chūsei has stressed as well that there were many land-owning peasants, village headmen, and minor local officials in late eighteenth century White Lotus religion.[13]

I have not investigated the correlation of disasters with rebellions in China, but it cannot be denied that a great variety of natural and man-made calamities was frequent, while only a relatively small percentage of them was related to any recorded social disturbance. Indeed, the Chinese peasantry developed a highly complex belief system which enabled them to accept most disasters, a system centered around fate and the propitiation of deities.

Dissenting movements flourished at all times in post-Han China, particularly after the T'ang dynasty. There may be a rough correlation between social decay and religious *uprisings*, but the sects themselves continued to exist and grow in quiet periods as well. On the other hand, in T'ao Hsi-sheng's exhaustive listing of "violent outbreaks" in the turbulent end of the Northern Sung, only 10 percent had any known connection with religion.[14] Though some Chinese sects had social programs of sexual equality, property sharing, and redistribution of land (see Russell's second point above), these programs can be understood in part as expressions of religious utopianism.

Of course, interpretations of European groups cannot be conclusive for Chinese data, but a look at these interpretations indicates the variety of approaches possible for similar groups elsewhere.

Representative Interpretations of the Chinese Movements

Most interpretations of Chinese folk sect religion have been hostile, moralistic, and political in tone, from early discussions of the second century Five Pecks of Rice sect to the approach of some contemporary scholars in China and the West. In addition to the approach which denies any religious validity at all to these groups, there has been a variety of "dualistic" interpretations. By "dualistic" I mean views which concede some authentic religious functions but which maintain that these functions existed together with other aspects considered less desirable. Thus, official reports often distinguish between pious and well-meaning members of the sects and their scheming leaders who deceive the people for private political ends; in 1800 the Chia-ch'ing Emperor made a quite sophisticated distinction between peaceful and rebellious White Lotus participants; Japanese Buddhist scholars like Shigematsu Shunshō separate the orthodox Buddhist phase of White Lotus religion from the degenerate and "superstitious" form which developed in the Yüan dynasty; and Western scholars such as Richard Chu differentiate between quiet "purely religious" phases and active "rebellious" phases.

In my opinion, these "dualistic" treatments do not give sufficient weight to a fundamental intention of sectarian folk Buddhism as it developed in the Chinese cosmos, that is, its intention to save all beings by a variety of interrelated means. These means could include preaching, the reading of scriptures, reciting mantras, distribution of healing charms, the invocation of divine assistance in the form of supernatural armies, or open eschatological warfare to place a pious emperor on the throne who would prepare the way for the advent of Maitreya. Soteriologically these methods were all of one piece and reflected the unity of the sect itself, based on its apprehension of divine grace. There is a hidden value judgment in the "dualistic" interpretations, which assumes that folk cult associated with political activity is somehow inferior to "pure religion," be it imperial Confucianism, orthodox Buddhism, or Christianity.

It is perhaps more useful to attempt to understand such phenomena on the level at which they present themselves, in the light of their own context, and their intentions and religious functions within that context. One can make historical and structural distinctions between Ch'an meditation and rustic devotion to a charismatic healer, but the historian need not decide which is better, and indeed cannot, without imposing an extraneous perspective.

There are a few modern scholars who are sympathetic to the groups in question, among them Joseph Edkins, Tsukamoto Zenryū, Suzuki Chūsei, and C. K. Yang. These men see the folk sects as an authentic expression of popular religion.

The Imperial Confucian background. Confucianism developed an emphasis on correct doctrine early in its struggle with other schools in the Warring States period, and actively opposed all other interpretations of the cosmos and history than its own from the time it was established as the state orthodoxy by the Han Emperor Wu (r. 140-87 B.C.). A distinction between orthodox and heterodox ideas goes back to Confucius (d. 479 B.C.) himself, in *Analects*, II, 16, which reads, "The study of heterodox teachings (*i-tuan*) is injurious indeed."[15] Mencius (d.c. 289 B.C.) amplified this distinction in his attacks on Yang Chu and Mo Tzu, the leaders of two rival schools.

He wrote:

> If the principles of Yang and Mo be not stopped, and the principles of Confucius not set forth, then those perverse speakings will delude the people and stop up the path of benevolence and righteousness . . . I _____ oppose Yang and Mo. I drive away their licentious expressions, so that such perverse speakers may not be able to show themselves . . . I also wish to rectify men's hearts, and to put an end to these perverse doctrines . . . and thus to carry on the work of the three [Confucian] Sages [Yü the Great, the Duke of Chou and Confucius].[16]

The fundamental sanction against non-Confucian belief and action is revealed in the *Li chi* (compiled in the second century B.C.), Book III, section 4:

> . . . using licentious music, strange garments, wonderful contri-

vances and extraordinary implements, thus raising doubts among the multitudes: all who used or formed such things were put to death, [as were] . . . [those] who studied what was wrong [and persisted in doing so].[17]

This doctrinal position in the hands of an imperial state led directly to attempts to suppress dissenting religious movements. Many modern scholars attempt to maintain that such suppression was really politically motivated, concerned not with doctrine, but with preserving the existence of the state, and hence was invoked only on politically active groups.[18] But, as the above quotes indicate, such opposition involved ideological factors as well. The state being protected was precisely the Confucian state, a state which claimed authority over every dimension of existence, including that which in the West is called religious or spiritual. The struggle with dissenting religions was a conflict of belief systems as well as a contest for power. Evidence for this view can be seen everywhere in official reports which decry the nonorthodox scripture texts collected in police raids, in the existence in the Ming and Ch'ing law codes of special sections on heresies, distinct from those on rebellions, and in repeated suppressions of entirely peaceful groups on the grounds that they were heterodox, privately built temples, and sponsored group worship. As C. K. Yang himself admits, "The traditional state was founded upon Confucianism as the supreme orthodoxy," and "[In case of rebellion] . . . the replacement of the Confucian orthodoxy by heterodox doctrine was always a central issue."[19]

An important factor in this situation was the unique status of the emperor, the only Son of Heaven and the focal point of the cosmos. The profoundly religious dimensions of this role, which are well known, have been discussed in detail by Marcel Granet, W. E. Soothill and many others.[20] The emperor was responsible not only for the peace and well being of the people, but also for the harmonious interaction of man and cosmos. Only he could worship Heaven and Earth, and only his appointed officials were authorized to worship the gods of the orthodox state pantheon on behalf of all the people. In this way the cultic role of Confucian officials continued that of the state diviners and *wu* priesthood in classical times.[21] This meant that local government representatives were also the priests of an established religious system. No religion outside this system could be granted more than a grudging, pragmatic recognition, for in theory everything else but ancestor worship and homage to deities of land and grain was unnecessary.

The beginnings of this perspective can be seen in the *Li chi* where we are given lists of the forms of sacrifice appropriate for each level of the hierarchical order, from Emperor to common people. Proper performance of these rituals contributes to universal order; improper performance to chaos. Thus we read, "A sacrifice which is not proper to offer, and which is yet offered, is called a licentious sacrifice. A licentious sacrifice brings no blessings."[22] For the period when popular sects were most active the Ming law code amplifies this position by first specifying the types of deities and spirits whose worship is to be officially encouraged. The list includes deities of land and grain, mountains, rivers, wind and rain, as well as holy emperors, enlightened kings, and loyal officials whose names are recorded in ritual texts. However, "Those who sacrifice to deities which they should not worship are to be given eighty strokes of the bamboo cane." Elsewhere in this same chapter of the Ming code we read that while other religious ceremonies are prohibited, spring and autumn sacrifices offered to publicly established local earth deities are permitted.[23]

A Ch'ing edict of 1812 makes this same point even more clearly, in the context of renewed prohibition of dissenting sects: "Imperial edicts are to be made clearly known, so that the common people in the countryside will all understand that there is no [proper] teaching (*chiao*) outside [the ethic of] the three bonds [between ruler and official, father and son, husband and wife], and the five constant virtues [humanity, righteousness, propriety, wisdom, trustworthiness]. Beyond the principles of heaven and the royal law there is nowhere to seek for blessings."[24]

This sort of perspective meant that the state tended to hold negative and defensive views of alternative religions, be they Manichaeism, Buddhism, orthodox liturgical Taoism, Christianity, or popular cults, though of course there were periods when Buddhism and Taoism received imperial support. The history of Chinese state persecution of Buddhism is too well known to require retelling here.

Suffice it to say that the first known violent repression was carried out by Sun Lin, a general of the Wei dynasty, in 258. Sun Lin "destroyed temples and had priests decapitated."[25] Other major persecutions occurred in 446, 574, 845, and 955.[26] While in modern accounts much emphasis is placed on economic and political motives for these repressions,[27] the above discussion should make it clear that doctrinal considerations were also important. This can also be seen in the long tradition of Confucian anti-Buddhist polemic, with its emphasis on Buddhism as a "barbarian creed," unmentioned by the sages, and in violation of the established familial morality. Erik Zürcher has stressed the importance of ideological factors in this conflict, noting that the Confucians were "exponents of a well-defined world-view," and that since state and ruler had an important cosmic role, "Insubordination or withdrawal from the influence of [the ruler's authority] is not merely illegal or asocial, but such actions contain an element of blasphemy, as is clearly shown in the discussion on the autonomy of the Sangha. [The conflict was] a conflict between two ideologies."[28]

For most periods in the history of imperial China the Confucian tradition rightly considered itself to be the legitimate carrier of high culture. At its best this tradition stood for ideals of integrity and justice which did much to strengthen and improve the quality of Chinese life. For a committed scholar official, particularly after the Sung revival of Confucianism, the orthodox tradition of society and thought was a necessary expression of cosmic order. It was his responsibility to communicate this tradition to the common people in such a way that they would understand and assent to it within, and thus conform in their outward behavior. From such a perspective dissenting ideas and movements could not but appear as threats to the stability of the whole system, which was sincerely believed to be for the benefit of the common people as well. There is thus a tragic dimension in the long and often bitter confrontation between state and sect, to which we now turn in more detail.[29]

Interpretation of the sects in official sources. There is no doubt that the Chinese government was particularly concerned about collective religious activities which could provide the opportunity for riots or illegal organization. Such activities might include group pilgrimages, temple fairs and processions, public preaching, or group worship. Some official reports are quite explicit about this concern. For example, a Yüan source, dated 1291, comments about "those who gather large groups of people together at night for religious ceremonies, pounding drums and making a disturbance. It is to be feared that this will produce banditry."[30]

Four hundred and fifty years later the Ch'ien-lung Emperor (r. 1736-1796) made the same point:

The common people . . . are constantly confused by teachings concerning ancestors and deities, praying and sacrificing . . . In such provinces as Chihli, Shantung, Shansi and Shensi . . . ,but particularly in Honan, in the first month of the year every day many hundreds of people gather together, first going to the temples of the city-god, where they present written prayers to the deities and burn incense . . . Then they form processions going out in every direction, filling up the streets, carrying flags and banners, beating on gongs and drums, led by Buddhist and Taoist priests. [In such gatherings] men and women mingle together, no one can distinguish evil people from the good, and fighting and stealing take place. Thus, problems arise. This sort of evil custom wastes money in the present, and I fear in the future will lead to heretical religion.[31]

Opposition to organized sects must be understood against this background of concern about collective ceremonies as a potential source of disorder. Nonetheless, as we have noted, prohibition of dissenting religion was based on ideological grounds as well, as can be seen for example in the Ming prohibition of any form of religious revelation outside the official system, whether or not it was related to the activity of a group: "All teachers and shamans who falsely call down heretical gods, write charms, make incantations over water [for healing purposes], who use the planchette or pray to saints, calling themselves [various kinds of] spirit-mediums, are prohibited."[32] Beyond this, the importance of ideological factors is revealed in the emphasis placed by officials and emperors on transforming the ideas of people. This theme is set by such phrases as *hua-min ch'eng-su*, "transform the people and perfect their customs," and is of course rooted in the fundamental Confucian concern for ethical reform through education and example. It is the rectification of the mind which leads to social harmony; this self-understanding was extended to the people as well. Thus, the thinking of heretics must be changed, as well as their overt activities suppressed, a perspective succinctly summed up by Ming T'ai-tsu in 1370: "If heretical teachings are not practiced, then the people will not be confused."[33] At a more specific level official interpretation of the sects ranges from straight-line opposition to a rather sophisticated sociological understanding of the poverty and despair which drive people to dissent.

The most common approach was well stated by the Chia-ch'ing Emperor in 1812: "Heretical religions which confuse the people and collect money are extremely injurious to the people's customs. If they are not prohibited and stopped immediately they will daily become more widespread."[34] This view of popular sects goes back to comments about a late second century Taoist movement in Szechwan, the Religion of the Heavenly Master, or the "Five Pecks of Rice" sect (so named because members were supposed to contribute rice to meet expenses). Members of this group were called "rice bandits" (*mi-tsei*). A fifth century historian had this to say about their healing rituals: "Really they didn't heal illness; this was all nothing more than evil and lying talk. But the common people were confused and stupid, and followed them with great dedication."[35]

Since the whole of J. J. M. DeGroot's *Sectarianism and Religious Persecution in China* (Amsterdam, 1903) deals with official opposition to the sects, and since I have already discussed a detailed example of such opposition in Chapter 2, I will simply note a few more illustrations of this generally hostile perspective. For example, a T'ang dynasty edict of 715 concerning the Maitreya sect reads as follows:

Now there are those with white clothing and long hair, who falsely claim that Maitreya has descended to be born. By means of supernatural and deceitful actions they have gathered followers from a wide area. They say they understand Buddhist concepts, and irresponsibly speak of good and bad omens. They have written short sūtras which they falsely claim were spoken by the Buddha himself. They collect disciples and call themselves monks. They do not marry. They mislead and confuse the villagers and cause great trouble for the government.

This edict closes with a threat that officials who do not expose and arrest such groups will be demoted.[36]

There is no mention here of any violent activity, though the Maitreya sect had been involved in such activity before. The emphasis is rather on disruption of the established belief system by an independent religious group. Nonetheless, much valuable historical data can be elicited from such passages. That the government did not or could not comprehend any authentic religious drive behind such groups is obvious. This is also revealed by repeated use in the reports of such phrases as "misled the multitudes by burning incense (*shao hsiang huo chung*)" or "deceived the people by means of the Buddhist dharma (*i fo-fa huo chung*)," or, often in relation to groups with numerous followers, "those who were coerced into following him [the sect leader]."[37] The idea that such religious activities could be carried out in good faith is usually not considered.

In 1386 a Ming official named Lien Tzu-ning stated the Confucian view with great clarity and vigor:

Unscrupulous and obstinate elements falsely take the name of burning incense and chanting the Buddha's name in order to attract vagrants, and ignorant folk follow them in confusion. This is the beginning [of the problem]. Misled by strange and superstitious teachings [the people] hope thereby to escape from disasters and suffering. [However] these robbers and bandits intend only to rob, attack, and plunder. Therefore, when the nation is in a period of stability and prosperity it should [not relax its vigilance], but mow them down like grass and hunt them like animals.[38]

The results of exhortations like that of Lien Tzu-ning can be seen in a characteristic Ming account:

In Hu-kuang a heretic of Lo-t'ien county named Wang Fo-er [Wang, Son of the Buddha], said of himself that he was the reincarnation of Maitreya Buddha. He deceived the people by preaching and writing of Buddhism, hoping to gather a multitude together to rebel. Government troops seized and beheaded him.[39]

The reader is referred to DeGroot for similar accounts from the Ch'ing period.

The perspective of "straightforward opposition" is of course summed up in the imperial law prohibiting sectarian activity, a law which investigating officials were obliged to follow. Perhaps the best example of such prohibition is found in the Ming code:

[As for] all [groups] recklessly calling themselves the White Lotus society of the Buddha Maitreya, the Religion which Honors Light (tsun-ming chiao) [Manichaeism], or the White Cloud school, and so forth, and all those methods of the left way [heresy] which cause disorder, and those who conceal pictures and images [of deities], offering incense, gathering the people at night to disperse by day, pretending to practice good deeds [but in fact] stirring up and deceiving the people, the leaders [of all such groups and activities] shall be strangled, and their followers given 100 blows [of the bamboo cane] and banished 3,000 *li*.[40]

Sections in the Ch'ing code proscribing heretical groups are somewhat expanded. For example, in an appended edict of 1813 officials are threatened with demotion (as in the T'ang edict quoted above) if they neglect to prosecute "local heretics who call themselves gods or Buddhas, promote and establish heterodox religions, employ charmed water . . . to deceive the people, and so on," and promised promotion if they arrest sect leaders: "If local officials . . . can decapitate one leader [of a heretical sect] they will be promoted one level [in the civil service system]." If ten or more such rebels were arrested the official was promised a direct recommendation for his promotion to the emperor himself.[41]

Fortunately for the sectarians such law was not always literally followed or enforced, in part perhaps because some officials felt that it was the responsibility of government to deal with the causes of unrest rather than simply seek to repress it. In the statement of Lien Tzu-ning quoted above we see a fleeting attempt to attribute popular support for the sects to social and economic causes. Other officials also held that most sect members were desperate folk who turned to religion and violence as a way of improving their lot. This interpretation is, of course, related to the Confucian conviction that the common people could not be expected to act in a morally

disciplined manner until their physical needs were first taken care
of. One of the most complete statements of an early Chinese version of a theory of "relative deprivation" was made by an official of
the Ming censorate named Lü K'un (1536-1618). In 1597 Lü K'un
wrote a memorial to the throne concerning the situation of the empire. After summing up signs of disorder and incipient rebellion
among the people he continues:

From antiquity there have been four types of people who have
sought to take advantage of disorder [lit. "who consider disorder to
be good fortune"]. The first are those who have nothing to rely on,
and have no source of food or warmth. Because they and their families are in desperate straits, they harbor thoughts of acting in rebellion, hoping to delay imminent death.

The second are immoral and reckless men, arrogant and cruel,
who play with the law and treat life with contempt. They constantly desire jade and silk, sons and daughters, but are unable to obtain
them. [Thus,] when there is an opportunity they immorally plan to
seize what they want.

The third are "those who propound heresies, such as the White
Lotus society" (this part of Lü's statement will be cited in Chapter
5), and the fourth, political adventurers looking for power. Then
the memorial continues:

If your majesty would be economical [in relation to your own
needs] and love the people, diminishing the [power and advan-
tages] of superiors in order to benefit those in inferior positions,
then the four classes [of common people] will be like innocent children. If you do not, then they will be like bandits and enemies [of
the throne]. The poverty and distress of the masses are easy to see;
from [1582] on there have been natural disasters every year, and
yet the people are pressed for taxes as before.

Your servant was a provincial official for a long time [in Shan-
si] and has observed your majesty's children. Though they are
frozen to the bone they have no warm clothing; though they are
starving, they have nothing to eat. Their houses are in disrepair.
[Thus] daily more of them abandon their land to become vagrants.[42]

Perhaps in part because of the sort of understanding displayed by Lü K'un, there were also some government inspectors who removed corrupt local officials responsible for popular discontent, or who arrested only the leaders of a movement, releasing the followers with an exhortation to obedience.[43]

In all fairness in this discussion of official opposition, it should also be mentioned that when a White Lotus group did succeed in setting up an independent, if short-lived, political base, it promptly became the state religion and proscribed orthodox Buddhism and Taoism. Li Shou-k'ung notes that when Ming Yü-chen established the Ming Hsia state in the turbulent period at the end of the Yüan, the new government "rejected Buddhism and Taoism and worshipped only Maitreya." The Ming Hsia kingdom surrendered to the armies of the new Ming dynasty in 1371.[44]

In sum, the official view of sectarian activity was both hostile and understanding, a perspective which relates directly to the value of traditional historical sources for a study of our topic. In comparison with most premodern historiography the traditional Chinese approach to history is relatively rational. Implicit in the style of many Chinese scholars is a sustained attempt to present history as the narration of objective events, unrelated to the personal concerns of the writer. This means that official accounts of sectarian activity can be used with profit. But they must also be used with care. The literati were trained in Confucian orthodoxy and committed to uphold its particular view of life and government, a view which they felt the sects violated. As a result their descriptions are a mixture of data, value judgments and stereotyped phrases intended to identify present groups with proscribed heretics of the past. However, whatever their faults and biases, the Confucian historians have preserved for us a fascinating aspect of folk culture, which without them would have been almost entirely lost.[45]

Huang Yü-p'ien. The most important source for Ming and Ch'ing White Lotus religion is the *P'o-hsieh hsiang-pien* (A detailed refutation of heresies) which was written in 1834 by a Hopei magistrate named Huang Yü-p'ien (f. 1830-1840). While in office Huang conducted several investigations of heretical sects and temples in areas which had long been centers of sectarian activity. In the course of these expeditions Huang collected a total of sixty-eight sectarian scriptures, most of which were written near the end of the sixteenth century. Between 1834 and 1841 he wrote four books intended to refute the teachings of these texts, the latter three being continuations of the first. Fortunately for us, in his treatment Huang quotes long passages verbatim, so that in his officially approved critique is preserved rich material concerning sectarian belief and ritual. We will rely heavily on this material in Chapter 7; at this point we are interested in Huang as an unusually sensitive and learned exponent of the imperial Confucian position in the struggle with folk Buddhist movements. Since he was a loyal official who accepted the Ch'ing law quoted above as the basis of his interpretation, we will here deal briefly with Huang only as a Confucian rationalist defending doctrinal orthodoxy. Huang deals seriously with ideas and beliefs on both sides:

> If we do not carefully refute the contents of these heretical scriptures (*hsieh ching*), then the people, not knowing the errors of these scriptures will not understand the heretical nature of the sects themselves. Even if we do all we can to punish and correct them, the people have already been deeply ensnared [by their teachings], and it is very difficult to win them back. So, I have selected the more important sections of these texts, in order to refute them in detail. I am most concerned that wherever there is heresy it be rejected, and that all evil practices be investigated. I have titled my investigations the *P'o-hsieh hsiang-pien*, having judged that in general [everything in these texts] should not be believed (*pu k'e hsin*).[46]

In the *Hsü-k'an p'o-hsieh hsiang-pien* (A continuation of the P'o-hsieh hsiang-pien) Huang expands upon his conviction that misguided and incorrect beliefs are the heart of the problem. The reason why good people support the sects is that heretical leaders use the names of all sorts of orthodox deities in their texts, thus deluding the ignorant into thinking that the religions themselves are legitimate. He also writes that, since the sects tell people they will go to hell if they don't join and promise direct access to heaven if they do, and since this approach seems to work so well, officials should do the same but in reverse. Because Confucian exhortations to orthodoxy seem ineffective, perhaps it is better to demonstrate the errors of sectarian teaching and threaten those who follow them with punishments in hell. This Huang does, in the latter case chiefly by citing the work of a reformed heretic who claimed that he was told by the spirit of his deceased father that well-known sect leaders were suffering in purgatory.[47]

The basic accusations in Huang's critique are irrationality, vulgarity, and deviation from classical Confucian mythology, with an occasional reference to sectarian usurpation of imperial or official prerogatives. Thus, in discussing a characteristic folk passage in which five relatively recent historical emperors are portrayed as culture heroes who first introduced grains and fruits, he comments, "This passage is the extreme of wild superstition, disobedient error, vulgarity and confusion." When dealing with a sectarian precious scroll (*pao-chüan*) which interprets the self in Taoist alchemical terms, he reproaches the text by saying, "This is all utterly irrational; the crude vulgarity of their concepts is extreme."[48]

But though class-conscious epithets like vulgar and common are used often and indicate Huang's alienation from the folk consciousness, he does not confine himself to such name calling. On several occasions he reasons with the texts (though not always without a hint of ridicule), as when confronting a passage which describes the "3,600 golden boats, 12,000 medium sized boats, 84,000 small golden boats, etc.," which have been provided to save the Eternal Mother's ninety-six myriads of children (that is, mankind) to ferry them to paradise. Huang says, "If there were this many boats and pilots, every one would have already been saved." A clearer statement of Confucian rationalism comes in his attack on sectarian ideas of heaven: "Human happiness on this earth is real and has a proved basis (*shih er you chü*). Happiness in heaven is empty, and has no basis in fact (*hsü er wu p'ing*). The heretics hope for heavenly joy, but in the process they lose human happiness, and bring suffering on themselves. No one has ever seen a man who died in suffering reach a realm of joy after death. This cannot be believed."[49] In both these statements we see Huang's inability to appreciate the symbolic and mythical nature of *pao-chüan* thought.

But Huang's basic attack is on the grounds of sectarian rejection of established Confucian tradition. Thus, he denies that Fu-hsi and Nü-kua could be the children of Wu-sheng lao-mu (Eternal Mother, lit., Unbegotten Venerable Mother) because in the traditional historical mythology they were sovereigns who ruled consec-

utively after mankind and other sages had appeared. Again on the
subject of heretical visions of paradise, Huang gives a long, detailed
description of the Confucian heaven, with its nine levels, twenty-
eight constellations, and twelve divisions of the zodiac. He concludes by saying that the Confucian understanding of heaven is
detailed and complete and everything in it is based on astronomy.
There is no resemblance between this heaven and that of the heretics, nor is there any record of any such beings as the "Old Buddha"
or the "Eternal Parents" existing in heaven. In addition, none of
these beings existed in antiquity either; there is no trace of them in
the Classics. Then he again summarizes the orthodox creation
mythology and the work of the culture heroes, and continues:
"Since all educated men know [the traditional story of the universe]
and have never heard of the "Old Buddha," and Wu-sheng [lao-
mu], we can see that these beings never existed, and further that
they were created in a later period by ignorant, uneducated men."[50]

Huang's strongest reaction on the grounds of authority comes
in his response to an eschatological description of a new universe
including new categories of time, absence of distinction between
the sexes, and the abolition of birth and death. Our scholar-official
is plainly horrified and writes with some vehemence that the existing order of hours, days, and months was established by such
founders as Fu-hsi and the Yellow Emperor.

> The natural course of Heaven and earth was established in an-
> tiquity by the sages, and forever cannot be changed . . . The dura-
> tions of years, months, and days are . . . thus absolutely unchange-
> able. [From this we can see that the teaching of heretical scriptures
> on these matters] is empty and false . . . [and] cannot be believed.[51]

Here the issue is joined. It was this belief system backed up by
imperial power against which the sects rose unsuccessfully time and
time again.

Modern Republican Chinese approaches. Early Republican
Chinese who wrote of the White Lotus tradition, like T'ao Ch'eng-
chang and Sun Yat-sen, were partially sympathetic because they
saw the sects as carriers of an indigenous revolutionary tradition.[52]
However, later non-Marxist Chinese scholars have taken a more

critical view, and appear, in fact, as a continuation of the old imperial Confucian interpretation in modern dress.[53]

Two of these writers are T'ao Hsi-sheng and Li Shou-k'ung, neither of whom devote much time to methodological issues. Their work consists mostly of long quotes from original texts, connected with short summary comments. This approach in itself indicates a certain lack of critical distance between these writers and their sources. When they do make interpretive remarks both T'ao and Li emphasize the importance of socioeconomic factors and see religion merely as the mode of expression for popular discontent. Thus, T'ao, after quoting a Yüan folk verse critical of corrupt officials, says: "Under such social conditions, and [because of] oppression by the Confucian and [Mongol] Buddhist classes, the people arose in revolt, and their revolts took the form of religion." And at the end of this same article he writes: "From this we can see that the White Lotus was a movement in resistance to the power of the rich gentry . . . and therefore easily found occasion for revolt."[54] Though T'ao's point of view is not that of an imperial official, yet it is purely political, and does not see these movements as an authentic alternative tradition. In this connection it is of interest to recall the titles of a few of his articles: "The Maitreya and White Lotus Sects of the Ming Dynasty and Other Religious Bandits (*Yao tsei*),"[55] "Various Violent Movements in the Sung Dynasty,"[56] and "The Violent Activities (*pao tung*) of the Maitreya and White Lotus Societies in the Yüan."[57] This interpretation of the sects as sources of sporadic violence is rooted in the pre-Republican tradition.

In his article Li Shou-k'ung's own attitude is not expressed directly except in the statement, "In the Yüan, anti-Mongol nationalistic movements used the Maitreya ideology as a cover for their own ends."[58] Otherwise his interpretation can only be inferred from his close adherence to the perspective of the sources.

The view that sectarian religion is but a cover for political subversion is expressed more clearly by the later writers, Tai Hsüan-chih and Chan Hok-lam.[59] In 1967 Mr. Tai expressed the following view of the Maitreya and White Lotus societies:

The Maitreya society's political nature far exceeded its religious nature; it falsely used the name of religion, but in fact was an attempt to take over political control . . . [Its] basic purpose was to oppose the government . . . The White Lotus then carried on this political revolutionary tradition. [Its] basic purpose was to usurp government power . . . The White Lotus used religion as a pretext for hoodwinking the people . . . The Chinese people were molded by a long tradition of belief in the power of gods and spirits, and were very deeply superstitious, particularly the country yokels (*hsiang-yü*) . . . The White Lotus society, in order to attain its private ends, cheated the ignorant folk, utilized this tradition of superstitious thought, and by means of heretical techniques (*hsieh-shu*) commanded the people's belief . . . The White Lotus was really a political revolutionary group, and not a religious society . . . Its failure to succeed in taking over the government should serve as a warning to all those who are up to no good.[60]

This article continues much of the attitude of the traditional Chinese elite, fortified by more modern research techniques.

Chan Hok-lam's article on "The White Lotus-Maitreya Doctrine" is all the more interesting because though it was published in a Western Sinological journal in 1969, its interpretation is basically a restatement of the 1,800 year old traditional view, even to the use of specific words and phrases such as "seditious activities," "degenerate religious sect," and "fabricated scriptures." To these he adds terms from modern theories of psychic distress and relative deprivation, all in the context of treating "millennial doctrine . . . as an effective base for movements of rebellion and revolution."[61]

Orthodox Buddhist interpretations. Though some Buddhist monks were sect leaders and wrote on their behalf, the sangha on the whole rejected the folk movements on both doctrinal and political grounds. While orthodox leaders were sincerely concerned with the popular misunderstanding of karma and the people's use of devotion to the Buddha as means to solve immediate problems, their own precarious position made it politically necessary to sharply distinguish themselves from active sectarian dissent.

From the beginning there had been Buddhist scholars who were concerned with stating the differences between Buddhism and the Chinese *Weltanschauung* as well as their points of harmony. In relation to the government this position was most clearly stated by Hui-yüan (d. 416) in his refusal to submit to Emperor An and other powerful officials of the Chin dynasty, and in his emphasis to the

dictatorial Huan Hsüan that "those who had left the household life
to become monks had transcended society and had no concern with
worldly affairs [and thus] should not be judged by the ordinary
rules of society."[62]

But at least as early as Shan-tao (d. 681), orthodox Buddhist
opposition to the syncretizing pressures of Chinese culture was expressed in the other direction, against the growing tendency to
absorb folk beliefs. Criticizing the popularity of sacrificial rituals
and prayers for long life, Shan-tao wrote:

> The length of a man's life is already predestined. Why pretend
> that ghosts and spirits will lengthen it? If one who is ignorant and
> confused believes in heterodoxy and kills living beings in order to
> sacrifice to gods and spirits, this merely increases bad karma and
> shortens one's life. And when life is ended, what can little ghosts
> do?[63]

We have interesting criticisms of heterodoxy by two Southern
Sung (1127-1279) monks, Tsung-chien (f. 1230-1240) and Chih-p'an
(f. 1260-1270), whose perspectives will be discussed below in the
treatment of the White Lotus and White Cloud sects. At this point
suffice it to say that these scholars considered the teachings of both
groups to be false and misleading and thus harmful to the people.
Thus, Tsung-chien, for example, says of White Cloud members
that "they fell into evil ways, [becoming just like] those evil 'vegetarians who serve the devil' . . . They were neither Buddhist nor
Taoist . . . [but] upheld superstitious teachings in order to stir up
ignorant commoners. Taking the name of repairing roads and
building bridges, or reciting sūtras and burning incense, they
gathered at night and dispersed during the day, with no distinction
between men and women."[64]

In addition, Mao Tzu-yüan (1086-1166), who has been considered by some to be the founder of the White Lotus sect, vigor-
ously attacked those who chant Amitābha's name for immediate
blessings rather than for eternal salvation in his paradise. These
people are to be pitied rather than condemned:

> Alas, when believers join a Buddhist society today, they do so
> because of illness and difficulty, or to repay a vow [made on behalf

of a relative], or to seek protection for their families. They practice vegetarianism because they are afraid of disasters; even though they believe, they don't carry out their [proper] vows; even though they chant the Buddha's name, they don't understand its true meaning . . .

Though they say they are accumulating goodness and honoring the Buddha, yet in their worship and burning incense they merely desire riches, high position, fame and long life . . .

They want good crops and famous descendants . . . and if there is one thing that does not go as they wish they complain that the Buddha is not protecting them![65]

Orthodox attacks on folk Buddhism continued during the Ming dynasty (1368-1644). For example, in the mid-sixteenth century a Chekiang monk named Tsung-pen, in a section on "deciding doubts and clearly distinguishing between heresy and orthodoxy," discusses at length a variety of heterodox teachings and groups, all introduced by the sentence, "Today there are heretical teachers who propound devilish and superstitious teachings." He concludes most of his brief descriptions by roundly condemning to hell the heretics at hand, with such statements as "Their teachings vilify the Three Jewels (Buddhism) and destroy the orthodox tradition . . . They will certainly fall into Avīci hell, and, being reborn as animals or hungry ghosts, revolve in samsāra without end."

Though Tsung-pen unfortunately does not give the names of groups or leaders he discusses, it appears that in some cases he is referring to sects we know of from other sources. Thus, he criticizes those who, confusing Taoist "circulation of *ch'i*" with Buddhist meditation, say that they can "revert to the root and return to the origin" (*fan-pen huan-yüan*), a Taoist phrase common in *pao-chüan* texts.

Elsewhere in this fascinating section Tsung-pen attacks "others who set up every sort of superfluous teaching, wildly deceiving men and women who do not really know how to seek true enlightenment." He criticizes those who claim they have marvelous visions of paradise, those who call themselves Śākyamuni, Maitreya, or the Supreme Dharma King, and heretical teachers who "habitually practice magic, or who say that if one meditates quietly for a long time a powerful demon will take possession of his body. These men are good talkers, saying 'I have attained perfect wisdom and thus know both the past and the future.' They recklessly predict the fortunes of others, saying that today a certain person will arrive, or that tomorrow a certain event will occur."[66]

A better known Ming critic was Yün-ch'i Chu-hung (1535-1615), also from Chekiang, who wrote of the White Lotus:

> In the world there are vagrant evil elements who falsely use the Buddha's name to assemble the people and plot illegal and rebellious activities. Their false statements include, "Śākyamuni Buddha has declined; Maitreya Buddha shall govern the world." This is certainly not the Mount Lu Lotus Association (*lien she*) of Hui-yüan.[67]

Chu-hung also bitterly attacked the Lo Sect as he found it in the early seventeenth century:

> A man named Lo [Lo Ch'ing—founder of the Lo sect] wrote a book . . . called the *Wu-wei chüan* [Book of nonaction]. The ignorant followed him in great numbers, but [the book's] teachings are false . . . He talked about purity and emptiness, but in fact in his heart he was plotting for his own advantage. In name he was nonactive, but in fact he was active (*yu wei*). When people saw him quoting from many Buddhist sūtras, they supposed him to be orthodox, not realizing that he falsely used orthodox texts to support [his own] heresy . . . All Buddhists should firmly reject him.[68]

Thus, the sects were buffeted by doctrinal criticism from Buddhists as well as Confucians. Both forms of criticism are legitimate expressions of differing points of view, united by a common conviction that salvation is best attained by being part of an elite community, be it a literate class of superior men, or the celibate sangha. Because of this conviction, both the Confucians and Buddhists were unable to fully understand the religious aspirations of the people, and hence dealt with them in a distorted manner. The similarity of Buddhist and Confucian criticisms demonstrates that the alienation between these traditions and popular cult was due not so much to class distinctions as to different types of spirituality.[69]

Dualistic interpretations. Because there is such a variety of what I call dualistic interpretations, I will attempt to characterize these perspectives in summary form as much as possible. By dualistic I mean an approach which allows some validity to sectarian religion, but which sharply qualifies this validity. There are four types of such ambivalent approaches, which make distinctions between leaders and followers, political and religious functions, orthodox and heretical belief, and between peaceful and rebellious phases of activity.

1. Leader/Follower dualism. It was a fairly common practice in China for officials to arrest only sect leaders, or to release the members after they had been cleared or pardoned. For example, in 1420, after T'ang Sai-er's revolt had been put down, the *Ming shih* records that "more than 3,000 of those who had been compelled to follow her were captured, but Hsia Yüan-chi [the official in charge of the case) asked the Emperor to pardon all of them." Elsewhere in the same history, we read that when Li Tao-ming led an uprising in about 1500, only he was punished, while his followers were all released. His group had first been arrested for merely "assembling to burn incense," but a local military official then accused them of being in league with bandits. An investigating official could find no evidence for this charge, so he released the prisoners and arrested and disgraced the officer who had made the false accusation.[70]

While such fair-minded investigation was not always the case, it is clear that officials were often reluctant to punish great numbers of people, either because they feared more trouble or because they sincerely believed the people had been duped. The constant emphasis on the "ignorance" and "confusion" of the people made it easy to believe that they had unwittingly fallen into a trap in search of their own well-being.

In 1800, four years after a powerful White Lotus outbreak began in 1796, the Chia-ch'ing Emperor issued a remarkable edict which in effect put the leader/follower distinction on a new and more positive basis. While there is no doubt that the edict was largely intended to be a tactical weapon aimed at separating sect leaders from their popular base of support, it is also significant as the first official recognition of the validity of sectarian religion, by the chief opponent of such lay piety. For our purposes the focal point of the edict is the following statement:

As to the name "White Lotus religion," it originated long ago. The scriptures which Liu Chih-hsieh [the best known leader of this uprising] recited are in general concerned only with urging people to do good; they do not contain any rebellious words. The crime of Liu Chih-hsieh . . . lay in his taking the name Niu-pa [a symbol of imperial pretensions] and secretly plotting to rebel. He brought retribution on himself; it had nothing to do with the White Lotus religion. [The emperor goes on to compare this situation with the unfairness of condemning all Confucians just because one or two literati might be involved in illegal activities, and then continues] Those who practice the White Lotus religion maintain vegetarian diets and recite sūtras, being originally no different from ordinary common people. How can one say that all those who practice this religion are bandits, and rigorously search them out [simply] because there is a Liu Chih-hsieh in [their midst]? In sum, members of the White Lotus religion who are peaceful, quiet and obey the law are good subjects. It is useless for local officials to investigate and arrest them. [However,] if they gather in large groups and stir up confusion they are not ordinary members of the White Lotus religion, and should be prosecuted according to the law.[71]

In another statement made the same year the emperor said, "The White Lotus religion is for obvious reasons not the same as rebellion," again distinguishing between the leaders and "sect members who [merely] practice their religion at home, who were originally innocent."[72]

There is truth in the emperor's comments, as Susan Naquin has demonstrated in her recent study of the Eight Trigrams rebellion which erupted a few years later. In the sects involved in that uprising scripture texts were evidently the property of hereditary leaders, making possible for them a more thorough knowledge of myths and charms than was available to ordinary members. Though at first relationships between teachers and disciples were quite close, once final preparations for overt rebellion began the discipline of recruitment and initiation broke down in the quest for more troops. During the warfare which followed, only a minority of the rebels were sect members, and there seems to have been little concern for religious teachings among the nonmember majority.

Nonetheless, the basic structure of the movement was provided by the religiously oriented bonds of master/disciple relationships and congregational life. Most of the members seem to have been attracted by promises of a better life after the dawn of a new kalpa (world era). These promises were proclaimed by sect leaders, based on scriptural authority and seemingly confirmed by their healing powers in the present.

In a founded religious movement leaders may have different roles and status but risk losing contact with their followers if their beliefs and behavior patterns are completely at odds. An approach which makes a sharp distinction between leaders and followers fails to understand that in the long run charismatic leadership is possible only in the context of group recognition and support;[73] in addition, this interpretation does not give sufficient weight to the basic unity of White Lotus religion discussed above. Maitreyan eschatology was an integral part of the whole system from the fourteenth century on, not a propaganda line to be used in emergencies. It is fundamental to the doctrine of salvation which runs through all the *pao-chüan* literature. Maitreya was a savior given sanction by the Buddha himself, not a sublimated revolutionary; as such his religious role was constant and always available to the sectarian faithful. For late eighteenth century movements Suzuki Chūsei emphasizes how well the Maitreya ideology fit in with the real needs of the common people and thus penetrated deeply into the popular consciousness. He denies that religion was simply utilized by the leaders for their own political ends. Rather, "They all were men who had extremely strong and ardent religious tendencies . . . These sect leaders supported the Maitreya reincarnation belief in order to even more strengthen the religious coloration [of their movements]."[74]

At a more practical level, the Chia-ch'ing Emperor's "dualism" fails to account for the great popularity of the White Lotus movement, of which he himself admitted, "Yet, despite the vastness of the empire, there is nowhere they are not [found within it]."[75] The power and tenacity of this tradition cast doubt on attempts to portray the leaders as mere opportunists, as do its record of hereditary leadership and careful transmission from master to disciple.[76] Furthermore, the sources indicate a high level of devotion and obedience to sect leaders by the members, including the veneration of them as saving beings. It is instructive in this regard to note that the outwardly magnanimous decree of 1800 did not attain its desired result. Very few sect members repented and dropped out during this campaign. Contemporary officials reported that "There is no way to cause the people to recant; they look on death as a return home." In general official edicts calling on the sectarians to recant and return to orthodoxy "had not the slightest effect."[77]

2. Political dualism. This position is the most ambiguous of the dualistic interpretations from my point of view because while it affirms the positive historical role of the sects as a whole, it finally denies any lasting validity to their religious dimension. To this approach sectarian religion is temporarily valid as an expression of popular thought, but must eventually be superseded by a more scientific understanding of revolutionary organization and the historical process.

The first Chinese exponents of this point of view were the early Republican revolutionaries T'ao Ch'eng-chang (d. 1911) and Sun Yat-sen (d. 1925). While the anti-Manchu T'ao firmly approves of sectarian political dissent, he sees religion as but a necessary cover for this dissent. He holds that the reason why the White Lotus borrowed (*chia-chieh*) Buddhism in the Yüan dynasty was that the Mongols were devout Buddhists, and all Buddhists could avoid careful government surveillance no matter what plots they were up to. The orginal purpose of the White Lotus was to "get rid of the Mongols," for which they "utilized (*li-yung*) religion as a means of deceiving the people," but their "real ideology was nationalism (*min-tsu chu-i*) . . . They relied completely on religious belief and magical techniques to gain followers and support."[78] Sun Yat-sen also saw these groups (though he was referring primarily to the Heaven and Earth society) as China's own indigenous exponents of nationalism, who were a minority but still actively present in history. They used ritual to dramatize Han nationalism among the people.[79]

While there were definite nationalistic elements in the Heaven and Earth society, the motives of the White Lotus tradition were perhaps more eschatological than political, though of course the two were intertwined. The whole racial-nationalistic argument is based on the fact that sect leaders often proclaimed themselves or others to be the reincarnation of ideal emperors from past dynasties, which in the Yüan case meant Sung or T'ang and in the Ch'ing, the Ming, in both cases seeming to indicate a desire to replace foreign emperors with Han Chinese. But as Tai Hsüan-chih has already pointed out, this pattern is not consistent along nationalistic lines, for there were Ming rebels who proclaimed themselves "King of the Ming," such as T'ien Chiu-ch'eng in 1409, and others who allied themselves with aboriginal tribes against the ruling Han Chinese house. The very fact that White Lotus uprisings continued all through the Ming dynasty and contributed to its overthrow by the Manchus is also most instructive. Tai notes that Chu Yüan-chang, soon to be the founder of the Ming house, did not proclaim a nationalistic crusade against the Mongols until 1366, after he had already broken with the White Lotus movement. Tai further maintains that sectarian "Emperor of the Ming" titles in the Ch'ing period refer to the Manichaean tradition of ideal kingship, which first appeared as a part of White Lotus religion in 1351. He sums up by saying, "The White Lotus . . . made no racial distinctions, so all theories about it being the leader of racial or nationalistic revolutions are false."[80]

The view that the sects promoted Han political consciousness seems to have been suggested primarily by nationalistic Chinese leaders concerned to strengthen resistance to foreign aggression. To some extent it represents an attempt to read nineteenth and twentieth century conditions back into medieval Chinese history.[81]

The Chinese Marxist refinement of T'ao Ch'eng-chang's position holds that religion is not an instrument of national struggle, but of class struggle.[82] Mainland historians since 1949 have given much attention to what they call "peasant wars," because Mao Tse-tung himself sees them as important indigenous precursors of his own peasant based Communist revolution. The chief value of Marxist interpretation for our present purposes is its affirmation of the creative possibilities of peasant culture; its chief drawback is an external analysis of class conflict which does not adequately distinguish between religious sects and other forms of potentially violent social movements. It is not my purpose to discuss the general Marxist theory of religion to which all the Chinese writers consulted adhere. They agree that religious belief is an illusion that is necessarily replaced by scientific thought as history progresses.

Within this framework the mainland historians are divided into two schools, those who see eschatological religion as the product of peasant class consciousness, and therefore valuable and omnipresent in the class struggle, and those who deny that even peasant religion had any useful function in historical development. This second school emphasizes the reactionary character of much sectarian doctrine, and the fact that many resistance movements in China had little or no religious coloring. My own position is closer to that of the second group.

The first school is represented by Sun Tso-min and Yang K'uan of Shantung University. Sun emphasizes that "a special characteristic of Chinese peasant rebellions was their relationship to religious sects . . . [for] the great majority of these rebellions was closely linked with religion." The reason for this is that in a class society, because of different economic and social interests, each group produces a distinctive class consciousness, and thus "the oppressed classes produce their own thought, which stands in opposition to the thought of the ruling classes." Thus, peasant class religion has several positive functions in a premodern context. It serves to organize the people by giving them a unifying goal and ideology, to arouse them and give them courage by promises of divine assistance and predestined victory, and to provide a cover for resistance movements after their defeat, so they can maintain their revolutionary potential in a cultic guise. Nonetheless, whatever value religion had under feudal conditions, it was fundamentally superstitious and backward, and in fact "every peasant war under religious banners was at its deepest levels a class war."[83]

Yang K'uan continues Sun's distinction between peasant religion and the religion of the ruling class, with an emphasis on the positive historical value of the former. He holds that religion was constantly utilized (*li-yung*) by peasant wars; the people "took the outer garment of religion" and used its organizational forms in their attempts to resist and overthrow the oppresive feudal system. The desperate economic and social position of the peasants forced them to become a revolutionary class and to develop forms of thought which would express their own interests. This thought in turn was expressed as religion, which gave them courage and freed them from the shackles of feudal ideology. Thus, the peasants created their own dissenting religion and readily adopted other belief systems such as Maitreyan Buddhism to express their own claim to political power. While "there were many different sects, they were united by their primary emphasis on revolutionary beliefs."[84] It follows that Yang K'uan sees all Chinese peasant based movements as one subject and one tradition from the Yellow Turbans on; all are "peasant wars."

The second Chinese Marxist position is exemplified by Shao Hsün-cheng of Peking University, who writes: "I do not agree with Yang K'uan's opinion that there was a peasant class religion which was used as an ideological weapon in peasant wars . . . There were a great many large scale peasant wars in Chinese history that had no relation whatsoever to religion . . . The religion of the secret societies at bottom impeded and concealed revolution." While the debates of Marxist historians are not my central concern here, it is nonetheless most interesting to follow the development of Shao's position.

To begin with, Shao rejects Yang K'uan's claim that the White Lotus sect had a "revolutionary theory with an outer garment of religion," and with it rejects any essential connection between religion and class war. He holds that the White Lotus emphasis on returning to the "True Void Native Land" was not revolutionary in nature but rather reflected the general religious concern for a better life after death. So also the doctrine of saving beings coming down to rescue man is the antithesis of revolutionary thought. Further, there is a fatalistic trend in White Lotus belief; the movement from one world period to another is predestined and beyond man's control. Shao stresses that officials like Huang Yü-p'ien often commented on the fact that there was no rebellious content in sectarian texts, and that in the Yüan and again in the late Ming the White Lotus strove for and attained a measure of official recognition and support. It follows that "the only reason these groups were secret was because the ruling classes prohibited associations among the people."[85] On these same pages Shao also discusses the varied urban and artisan make-up of the Heaven and Earth society and the late Ming involvement of court eunuchs in the White Lotus as evidence that these groups did not have a class consciousness. Thus, without intending to, Shao Hsün-cheng gives support to a perspective which seeks to understand sectarian myth and ritual as having a certain coherence of their own, not completely subject to social factors. His emphasis on the secular nature of many Chinese rebellions also saves us from trying to prove too much.

3. Doctrinal dualism. This position can be briefly stated. The White Lotus sect began as a purely religious offshoot of orthodox Amitābha Buddhism, which was penetrated by Taoism and folk religion and took on rebellious and violent characteristics. This interpretation is represented by Shigematsu Shunshō, a Buddhist priest-scholar, and Suzuki Chūsei in his 1941 article on Buddhist religious societies in the Sung dynasty. In his *Shinchō chūkishi kenkyū* (A study of mid-Ch'ing history), published in 1952, Suzuki takes a less restrictive view, though echoes of his earlier position remain. Both these scholars assume the fundamentally religious nature of the White Lotus tradition but hold that the absorption of folk elements constituted a degeneration and vulgarization.

Shigematsu sees the original White Lotus sect as an integral development of the T'ien-t'ai and Pure Land orthodox traditions:

> At the beginning the White Lotus was a religion based on T'ien-t'ai doctrine, followed the Amitābha tradition of chanting the Buddha's name, and was dedicated to the ascetic suppression of desires and developing pure karma (*ching yeh*) . . . However, when the sect met with the violent opposition of government officials and religious [that is, orthodox Buddhist] enemies, it began to recruit members from the restless elements of society, and its doctrines and behaviour of necessity began to change.

Shigematsu attributes the early prohibition of the sect and Mao Tzu-yüan's exile to its "great popularity and strength among the people, which alarmed the officials . . . This was the same sort of difficulty encountered by every new Chinese religion in its formative years."[86]

In general Shigematsu's treatment is very sympathetic, and gives full weight to both social and doctrinal factors. He treats the White Lotus and White Cloud sects much as Leff treats the Waldensians. However, his orientation toward the Buddhist great tradition is revealed by his concluding comments concerning why the White Cloud declined. Here he maintains that while Ch'ing-chüeh, the

White Cloud founder, was devoted to the ideals of compassion, ethical purity, and suppression of desires, unfortunately, after he died his followers lived so much in the world that they were blinded by sensual concerns. Thus, they forgot Ch'ing-chüeh's original ideals, and the sect lasted less than 200 years.[87]

Suzuki's purpose is to get at the Sung origins of late Yüan White Lotus political activity. His basic position is that the peaceful Sung Amitābhist devotional groups became secretive and violent because of the amalgamation with Amitābhism of three other traditions: Ch'an Buddhism with its hierarchical master/disciple relationship; folk Taoism with its quest for immediate, concrete results; and Maitreyan eschatology. It was the latter that gave cohesiveness and overall political direction to the practical concerns of popular religion. The syncretic process itself was made possible by the lay oriented, nondoctrinal nature of Pure Land Buddhism.

Suzuki's excellent and valuable treatment is vitiated from my point of view only by his repeated references to Taoism as "superstition" in which he includes breathing exercises and other methods for attaining long life. The problem here is that what Suzuki calls superstition was a part of the mainstream of folk piety. He also gives full credence to allegations of sectarian sexual immorality in the official reports, adding, "Naturally, a government concerned with supporting public order and good customs would prohibit such activities."[88] Generally, in this article Suzuki stays very close to his sources and accepts their judgments as his own, all of which is detrimental to an empathetic understanding of popular religion. His later work, which we shall describe below, is more sophisticated.

The problem with "doctrinal dualism" is that of the relationship of great and little traditions, or classical and folk religion. That the two are different is obvious; the question is, does the scholar choose to affirm or regret the diversity? This is a crucial issue in discussing the history of folk Buddhist sects, for if the monastic great tradition is considered superior, the scholar is forced to denigrate the whole development of popular cult in China after the T'ang dynasty and is left without the methodological foundation necessary to understand the role of such folk expression. Thus, the quite understandable negative attitude of a Buddhist scholar toward a

sect whose members "lived too much in the world" by implication
denies spiritual validity to several hundred years of lay piety and
evangelism. One cannot remain satisfied with such a result.

4. Temporal dualism. This approach is well represented by
Richard Chu in his dissertation on the White Lotus: "In ordinary
times the White Lotus sect engaged in purely religious activities,
but during times of crisis, economic hardship or disorder, the sect
easily became politically active . . . it could be organized as a sectarian religion, or attempt to form an established political regime."
Chu is clear about the religious nature of this tradition; it was a
"folk religion," a "very old syncretic religion."[89] In contrast to
Chan Hok-lam, who says that the White Lotus was able to survive
because it could hide out in the villages,[90] Chu writes: "[The White
Lotus had] many qualifications to satisfy [the religious] needs [of
the poor]. This quality of spirituality alone is, perhaps, more than
sufficient to explain why the sect survived through centuries in the
face of severe organized persecution."

On the other hand, Chu's work is essentially that of a very
thorough political scientist who is interested in the White Lotus because of its relationship to peasant movements, that is to say, in the
relationship of religion to rebellion. This means that though he devotes some attention to the origins and religious aspects of the sect,
his overall emphasis is on political implications; when Chu writes
about "White Lotus activities," he refers primarily to violent uprisings. The resulting picture of the sect has a certain sporadic and
fragmentary quality.

Though Chu occasionally slips into disparaging language, as
in his statements that most White Lotus leaders were "common sorcerers" and that Hsü Hung-ju had magic skills "which were sufficient for him to attract the ignorant," this is balanced by his generally empathetic attitude. He also writes that "to follow the White
Lotus for the poor also means to have hope."

But my chief problem with Chu's treatment is that he does not
deal adequately with the relationship of the White Lotus to the history of Chinese Buddhism. Though he discusses Mao Tzu-yüan and
his possible relationship to Hui-yüan and the "Lotus School," he
holds that Maitreyan eschatology is the chief Buddhist element in
the sect.[91] This emphasis of course helps set the stage for a discus-

sion of political rebellions and vice versa. Perhaps because he evidently was not familiar with Suzuki's article on Sung dynasty Buddhist associations, he neglects the importance of the Amitābhist tradition of lay piety and salvation by grace.

I have said that White Lotus religion was radically syncretic. Though its congregational structure and concept of a lay priesthood were based on the orthodox Pure Land tradition, it soon came to incorporate elements of folk shamanism, Taoist cult and magical techniques, and Manichaean eschatology. More important, beginning in the mid-fourteenth century, White Lotus folk Amitābhism blended together with popular Maitreyan eschatology and in the process acquired a much more militant political stance. From then on the general theoretical structure of the sect's mythology was Maitreyan, though it retained such Amitābhist characteristics as ritual repetition of mantras, hope for rebirth in paradise, and an emphasis on divine compassion. It should also be stressed that the White Lotus movement became syncretic at the social structural level as well, with the result that sect leaders could both be evangelists and hold titles with imperial pretensions. Local congregations easily made the transition to local political units when the social situation and eschatological signs were favorable.

Nonetheless, while it was immersed in a folk context, it can be maintained that the basic theoretical and soteriological structure of White Lotus religion was rooted in Mahāyāna Buddhism, so that, for example, the role of the indigenous Eternal Mother was merged with that of Amitābha and thus shaped by the bodhisattva concept. If this fundamental soteriological unity is not grasped, then it is not possible to discuss the sect as a coherent religious structure; hence a fragmentary and dualistic picture appears. From a political point of view it is valid to describe quiet and active phases of sectarian activity, but in fact both armed rebellion in the name of Maitreya and quiet invocation of the Eternal Mother's aid were integral aspects of the same belief system.

More empathetic interpretations. The first wholly affirmative comment about the Chinese folk sects was made by the nineteenth century scholar-missionary Joseph Edkins in 1887: "There is another way of looking at these sects. This is the sympathizing and favorable view . . . If we would know where the movement of religious thought is most active in modern China, can anyone say that it is not among these sects, obscure as they are, and despised by the ordinary literati?"[92]

Of the Wu-wei (Nonaction) sect, a branch of the Lo chiao, Edkins wrote: "[It] is usually spoken of by the Confucians as a corrupt sect, with secret political designs; but its adherents appear at present to be entirely innocent of any illegal aims. They are, so far as can be seen, intent on religious objects, and sincerely attached to their system."[93]

Though in the last analysis J. J. M. DeGroot was more interested in persecution than in sectarianism, because of his concern about Chinese attacks on Christian missions, his view of sectarian religion is also most positive. He wrote of the White Lotus as a "mysterious powerful community, accommodated to the religious instincts of the masses, and by satisfying their cravings for salvation, able to hold its own, in spite of bloody persecution and oppression." This sect "had Maitreya for its patron saint, the Messiah, for whom all longed, who was to bring deliverance to the suffering militant church and reinstate it in its glory." The vocabulary is from another century, but DeGroot certainly cannot be faulted for lack of empathy.

Because the Dutch scholar held that the folk sects originated in state suppression of the sangha with the resultant returning of thousands of clergy to lay life and leadership, he wrote:

Thus, religious lay communities were created, in the main of a pronounced Buddhist colour, with the Buddhist doctrine of salvation for their backbone . . . They are religious sects in the fullest sense of the word, the upholders of Buddhism and Taoism among the people . . . They possess everything appertaining to a complete religious system: founders and prophets, a pantheon, commandments, moral philosophy, initiation and consecration, religious ritual, sacred books and writings, even a theology, a Paradise and Hell . . . everything borrowed from Mahāyānistic Buddhism, and partially from old Chinese philosophy and cosmogony.

The secrecy of these sects was imposed by persecution and hence they must be clearly distinguished from the

. . . various secret societies and seditious clubs . . . Against

such preposterous identification [of the sects with secret societies]
we must earnestly raise our voice. Only from the Confucian political point of view can there be a semblance of correctness in it . . .
[It is true that it is the custom for such political clubs] . . . to worship some deity . . . as patron saint, and to bear the name of the
same. But this is done by almost all associations, no matter what
their purpose or tenets, so that here again it is the appearance
which deceives.[94]

Edkins and DeGroot set the stage for a new, positive appre-
ciation of the sects, which was picked up by such scholars as Max
Weber[95] and Tsukamoto Zenryū. Nonetheless, DeGroot's work is
flawed by his passionate attack on the Confucian state, which he
saw as an evil Chinese form of medieval inquisition. This approach
is too moralistic and does not grant the Confucians the right to defend their own world view. To speak of Chinese officials as "arch-
persecutors . . . embued with fanatical animosity . . . [who supply]
victims and martyrs for the blood-drenched altar of intolerance"
does not contribute to an understanding of the cultural dynamics
involved. This same stress leads to an overly simplified and external interpretation of sectarian uprisings as being solely reactions to
what might be called "pre-emptive persecution."[96] There is truth in
this view, but it does not deal adequately with the internal and theoretical preconditions for revolt.

Tsukamoto discusses the Lo chiao as a full-fledged sect, assisted in its early period by orthodox Ch'an monks. He gives much
consideration to doctrinal developments and quotes Edkins and
DeGroot with approval. To Tsukamoto, Lo Ch'ing was "a prophet
of people's religion" whose teachings promised equality and an
easy means of deliverance for the poor and ignorant. He maintains
that the Lo sect eventually went underground only because of government suppression.

All of this clearly places Tsukamoto in the "empathetic"
school, though he is still ambivalent about sectarian political
involvement which he attributes to such external factors as the
political ambitions of sect leaders and official opposition.[97] At this
point Tsukamoto's interpretation of the Lo sect resembles Shigematsu's view of the White Cloud. The difference is that Tsukamoto
is willing to affirm the validity of syncretic religion.

I have also already introduced the sympathetic interpretation of Suzuki Chūsei. He sets the stage for his treatment by noting elements of religious conversion, training, and piety in White Lotus leaders of the 1796 uprising.[98] Other writers have tried to distinguish the White Lotus movement of this period by the relative absence of ideological factors.[99] Suzuki then emphasizes that the aspect of White Lotus religion most appealing to its members was the stress on healing and a prosperous life in the present. Most of the contents of sect scriptures dealt with avoiding illness and natural disasters, and even such statements as *huan shih-chieh* (change the world) were essentially concerned with avoiding the consequences of change and disorder, and did not imply a positive revolutionary spirit.

In discussing sect membership Suzuki agrees that most were farmers who were authentically pious and sought salvation in a disciplined manner. While there may have been some charlatans, on the whole White Lotus members were sincere and had good intentions. He continues, "White Lotus religion was essentially concerned with reaching salvation by observing vegetarian diet, ritual activity and ethical precepts, and thus attaining felicity in one's next existence." Thus "a person entering the sect became involved in a situation of very ardent belief and piety." Suzuki also maintains that the Maitreya belief and popular emphasis on a religion of immediate practical results provided the background of militant activity, though this activity was always aroused by sociopolitical conditions of extreme poverty, oppression by corrupt officials, ravages by government troops, and so on.[100] Suzuki's comments on the sects are of course but part of a detailed historical study.

We have already noted C. K. Yang's interpretation of the sects as the third form of institutional religion in Chinese history. From the above discussion it should be clear that my own understanding as it has developed is in harmony with many of Yang's positions, such as his comments that the political activity of organized religion can arise from "the conception of a new ideal world to replace the existing social and moral order," that "The Buddhistic goal of universal deliverance was consistently present," and all politically involved religious movements "closely identified their political cause with the divine mission of universal salvation." His understanding of the power of "emerging deities" is also most valuable in the Chinese context. In addition, Mr. Yang has a careful and balanced treatment of the relation of religion to the state and of the importance of socioeconomic factors in the stimulation of uprisings.[101]

There has been a rich variety of interpretations of Chinese folk religious movements. This variety demonstrates not only how basic attitudes affect scholarship but also the complexity of the movements themselves. An understanding of these factors can perhaps bring more flexibility to our own approach.

4
Cross-Cultural Perspectives

The scale creates the phenomenon.
Henri Poincaré

The Chinese folk Buddhist sects share many characteristics with similar phenomena elsewhere, particularly in medieval Europe and Kamakura Japan. Given these similarities, it is possible to develop a cross-cultural perspective which helps clarify just what the Chinese groups were and what they were not. The point of such cross-cultural work is not comparison but a multiplication of perspectives which can perhaps lead to better understanding. In taking this approach one is forced to think structurally as well as causally, though the types thus discerned must be kept in intimate dialogue with the historical subject at hand.

There are several types of religious association which provide starting points for cross-cultural analysis of the Chinese movements. They include: primitive secret societies, secret societies in more complex cultures, Hellenistic mystery cults, sectarian movements in medieval Europe, and Buddhist denominations in Japan. We will look briefly at each of these types in turn in order to understand their structural similarities and dissimilarities with the Chinese folk religious associations. In addition, I will attempt to distinguish from religious sects another phenomenon which almost seems to constitute a category in itself, religiously influenced peasant rebellions. At every point I am concerned with the implications of this analysis for interpreting the Chinese situation.

Primitive Secret Societies

> The [White Lotus] has branched out into many secret societies. In the North, its branches include such groups as the Way of Pervading Unity, The Big Sword Society—the Non-Ultimate Society —[and] the Eight Trigrams Society . . . In South China, the main branches of the White Lotus are the Triad Society and the Elders Society.
>
> Basically these secret societies belonged to two major systems, two big "families": the White Lotus, established mainly in North China, and the Triad, influential in the South.[1]

These statements by contemporary scholars illustrate the typological ambiguity surrounding discussions of these Chinese associations, and the extent to which the category of secrecy contributes to that ambiguity.[2] We have noted that there were secret societies, which kept secret both their myths and rituals and in some cases membership as well. However, these associations were different from the folk sects in origin, teachings, and practice, differences which come into sharper focus from a cross-cultural perspective.

Primitive secret societies are of course not culturally comparable to Chinese associations, but they show several interesting points of typological similarity and divergence. There are two main differences. First, most secret societies in primitive cultures are exclusively male, or in a lesser number of cases, particularly in Africa, exclusively female. Loeb notes that in Australia "all the men of the tribe form a secret society from which the women are excluded."[3] Hutton Webster emphasizes the close relation in aboriginal America and elsewhere of secret societies to mens' houses, and his whole discussion assumes the separation of the sexes and the predominance of male membership.[4] To be sure, there are exceptions to this characteristic, as there are exceptions in the definition of any type, but the stress on sexual exclusiveness is clear. This sexual distinction is not in evidence in China, except perhaps in the Triad tradition.[5] On the contrary, the folk sects were characterized by the role of equality and even leadership which they afforded women. At times a man joined with his whole family.[6]

The second chief difference is the much greater emphasis on

initiation in the primitive groups and the sense of separation and rebirth which initiation imparts. In the primitive societies, the initiation rite is an intensification of tribal or puberty initiation, and its basic motif is the death and resurrection of the candidate into a new mode of being.[7] Such an initiation sets a man off from women, children, and uninitiated men as a being apart. He is given a new name, known only to other fully initiated men, and he may use a form of speech esoteric to the rest of the tribe, not used in the presence of women or the uninitiates. In the history of these archaic secret societies, "The tendency . . . is to widen the gap between the initiated and the uninitiated . . . [The result of this] is that secret societies . . . are organizations more or less limited in membership, divided into degrees, and localized usually in some definite lodge."[8]

This whole separatist tendency in the primitive groups is the antithesis of the pre-Triad Chinese sects. In China membership was usually a rather simple matter that included such things as recommendation by other members, payment of a fee, approval by the leader or by a deity itself through divination or use of the planchette, and registrations of one's name on the heavenly rolls by burning a piece of paper on which it was written. To be sure, in the Lo sect and other groups, members took the *upāsaka* vows and were given dharma names, but this was in direct emulation of the orthodox sangha rite. Furthermore, the new names were not secret, but proudly used. This absence of developed initiation rites is typologically crucial, for as Joachim Wach says, "[only groups] connected with initiation . . . are true secret societies."[9]

The Heaven and Earth society had a complex initiation ritual, full of the symbolism of death and rebirth, and the transition from darkness to light, all girded about with oaths of secrecy. This death/rebirth motif is not present in other Chinese groups in the same way, though, to be sure, a member of the White Lotus society could hope to go directly to the Eternal Mother's paradise at death. However, this salvation was available to all who would accept it. It did not involve an ordeal, nor did being saved imply a rejection of those who were not. Rather, it was a summons to evangelism.

The secret society use of esoteric language is also instructive, for the non-Triad Chinese sects were characterized by their use of the vernacular, popular preaching, and propagation by means of signs and tracts. Their thrust was in the other direction, toward making the means of salvation as simple and easily available as possible. Here again the highly symbolic writing, codes, and gestures of the Heaven-Earth groups are atypical.[10] Thus, even at the primitive level the secret society is a type different in intention from the Chinese sects. Its concern is with the guarding and concentrating of sacred experience, while that of the sectarian movements is to share their message with all who will listen.

However, there is also an instructive similarity between these two types, because both were constituted by voluntary association in contexts heavily oriented toward tribal and family relationships. Commenting on the Australian Kurnai initiation society, Webster wrote, "It is a brotherhood including all the descendants of the male and female [mythical] ancestors Yeering and Djeetgun. All initiates are brothers [who] call each other's wives as 'wife' and children as 'child.' "[11] Fortune says that while membership in Omaha secret societies could be passed on from father to son, this could only be done by telling the initiate of the traditional vision of the society. The goal and norm were membership by individual vision without human intermediaries. It was this shared religious experience which constituted the society.[12] So members of the Chinese sects called each other "brother" and expressed their new horizontal relationship in communal living and shared ownership of property. The source of their cohesion was the rediscovery that they were in fact the primeval children of the Eternal Mother. This rediscovery meant that in principle their earthly parents were incidental. Their real home was the paradise from which they came, the "True Void Native Land."

Secret Societies in More Complex Cultures

In the introduction to his book *Secret Societies*, Norman MacKenzie writes:

Every organization has secrets of its kind. The hallmark of a secret society is that it places a premium upon secrecy, and that its formal rituals are designed to seal that secrecy. In the case of such groups as . . . the Assassins, the Thugs, Mau Mau or the Rosicrucians, we are dealing with a very special type of secrecy. We can say that without secrecy, the organization could not exist . . . A secret society . . . is organized around the principles of exclusiveness and secrecy. It places very strict limitations on recruitment and will often go to great lengths to screen its activities from public gaze . . . [Its] whole outlook is colored by secrecy.[13]

In this definition MacKenzie is echoing the position of Georg Simmel, who wrote that in secret societies secrecy is:

a form of the existence of the group; the secret element in societies is a primary sociological fact . . . the secret society is itself characterized by its secret . . . [Its principle of membership is that] whoever is not expressly included is excluded . . . The structure of [many such groups is often aimed at] keeping certain subjects from general knowledge . . . [In gnostic type groups] . . . the issue turns upon a body of doctrine to be kept from publicity.[14]

MacKenzie lists four major characteristics of secret societies, in addition to the central factor of secrecy: 1. They are exclusively or predominantly male, though women are often allowed roles in a subordinate association. 2. They are very hierarchical in structure, with an elaborate system of ranks and degrees through which the novice progresses from novice to senior official. Their titles are often elaborate and esoteric. 3. Such a group has a specially created story of its origins. 4. They place great emphasis on rituals of initiation. The novice is often made to take a symbolic journey, which involves the themes of death and resurrection, and his rebirth as a new man in a new environment. This ritual often includes fearful oaths of secrecy which invoke death on the betrayer.[15]

Of these characteristics, only the third is wholly applicable to the Chinese folk movements, since every religious group has a "story of its origins." The second point is applicable in part because sects in the White Lotus tradition did have hierarchical leadership. But their titles and responsibilities are characteristic of any cultic association in a complex social setting. At times sect leaders assumed titles such as "Incarnation of Maitreya" or "Emperor of the Sung," which were certainly grandiose in relation to their actual status, but these were eschatological signs publicly proclaimed.

Again, it is the Triad societies that fit nicely into MacKenzie's scheme, not the folk Buddhist sects.

The type "secret society" simply doesn't work for the Chinese groups under discussion. The Mahāyāna based movements were expressions of the bodhisattva ideal of universal salvation at the popular congregational level. Their texts are shot through with such phrases as *tu-hua chung-sheng* (save all living beings). That they were often forced to go underground and assume temporary secrecy is a function of their relation to the all-encompassing Chinese state, not an attribute of their own being. As Favre wrote, "Si elles sont secrètes, c'est uniquement pour échapper aux persécutions."[16] To be sure, when they were involved in open warfare they tried to keep secret their military plans, but even then the sources tell us over and over again that *shih lou* (the affair leaked out), and uprisings were cut off in the bud. There is nothing to indicate that they had more secrets than any normal men in similar political circumstances, or that they kept them any better.

Mystery Societies

Joachim Wach lists three main types of "specifically religious organizations," secret societies (in which category he includes only primitive phenomena), mystery societies, and founded religions, with congregational Hinduism, the *sampradaya*, as an intermediate type between the mystery society and founded religions. He classifies the Chinese Lo sect discussed by Edkins as a mystery society.

This classification distinguishes the Chinese groups from secret societies and recognizes that they never became full scale, officially recognized sectarian denominations, as in Japan, but it doesn't do full justice to their historical and intentional differences from Hellenistic mystery cults, the classic example of this type.[17]

There are three chief differences. First, the Chinese sects were "second generation" voluntary associations. They were vehicles of popularization which can only be understood against the background of established monastic Buddhism. Thus, their structural role in history was different from that of the mystery societies which were a *primary* voluntaristic reaction to Greek and Roman family/state cult and organization.[18] It follows that the mystery societies were typologically closer to primitive secret societies; at different cultural levels their function of individualizing and concentrating sacred experience against a background of tribal or national cult was the same. Simmel holds that secret organizations are a transitional type that appear only within fully developed social contexts. They are the "antithesis of generic societies," whose secrecy is necessary to protect weak new structures and beliefs from the "opposition of the powers that be."[19] Without accepting Simmel's analysis *in toto,* perhaps we can say that the element of secrecy surrounding the initiation rite of both primitive secret societies and the mystery cults is related to their direct apposition to "genetic societies." The Chinese groups, in contrast, always had the model of the sangha existing in a sense *between* them and the traditional social order, a model in which personal religion was officially recognized and openly propagated. From this perspective, one might say that the Chinese sects had a dual role; in relation to the traditional order they were primary voluntary associations at the popular level; as viewed through the existence of the sangha they were a secondary development. Insufficient emphasis on the ground theme of Mahāyāna salvation in these associations contributes to their being interpreted primarily as secret societies opposed to the established order.

The second difference between the Hellenistic and Chinese cult groups is the strong emphasis on initiation in the mystery societies. We have already discussed the absence of highly structured initiation rites in pre-Triad China. While there was evidently some amalgamation of Triad and White Lotus groups in the nineteenth century, the sectarian religious tradition remained essentially distinct from that of the more politically oriented secret societies. Thus, membership ceremonies, as distinguished from the more rigorous initiation rites, were characteristic of the Hsien-t'ien and Lung-hua sects in Amoy investigated by DeGroot in 1887. This characteristic was continued into the twentieth century by the I-kuan tao sect and is still operative in Singapore groups related to the White Lotus tradition.

In the Hellenistic cults, on the other hand, elaborate, graded initiation rites, which could take several days to complete, were of central importance. Through these rites the initiate was reborn into a new and higher level of being. This new being was constituted by a revelation of sacred truth unavailable to the uninitiated and thus led to a sharp distinction between the elite and those who still groped about in darkness. In the cult of Mithra, which Wach calls the "most striking example of a mystery religion,"[20] there were seven degrees of initiation, each degree corresponding to symbolic ascent through the seven planetary spheres toward the sun, each involving passwords known only to the initiate. Only after passing the fourth stage was the member admitted to a revelation of the mysteries. When he became a "lion," honey was poured on his hand and tongue, as was customary with newborn children, symbolizing his rebirth. Attainment of this fourth level also allowed one to participate in the sacrament of Haoma. Franz Cumont says that such participation "was not granted until after a long novitiate . . . [There] were genuine trials imposed upon the candidate. To receive the sacred ablutions and the consecrated food, the participant was obliged to prepare for them by prolonged abstinence and numerous austerities."[21]

This emphasis on rigorous initiation is echoed in Apuleius' second century account of Lucius' entry into the cult of Isis. A priest said to him, "The day you have so long asked for by your unwearied prayers has come." He was then bathed and given secret instructions, and he sat before the image of the goddess for ten days, taking no meat or wine.[22]

Of these rituals Cumont writes, "In the initiation the mystic was born again, but to a superhuman life, and became the equal of the immortals."[23] So Plutarch of Athens (fifth century) wrote: "Thus death and initiation closely correspond . . . [After the darkness and terror of the ritual death] . . . a strange and wonderful light meets the wanderer; he is admitted into clean and verdant meadows . . . Here the now fully initiated is free . . . he is the companion of pure and holy men, and looks down upon the uninitiated and unpurified crowd here below in the mud and fog."[24]

This experiential dualism was both the result and a continuing source of the ontological dualism which permeated the mystery society tradition, a position rooted in Orphism and Platonic philosophy. Ontological dualism was the background of the mystery society emphasis on secret truth or on revelatory actions hidden from all but the initiated. We have seen the first seed of this distinc-

tion between old and new being in primitive secret societies. Such
an emphasis is the third main difference between Hellenistic mystery cults and the Chinese sects. Though, as we shall see, a Manichaean element entered the White Lotus tradition of the Yüan dynasty, the primary philosophic background of the folk Buddhist
sects was the T'ien-t'ai emphasis that "all phenomena are the manifestations of the Mind of Pure Nature,"[25] with the result that "the
phenomenal life . . . is affirmed absolutely. The everyday life of the
layman is part of the life of the Buddha."[26]

This radical emphasis on the unity of all things was the ground
of sectarian affirmation of the world and of lay existence in both
China and Japan. The two principal sect founders, Mao Tzu-yüan
and Shinran, were both Pure Land monks trained in T'ien-t'ai philosophy. Their evangelism was rooted in their ontology.

But in the Hellenistic world, Grant says:

> There was . . . a notable tendency in the direction of dualism,
> to be seen especially in the revival of Orphic and Pythagorean doc-
> trines and practices [and in their successors—the Gnostics, Mani-
> chaeans and Neoplatonists] . . . [In later Platonism, the Platonic
> epistemological distinction between invisible realities and their
> copies or shadows in the visible world] had become an out and out
> ontological principle.[27]

The expression of this dualism in religion was a quest to gain personal knowledge of hidden spiritual reality and then to defend its
secrecy at all costs to preserve the precious manifestations of
sacrality in an impure world.

There was a sense of holiness in the Chinese folk sects, expressed in their veneration of images, and in the solemn rituals
which invariably accompanied the reading of a sacred text. But
their awareness of the *numinous* was in a monistic context which
affirmed that all levels and types of being participated in sacred
reality; that all things, in Paul Ricoeur's words, were "fragments of
the cosmos."[28] Further, their experience of holiness was closely tied
to divine beings who were the embodiment of the Mahāyāna thrust
toward universal deliverance. Thus, in principle, the Chinese
groups had no ground for a sharp distinction between initiated and
uninitiated, ordinary and hidden truth, public and secret ritual.[29]

To sum up, the Chinese groups cannot be typed as mystery societies in any accepted sense of the term. While they filled the same need for personal salvation at the popular level, they are distinguished by their different cultural and philosophical contexts. Though both were potentially universal in scope, the mystery societies were exclusivist and Pelagian in principle, for only those who had worked their way through initiatory death and rebirth were eligible for salvation. Their new being gave them an elite religious status. The Buddhist sects, on the other hand, were populist and Augustinian in principle; all could be saved by the power of Amitābha or the Eternal Mother. All persons on earth were really her primeval children, and thus the distinction between them could not be ontological, but was only between those who believed and those who did not.

Sects

I use the word sect to mean "a founded voluntary association, oriented toward personal salvation, which arises in reaction to a larger, founded religious system, which though it is established, was itself voluntary in origin." Since the factors of exclusiveness and detachment from the world stressed by Ernst Troeltsch are an echo of Western dualism, they are not relevant to a definition which intends to be universal. His emphasis on the objective established character of a church, into which a person is born, neglects the inherent voluntary element in the soteriological system of a founded religion, and the extent to which monasticism, lay fraternities, and the sects maintained and tried to strengthen that original voluntarism. Troeltsch's definition, like H.R. Niebuhr's statement that the church is a "natural social grouping," is essentially parochial because it is not formulated from the perspective of the world history of religions, and thus does not structurally distinguish a founded religion from the tribal or classical types.[30] Niebuhr's contention that a sect, properly speaking, can exist for only one generation is even less tenable, as Wach has pointed out.[31] "Sect" and "denomination" are two aspects of the same type, the difference being the more advanced institutionalization and broader social acceptance of the denomination. As a matter of fact, it is possible to define the sect as a type precisely because it maintains itself as an independent tradition and thus can be distinguished from sporadic cult groups or rebellious movements which fade away when the leader dies or when the movement is defeated.

As every founded religion becomes established and thus more rigid and more oriented toward the ruling elite, there arises a tendency within it to form sects. These sects are essentially a quest for more immediate and personal assurance of salvation at the popular level. Though the sect is a new type, it sees itself as an attempt to restore the original vitality of its mother tradition, through congregational cult, charismatic leadership, and popularizations of scripture.

A dialogue with Europe and Japan. The Chinese folk sects were similar in structure to dissenting religious associations in medieval Europe, though in their beginnings they were parallel to the Buddhist denominations which developed in Kamakura Japan.[32] The great difference between China and both Europe and Japan is that in the Chinese situation, incipient "denominational" or "church" structures were never allowed to develop to their full potential because of official hostility, an opposition present even during periods of political disunion. In Sung China, when the White Lotus began, there was rich social and economic differentiation but in the context of increasing political centralization. The state became even further centralized during the Ming and Ch'ing periods when the sects were most active. In China, feudal lords had been done away with, merchants' guilds were fragmented, and monasteries placed under governmental control. The fate of popular religious groups was that of all private associations.

In both Europe and Japan, on the other hand, a divided political situation made possible the secular recognition and support which is vital to the establishment of a denomination. In both cultures, the absence of a strong central power over long periods of time permitted the development of many relatively independent forms of social differentiation, including hereditary landowning aristocracy, free cities and towns, artisans' guilds, peasant unions, and autonomous monastic establishments. In this sort of context Luther could gain the support of Philip of Hesse, while Shinran's Jōdo sect could establish its own town at Ōsaka[33] and enjoy the devout favoritism of Ieyasu, the founder of the Tokugawa shogun-ate.[34]

A key result of this recognized public status was that both the European and Japanese reformations were led and sustained by an educated professional clergy. While for a time Luther was forced to hide in Wartburg castle, and Shinran was exiled to Echigo, yet both returned to a political favor from which their movements were thenceforth never completely dislodged. Their successors were trained leaders, given a special status by their communions to consciously carry on a unified theological and cultic tradition.

In China, by contrast, while ordained monks were involved in the founding of such sects as the White Lotus and White Cloud, and while monks were frequently allied with the folk movements all through their history, yet their role was illegal, and they were vehemently rejected by both government and the celibate sangha. This double rejection meant that their chief available base was the peasants and other folk at the bottom of the social system, and thus what organizing and training they did was limited by the poverty and lack of education of the people. More often than not an ordained monk was not available for the leadership of a local congregation, and even if a sympathetic priest could be found, the chances were that his own education was sadly deficient. Repressions of the sangha and sale of ordination certificates by the government made such a situation only too common in post-T'ang China. Thus, the Chinese sects of necessity turned to a variety of "folk intellectuals" for guidance. While many of these men and women were devoutly religious, they often had only a vague understanding of Buddhist doctrine, thoroughly mixed with Taoism, popular demonology, geomancy, and other traditions.

As such folk leadership took a more active role, the sects became more syncretic. Yet this syncretism never erased the signs of their Buddhist origin with its promise of total salvation. In addition, it was precisely their syncretism which gave the movements their vitality and widespread appeal among the people. The sects offered everything available in the general popular religion, and added to it a new orientation for faith and social existence. But when all this has been said, it must be admitted that the Chinese groups at their full flower in the Ming dynasty were not straight-line Buddhist sects as in Japan, but folk sects of Buddhist origin and basic intention. At their best they were prevented by their social environment from ever developing an independent professional priesthood. The closest they came was hereditary lines of lay leadership. This relative absence of educated leadership had incalculable significance for Chinese religious and cultural history. It meant that popular movements lacked thorough-going intellectual formulation and that dissenting religious ideas rarely had the chance to find legitimate social expression. The Chinese state was never strong enough at the village level to prevent sectarian religious activity, but to the end it tenaciously kept them in a state of semisubjection and intellectual decapitation. From the point of view of European and Japanese church history, the Chinese sects, like Simmel's secret societies, were perpetually suspended between being and nonbeing.

There is no need to go into great detail concerning Chinese parallels with the European and Japanese experiences. Our concern here is with methodological and morphological considerations. More detailed comparative data will be used later to give perspective to a discussion of the folk sect tradition itself. At this point I will simply note a few general convergences of intent and structure in addition to those mentioned above.

Sects in all three cultures maintained that ordinary lay life was a most adequate context in which to attain salvation. It follows that all had a married clergy, stressed the equality of believers, and granted a higher status to women than was generally true in their social environment. In all the basis for such affirmation of lay existence was deliverance mediated through personal saviors such as Jesus Christ, Mary, Amida, Maitreya, and the Eternal Mother. In each culture, the sectarian means of grace were simplified rituals, short invocations, and popularized preaching based on vernacular scriptures. Thus, the Waldensians rejected all sacraments of the Roman Catholic church except baptism and annual communion; they repeated the Lord's Prayer 30 or 40 times a day and preached and read the Bible in local dialects.[35] In Japan, Hōnen and Shinran rejected all meditation techniques in favor of a simple ritual of re-

peating Amida's name, interspaced with group scripture reading.
Shinran wrote hymns and catechisms in the Japanese *kana* script,
and his hymns, along with the "Epistles of Rennyo," another Jōdo
Shinshū patriarch, are still used constantly in daily worship.[36]

The Chinese sects also quickly developed their own scriptural
traditions, beginning with Mao Tzu-yüan's popularizations of T'ien-
t'ai doctrine in verse and chart and extending into the proliferation
of "precious scroll" scriptures in the fifteenth and sixteenth centuries. White Lotus ritual consisted basically of burning incense,
reading sectarian and Mahāyāna scriptures, and chanting first
Amitābha's name, and later their characteristic mantra, *chen-k'ung
chia-hsiang, wu-sheng fu mu* (the true void native land and the
unbegotten [external] parents). The sect leaders preached in the
vernacular, following a long Mahāyāna tradition which began in
the monasteries of the T'ang period. The *pao-chüan*, in fact, began
as sermon notes, in the style of the traditional Chinese storyteller.
The European equivalent of an independent scriptural tradition
was lay use and interpretation of the Bible, though there was also
an abundance of sectarian catechisms, tracts, and prophetic writings.

The popular thirst for soteriological immediacy pushed the
sects toward the worship of their own founders along with the most
approachable figures in the orthodox pantheon. Lindsay emphasizes that when Jesus Christ was placed more and more in the role
of a stern judge, the people turned first to Mary and then to St.
Anna as mediators of grace. Hans Böhm said that his visions were
of the Blessed Virgin, and to her he dedicated his chapel at Niklashausen.[37] Tanchelm's followers worshiped him while he was still
alive and competed with each other for bits of his hair and clothing,[38] and Leff notes a Waldensian group discovered in 1458 which
worshiped Wyclif, Hus, and Jerome as saints in heaven.[39] In Kyoto
the central hall in the Jōdo Shinshu temple is reserved for Shinran's
image; Amida's is in a side building. In China Lo Ch'ing, the founder
of the Lo sect, came to be worshiped as the savior sent down from
the Eternal Mother's Native Land after Maitreya himself had failed.
His image was venerated in Lo sect homes and temples.[40]

An important difference between the European groups and
their Japanese and Chinese counterparts is the characteristic em-

phasis of the former on holy poverty and withdrawal from the world, which led to an insistent attack on the church for its wealth and its involvement with the political realm. The Asian sects, on the other hand, were fundamentally world affirming and always ready either to fight for their existence or to accept political recognition and power when it was granted. We have seen that the frequent expression of the sectarian religious vision in politico-military terms in China has led some scholars to interpret them simply as revolutionary movements. However, other interpretations are possible. The blending of authentic religious experience with the use of violence is attested all through human history, beginning at least as early as raids by primitive planters to get human heads, which had a profound sacred significance. In fact, only in the modern West has it been possible to neatly separate such categories as "religious," "military," and "political," and assign different realms and sets of motives to each. Such a distinction was surely not made in the city-states of ancient Babylonia and Assyria, whose battles on earth were patterned on the struggles of their gods above. Nor was such a distinction operative for the Egyptian pharaohs, or for Mohammed and the Islamic armies which swept across North Africa into Europe.

One of the fundamental philosophical reasons for the difference between the European and Asian sects is the dualism that runs all through Christian history, separating the spiritual and worldly realms. But even in Europe this dualism cut both ways; it could be used as justification for righteous war as well as for quietism. So Christian history, too, is full of the use of violence by deeply religious men, from the Inquisition and the Thirty Years' War to colonial campaigns against "pagans."[41]

Nonetheless, it remains true that as far as the European sects are concerned the quiet piety of Menno Simons was more characteristic than Melchior Hoffman's militant eschatology; the self-effacing preaching of Peter Waldo was more often emulated than the imperial claims of Tanchelm and his twelve apostles. The East is par excellence the center of sophisticated styles of withdrawal from the world, but in a fundamentally monistic context, be it expressed as Brahman, Emptiness, Dharmakāya, Tao, or the world of the *kami.* However dialectically this monism may have been understood by a Theravada monk or a Taoist hermit, at the popular level it was appropriated literally; in principle, everything was affirmed. At bottom there was no reason why Zen monks should *not* have directed the government department of shipping and commerce in the Ashikaga period,[42] or why the Shinshū sect should *not* have established fortified towns and engaged in twenty major wars in the sixteenth century alone. Such blending of piety and the sword was simply an expression of the way things really were in the universe itself.

The White Lotus religion not only shared a monistic world view and T'ien-t'ai ontology with its Japanese counterparts but in addition by 1351 had appropriated Maitreyan eschatology under the leadership of Han Shan-t'ung and his family. Here again, it is important to get at the intentions included in a particular eschatology, not simply to attribute all to utopian dreams fed by the tensions of relative deprivation. In Buddhist legend the Indian Emperor Aśoka (d. 232 B.C.) provided a historical model for the ideal universal monarch who would prepare the world for the coming of Maitreya, a monarch whose role is described in Pali texts. Already in the pre-Mahāyāna tradition it was held the Gautama himself in his last existence before attaining Buddhahood was a Universal King. As king he had made a vow to "become a guide to the world, teacher of gods and man."[43] Sarkisyanz states:

> Against the background, the birth as an ideal universal king . . . came to be seen as the last stage before birth as the Future Buddha . . . [The] political realization of the Buddhist Dharma came to be associated with the unification of the universe under the perfect Buddhist king of the future. [This] vision [of the ideal ruler] was and still remains associated with the Golden Age of the future [which sets the stage for Maitreya].[44]

A large number of Maitreya sūtras had been translated and were popular among the Chinese people by the Northern Wei dynasty (386-534), and, in addition, several kings of this state deliberately adopted the Asokan model of kingship, as did emperor Wu of the (southern) Liang dynasty, and emperor Wen of the Sui (581-618).[45] It is important that this Buddhist concept of universal rule, so closely related to Maitreya's mission, was known among the people by the fifth century. Ch'en writes of a lay inscription in a Yün-kang cave, dated 483, in which prayers were offered for the ruling house, that "its power be like that of the universal monarch."[46] It was but a short step for the leader of a messianic sect to apply this model to himself.

Thus, there was a "political" element deeply imbedded in Maitreyan eschatology itself, and White Lotus uprisings cannot be understood apart from this intentionality of their religious vision. Their linking of the Buddhist Messiah with the descendant of an idealized past emperor was not just clever propaganda, but a practical expression of their understanding of how the new order was to be brought about. For Maitreya's mission to succeed, there had to be a pious emperor on the throne who would prepare the people with his teaching and benevolence. This ancient Indian concept was still preserved in the Singapore Hsien-t'ien tao sects investigated by Marjorie Topley in 1955.[47] That some White Lotus leaders may have used this doctrine for their own private ends is certainly possible, but since bad faith can be found anywhere, it explains nothing. One must still explain why the unscrupulous leader chose this particular ideological cover for his ambitions and why it had an impact on great numbers of people who did not share his private concerns.

Peasant Rebellions

In his *Heresy in the Later Middle Ages*, Gordon Leff writes: "Finally, heresy is to be distinguished from mere disaffection . . . Risings like . . . the Peasants' Revolt were not primarily the work of doctrinal or religious dissent, nor did they leave behind any distinctive outlook. On the other hand, this is not to deny that religious outbreaks could become social risings, as with the [eschatologically oriented] Taborites."[48] George H. Williams makes a similar distinction between the Peasants' War of 1524-1525 and the radical Anabaptist experiment at Münster: "Whereas the earlier movement started out as a social protest . . . the Münsterite . . . episode of 1533-35 started out with a powerful sense of evangelical, eschatological expectancy and became socially revolutionary."[49] I don't fully agree with the language employed in these statements, but the basic distinction they make applies equally to the Chinese scene. I have noted that there were all kinds of voluntary associations in China which occasionally engaged in violence: organized robber bands, refugees forced off their land by famine, salt smugglers, and disaffected peasant groups organized around village militia, to name just a few. These groups tended to be particularly active in times of political and social deterioration. Many of them also contained religious elements, as did just about every association in traditional China, from artisans' guilds to hostels for unmarried women. But peasant uprisings with religious overtones are not the same as sectarian movements engaged in eschatological warfare. The intention of the first is primarily to solve local socioeconomic problems; of the latter, to bring about a new order for the whole empire. This intentional difference holds even if the peasant rising spreads to a whole province and the messianic movement is cut off in its home village. Of course, the sects, too, were very much concerned with the socioeconomic situation of their members, but we are concerned here with central motives that give structure and continuity to the enterprise as a whole.[50]

It is the lack of a dominant and cohesive theoretical direction, coupled with a lack of strong, self-conscious leadership and organization that distinguishes the peasant revolt. Equally important is the collapse of the movement after it is put down and the absence of a continuing cultic structure, scriptural tradition, preaching, and a sense of group history. For example, Western scholars writing about the uprising of German peasants in 1524-1526 stress that it lacked cohesive organization and effective, generally recognized leaders, and thus disintegrated in the face of strong opposition.[51] It is true that the Chia-ch'ing White Lotus movement in 1796 had no universally recognized leader, but there were many strong local leaders, religiously connected by generations of master/disciple relationships. At other periods, generally recognized chiefs were the rule, and White Lotus organization was certainly not "improvised." As T'ao Ch'eng-chang wrote, a White Lotus leader could control his followers from hundreds of miles around "like a body moving its arm, and a hand its fingers."[52]

There is an intermediate type here, namely the localized folk religious cult which is stamped out before it has a chance to establish a scriptural tradition or a system of continuing leadership. Such a group shares some of the improvised nature of the peasant social movement, but is distinguished by its clearly religious impetus. I have in mind such phenomena as the "proto sects" begun by Hans Böhm at Niklashausen in 1476 and Sun Ta-yu in Hupei in 1768. Both these movements were led by laymen who claimed special revelation, both never got beyond their local village area, and both ended in less than a year with the execution of their leaders. The adherents of their leaders were primarily poor peasants, who eagerly believed Böhm's visions of the Virgin and Sun's preaching from a Heavenly Book (*T'ien shu*). To be sure, the Chinese group was more explicitly "political" in its orientation; Sun claimed that he was the reincarnation of Chu T'ung-t'ai, a man with the same surname as that of the Ming royal house, whose advent was predicted in the Heavenly Book. His followers obtained imperial style robes from a traveling opera company and venerated Sun as emperor. But Böhm's blessing of his followers in the name of the Virgin and his denial of all priestly power and secular privilege were just as pretentious in the European context, and even Böhm urged his followers to bring their swords on the day he was arrested. In any case, both Böhm and Sun moved out of intentional and theoretical self-understandings which included local social discontent but transcended it as well.

Both Sun and Böhm were influenced by the larger popular traditions around them, Sun by folk Taoism with its faith healing and expectation of a righteous emperor; Böhm by the Mary cult and (probably) Hussite ideas picked up during his wandering in Bohemia. But though Böhm's influence lingered on, in both Germany and Hupei the movements as such died with their leaders. Thus, they did not become established sects.[53]

In sum, the Chinese groups in the folk Buddhist tradition were religious sects in origin and intent, and only an approach that recognizes the central role of their religious vision can deal with them adequately. An important segment of the Chinese tradition took a path similar to that of the Anabaptists after Münster. The quiet devotional sects in Lo chiao tradition which DeGroot discovered in Amoy are in some ways parallel to peaceful Anabaptist conventicles after the unifying work of Menno Simons. But even at this devotional level the Chinese sects never attained the public recognition and support which eventually permitted the Anabaptists to develop into denominations with trained leadership.

The development of popular sects in Mahāyāna Buddhism is the social expression of an affirmation of the religious possibilities of lay existence. From the beginning Buddhism has taken social forms appropriate to the form of its message. In China the full development of this inherent tendency was inhibited, and the lay sangha was to a large extent kept submerged in the folk consciousness. It is in Japan that the social implications of Mahāyāna Buddhism were fully expressed. In the great Jōdo temples of Kyoto we see what the White Lotus might have been.

5
An Outline History
of the White Lotus Tradition

The best known of the sectarian traditions is the White Lotus, which was active in various forms from the twelfth to the nineteenth centuries. Its combination of piety with politics and rebellion makes it the classic example of Chinese folk Buddhist sects. There were, of course, many earlier popular religious movements that influenced the White Lotus, including Taoist and Manichaean groups, and two Buddhist traditions, the Maitreyan and Pure Land. Nonsectarian influences such as T'ien-t'ai thought and aboriginal mythology as well as a number of other background factors will be discussed where relevant. There were also folk sects such as the Lo and White Cloud which began independently of the White Lotus; these groups will be described in Chapter 6. My purpose in dealing with background traditions is not to describe them exhaustively but to better understand their relationship to White Lotus development and to see that development in context.

Antecedents

Taoist groups. The earliest organized popular religious movements in China were Taoist groups which appeared in the late second century during the decline of the Han. The best known expressions of this "collective Taoism" were the T'ai-p'ing tao or Way of Great Peace in Hopei and the Heavenly Master or Five

Pecks of Rice sect in Szechwan. Both these groups were concerned to realize ideal theocracies on earth and rebelled in the name of this ideal in 184. The Szechwan movement in the west was eventually able to establish an independent state which persisted until it was absorbed by the new kingdom of Wei in 215. In the east the T'ai-p'ing tao (otherwise known as the Yellow Turbans) was both more ambitious and less successful. This sect attempted to take over the whole empire in a revolt which spread rapidly to eight provinces, but its efforts were largely checked in the same year the rebellion began. However, though their founding leaders were killed in 184, T'ai-p'ing units were still involved in rear guard actions until 205. Although these movements evidently began separately, they show many similarities, and by the third century their remnants had blended together to become a primary source of the Taoist religious tradition.

Since the history of religious Taoism is extremely complex and as yet only partially explored we cannot go into much detail here.[1] The late Han movements were characterized by leadership that combined religious and administrative functions, collective ritual, and the belief that illness could be cured by penance. In all this these groups seem to have been an attempt to recover in a more limited setting the Han cosmological and political synthesis which had disintegrated around them.

R. A. Stein lists the following shared characteristics of the Celestial Master and T'ai-p'ing sects: 1. Taoist orientation revealed by reciting the *Lao Tzu* (Celestial Master) or venerating Lao Tzu deified as Huang-Lao (T'ai-p'ing). 2. Concern to realize utopia through politico-religious administration. 3. Understanding of illness as a sign of sin to be healed by confession. 4. The source of healing power in three deities representing Heaven, Earth, and Water (Celestial Master) or Heaven, Earth, and Man (T'ai-p'ing).[2] One could add to this list the use of magic charms and charmed water to heal illness. In addition, the Yellow Turbans employed eschatological symbolism based on recurrent sixty-year cycles, staging their uprising in the first year of a new cycle and proclaiming themselves representatives of a renewed cosmos. Stein has demonstrated that the prototypes of all these characteristics and the background of collective Taoist terminology can be found in earlier Han dynasty religion and village administration.[3]

By the mid-fifth century a split developed in religious Taoism between elite and popular levels of apprehension, based in part on the proclamation of Taoism as the state religion by the Toba Wei kingdom in 444. From that time on the elite level moved toward officially established status based on hereditary leaders, the formation of a canon of scripture, metaphysical speculation and an elaborate liturgy known only to an initiated priesthood. Popular Taoism seems to have moved in two directions, eschatologically oriented sectarianism or absorption by folk religion.[4]

It is of course the popular sectarian tradition that is of most relevance for us. Since this tradition has recently been described in some detail by Anna K. Seidel, suffice it to note here that these Taoist groups were characterized not only by concern for healing and the use of charms but also by their expectation of the return of a messianic figure who would establish an ideal state on earth. Such a figure was not prominent in the Han movements but evidently developed out of the old Chinese belief in sages who descend from the mountains to assist rulers in time of need, perhaps stimulated by interaction with the intrusive bodhisattva ideal.

Popular Taoist sects continued to exist throughout Chinese history, but their later development needs further investigation. Though this form of Taoism remained a distinct tradition centered on its own deities and rituals, it had a strong influence on other groups, including models of theocracy and eschatological warfare and an emphasis on healing and magic charms. All the later folk Buddhist sects adopted these characteristics in greater or lesser degree.[5]

Manichaeism. In his *Daily Life in China*, Jacquest Gernet describes a twelfth century sect very popular in Fukien and Chekiang called the Demon Worshipers. This group was directed by a Demon King with the aid of two assistants called the Demon Father and the Demon Mother. They observed prohibitions against meat and alcohol much more strictly than the Buddhists, and "proscribed the worship of all Chinese and Buddhist deities, as well as the ancestral cult, and the only gods they recognized were the sun and the moon, which they considered to be 'true Buddhas.' " They buried their dead naked to resemble a foetus, and maintained "that death itself brought final liberation. Hence to slay one's heretical neighbor was to ensure his salvation."[6]

This Fukien movement described by Gernet was a sect of popular Manichaeism. Manichaeism entered China in 694 with the Uighurs, a Central Asian tribe which had great military and political influence in China during the first part of the T'ang dynasty. Until 843 Manichaeism was chiefly active among Uighur merchants, troops, and government officials, because the Chinese themselves were forbidden to support it. However, in 719 a Manichaean scholar noted for his knowledge of astronomy assisted at the Chinese court, and in 768 the Uighurs were permitted to build temples for their religion in which monks and nuns lived.

When the Uighur kingdom collapsed in 843, Manichaeism was immediately proscribed, its temples destroyed, and its priesthood executed or scattered. It never again existed in China as an officially recognized religion. However, it went underground and appears several times in later sources as a militant popular movement, heavily influenced by Chinese ideas and terminology.[7]

The first known appearance of Manichaeism as a Chinese folk sect was in 920 in Honan. In the *Fo-tsu t'ung-chi* we read:

> The Manichaeans of Ch'en-chou rebelled, and set up Mu-i as emperor. The court sent troops which captured and beheaded him. The members [of this sect] did not eat meat or drink wine. They assembled at night to carry out obscene activities, and had a picture which depicted the seated Mo Wang [Manichaean King] with the Buddha washing his feet. They said that Buddhism was only the great vehicle (*ta-sheng*), while their religion was the supreme vehicle (*shang-shang-sheng*).[8]

Fang Ch'ing-ying lists four other Manichaean related uprisings in 1120, 1130, 1133, and 1233,[9] while Wu Han notes that in 1366 there was a Ta-ming chiao (Great Light religion) in Wen-chou (in modern Chekiang province), which built temples and was eagerly supported by the people. At about the same time there was another sect in Ch'üan-chou of Fukien province which had a temple first

built in the Yüan period. In this temple worship was offered to a
Manichaean Buddha (Mo-ni fo), for which another name was
Mo-mo ni kuang-fo (Manichaean Buddha of Light). There was also
another image (*fo*) called the All-Wise Great Messenger of Light
(Chü chih ta ming-shih).[10]

It should not be necessary to discuss here characteristic Manichaean beliefs which have long been described elsewhere.[11] It is
enough to point out that despite amalgamation with Buddhism and
Taoism, Chinese popular Manichaeism retained the dualistic core
of its original doctrines. This can be seen in a statement attributed
to Hung Mai (d. 1202), which is quoted by Chih-p'an:

> Those who eat vegetables and worship Mo [Mani] are espe-
> cially numerous in San-shan [Fukien province]. Their leaders wear
> purple hats and clothing with wide sleeves. Their women wear
> black hats and white clothing. They are called the "Religion of
> Light (Ming-chiao hui) . . . [They have a] scripture text called the
> *Sūtra of the Two Principles and Three Stages* (Er-tsung san-chi
> *ching*). The two principles are light and darkness, and the three
> stages mean past, present and future.[12]

Though there was much in the White Lotus tradition that had
no precedent in what we know of popular Manichaeism, it is probable that the Manichaeans influenced their folk Buddhist counterparts indirectly at several points, and directly at one. First, Manichaeism provided a precedent for the full-time lay vegetarianism
which led Mao Tzu-yüan's contemporaries to label his group the
Pai-lien ts'ai (White Lotus Vegetarians). Though Buddhist monks
had long eaten an exclusively vegetarian diet, the common practice
in lay Buddhism was intermittent vegetarianism on regular
stated days of the month in fulfillment of vows for wishes
granted, or meatless feasts on the occasion of anniversaries, birthdays, arrivals and departures, and other special days.[13] Second, the
Manichaeans offered a well-known model of an independent religious sect composed of laymen, possessing its own scriptures, tightly
organized around hierarchical leaders, and accomplished in the
practice of mutual aid.[14] This model may have served as an encour-
agement to Buddhists inclined to form similar groups.[15] Third,

Manichaean three-stage chronology may have served to reinforce the influence of the similar time scheme which had developed independently in Chinese Buddhism.

The possibility of Manichaean influence on such groups as the White Lotus was of course strengthened by the fact that Chinese Manichaeans came to describe their beliefs in heavily Buddhist terms. As Hung Mai wrote of them, "The Buddha they worship is dressed in white, which they took from the so-called White Buddha spoken of in the sūtras . . . They took the list of five Buddhas from the *Diamond Sūtra*, saying that the fifth Buddha is also called Mo-mo ni. This is all [based on] the [Lao Tzu] *Hua hu ching* [The sūtra concerning Lao Tzu's conversion of the barbarians]."[16] Manichaean three-stage eschatology is discussed in a scripture in this same volume of the *Taishō Compendium*, the *Mo-ni kuang fo chiao fa i lüeh* (A summary of the teachings of the Manichaean Buddha of Light), which was translated in 731. This text also says that 1,300 years after Śākyamuni entered Nirvāna, Mo-ni kuang-fo appeared in the world, "constantly shedding a brilliant light, in order to carry out a Buddha's tasks (*i tso fo-shih*) . . . When the third stage arrived . . . he descended from the world of light on high into that of darkness and filth, and from this all sentient beings will be saved. After Mo-ni [appeared] our religion flourished [for a long time] and then reached China. In the second year of the T'ai-shih period of the Chin dynasty [266] . . . he entered Nirvāna, but his teaching reached everywhere, saving all people."

Though the Buddha of Light has already come, his work continues on earth, and the text ends with a description of the culmination of the third stage. Then: "The work of salvation will be completed, and both truth and falsehood will return to their original source, light to the Great Light, and darkness to where darkness is gathered up."[17] All this eschatology was available to those interested in parallel teachings concerning the future Buddha, in terms which must have sounded quite familiar.

An important Manichaean characteristic was their worship of the sun and moon, which for them were "ships which ferried in turn the [liberated particles of light] to the luminous abode."[18] Their faith in the Sun and Moon as representatives of the realm of light was second only to faith in the God of Light himself. We have noted that Chinese popular Manichaeism continued this belief.

In this context it is interesting that there were some White Lotus related groups which also worshiped the sun, with names such as Hung-yang chiao (Red Yang religion). A memorial submitted to the emperor in 1775 describes a Green Yang sect (Ch'ing-yang chiao) in Honan. The reporting official notes that "They worship the sun (hsiang t'ai-yang li-pai) . . . and have a Green Yang Sūtra." Since we are also told that these sectarians worshiped the Mother and had such slogans as "All recover the origins" and "The sons and daughters preserve perfect unity," we know that they were in the White Lotus mythological tradition.[19]

A report dated 1813 describes sun worship in the Eight Trigrams Sect led by Lin Ch'ing:

> Lin Ch'ing [confessed] that . . . the original name of his religion was the Three Yang Sect (San-yang chiao), which is divided into Green, Red and White Yang groups. It is also called the Dragon-flower Society, and because it is divided into eight sections named after the eight trigrams it is also called the Eight Trigrams Society. Later the name was again changed to the Society of Heaven's Principle (T'ien-li hui). Every day at dawn they worship the sun and chant scriptures, saying that thus they can avoid harm from weapons, water and fire.[20]

The Manichaeans provide the clearest precedent in China for the sun as a main object of worship. Sun worship is mentioned in the *Li chi* as part of imperial ritual,[21] but here the sacrifice to the sun is but one part of the whole state cult, which involved propitiation of symbols representing every aspect of the cosmos. The sun as the preeminent *yang* symbol was important in this system, but not as central as it appears in the eschatology and worship of the Green Yang and Eight Trigrams sects. It thus seems reasonable to conclude that sectarian sun worship is related to Manichaean influence, however indirect.[22]

The one Manichaean influence on the White Lotus that can be clearly demonstrated is Han Lin-er's title Hsiao Ming-wang (Lesser King of Light) in Han Shan-t'ung's 1351 uprising. Wu Han and others have shown that this title is taken from a Manichaean text named the *Ta-hsiao ming-wang ch'u-shih ching* (Sūtra of the Incarnation of the Greater and Lesser Kings of Light). The character *ming* is the same one used by Hung Mai to describe the two basic principles of Manichaeism.[23] Since Chu Yüan-chang, the founder of the Ming dynasty, kept part of Han Lin-er's old title as the name for his new regime, the Ming period was in fact named after the Manichaean principle of light.[24]

Tai Hsüan-chih maintains that the White Lotus originated in sectarian Manichaeism,[25] but other modern writers agree that while the White Lotus was influenced by several different traditions, its original impetus came from Amitābha pietism. Even Wu Han, who wrote a well-known work on Chinese Manichaeism, says that "Manichaeism . . . blended together with the Pai-lien she which arose out of the Buddhist Pure Land School."[26] After fully considering the role or Manichaean influence, Fan Ch'ing-ying maintains that "the White Lotus clearly did not originate in Manichaeism." It is mentioned in the sources as a parallel contemporary sect, not as a branch. The identification of the two probably arose out of the Confucian habit of grouping all such sects together as heretics.[27] We have seen that while the White Lotus was influenced by Manichaeism, this influence was largely indirect and peripheral.

Maitreyan Buddhism. The first independent, lay-oriented Buddhist popular movements appeared in 402. Tsukamoto discusses ten different monk-led popular movements in the Northern Wei kingdom (386-532), dating from 402 to 517. Though the official records are characteristically laconic, one can still sense the religious and eschatological vitality they reflect. The first known rebel monk, Chang-ch'iao (d. 402), called himself King without Superior (Wu-shang wang). Fa-hsiu, who was active in 481, "plotted rebellion" with the support of over one hundred close followers including an imperial censor named Chang Ch'iu, who recruited slaves to the cause. Fa-hsiu was accused of using religion to deceive the hearts of the people, which is perhaps the first mention of this hoary condemnation in connection with a popular Buddhist movement. An abbot named Seng-ming gathered together several hundred monk followers, "who bound themselves tightly together [as with] ropes, with Seng-ming as their leader." They are described as bandits and were all beheaded.[28] An official during the reign of

emperor Hsiao-wen (r. 471-500) reported in connection with these
groups that

. . . the people compete with each other to establish vegetarian
feasts. They falsely give themselves noble titles, and stir up each
other . . . With an arrogant spirit they [seek to] usurp royal prerogatives . . . [I urge that] we should immediately execute their
leaders. If we don't, I fear that they will become as bad as the Red
Eyebrows and Yellow Turbans [of the Han dynasty].[29]

We also read of the monks Liu Hui-wang (d. 509) and Liu Seng-
shao (d. 514) that they both "assembled a multitude to rebel (chü
chung fan)," and that Liu Seng-shao called himself the Dharma
King Light of the Nation Who Dwells in Purity (Ching-chü kuo-
ming fa-wang).[30]

That such independent Buddhist associations were present in
south China as well is illustrated by Lu Fa-he's movement during
the reign of Emperor Yüan (r. 552-555) of the Liang dynasty (502-
557). Lu was a *chü-shih* (lay devotee) who commanded many thousand troops and set up his own government covering the area of
several departments. Liang Ch'i-ch'ao writes of him that "from his
youth to old age he rigorously adhered to Buddhist law and discipline. All his followers were called disciples."[31] By T'ang times
most of these sporadic movements were absorbed in the Maitreya
tradition. Though the evidence is scanty, they do not appear to
have had cohesive scriptural or cultic traditions, and thus might be
called protosects.

In Indian Mahāyāna Maitreya is the Buddha of the future who
waits in Tushita heaven until it is time for him to descend to earth
many thousands of years hence. He is born after a world ruler has
"made the dharma prevail," incarnate in the womb of the wife of a
Brahman adviser to this pious king who has prepared the way. For
60,000 years he will "preach the true dharma, and save hundreds
and hundreds of millions of living beings." After he finally enters
Nirvāna, his "true dharma still endures for another 10,000 years."[32]

The first known Chinese translation of a sūtra describing Maitreya is the *Fo shuo Mi-le hsia-sheng ching* (Sūtra of Maitreya's rebirth), translated by Chu Fa-hu (Dharmaraksha) in the T'ai-shih

reign period of the western Chin (265-275). Fifteen other sūtras concerning Maitreya were translated into Chinese during the Six Dynasties period (222-589).[33] In 380 Tao-an (d. 385), Hui-yüan's teacher, organized a Maitreya cult with eight of his disciples, vowing to be reborn in Tushita heaven. All during the Northern Wei dynasty (386-534) the Maitreya belief was very popular among the people. Images of Maitreya and Śākyamuni dominated the Yün-kang cave sculptures in this period. Ch'en notes that devotion to Maitreya in the Northern Wei had two aspects: a wish to be reborn in Tushita and meet him face to face and a wish to be reborn on earth when Maitreya made his descent and thus benefit from the peace and prosperity he would bring. "It was also hoped that this descent would occur during the reign of the Northern Wei, so that Maitreya would make use of that dynasty to pacify and unify the world."[34]

In addition to this rich orthodox background of Maitreya belief, there were dissenting popular movements in this period based on similar eschatologies. For example in 516 a monk named Fa-ch'üan said that a nine-year-old boy was the reincarnation of Yüeh-kuang P'u-sa, the Bodhisattva of Moonlight, a proclamation based on the *Sūtra of the Moonlight Child* (*Yüeh-kuang t'ung-tzu ching*) in which the Buddha predicts that the son of an elder of Magadha will be "the king of China in a future incarnation, when all of China and the central Asian peoples would be converted."[35] Fa-ch'üan led an uprising in Shansi which was soon put down. In 515 a Hopei monk named Fa-ch'ing started a rebellion along with a layman named Li Kuei-po. Fa-ch'ing proclaimed that he himself was the Mahāyāna Buddha (Ta-sheng fo) and that Li was a Bodhisattva of the Tenth Abode (Shih-chu p'u-sa). Li was also given the titles Commander of the Army which Pacifies Devils (P'ing-mo chün ssu) and King of the Han (Han Wang). Fa-ch'ing's movement was exceedingly violent, specializing in the slaughter of Buddhist monks and nuns and the destruction of temples and pagodas. The leader claimed to be a new manifestation of the Buddha, whose task it was to wipe out the old devils, principally the clerical enemies of the sect.[36]

With this strong "political" emphasis in both orthodox popular belief and dissenting movements, it is perhaps not suprising that Maitreyan sectarianism first appears on the scene as an attempt to implement the advent of the new age by an attack on the imperial palace in Ch'ang-an. In 610, near the end of the Sui dynasty (581-618), the *Sui shu* records that "several tens of bandits (*k'ou*) [who were of a group in which all wore] dark hats and white robes, burned incense, held [offered] flowers and called [their leader] Maitreya Buddha, entered [the palace by] the Chien-kuo gate and decapitated all the guards." The attack was foiled and more than 1,000 households of those supporting this group were arrested.[37]

In 613 Sung Tzu-hsien proclaimed himself to be Maitreya manifest anew and founded a sect in Hopei. In a short time he and several thousand followers rebelled, but their plans leaked out and Sung was captured. In that same year a Shensi monk named Hsiang Hai-ming said that he was the incarnation of Maitreya and led a revolt aimed at establishing a new dynasty. He proclaimed himself emperor and established the new reign title Pai-wu (White Crow). The movement was suppressed that same year.[38]

The basic time scheme of fully formulated White Lotus belief in the sixteenth century was the doctrine of three successive world stages, the past, controlled by the Lamplighter Buddha (Dīpamkara), the present, dominated by Śākyamuni, and the future, to be ushered in by Maitreya. The sects believed themselves to be at the very end of the second period, the date of which was continually revised over a period of at least a thousand years. The first clear statement of this doctrine in the sources is attributed to Wang Huai-ku who was active in the T'ang K'ai-yüan period (713-741). "Śākyamuni Buddha has declined; a new Buddha is coming. The house of Li [that is, the T'ang dynasty] is ending and the House of Liu will arise to take its place. This winter a black snow will fall in Pei-chou." Wang then launched a revolt which soon failed. Shigematsu says that there is no doubt that the "new Buddha" in this passage is Maitreya.[39]

One of the earliest more detailed references to a Maitreya sect is the passage from the *T'ang ta chao-ling chi* quoted in Chapter 3, dated 715. In the Sung dynasty, the best known Maitreya sect was that led by Wang Tse, in the Pei-chou area of Hopei. That this movement in 1047 was active in the same area as the Maitreya sect led by Wang Huai-ku 300 years previously perhaps indicates that even the militant Maitreya belief was rooted in continuously exist-

ing cultic life and was not merely propaganda for sporadic uprisings.

Wang Tse was a major in the army who after his conversion
formed a movement whose slogan was "Śākyamuni Buddha has
declined. Maitreya Buddha shall rule the world." After his troops
occupied Pei-chou they imprisoned the district magistrate, killed
the yamen officials, burned the county administration buildings,
raided the armory, released prisoners, and plundered rich gentry
estates. Wang proclaimed himself King of the Eastern Plain (Tung
p'ing chün wang) and established Te-sheng (Attained Sainthood) as
his reign title. He appointed a whole panoply of officials and called
his army *i-chün*, the Army of Righteousness. All their battle flags
had the character *fo* (Buddha) on them. However, after two battles
Wang Tse's uprising was put down in less than sixty days.[40]

After Wang Tse's movement was suppressed, the Maitreya
sect went underground and does not reappear in the records until
the early fourteenth century. A memorial of 1325 says that two
Honan men, Chao Ch'ou-ssu and Kuo P'u-sa (Kuo the Bodhisattva), from Hsi-chou (modern Ju-yang county) preached heretical
doctrines, saying, "The Buddha Maitreya should possess the
world." This group did nothing violent, but nonetheless Kuo was
executed and his followers beaten and exiled.[41]

The first known Maitreya uprising after 1047 took place in
1337 in Honan, southeast of Kuo P'u-sa's movement, in Ju-ning fu
(modern Ju-nan county). It was led by Pang Hu, of whom it is recorded that he "burned incense to deceive people," used heretical
words (*yao yen*), and emblazoned his banners with the word Maitreya. He also had a *liang t'ien ch'ih*, an instrument used by the emperor to measure the precession of the equinoxes at the beginning of
each reign, in preparation for a new imperial calendar. Possession
of such astronomical instruments by a commoner was considered
blasphemy and treason and further indicates the militant nature of
Maitreya sect activity.[42]

Thus, when Han Shan-t'ung's White Lotus movement proclaimed the Maitreyan eschatological hope in 1351, it drew on a
tradition which had been developing for over 700 years. In view of
the consistent tendency of this doctrine to seek expression in violent
revolution, it is no wonder that the White Lotus itself became more

militant after the late Yüan period. From that time forward the
Maitreya belief was a cornerstone of White Lotus theology. While
much of the Maitreya sect impetus was absorbed by the larger
movement, it continued to exist independently until at least the sixteenth century.[43]

Pure Land Buddhism. "[Whoever] shall make mental prayers
for the Buddha country of that blessed Amitāyus . . . all these will
never return again . . . They will be born in that Buddha country."[44] This passage from the *Smaller Sukhāvatī-vyūha Sūtra,* with
its promise of a simple and direct means of salvation, had a profound impact on the development of Chinese Buddhism. The earliest known Pure Land devotees were Ch'üeh Kung-tse (d. c. 265-
275) and his disciples in Lo-yang. Chih-tun (d. 366) made an image
of Amitābha, and vowed to be reborn in his Western Paradise.[45] In
402 Hui-yüan gathered at Mount Lu in Kiangsi a group of hermits,
retired scholars, and gentlemen in seclusion who sought rebirth in
the Pure Land by meditation, vows, and disciplined living.[46]

However, the first man to propagate Pure Land teachings at
the popular level as a means of universal salvation was T'an-luan
(476-542). It was he who first emphasized the oral invocation of
Amitābha's name in lay societies. His work was carried on in the
Sui (581-618) and T'ang (618-907) periods by Tao-ch'o (d. 645) and
his disciple Shan-tao (d. 681). These men preached actively among
the people, wrote devotional books, and encouraged the mass distribution of the *Pure Land Sūtra.* The acceptance of *nien-fo* (reciting Amitābha's name) as the principal means of salvation in Chinese Buddhism was established by the work of these two men.

In the Sung dynasty the *nien-fo* movement coalesced with a
long tradition of lay devotional groups attached to monasteries
which began in the mid-fifth century. These groups were founded
by monks or in some cases by pious laymen with monk advisers.
Their activities centered around congregational chanting of the
Buddha's name, but often included vegetarian meals, printing and
distribution of scriptures, and evangelistic preaching. In their congregational form and concern for the salvation of all, these devotional fraternities were the forerunners of the independent sects,
much as was the case in Japan. There in the Heian period, Kitagawa
tells us, the beginning of Amida pietism was in loosely organized

fraternities, such as that founded by Genshin in 986. Though these groups included priests, nuns and laity, they did not wish to split the ecclesiastical structure but to develop "a core of spiritual elite within the larger religious groups." It was not until the thirteenth century that "full-fledged Amida pietism . . . developed through independent ecclesiastical organization."[47] At first, most of the members of the Chinese groups consisted of literati, gentry, and clergy, and many had imperial support or enjoyed the patronage of government officials. But by the mid-T'ang period many fraternities had commoners among their membership. This "democratization" was fostered by egalitarian Pure Land soteriology. In the Sung several such associations took the name Pai-lien she in imitation of Hui-yüan's fellowship as it was described in contemporary legendary accounts.[48]

The general popularity of Ching-t'u (Pure Land) piety in the Northern Sung is revealed in a passage from the *Le-pang wen-lei:*

At present teachers of [the various Buddhist] schools, being ecumenical without distinction, and non-partisan, all employ the [Pure Land teaching] to instruct and attract disciples. Because of this everywhere they build temples, make images and form societies and associations. Thus, without distinction between rich and poor, young and old, there are none who do not devote themselves to the Pure Land.[49]

A number of Pure Land devotional societies grew out of this general salvation movement. For example, in the *Ching-t'u chih-kuei chi,* we read of a monk named Hsing-ch'ang who organized a Society for Pure Conduct (Ching-hsing she) at Hsi-hu in Chekiang. This group had a layman as its head (*she-shou*); its lay members, who are described as literati, were called "disciples of the Ching-hsing she." There were 80 such members, along with 1,000 monks. We are told that Hsing-ch'ang "pricked his finger and with the blood wrote an oath for the group called the 'Hua-yen [vow] of Pure Conduct' . . . Because he admired Hui-yüan's society on Lu-shan, [he later] changed the name Ching-hsing to Pai-lien [she] (White Lotus society)."[50]

Suzuki Chūsei describes a number of similar groups in the

Sung, such as a Nien-fo she (Buddha Recitation Society) established by Chih-li (960-1028) in 1013, which held assemblies to chant Amitābha's name and reaffirm the vows of upāsaka and clerical discipline. We read also of Pen-ju (982-1051), a monk known for his lectures on the *Lotus Sūtra*, who established another Pai-lien she in 1042, which within a few years built a large temple for itself. Emperor Jen-tsung (r. 1023-1064) himself bestowed the title Shen-chao (Divine Light) on Pen-ju and gave his group an imperial signboard inscribed with the words Pai-lien. This seal of imperial approval of the Lotus society name in an orthodox context was repeated by Emperor Kao-tsung (r. 1127-1163), who wrote Lien she on a signboard in his own hand for a *nien-fo* society founded by an official named Chang Lun. Chang Lun dug a pool and planted a lotus in it in imitation of the Hui-yüan legend and led his association in a ritual consisting of 10,000 repetitions of Amitābha's name. There were other fraternities founded by pious officials, such as Wen Yen-po, a well-known minister and general who served under four Sung emperors, who told everyone he met that he should *nien-fo*. With the support of a monk, Wen is reported to have formed a Pure Land society with 100,000 members. Deep in the Northern Sung, Chiu Ting-kuo (d. 1211), an official in a provincial Bureau of Education, established a "Society for Returning to the Western Paradise" (*hsi-kuei she*) and printed *nien-fo* tally sheets which he distributed gratis. He also built a Buddha recitation hall (*nien-fo yüan*) on the grounds of a monastery, in which laymen and monks gathered together every second and eighth day of the month for congregational worship.[51] All this support by officials no doubt served to encourage popular participation in *nien-fo* societies.

These groups ranged in membership from a few score to several thousands, including women as well as men. We read less and less of the imposition of semi-monastic discipline; rather the sources mention a Pai-lien she founded by a certain Wang Chung, who said: "All those who wished to prepare themselves I invited to enter this society, without distinction between rich or poor, noble or humble, gentry or common people, monks or nuns, if only they vowed to return to the West."[52]

As the societies increased in size they became unwieldy and had to be subdivided, like a Chekiang group in 1202, which had:

. . . 10,000 members, clerical and lay, male and female, who devoted their whole lives to calling out Amitābha's name, seeking to be reborn in the Pure Land. They met together on the fifteenth of every second month for preaching and a vegetarian feast, and prayed for long life for the emperor and prosperity for all people. The method of establishing this association was to enlist 210 group leaders, each of whom in turn recruited 48 persons.[53]

There was a strong effort made to maintain a sense of solidarity in the larger group through annual presentation of individual recitation records, prayers for deceased members, and regular monetary contributions. In the above described association there were at least four levels—master evangelist (*ch'üan-chu*), chief evangelist (*chüan-shou*), group leader (*hui-shou*), and disciple (*ti-tzu*). In general the leaders were laymen, though one also reads of *she-seng*, which might be translated as "society chaplain," regular clergy who served as teachers and advisers. Characteristically the subgroups met once a month and the general assemblies one to three times a year.

This tradition of Pure Land devotional societies is the immediate context in which the earliest White Lotus sect developed. Many elements in this orthodox tradition prefigured those in the sectarian movement, notably the combination of T'ien-t'ai philosophy with Amitābhist piety, lay leadership and the mass involvement of ordinary people, congregational worship, simplified ritual, and the use of vernacular scriptures and ritual for evangelistic purposes.[54]

But the chief contribution of the Pure Land associations to the sects was a concern for universal salvation. The Amitābha tradition had always been directed toward salvation both for the self and others, and with the development of congregational life the movement toward others was strengthened. So, the *Ssu-ming chiao-hsing lu* notes that: "chanting the Buddha's name 1000 times a day, repenting of sin and vowing to attain *Bodhi* is for the purpose of (*wei*) saving all living beings and [leading them] to the Pure Land (*tu chung-sheng ch'ü yü ching-t'u*)."[55]

One of the most interesting examples of Pure Land evangelistic concern is found in the life and work of Wang Jih-hsiu (d. 1173), a layman who dedicated himself to writing and distributing popularized scriptures.

Wang classified all professions and character types into thirty-six groups, including officials, farmers, artisans, wine sellers, wives, unmarried maidens, the intelligent, evil, and filial, all of whom he urged to work for salvation in their own situations:

Pure Land devotees should do good according to their positions, in order to produce merit . . . The illiterate depend completely on good and compassionate gentlemen to explain [the teaching] to them with a bodhisattva's devotion. This is the greatest form of evangelism. The process [of teaching] should always begin with the near and extend to the far, from the urgent to the less important, with no regard for the high or low social position of others (*pu chü ch'i jen chih kao-pi*).[56]

Though orthodox lay devotional societies have continued to exist down to the present, after the Sung their concern for mass salvation was largely carried on by the sects. They were a vital halfway house between celibate monasticism and independent lay movements. The scope of their activity in the Sung shows the Mahāyāna salvation tradition changing its institutional form to meet the needs and pressures of the Chinese world. The sects were an extension of the bodhisattva's "skill in means."

The White Lotus Tradition

It is not surprising that independent sects such as the White Cloud and White Lotus should appear in the mid-Sung dynasty, for the Sung was a time of increasing social differentiation and economic specialization in the context of rapid urban growth. Many new forms of voluntary association developed in this period, of which the sects were just one.[57]

Particularly after the fall of the north to the Jurchen in 1127, peasants in the south left the land by the thousands to go into other occupations in towns and cities. They became a mobile urban labor pool with such specialized jobs as servants, porters, entertainers, shopkeepers, and clerks. There was also more social interchange in the countryside; local markets and fairs increased, as did the number of traveling peddlers, healers, and fortune tellers. Great numbers of farmers took work as part-time hired laborers or developed trades of their own.

By the twelfth century there were many people who because they had left traditional social ties were ready for integration into new forms of voluntary association, and indeed, such associations flourished in the Sung particularly in the form of guilds for trades and professions.[58]

An abundance of voluntary societies for a variety of purposes is a well-known characteristic of traditional Chinese life which appeared long before the Sung, so there is no simple causal relationship between such groups and the development of religious sects. However, it is clear that conditions for such development were particularly good in a period so full of social and commercial ferment. In this context it is interesting that many of the common people became Taoist or Buddhist priests, while on the other hand there were Buddhist monks who became pawnbrokers or shopkeepers.[59] Such interaction perhaps helped provide cultural support for sects which contemporaries called "neither clerical nor lay" (pu seng, pu su). One of these groups was the White Lotus.

Shigematsu Shunshō says that the White Lotus sect was founded by a Buddhist monk named Mao Tzu-yüan (1086-1166) in 1133 just after the beginning of the Southern Sung period (1127-1279).[60] However, there is conflicting evidence on this point from the earliest available sources. In the Pure Land tradition Mao Tzu-yüan is considered an orthodox patriarch of the school, whose writings are quoted approvingly all the way down through the Ming dynasty. While he is noted for his popularization of Amitābhist and T'ien-t'ai teachings, he is not associated with a new form of sectarian activity. On the other hand, to T'ien-t'ai and Ch'an historians Mao is an execrable heretic who founded an independent lay association in which men and women mingled indiscriminately together. The contrast could not be stronger. A further problem is that Yüan and early Ming accounts of the White Lotus do not mention Mao Tzu-yüan, in fact do not discuss any founder at all. This may be significant because remembrance and even deification of branch founders was an important characteristic of later White Lotus tradition, a characteristic even more prominent in the Lo sect (to be discussed in Chapter 6). Yet from the mid-Sung on there is an independent folk Buddhist tradition, influenced by the Amitābha cult, variously called the White Lotus Vegetarians (Pai-lien ts'ai), White Lotus Way (Pai-lien tao), White Lotus Association (Pai-lien hui), or White Lotus religion or sect (Pai-lien chiao) and so on, all located in east and south China. By the mid-fourteenth century this tradition was given new impetus by Maitreyan eschatology from Hopei in the north and from then on began to appear all over China. However, even then there does not appear to have been a generally recognized founder but rather groups of sects united by similar beliefs and scriptures and in some cases by connections between leaders. The most cohesive of these groups was that begun by Wang Sen at Shih-fo k'ou in Hopei in the late sixteenth century.

All this means that if Mao Tzu-yüan did found an independent association it may not have been the lineal progenitor of later groups having the same or similar names. The sources permit us to talk about a White Lotus tradition to the extent that they describe independent lay Buddhist associations of that name appearing fairly regularly from the Sung on. We have evidence that some of these groups were directly related to each other, but about others we cannot be sure. Now let us look in more detail at Mao Tzu-yüan himself.

The Pure Land historian P'u-tu (f. 1300-1312) has this to say about the life of Tz'u-chao tsung-chu, Master of the Light of Compassion, as Mao came to be called in the Ching-t'u school:

> Master Tzu-yüan, whose sobriquet was Wan-shih hsiu, was of the Mao family of K'un-shan in P'ing-chiang [in modern Sung-chiang county in southeastern Kiangsu]. His mother . . . once dreamed that a Buddha image entered the door, and on the next day she gave birth, so she called him "the Buddha has come" (fo-lai). His father and mother died early, so he entered the Yen-hsiang monastery [of this same area], his will set on becoming a monk. He regularly chanted the *Lotus Sūtra*. At the age of 19 (*sui*) he cut off his hair [was initiated as a novice] and began to meditate regularly according to the [T'ien-t'ai] method of cessation and contemplation. One day as he was in a meditative trance he heard a crow's call and reached enlightenment.
>
> He later wrote verses [concerning his enlightenment] which

said "For more than twenty years I sought [enlightenment] on paper [by reading books], but though I looked everywhere I simply became more lost and confused. Then, suddenly I heard the call of a compassionate crow, and realized for the first time that I had been using my mind in the wrong way. Then to benefit the minds of others, I vowed to work for the salvation of all. In admiration of the spirit of [Hui] Yüan's Lotus society [Lien-she] on Mount Lu I urged others to take refuge in the Three Jewels, observe the Five Prohibitions [of the Buddhist novice] . . . and to recite Amitābha's name five times . . . in order to bring about pure karma everywhere." . . . He [also] collected the most important teachings of the *Compendium* to compile the *Morning Penance Ritual of the Lotus School* (*Lien-tsung ch'en-chao ch'an-i*), to be for all living beings [a means of] worshiping the Buddha, confession and praying for tranquillity and good health.

Later [Mao] went to Lake Tien-shan [in modern Ch'ing-p'u county of Kiangsu] where he built a Lotus School Confession Hall (Lien-tsung ch'an-t'ang) [where all could] together cultivate good karma. He wrote the *Yüan-jung ssu-t'u san-kuan hsüan fo t'u* (Diagram of the three meditations and complete interpenetration and identity in all the four regions) . . . At the age of forty-six *sui* . . . he travelled everywhere to convert others, and wrote a collection of hymns entitled "Going to the West" [Amitābha's paradise] (Hsihsing chi).

In [1166] Emperor Kao-tsung summoned him to court to lecture on Pure Land teachings and gave him the special honorary title of Most Honored Master of the Light of Compassion, Guide and Teacher of the Lotus School, who Urges [Others] to Piety and Good Works . . .

He then returned to P'ing-chiang, where he vowed [that he would help] everyone on this great earth to realize the wonderful Tao. He used four-character phrases to teach people to attain rebirth together in the Pure Land by reciting only the name of Amitābha. From this [our] school became very influential. He collected texts such as "Essentials of Amitābhism" (*Mi-t'o chieh-yao*) . . . [and] "The Song of Verifying the Way" (*Cheng-tao ke*) . . . and circulated them [throughout] the world.

[Later that same year] . . . he said to his disciples, "My present incarnation has reached its end, and it is time for me to go." As he finished speaking he folded his hands, took leave of all, and died.

Elsewhere P'u-tu says of Mao: "The transforming influence of Tz'u-chao tsung-chu was felt all over the land. Princes, ministers of the court, monks and laity, all venerated him. There were very many who [through his influence] were converted by reciting the Buddha's name. The records of his activities are too numerous to recount."[61]

In chüan 2 of the *Lien-tsung pao-chien* Tz'u-chao's teachings are quoted and described in detail, and they appear to be uniformly orthodox. As such they are quoted with approval by Wang Jih-hsiu.[62] In Ming Ching-t'u sources Mao appears as a pillar of the Pure Land tradition; his autobiographical hymn (quoted above) is reproduced several times. I have already discussed his attack on folk distortions of reciting the Buddha's name. In addition, in I-nien's *Hsi-fang chih-chih* (Pointing directly to the western land) Tz'u-chao is quoted in sharp criticism of "ignorant folk" who do not understand the proper way to seek rebirth in the Pure Land, who recite Amitābha's name to ward off illness and in times of difficulty call on gods and ancestors, burn paper money, and kill living beings for sacrifice. He concludes, "[Such folk] will not be protected by the Buddha, but will fall into the [lowest levels of purgatory]."[63] After reading this material it is extremely difficult to conceive of Mao Tzu-yüan as the founder of a syncretic folk sect! If he had been involved in dubious or heretical activity, why would the Pure Land school have so venerated him as an orthodox saint of the tradition, described alongside Hui-yüan and Shan-tao?

Nonetheless, it is as just such a subversive sort that Mao Tzu-yüan is viewed by writers from rival schools. In the words of Chih-p'an, a T'ien-tai writer,

The monk Mao Tzu-yüan was from the Yen-hsiang monastery in Wu-chün (the area around Wu-hsien in Kiangsu). He first studied with the Dharma Master Fan [d. 1127] and in imitation of T'ien-t'ai [teachings] he wrote the *Yüan-jung ssu-t'u t'u* and the *Ch'en-chao li-ch'an wen* . . . and urged all men and women to together cultivate good karma. He called himself the White Lotus Master Teacher (Pai-lien tao-shih), and while seated received the veneration of his many [followers]. Because they were careful about onions and milk and neither killed [animals for meat] nor drank wine, they were called the White Lotus Vegetarians. Those who were taught his heretical religion (*hsieh-chiao*) called it transmitting the Tao. Those who had illicit sexual relationships [with each other] called it the Buddhist dharma (*fo-fa*). Arrogant and rude, they stopped at nothing. [In this group] ignorant men and women took turns in deceiving each other, and [when] assembled

in the fields and villages they all took pleasure in [the sect's] reckless teachings. Because of this, those in authority banished [Mao
Tzu-yüan] to Chiang-chou, finding him guilty of worshiping the
devil . . . The White Lotus [sect] falsely ranked [its leader] along
with [orthodox] patriarchs . . . calling him a Master Teacher equal
to the Buddha. They falsely say they are practicing pure religion
while in fact they are solely devoted to immorality. There is
nothing good in what they do. How can they possess the way? Oh,
my![64]

Tsung-chien gives a condensed version of this account in his
section on "Rejecting Falsehood," sandwiched between attacks on
the Manichaeans and the White Cloud sect.[65]

Is it possible that the "Lotus School Penance Hall" referred to
in the Pure Land sources became the focal point for a new lay society? Language describing devotional activities for both sect and
penance hall is identical at this point: "together cultivating pure
karma" (t'ung hsiu ching-yeh). Perhaps after Mao died the originally orthodox group became less so? Tsung-chien indicates at least
this possibility when he says that "after Mao Tzu-yüan [died] a
Buddhist priest [named] Hsiao Mao (little Mao) gathered together
the remaining members, but his teachings were not equal to those
of [Mao] Tzu-yüan [himself]. White Clothing (Pai-i) [sects] spread
their teaching everywhere, but they are all in error, [because they]
retain only the prohibition against killing."[66] Hsiao Mao was probably Mao's son, which would indicate that Mao himself married,
thus making possible a form of hereditary leadership new to Amitābhism but common in later sectarian tradition. Tsung-chien's
accusation that the sect retained only one of the five prohibitions
may have been intended primarily to point out that they had aban-
doned celibacy.

It was evidently the fact that White Lotus clergy did marry
that most aroused the hostility of Chih-p'an, as we can see from his
language about "immoral sexual relations," while Tsung-chien
states that the most important distinction between the White Lotus
and White Cloud groups was whether or not their members married, with the implication that only the White Lotus did.

Nevertheless, other than this there is nothing in these hostile
descriptions of the Pai-lien ts'ai which really indicates heterodoxy.

There is no doubt that Mao Tzu-yüan was (at least) a successful popularizer, but this is not the same as veneration of non-Buddhist deities or complete acceptance of folk concern for a religion which promises immediate physical benefits. These are not mentioned.

Whatever the role of Mao himself, Chih-p'an, writing about 130 years later, says of the White Lotus Vegetarians that "they are still numerous and active today,"[67] which indicates continuous existence at least to the end of the Sung. It seems reasonable to suggest, therefore, that an independent lay group developed out of Mao Tzu-yüan's evangelizing efforts, perhaps centered on the Penance Hall. Led at first by his son, this group was able to maintain itself, sustained by hereditary leadership and by the catechisms and ritual texts which Mao had prepared. This association was distinguished by the fact that it permitted its members to marry, which is just the situation we find in the next detailed description of a White Lotus group, in the Yüan dynasty.

There is no further source material which refers directly to White Lotus activities in the Sung period. However, there was an edict in 1257 which said, "It is prohibited for heretics to form societies [of those who wear] white clothing (*pai-i hui*)." And in 1273 another imperial decree states, "It is prohibited for heretics to recklessly establish associations and to privately build temples and hostels in order to escape corvée labor."[68] From Tsung-chien's comments above perhaps we can assume that at least the first of these edicts refers to the White Lotus, though the second could apply to other groups as well.

The White Lotus sect thus began as an independent association of clergy and laymen, devoted to attaining rebirth in the Pure Land. Its vegetarianism, abstinence from wine and killing, and disciplined piety all mark it as a part of the Mahāyāna tradition.

Syncretism and institutionalization in the Yüan Dynasty. The first reference to a White Lotus group in the Yüan (Mongol) dynasty (1280-1368) is a memorial submitted to Kublai Khan in 1281. The reporting official says that in that year there was a White Lotus society (Pai-lien hui) active in Tu-ch'ang county of Kiangnan (modern Tung-hai county of Kiangsu), led by a "bandit chief" named Tu Wan-i, who with others "has led a rebellion . . . [This group had] a Five Dukes charm (Wu-kung fu), a prognostication book

(Tui pei t'u), a "blood basin" (Hsüeh p'en) [exorcising implement], and an illegal book of astrological charts (*t'ien-wen t'u-shu*), and all sorts of [such] heretical implements and arts which cause disorder."[69] The memorial asks that the White Lotus be prohibited because of its possession of such objects. No details are given about the extent of Tu Wan-i's uprising, but presumably it was a very minor affair. What is most important for our purposes is the religious syncretism implied by the presence of such popular Taoist ritual implements, 150 years after the founding of the sect.

The next Yüan mention of the White Lotus indicates not only further syncretism but also an advanced state of institutionalization. In the *Yüan shih* there is an edict of 1308 which reads, "Prohibit the White Lotus association (Pai-lien she), destroy its temples, return its members to their homes."[70] A memorial of the same year describes a group called the White Lotus Way (Pai-lien tao) in Chien-ning lu (modern Chien-ou county of Fukien province). The members were all married, had their wives and children with them, built their own monasteries (*ssu*—perhaps "temple hostels" is a more accurate term in this context), assembled large numbers of men and women together for worship at night, and practiced good works. They also prayed for the emperor's long life. The imperial response to this report was: "All the White Lotus temples (Pai-lien t'ang) should be destroyed, along with all the images (*shen-hsiang*) in them. All the members (*tao-jen*) should be dispersed to their original registered places of residence . . . Those who don't reform are to be severely punished. Other similar groups are [also] prohibited."[71]

Since the Mongols were generally sympathetic to Buddhism, it is reasonable to assume that the investigating official was aware of the differences between Buddhism and folk religion and therefore consciously chose the terms *tao, tao-jen* (Taoist practitioner), and *shen-hsiang* (image of a god, as distinguished from *fo-hsiang*, image of a Buddha). All this further indicates the development of White Lotus syncretism. Even more important is the evidence that by the early fourteenth century the White Lotus sect was based on a system of lay monasticism. This communal living in temple hostels was continued all through sectarian history, including Lo sect hostels for canal boatmen in the sixteenth century and permanent residence in vegetarian halls in Singapore as late as 1955.[72]

One of the most interesting indications of the nature of the early White Lotus tradition is the fact that for nine years in the Yüan dynasty (1313-1322) the sect was officially recognized and supported by Emperor Jen-tsung. Nothing more clearly indicates that we are dealing not with a rebel movement but with a religious voluntary association which in its beginnings had a strong tendency toward full-scale denominational development. By 1313 the White Lotus had produced a religious and economic "subculture," similar to that of the Jōdo sects in Japan. But after 1322 the movement was never again officially permitted to operate openly, so the tendencies visible by that time were not able to come to mature and independent fruition.

Jen-tsung was favorably influenced toward the White Lotus by a sympathetic official, who introduced him to a sect leader named Hsiao Chüeh-kuei. Hsiao turned to the emperor for protection because he knew he was a devout Buddhist. The decree of recognition directed to all the officials, clergy and people in the realm, reads in part as follows:

... in the mountains behind Chien-ning lu ... there are White Lotus "Respond to Compassion" temples (Pao-en t'ang) ... There are those who don't understand Buddhism who have destroyed some of these temples ... In these Buddhist temples (fo-t'ang), built with their own contributions they regularly chant sūtras, pray for prosperity and long life for those in higher positions, and carry out other beneficial activities ... These *fo-t'ang* are to be called, "Respond to Compassion Hall of Eternal Life" (Pao-en wan-shou t'ang); each such temple is to have a director in residence ... Another temple belonging [to the sect] is called the Hall of Pure Response. Every locality [in the Fukien area] has these Lotus Halls (Lien t'ang) which ... carry out charitable activities. [All responsible officials] are hereby ordered to stop prosecuting and suppressing this religion ...
Further, all the Lotus temples, water and land, people, rolls of cloth, gardens and forests, mills, shops, [supplies for] feasts, sūtra storehouses, bathhouses and boats which belong to this sect are neither to be molested nor confiscated.

This edict concludes by saying that sect temples are to be tax exempt and by warning officials who do not comply.[73]

The public recognition which the White Lotus sought and won

lasted only until 1322. In that year the new emperor Ying-tsung proclaimed, "White Lotus Buddhist activities are prohibited (*chin Pai-lien fo-shih*)."[74]

With the exception of a small local outbreak led by Tu Wan-i, the White Lotus was involved in no violent activities from the time of its founding until the mid-fourteenth century. It did not participate in a general rebellion until Han Shan-t'ung's movement in 1351, a period of 218 years. The structure that appears in early fourteenth century sources is a full-scale religious system, supported by a variety of economic enterprises, operating openly at the local level, a structure clearly not intended as a base for guerrilla warfare. It is significant that only when the forces of imperial Confucian orthodoxy were temporarily eclipsed by a non-Chinese Buddhist emperor could the White Lotus emerge into public recognition. When it did, far from threatening the government, the sect prayed for the emperor's well being.

But even such moderate and inoffensive behavior was not long to be tolerated. Perhaps in part because of repeated prohibitions, the sect developed a new openness to the "radical left" of medieval Chinese culture, Maitreyan eschatology. When it next appears in the sources the White Lotus is proclaiming the advent of Maitreya and the descent of the Manichaean King of Light.

White Lotus religion from the fourteenth to the sixteenth centuries. In the mid-fourteenth century the White Lotus religion entered a new phase under the leadership of Han Shan-t'ung (d. 1355) from Hopei in north China, who brought the Maitreya cult with him south and east to where the White Lotus had begun. Of him we read in the *Yüan shih*:

> Han Shan-t'ung's grandfather [was a leader of] The White Lotus Society (Pai-lien hui), who deceived the people by means of conducting worship services (*shao-hsiang*, lit. "burning incense"). [For this] he was banished . . . As for Shan-t'ung, he said that the empire was in great disorder, and that the Buddha Maitreya was about to descend to be reborn. All the ignorant people of [the present provinces of] Honan, Kiangsu and Anhwei eagerly believed him. Liu Fu-t'ung [and six other sect leaders] proclaimed that Shan-t'ung was really the eighth generation descendant of the Sung Emperor Hui-tsung [reigned 1101-1126], and that therefore he should

be the lord of China. Fu-t'ung and the others then slew a white
horse and a black ox, and took oaths before Heaven and Earth that
they would rise together in rebellion. However, the news leaked
out . . . Liu Fu-t'ung rebelled, but Shan-t'ung was captured. [How-
ever] . . . his wife and son, Lin-er, escaped to Wu-an shan [in modern Wu-ning hsien, Kiangsu].[75]

These events are described in some detail in the *Ming shih*
biography of Han Lin-er. Liu Fu-t'ung successfully occupied Ying-
chou and a number of other places in the same area. As a result his
army increased in size to over 100,000 men, which Yüan troops
were unable to suppress. At this same time other White Lotus-
related leaders rose in revolt, such as Hsü Shou-hui in Ma-ch'eng
in Hupei and Kuo Tzu-hsing in Hao-chou (modern Feng-yang
county, Anhwei). All these forces were collectively called the Red
Army (from the red turbans they wore) or the Incense Army
(Hsiang-chün).

In 1355 Liu Fu-t'ung located Han Lin-er and designated him
both emperor and Lesser King of Light (Hsiao Ming-wang). Together they established a state with its capital at Po-chou [modern
Po-hsien, Anhwei], where they built a palace; the name of this state
was Sung, and Han's reign title Dragon Phoenix (Lung-feng). Lin-
er's mother was honored as empress dowager. Kuo Tsu-hsing
became a general in the Sung armies.[76]

It is not my task here to describe all the complex events at the
end of the Yüan dynasty culminating in the founding of the Ming in
1368, events which have been dealt with in detail by John W. Dardess.[77] Suffice it to say that after years of struggle with both Yüan
armies and other rebels, and after much internal competition between rival factions in Sung, in 1363 Liu Fu-t'ung was killed, and
Han Lin-er appealed to Chu Yüan-chang for help. Chu, who was
soon to found the Ming empire as Ming T'ai-tsu, had for several
years been a successful officer in Kuo Tsu-hsing's command and
was able to save Lin-er for awhile. However, the erstwhile emperor
died by drowning in 1366. In that same year Chu Yüan-chang publicly denounced his old Red Army associates and denied the Maitreya hope.

Other histories of this period provide additional detail about

White Lotus symbols and beliefs. In his account of the last reign of the Yüan dynasty, Ch'üan Heng writes: "[In 1351] the Red Army of Ying-chou rose in revolt. [They were also] called the 'Incense Army' because they burned incense in worship of the Buddha Maitreya."[78]. In another source we read that Han Shan-t'ung proclaimed, "The empire is in great disorder, Maitreya Buddha has descended to be reborn and the King of light has appeared in the world." (*T'ien-hsia ta luan, Mi-le-fo hsia-sheng, Ming-wang ch'u-shih*).[79]

Here we have a passage almost identical with that in the (Ming edited) history of the Yüan, except for the title Ming-wang. Wu Han says that the new Ming emperor did not want to recall his common origins and his debt to Manichaean eschatology. The King of Light was none other than Han Lin-er, as we can see in the work of another historian: "As for the Lesser King of Light (Hsiao Ming Wang) Han Lin-er, he was the son of Han Shan-t'ung. His ancestors had deceived the multitudes by means of the Pai-lien hui, and the people all followed them. At the end of the Yüan, Shan-t'ung proclaimed . . . the King of Light has appeared, etc."[80] In these quotes we can clearly see White Lotus blending of Maitreyan, Manichaean, and Confucian-traditional eschatologies as the basis for messianic warfare. From this point on the potential for such warfare was always present, though not always expressed.

In 1370, two years after proclaiming himself emperor of the Ming dynasty, T'ai-tsu promulgated the strict laws against heresy which became the backbone of official suppression until 1911. But the White Lotus continued on as before and staged numerous uprisings all through the dynasty which it had helped name.

Liu Fu-t'ung's short lived state of Sung was in Anhwei, while Hsü Shou-hui occupied an area of Hupei and Kiangsi. In 1359 one of Hsü's own subordinates, Ch'en Yu-liang, took over real power in his movement and established the kingdom of Han (Ch'en Han). This kingdom was defeated by Chu Yüan-chang in 1364 and absorbed into the growing area under his control which in 1368 became the Ming dynasty.[81]

Further west in Szechwan a third center of activity was led by Ming Yü-chen, who established a kingdom of Hsia (Ming Hsia), taking the ancient name of a legendary kingdom which is said to

have preceded the Shang dynasty. It is in this state that the worship
of Maitreya was established as the official religion. Ming Yü-chen
surrendered to T'ai-tsu in 1371.[82]

Despite their rivalry, these three White Lotus centers all called
their armies Hung-chün, Red Army, thus perhaps indicating their
unity at the theoretical level. It is true that all three were soon elim-
inated geographically and politically, but their religious legacy
lived on, for it is in these areas that the sources note sectarian activity again and again all through the Ming dynasty. For example,
there was an uprising in Shensi in 1409 led by a man who called
himself Chin-kang Nu, Slave of the Diamond (Sūtra). He was a
Buddhist who took the title Kings of the Four Heavens (Ssu T'ien
Wang), a title which originated in the *Golden Light Sūtra* (*Chin
kuang-ming ching*). In this text the four kings pledge to defend the
nation against plague, famine, and enemies if the sūtra were read
and if the ruler himself would support Buddhism.[83]

One of Chin-kang Nu's followers was given the title Emperor
of the Han Ming and took Han Lin-er's old reign title Dragon Phoenix. Thus, this movement claimed to continue the Han family
White Lotus tradition.

In the Ming Cheng-t'ung reign period (1436-1450) a rebellion
broke out, led by a man named Liu from Hsi-hua in Honan who
established his group in Ching-chou and called himself King of
Han. As Li Shou-k'ung points out, Hsi-hua was in Han Lin-er's old
bailiwick, and Ching-chou in Hupei was the area of the Ch'en Han
state. So both geographical connections and royal title indicate that
Liu may have been continuing the earlier White Lotus activity.
Thus, "these mid-Ming White Lotus movements operated in roughly the same area as those at the end of the Yüan."[84]

Sectarian continuity can also be seen in the case of a Szechwan
White Lotus leader in 1566, who when captured confessed that he
had studied with Li T'ung in Shansi, far to the north. When Li T'ung
was arrested, he said that he was the son of Li Ta-li, who in turn
was the son of a famous sectarian leader named Li Fu-ta, who had
been active in Shansi in 1526. Li T'ung said that his family had been
leaders in the White Lotus sect (Pai-lien chiao) for generations.[85]

Of course there were also other Ming White Lotus groups
which were not clearly related to any of the late Yüan centers,

though records concerning them are so brief that one cannot do much with them. Most interesting for our purposes is a reference to a 1565 White Lotus group in Shang-he county of Hopei province, which "privately established forty-five temples and had over 10,000 riff-raff (wu-lai) followers who came from all directions to worship [in them]. Day and night they preached the dharma and recited sūtras, with men and women participating together." Though this branch did not engage in any violent activity its leader was executed, and "those who had been forced to follow him were released."[86] All this is summed up in Lü K'un's memorial to the throne in 1597 which complained: "The White Lotus society (Pai-lien chieh-she) is active everywhere. Wherever there are sect leaders (chiao-chu) or head evangelists (ch'uan-t'ou) there they gather the people in groups. If there are leaders to summon, there are folk [inclined to heresy] who respond in allegiance to them."[87]

Later White Lotus activity. The most important new development in White Lotus tradition during the sixteenth century was the appearance of the Wu-sheng Lao-mu myth, the story of the creation of mankind by the son and daughter of a primordial mother deity. This myth and its background will be discussed in Chapter 7. Since there were few religious innovations after the sixteenth century and since the later period has been more extensively dealt with in English by scholars like DeGroot and Chu,[88] I will note here just the salient events in seventeenth and eighteenth century White Lotus history. After the Eight Trigrams uprising was put down in 1813, the movement was further fragmented into a number of small groups with many different names. The history of these groups is extremely complex but their basic organizational and belief systems seem to have been similar.

The sources record a number of White Lotus groups active at the end of the Ming, the most important of which was led by Hsü Hung-ju. In 1622 Hsü's movement was involved in a six month civil war in Shantung province but was defeated by the government.

What is most significant for us is that the official records note an increase in sectarian activity in the Wan-li period (1573-1620), which corresponds to the sudden increase in *pao-chüan* literature at the same time. I have already quoted a memorial from 1597 which noted that "the White Lotus society is active everywhere," while

Huang Yü-p'ien says that "All these *pao-chüan* were published in
the Ming Wan-li and Ch'ung-chen (1628-1644) periods."[89] This was
just the time of final dynastic decay and disorder in the face of
Manchu pressure. Richard Chu writes: "After 1600, as the internal
situation further deteriorated and as foreign pressure continued to
increase the White Lotus activities became more evident . . . During
the T'ien-ch'i period (1621-1627) alone, there were twenty uprisings
in the White Lotus category."[90]

But, just in this tumultuous period, when from a external point
of view White Lotus activities are difficult to distinguish from the
numerous disturbances caused by "roving bandits" (*liu-k'ou*) and
military opportunists, there is evidence that the sects in fact were
operating out of a long established religious tradition. For Hsü
Hung-ju was a disciple of Wang Sen (d. 1619), and Wang Sen was
the leader of a White Lotus group based in Stone-Buddha village
(Shih-fo chuang or Shih-fo k'ou) of Luan-chou, Hopei province
(Modern Luan-hsien). We are told that "Wang promoted the
White Lotus religion, and called himself the leader of the 'Incense
Smelling Sect' (Wen-hsiang chiao). Among his followers there
were those with such titles as 'greater evangelist,' 'lesser evangelist' (ta hsiao ch'uan-t'ou) and 'chief of congregation' (hui-chu).
His movement was widespread in the area of the imperial capital,
and in Shantung, Shansi, Honan, Shensi and Szechwan." Wang
was also involved in intrasect rivalries and had some converts
among court officials, particularly eunuchs and relatives of the
empress. He was arrested twice, in 1594 and 1614, and finally died
after five years in prison. After he died his son Hao-hsien and Hsü
Hung-ju succeeded him in sect leadership, and in 1622 Hsü proclaimed himself Blessed and Eminent Emperor of the Restoration
(Chung-hsing fu-lieh ti) and called the first year of his reign the First
Year of Great Achievement and Joyous Victory (Ta-ch'eng hsing-
sheng yüan-nien). According to the records he had some 2,000,000
followers, who are called not troops but *t'u-tang*, disciples or members. He was eventually defeated and "sliced to pieces in the mar-
ketplace."[91]

The religious base of this eschatological war is further revealed
by the fact that the Stone Buddha village White Lotus community is
discussed in what Huang Yü-p'ien considered to be the pre-eminent

pao-chüan among the twenty he collected in 1833, the *Precious Dragon Flower Scripture Examined and Corrected by the Old Buddha*. This text contains the most complete statement of the Eternal Mother mythology. In a chapter entitled "Going East and West to Get Scriptures" we read that at Wu-sheng lao-mu's request "The Venerable Buddha King (*Lao fo-wang*) of Stone Buddha village, personally went to the Dragon Temple and took a scripture back to the village. Kung Ch'ang [a sect leader] then went to Shih-fo where he obtained this true scripture. [He also] got a copy of the *Old Buddha Scripture* [which deals with] Arranging Heaven and Establishing Earth and a copy of the *Unborn (Eternal) Scripture (Wu-sheng ching)*."[92]

Thus, the Shih-fo village produced at least three scriptures, including one dealing with creation mythology. It is not surprising that Huang found this Dragon Flower text, for we know that the Stone Buddha congregation continued to be a center of White Lotus activity for at least 200 years, led by the same Wang family. In 1815, Na-yen-ch'eng (1764-1833), the governor-general of Chihli, who had put down the Eight Trigrams sect uprising in 1813, reported:

> As for the Wang family of Shih-fo k'ou of Luan-chou, their ancestor was Wang Sen. From the Ming [dynasty] on they have propagated the White Lotus religion, calling themselves masters of the Incense Smelling Sect. [This religion] has been continued down to the present for more than 200 years. I have discovered that they have repeatedly been prosecuted for ten generations yet their sons and grandsons still continue this evil without reform, changing their name to the Pure Tea School (Ch'ing-ch'a men).[93]

In that same year Na-yen-ch'eng described a book owned by the Wang family of Shih-fo k'ou entitled *A General Interpretation of Response to Kalpic Change According to the Three Religions (San-chiao ying-chieh tsung-kuan t'ung-shu)*, which discussed the Lamplighter Buddha, Śākyamuni Buddha, and the Buddha Yet to Come (*wei-lai fo*), each related to successive kalpas as follows:

> In the past the Lamplighter Buddha ruled the religion (*chang-chiao*), and [then] each year had six months, and each day [only] six [Chinese] hours. Now Śākyamuni Buddha is dominant, and the

year has twelve months, with twelve hours to the day. In the future, the Buddha of the Future, Maitreya, will control the religion; then each year will have eighteen months and each day eighteen hours. The Buddha of the Future will be reborn in the Wang family of Shih-fo k'ou.[94]

Other sources indicate that until 1815 the Wang family was still actively propagating the religion, still preparing for the imminent advent of a new age, led by generations of hereditary lay leaders.

White Lotus activity is noted all through the Ch'ing dynasty. The most powerful and long lasting of all sect-led rebellions occurred in 1796 under the leadership of several men, the most famous of whom were Liu Sung and Liu Chih-hsieh. The uprising began in Hupei, spread to five provinces, and lasted nine years. It was this period that the Chia-ch'ing Emperor proclaimed his distinction between peaceful White Lotus members and rebellious leaders, a distinction I have discussed in Chapter 3. Since I know of no new contribution by this movement to White Lotus religious development, I will not discuss it in detail, though Suzuki's valuable research concerning this period has been mentioned above and will be referred to again.

Another White Lotus related outburst came in 1813, only nine years after the first Chia-ch'ing uprising was put down. It was led by Lin Ch'ing and Li Wen-ch'eng under the name "Eight Trigrams Sect" or "The Religion of Heaven's Guiding Principle" (T'ien-li chiao), and began, as did the Maitreya rebellion in 610, with a direct attack on the imperial palace. Of Lin Ch'ing we are told that when he entered the religion he was taught the sacred mantra, *chen-k'ung chia-hsiang, wu-sheng fu-mu.* The movement was full of cosmological and eschatological symbolism, all based on the theory of kalpic change. Because of the threat to the emperor himself, it is understandable that this uprising was put down with great ferocity. The suppression was so thorough that the White Lotus tradition was further fragmented at the organizational level and continued to exist only in small groups under a variety of new and changing names.

In this connection it is interesting that there were several sects which continued the Eternal Mother mythology and other aspects of White Lotus belief structure deep into the twentieth century. Among them are the I-kuan tao, "The Way of Pervading Unity," and the Hsien-t'ien tao, "The Way of the Former Heaven."

The I-kuan tao is said to have been founded by a Wang Chüeh-i in the middle of the nineteenth century. This group was particularly active during the period of Japanese occupation, 1937-1945, and was still being attacked by mainland writers and officials as late as 1956.[95] In 1968 an I-kuan tao sect adherent in Taiwan gave Kristopher Schipper a manuscript titled *I-kuan tao i-wen hsiang-ta* (Detailed answers to doubts and questions concerning the I-kuan tao). This catechism claims that the sect was founded by Wang Chüeh-i, and that the highest god, Ming-ming shang-ti, "because he is also the mother of all things is called Lao-mu."[96]

While I-kuan tao doctrine is complex and shows Christian and Moslem influence, in it the Eternal Mother-Maitreya mythology remains essentially intact. The *I-wen hsiang-ta* catechism describes the three-stage chronology in the context of a concern for universal salvation.[97] I-kuan tao groups active on the mainland in the 1950's taught that:

> Now the last era of the three time periods approaches, when a violent wind will sweep the earth, and the world will be in great disorder, with the dead beyond counting. Only by joining the I-kuan chiao can one escape these disasters, thereby transforming evil into good fortune. After the trials of this time have passed, an incarnation of the Buddha of the White Yang will put this world in proper order, so that it becomes the White Yang world. At this time members of the religion can ascend to heaven [at death] . . . and while they are alive can be at ease as officials.

Wu-sheng lao-mu was the supreme deity of these groups as well.[98]

The I-kuan tao texts collected by Grootaers in and before 1946 also discuss the Lao-mu myth. The supreme being is called Mu (mother). The five character invocation taught all members is Wu-t'ai fo Mi-le (Oh, Great Buddha Maitreya). A scripture which Grootaers translates as *Instructions pour rentrer á la maison* (*Chia-hsiang hsin-chu*), written in 1919, speaks of Shang-ti's great mercy in the time just before the arrival of the third age. In order to save all men and their families from the sea of suffering and enable them to ascend to the other shore (*ch'u tz'u k'u-hai er teng pi-an*), he explains the Hsien-t'ien I-kuan tao (the Way of Pervading Unity of the Former Heaven).

The text goes on to say that the inhabitants of the earth are separated from the Venerable Mother by their ignorance. Because she wishes to save them from the approaching catastrophe, she indicates the means of salvation by sending down several "masters," including Maitreya. Men refuse to listen to Maitreya, who is then sent down again to show the way home to the Western Land. After he fails a second time, all the celestial spirits are sent down to save mankind, and finally Lao-mu writes a letter with her own blood, urging all men to conversion.

A scripture revealed by planchette in 1923, called a *New Introduction to the I-kuan tao* (*I-kuan tao hsin chieh-shao*), describes mankind's fall into disaster because they have forgotten their origins. The infinite, the Mother of Mankind, Lao-mu, loves them more than her own flesh and is broken-hearted. She sends the saints to teach people to recover their true nature, but they persist in recognizing the mothers of their bodies but not the Mother of their spirits. Now Heaven has revealed the way of fundamental unity to teach them that the origin of all is Wu-sheng lao-mu, who in her mercy has showed the way of salvation to men.[99] We shall see below that all these teachings are found in sixteenth century White Lotus texts.

In 1954-1955 Marjorie Topley investigated Hsien-t'ien tao groups among the Chinese inhabitants of Singapore. She reports that these sects were based in *chai-t'ang*, which she describes as "residential religious establishments in which inmates practice sexual abstinence and follow a vegetarian diet." The highest deity of this religion is Mother, otherwise known as Lao-mu, Wu-sheng lao-mu, or by other similar titles. As in White Lotus tradition, cosmic time for the Hsien-t'ien tao is divided into three cycles, each dominated by a Buddha, with Maitreya being the one to come. In fact, one of the Singapore groups "believes that the third major cycle, that of Maitreya, has already begun and that its own present patriarch is Maitreya incarnate."[100] For this group the key symbol of

Maitreya and his cycle is the white lotus. I will discuss Topley's fascinating discoveries in Singapore in more detail later; for now we have seen enough to verify the continuation of Ming dynasty sectarian thought into the second half of the twentieth century. How did this oft-suppressed White Lotus belief structure survive so long? Was this tradition transmitted by hereditary sect leadership during the nineteenth century, as it evidently had been earlier? To these questions there is still no certain answer.[101]

6
Other Groups:
An Introduction to the
White Cloud and Lo Sects

By describing the Ch'ang-sheng sect I have already indicated that the formation of sects in folk Buddhism was a general phenomenon not limited to the White Lotus tradition. In fact, the White Cloud society was founded as an independent movement in 1108, twenty-five years before the rise of the White Lotus. There is little material on White Cloud beliefs, but this association was a product of the general Sung tendency to form popular devotional societies. Suzuki lists it in his section on Pure Land groups, together with the White Lotus,[1] which is probably accurate, given the pervasive nature of contemporary Amitābhist piety. However, the fragmentary evidence we do have does not specifically mention *nien-fo* but rather indicates a form of popularized Ch'an practice based on T'ien-t'ai philosophy.

The Lo sect was founded by Lo Ch'ing in the Ming Cheng-te period (1506-1522), probably about 1509. While Lo Ch'ing may have been a reformer who split off from the White Lotus tradition, as Topley suggests,[2] the evidence indicates that the sect he established maintained an independent existence alongside the White Lotus until at least the nineteenth century. After that there was a general blending of sect names and doctrines, though the Amoy Lo groups investigated by DeGroot in 1887 do not seem to have been much affected by White Lotus practice, and their texts do not mention the Eternal Mother.[3]

It is interesting that except for a Lo sect uprising in 1748 to free an imprisoned leader, there is no record of any violent eschatological activity by either the White Cloud or the later group. In the White Cloud this is perhaps explained by an absence of Maitreyan messianism, and in the Lo by an early emphasis on Taoist-Ch'an nonaction. One of the alternative names used in the Lo tradition was Wu-wei chiao, the Religion of Nonaction.[4]

The White Cloud Religion

The White Cloud society was established in Hangchow by an ordained monk from Honan named K'ung Ch'ing-chüeh (d. 1121).

The *Bhiksu* Ch'ing-chüeh, whose sobriquet was Pen-jan, was born in Lo-yang . . . in the third year of the Ch'ing-li period of emperor Jen-tsung [1043], in the family of Confucius, of whom he was the fifty-second generation descendant. His great grandfather was [an official] in the Liang and Later T'ang dynasties [Five Dynasties period], and became the Grand Tutor of the crown prince. His father was a *chin-shih* degree holder [the highest degree in the state examination system] . . . [Ch'ing]-chüeh was an intelligent youth who studied Confucianism and attained [the *hsiu-ts'ai*] degree [the first degree] . . . In [1069] he for the first time read the *Lotus Sūtra* and resolved to leave home and become a monk, to which his parents consented. He subsequently was given tonsure by Master Hai-hui of the Pao-ying monastery in Ju-chou [modern Lin-ju county, Honan]. [Hai-hui] told him to go south to seek instruction . . . He [eventually] came to Fu-shan [in Anhwei], where . . . he built a small temple on the top of . . . a high cliff and there he meditated for twenty years. [In 1092] he began to travel about Chekiang, and the next year reached the Ling-yin monastery in Hangchow . . . Behind this Ling-yin establishment there was a White Cloud mountain monastery (Pai-yün shan an) where Ch'ing-chüeh stayed and attained enlightenment. Here he established his new school, which he called the White Cloud school (Pai-yün tsung) . . . [Later he moved on to another monastery at Hsi-hu] and there in 1104 [a group] of monks and laymen asked him to lecture on the *Hua-yen sūtra*.

Just at this time Emperor Hui-tsung began to support Taoism and to move against Buddhism. Ch'ing-chüeh wrote two tracts defending the religion against this new policy, one a discussion of the Three Religions, and the other called "The Song of the Ten Stages" of bodhisattvahood ("Shih-ti ke"). He continued to move about building small temples with such names as Shih-ti and Ch'u-lu (Transcend the world). In 1116 his enemies at court attacked him on the basis of his discussion of the Three Religions, which he had written in defense of Buddhism, and he was exiled to southern Kwangtung. His disciples finally succeeded in obtaining a pardon for him in 1120, but two months later he died at the age of seventy-nine *sui*. He was succeeded by his disciple Hui-neng, who in 1123 buried his master's bones in a mountain near Hangchow, where he built a White Cloud pagoda, with a temple named Universal Peace (P'u-ning). Ch'ing-chüeh's disciples then built nine temples on mountains all over Chekiang. The foundations of all of them included a sacred relic (*she-li*) of the founder. Thus, "his teachings flourished in Chekiang."[5] It is clear that the White Cloud was founded by an active and outspoken orthodox monk of good family. Its movement toward independence was perhaps furthered by the opposition Ch'ing-chüeh encountered.[6]

Ch'ing-chüeh's work was characterized by his evangelistic concern and his writing of devotional and doctrinal books in a popular style. In addition to "The Song of the Ten Stages," he wrote works with such titles as "The Attainment of the Four Realizations and the Ten Stages," and "The Difference between the Large and Small Vehicles." Chih-p'an says that all of his writings were "taught in accord with vulgar custom" (*chiao yü liu-su*), and that another name for his group was the Shih-ti ts'ai, the Ten Stage Vegetarians.[7]

White Cloud members were vegetarians who lived a simple life and did their own farming. Shigematsu characterizes them as an upāsaka sect, which came to have hereditary lay leadership beginning with Shen Chih-yüan, who called his followers *tao-min*, People of the Way.[8] They were also called monks with hair (*yu fa seng*). Members were forbidden to marry and lived a tightly disciplined life dedicated to attaining pure karma through piety and good works.

In 1202, Shen Chih-yüan, a *tao-min* of the White Cloud center near Hangchow, petitioned the court for official recognition. In response to his request an official protested to the emperor:

As for these "People of the Way," they are vagrants up to no good who "eat vegetables and serve the devil." They are indeed evil folk. They are organized in groups of 1000, and by means of heretical teachings stir up the ignorant commoners. They repair roads and build bridges, and devote themselves to chanting sūtras and burning incense in assemblies. They gather at night and disperse during the day, making no distinction between men and women. Each group has an established leader. Whenever they are prosecuted they unite their resources to bribe officials, and are determined to always win (chih tsai pi sheng). They hoard up provisions, and build private temple-hostels (ssu-an) which they use as hiding places to escape arrest. This Chih-yüan is the leader of these false people, and has confused the people by means of heresy (tso-tao). He has broken the law [and should be punished].[9]

Obviously, Shen Chih-yüan's petition for recognition didn't work out quite as he had planned! Nonetheless, this passage gives valuable information concerning the size and vigor of White Cloud organization.

There is not much material on the later history of the White Cloud. Available sources indicate that despite difficulties in the early thirteenth century, a later sect head named Shen Ming-jen was given the honorary title Ssu-k'ung by the Yüan court in 1315, which indicates a degree of public recognition and influence. However, within two years memorials were sent to the throne urging that this title be withdrawn, a move that was successful in 1320. In the process we are told that the White Cloud at this time had 100,000 members from among the common people and owned 20,000 ch'ing of land. Furthermore Shen Ming-jen had illegally ordained over 4,800 monks, for which he had collected a large amount of money. When he was arrested in 1320, he sent a disciple to the capital to bribe officials, but this disciple was also arrested. The next time we hear of the White Cloud is in Ming T'ai-tsu's edict against heresies in 1370, after which it disappeared from sight.[10]

Shigematsu indicates that after Ch'ing-chüeh's death the most important White Cloud center was the P'u-ning monastery on a mountain south of Hangchow, and that this monastery was also known as a center of T'ien-t'ai teaching for that whole area. In addition, there is evidence that Ch'ing-chüeh studied for a time on O-mei mountain in Szechwan with a famous T'ien-t'ai master, who included the titles of several White Cloud scriptures in an appendix he wrote for the Yüan *Buddhist Compendium.* All this indicates that T'ien-t'ai teachings probably formed the theoretical base of White Cloud activity.[11]

Thus, the White Cloud developed a full scale "denomination-al" structure of lay monasticism on a T'ien-t'ai foundation, contemporaneous with that of the White Lotus. The chief differences between the two are the celibate clergy of the White Cloud, the absence in it of any syncretic cult, and the fact that most of this sect's activity was in Chekiang. But even celibate clergy were called *tao-min* and "monks with hair," they were irregularly ordained by hereditary lay leaders and lived together with ordinary members in White Cloud temple hostels.

The Lo Sect

The most influential sectarian founder and writer in the Ming dynasty was Lo Ch'ing (f. 1509-1522). Lo Ch'ing, who is also variously called Lo Huai, Lo Tsu (The Patriarch Lo), Lo Hui-neng, and Wu-wei Tsu (Patriarch of the Nonaction Sect), established a sect with hereditary lay leadership devoted to simple piety and good works. Lo wrote five books which became the main scriptures of the sect, and he himself came to be worshiped in image form as a saving bodhisattva. By Ch'ing times the Lo sect was most popular along the canals and rivers of east and south China, where it established temple hostels for grain boatmen who lived in the hostels during the winter season. However, these temples also had local permanent residents who cared for the grounds, continued ritual activity, and supported themselves by farming.

The date of Lo Ch'ing's activity is in dispute, but the publication dates of the scriptures he wrote indicate that he must have been born well before the end of the fifteenth century. The Lo material collected by Edkins in 1858 indicates that his books were published in 1518.[12] Li Shih-yü emphasizes that the texts attributed to Lo Tsu were the earliest (of the Ming) *pao-chüan* to appear and themselves indicate that they were printed in the Cheng-te period (1506-1522).[13] For example, the *Cheng-hsin ch'u-i pao-chüan* (Precious scroll of rectification of belief which eliminates doubts), was published in the Cheng-te fourth year, 1509.[14]

The dating problem arises from the fact that the Lo texts collected by DeGroot in Amoy say the founder began his work in the Ming Wan-li period (1573-1620) and lived from 1563 to 1647. However, this discrepancy, which DeGroot admitted he was unable to explain, is systematically dealt with by Tsukamoto Zenryū, who demonstrates that Lo was active by at least the Cheng-te period.[15] Marjorie Topley's studies of Singapore Hsien-t'ien tao texts indicate that Lo was born in 1488, though one suspects it may have been earlier.[16]

There are brief biographical comments about Lo Ch'ing in both the *Cheng-hsin* and *T'ai-shan pao-chüan*, where we are told that he was from Lao-shan near Ch'eng-yang in Chi-mo county, not far from the eastern tip of Shantung. His family had for generations served in the military, which, as Sakai Tadao demonstrates, meant that he was in the grain canal patrol troops, guarding transport in the Grand Canal from the Yangtze delta north to Peking. Beyond this we are simply told that he was "enlightened and preached the dharma to save others," writing his five scriptures to "enable you to escape suffering in the realm of birth and death and obtain eternal salvation, never to return."[17]

Writing in the late sixteenth century a Ch'an monk named Mi-tsang Tao-k'ai reports that in 1581 he discovered a description of Lo Ch'ing and his books in the (unnamed) writings of a monk named Lan-feng:

> [Lan-feng] commented positively on all of the five scriptures of the Lo religion, and supported [Lo's] followers . . .
> In the Cheng-te period there was a member of the grain canal patrol troops from Chi-mo county in Shantung named Lo Ching, who many years ago became a devout lay Buddhist [lit. "maintained a vegetarian diet"]. One day he met a heretical teacher who taught him an [esoteric] oral tradition. After meditating for thirteen years he suddenly saw a light in the southeast, which he took to mean that he had attained enlightenment. Then, aimlessly quoting from various texts to support [his own views] he wrote his five books . . .
> There was a certain Ta-ning who became [Lo's] disciple, while Lan-feng also secretly supported him, so that today his teaching has stirred up the whole world, and there is no way to suppress it. This sect is also called Wu-wei, Ta-sheng, Wu-nien, and other such names.[18]

Ta-ning, whom Tsukamoto says was also a Ch'an monk, is described by Tao-k'ai as a writer of simplified moral and religious texts in the vernacular. Though Lo Ch'ing himself was evidently not ordained, it was in part with the support of monks like Lan-feng and Ta-ning that he began to preach and organize among the boatmen.[19]

From Lo Ch'ing's texts it is clear that his teachings are a combination of Ch'an and Pure Land, with an emphasis on the Pure Land being one's own "original face," in one's own mind. There is also sustained criticism of reliance on any form of external support, such as sūtras or images, on the ground that all such forms are empty. In fact, Lo's scriptures are for the most part orthodox popular Buddhism, full of quotes from such sūtras as the *Diamond* and *Hua-yen*, pervaded with an awareness of śūnyatā. There is nothing in them of the Eternal Mother, relatively few references to Taoist terms, and no mention of Maitreya except to list him as one of many saving figures, or to criticize the popular cult in his name.[20]

Since the titles of Lo's books are mentioned by Ch'ing officials[21] and since all through the eighteenth century the names Lo chiao and Ta-sheng chiao are equated with Wu-wei chiao, the sect's tendency toward a Ch'an point of view may have continued throughout this period. Additional evidence is provided by DeGroot's discovery of a Wu-wei group in 1887 which traced its origin directly to Lo Huai. De Groot gives an English translation of the traditional account of the patriarch's disputation with a Tibetan monk, which is an excellent statement of a sophisticated Taoist-Ch'an interpretation of worship.[22]

Whatever the role of Ch'an elements in Lo's teachings, the five scriptures he wrote are eclectic and based on a wide variety of sources, including not only Buddhist sūtras, but also vernacular catechisms, several earlier *pao-chüan*, miscellaneous Buddhist texts such as biographies, genealogies, and interpretations of texts, and Taoist and Confucian classics. As Sakai writes, "Lo was evidently a student of such books as these, which were very popular among the common people [in the Ming period]."[23]

Lo's syncretic approach was continued by his followers, several of whom wrote commentaries on his five texts in the Ming Ch'ung-chen reign period (1628-1644). The sources used for these commentaries are again extremely varied, including orthodox sūtras, Buddhist ritual texts, almanacs, and dynastic histories. The commentators themselves were educated laymen from the Nanking area in Kiangsu, three of whom were called *chü-shih* (Buddhist devotee).

The popular Buddhist orientation of those who donated money to reprint these scriptures is revealed in dedicatory passages appended to them. The donor for the *Cheng-hsin* text and commentary was a woman named K'ung from Nanking who describes herself as a "devout woman who venerates the Buddha" (*feng fo hsin-nü*). She continues, "I have given all I possess to have carved [new printing blocks] for this scripture . . . [so that from the merit accruing to this donation] those who have gone before can attain release [from purgatory] (*ch'ao sheng*), in this life I can accumulate happiness and good fortune, and in my next existence attain complete enlightenment. [I also hope by this act] to wash clean my bad karma, with a single mind move forward on the road ahead, and in the end leave the world to become a saint (*chuan-fan, ch'eng-sheng*).

The donor of funds for reprinting the *T'ai-shan pao-chüan* was a man named Chang, also from Nanking. He calls himself a "disciple of the Buddha, [who wishes] to urge the multitudes to goodness and faith." He continues, "I pray that in every home those now alive will have increasing blessings and long life, while those who have passed on will leave the bitterness [of hell] and ascend to heaven . . . [and that] all together will enter the realm of the Great Tao of Enlightenment."[24] Both these passages are dated 1629.

In sum, the Lo religion began in Shantung in 1509 as an independently founded movement of popular Buddhist origins. Since it was based on the mobile canal boat population it spread rapidly and by the early seventeenth century was well established, with an important center in Nanking. From the *Shih-liao hsün-k'an* we know that Lo activity reached a peak in the eighteenth century. It may be helpful to look at some of the lengthy reports to the emperor included in that collection.

We have learned that before his conversion Lo Ch'ing served in the grain canal patrol troops, while a nineteenth century Hsien-t'ien chiao account notes that for a time he lived and preached in Chekiang.[25] It perhaps should not surprise us then that the earliest

record of the Lo sect in the *Shih-liao* speaks of temple hostels
among canal boatmen in Chekiang:

> In Yung-cheng, the fifth year [1727], [a court official named]
> Li Wei learned that there were believers in the Lo religion among
> boatmen in Chekiang. He recommended that these activities be
> prohibited. However, at that time only scriptures and images of the
> sect were destroyed, and the temple hostels (*an-t'ang*) were pre-
> served because they were places of rest for the boatmen. But these
> temples still contain images and scriptures, [so it can be seen that]
> we have not yet been able to destroy the root [of this problem].
> There are still twenty-two temple hostels left.[26]

By 1768 this "mission to homeless sailors" was still going on.
Chüeh-lo Yung-te, governor of Chekiang, reports that a local
official had arrested one Hsing Hai, the director of a Lo sect temple
(sūtra hall, *Lo chiao ching-t'ang*), who confessed that there were
three other such temples in Hangchow. In investigating further,
Yung-te discovered more than ten more such places, "neither clerical nor lay," which "venerate the Lo religion and Lo scriptures." All
the temples were "resthouses in which grain boatmen stay in the
off season." The various temples were named after their respective founders, and several had branch hostels, each again
named after a particular leader. Yung-te located more than seventy
temples, all related to each other by a common faith and through
their directors. Since the boatmen living in them were mostly from
further north in Shantung and Honan, they had no place to stay in
the winter off-season or when they were old or sick, so they turned
to the temple hostels. Here they were converted to the religion by
other residents. The sailors returned to the temples every year and
while living there contributed four coppers a day for food. There
were normally only a few permanent residents who took care of the
premises.

Yung-te continues,

> The names of their scriptures are *K'u-kung, P'o-hsieh, Cheng-
> hsin,* and *Chin-kang* [the first three are Lo texts, the last is the *Dia-
> mond Sūtra*] . . . but there are no illegal or heretical statements in
> these texts . . . [Apprehended members say that] the leader of the
> sect is a man named Lo Ming-chung from Mi-yün county [in Hopei

north of Peking] whom they once saw in an inn [fifteen years ago]. At the time he was over seventy, and they were told he was a descendant of the Lo chiao [founder] . . . [on the whole] the permanent residents of the temples are boatmen who are too old and sick to work . . .

Their scriptures are written in common, vulgar language and generally deal with transmigration, hell and urging men to practice the religion. They contain no rebellious words nor [descriptions of] illegal heretical arts. But such heretical religion easily confuses the common people, particularly unruly grain boatmen . . . [I suggest that] the [1727] proscription be rigorously enforced, sect leaders be executed and their images and texts be destroyed . . . However, since the boatmen have nowhere else to stay, the hostels should be turned into public resthouses with the temple names removed, for temporary residence only . . . Furthermore, all boatmen should be prohibited from joining the Lo religion and the present members dispersed; [thus] this heretical teaching can be cut off.

The emperor approved these suggestions. But a few weeks later Yung-te submitted a second memorial recommending that sect buildings be completely destroyed for fear that members would simply "turn the public hostels back into temples."

The governor-general of Fukien and Chekiang also submitted a memorial concerning Lo activities among grain boatmen, which supports Yung-te's report. He adds that, "In each temple they worship Buddhas, maintain a vegetarian diet and chant sūtras." He lists the names of twenty-two temple directors (*k'an-shou*) all of whom were

boatmen who have taken refuge in [been converted to] the Lo religion, who are now old or ill . . . they all depend on cultivating land around the temples for food . . . They feed the boatmen who stay with them . . . [and in return] the boatmen contribute money for incense, candles, and vegetables which are offered to the gods . . . The temple directors recite several chüan of scriptures a day, as do members who can read. Those who cannot read participate by burning incense and bowing. Other than this they do not carry out any activities which would mislead or confuse the people, and neither do they gather at night and disperse during the day . . . [Apprehended members] state that when boatmen come in the slack season, they merely chant sūtras, worship and eat together in peace

. . . and do not carry out any banditry or illegal activities. They
also have no secret or hidden temples.

In the same year (1768) the governor of Kiangsu submitted
another report which describes Hsing Hai as a leader of the Ta-
sheng (Mahāyāna) and Wu-wei sects, which are equated with the
Lo chiao. Hsing Hai is described as a monk (*seng-jen*), but other directors of eleven sect temples discovered are called "neither Buddhist monks nor Taoist priests" (*fei seng, fei tao*). This report
makes it clear that the hostels functioned in part as retirement
homes for old sailors and that each temple was in fact a subsect,
giving allegiance first to its own founder. Leadership was handed
down from master to chosen disciple, as was often the case in orthodox Chinese monasteries.

However, eighteenth century Lo chiao membership was by
no means confined to grain boatmen. In 1729 a Lo group was discovered in Kiangsi whose membership consisted of 123 laymen
and 68 Buddhist monks. Some of the members were city artisans,
while others were farmers, all of whom devoted themselves to vegetarian living and the cultivation of piety. Among forty-one scriptures of this group were all five of Lo Ch'ing's *wu-pu* texts, all of
which were "put together from miscellaneous quotes from Buddhist
and Taoist works." The official reports that other names for this
group were Ta-ch'eng chiao and San-sheng chiao.

One of the lay leaders apprehended in 1729 said that he was a
boatman from Shantung and that his master in the Lo Tsu chiao
(Religion of the Venerable Lo) was named Li, a boatman from
Hangchow. The general sect leader at that time was named Lo Tao,
who was said to be the eighth generation descendant of Lo Tsu.[27]

Another report from Chekiang dated 1753 describes an investigation of Lo vegetarians. The dharma names (*fa-ming*) of all the
sect leaders began with the character *p'u*. The interrogated members said that alternative names for the sect were Lung-hua hui
(Dragon-flower Assembly), and Lao-kuan chi (Venerable Official
Vegetarians).[28] The branch founder in Chekiang, Yao Wen-tzu,
dharma name P'u-shan (Universal Goodness), was considered to be
a reincarnation of Lo Tsu (*Lo Tsu chuan-shih*). There were three

levels of spiritual attainment (*kung-fu*) in this sect, the first, called the Small Vehicle (*hsiao-sheng*), involved chanting the "Gatha in Twenty-eight Words" and the second, called the Great Vehicle (*ta-sheng*), The "Gatha of One hundred eight Words." The highest level, called the Superior Vehicle (*shang-sheng*), was characterized by seated meditation (*tso-kung*) with no chanting required. At each level the members were required to make an offering of incense and money to the temple.

P'u-shan left behind three branch congregations, each headed by successive leaders named P'u. One hundred years after Yao P'u-shan the leader of the central branch (*chung-chih*) was named P'u-yüan. The member witness adds: "And after P'u-yüan there were seven more leaders [he gives the names of the first six] . . . and P'u-tung. I am P'u-tung . . . In this religion we make no distinction between men and women, young and old [in the giving of] dharma names."

The official investigator comments concerning a text of this group entitled "Origins for Three Generations" ("San-shih yin-yu") that

the name of the first generation [leader] was Lo Yin, the second Yin Chi-nan and the third Yao Wen-tzu. In general [this book] is concerned with exhortations to goodness (*ch'üan-shan*). Its vocabulary is extremely crude. Only a few people have contributed incense and money, [though] it is easy to become a member . . . This Lo religion began in the Ming dynasty . . . [Its leaders] advocate establishing Dragon-flower assemblies and heretical religion (*hsieh-chiao*), and call upon men and women to enter their congregations to eat vegetarian food and chant sūtras. There are [even] soldiers who have joined the sect . . . These people build temples and preach their religion (*k'ai-t'ang, ch'uan chiao*) . . . [and cause] the old and young, men and women without distinction to enter their congregations, offer incense and money, become vegetarians, recite scriptures and urge others to do good. They do not carry out any other dangerous or secret activities.[29]

It is significant that the only record of violent activity by the Lo sect in the *Shih-liao hsün-k'an* is associated with Maitreyan eschatology. This outbreak occurred in Fukien in 1748. The reporting official says: "Normally this Lao-kuan chai group urges people to become vegetarians and join the religion saying that in this way they can be saved (*ch'eng-fo*). They have vegetarian feasts once or twice a month which are usually attended by no more than one hundred persons."[30]

He then goes on to describe the five Lao-kuan congregations in the area. Their leaders, too, all had the dharma surname P'u, and the group claimed descent from Yao P'u-shan in Chekiang. They also possessed the *San-shih yin-yu* text. But this branch saw Yao as the Heavenly Maitreya (T'ien-shang Mi-le), also called the Holy Ancestor (Patriarch) of the Limitless (Wu-chi sheng-tsu).

> They permit men and women without discrimination to enter the religion and become vegetarians . . . calling each other *Lao-kuan*. There are a great many members in Chien-an and Ou-ning counties of Fukien. [This particular congregation] has a vegetarian hall named the Vegetarian Hall of Light. Its leader is a man named Ch'en Kuang-yao, dharma name P'u-chao, who has attained enlightenment through meditation.

He then lists the names of the four other such halls in the immediate vicinity with the names of their leaders. The members of each congregation gathered together to offer incense and candles and chant the scriptures on the first and fifteenth of every month. In addition, descendants of Yao P'u-shan came to Fukien every year to meet with these groups. All who wished to be given a dharma name (become full members) had to contribute money to these visitors and offer incense in honor of Yao P'u-shan. The narration continues:

> In the eleventh month of Ch'ien-lung twelve [1747] the head of the Vegetarian Hall of Light congregation, Ch'en Kuang-yao, built a temporary shed of bamboo mats beside a street in which he gathered many people together to chant scriptures and light candles. He was arrested by the village chief [and other officials], along with four other persons, and put in jail . . . In the first month of this year [1748] several of the sect leaders . . . plotted together to arouse the people. [Their number included] a female medium (*nü-wu*), surnamed Yen, also called Lao-kuan niang (Mother of the Lao-kuan sect), whose dharma name is P'u-shao. She is the wife of a sect member named Chu, who is also called the Maitreya Club(?).[31]

P'u-shao then claimed that she had ascended to Heaven in

meditation, and that her master had ordered her to arouse and assemble the people in response to Maitreya's descent to rule the world. Then she and [other sect leaders] decided to gather the people to enter the city and attack the prison, in order to free Ch'en Kuang-yao. They also took advantage of the opportunity to attack wealthy families, forged official documents and military record books and made banners. [They gave themselves as well such military titles as] *yüan-shuai, tsung-shuai, tsung-ping, fu-chiang* . . . Each congregation gathered its old shotguns, muskets, knives and other weapons, including gunpowder. They also made colored scarves of silk with which they covered their heads, and emblems inscribed with Limitless Holy Ancestor. Each person was given [such an emblem] as a distinguishing mark. On the twelfth of the first month P'u-shao . . . uttered a prophecy she falsely said was given to her by a deity who had descended, saying that the Buddha Maitreya wanted to enter the city. [The various leaders] all agreed that on the fourteenth they would gather together the members of each congregation, and that on the fifteenth they would take up their weapons in order to welcome the bodhisattva [Maitreya]. After they entered the city they planned to guard all the streets and intersections . . . permitting no one to leave . . .

Early on the morning of the fifteenth this bandit army sacrificed to their banners in [a field], and P'u-shao seated in a sedan chair covered with a canopy, led them. They first ordered men of the village to carry images of the gods in sedan chairs and leap about all over the road. [All the various congregational leaders] rose in unison.

The account continues with an account of battles that raged for two days, ending in the destruction of 514 houses and the complete defeat of the rebels by a combined force of government troops, yamen police, militia, and local citizens. P'u-shao and the other leaders were killed and their bodies dismembered; their followers were either killed or captured, with their friends and relatives hunted down. Among the captured objects were: "Large and small banners of blue and white, all of which were inscribed with such slogans as 'The Great Way of Nonaction' (*wu-wei ta-tao*), 'Act on Behalf of Heaven' (*tai-t'ien hsing-shih*), 'Limitless Holy Ancestor,' and 'Exhort the Rich to Aid the Poor' (*ch'üan fu chi p'in*)." From the time of the uprising, no more Lao-kuan chai activities were permitted in that part of Fukien.[32]

One could scarcely hope for a better illustration of eschatological action stimulated by external oppression against a background
of messianic hopes. The 1748 Lao-kuan chai uprising was based on
a long tradition of congregational cult, which was rooted in turn in
a succession of leaders going back to the founder. The Fukien group
had emphasized the Maitreyan elements in this tradition and evidently had some sort of organization in his name. While their uprising was concerned to free an imprisoned leader and included
some elements of class conflict, it was enveloped in symbols of divine validation and eschatological expectancy. The expressed purpose for entering the city was not to release Ch'en Kuang-yao but
to welcome Maitreya, who had chosen them as the first heralds of
his new world order.

It is important that all of P'u-shao's actions and prophecies
were standard practice for mediums in southern Chinese popular
religion. Everything she did: sending her soul to Heaven, issuing
oracles in the name of a possessing deity, being carried as the incarnate god in a sacred sedan chair—can still be observed as a part of
normal mediumistic activity on Taiwan. Thus, there is no a priori
reason for accusing her of bad faith in misleading the people for her
own political goals. On the contrary, it is quite possible that she
herself and the sect members believed her messages implicitly, for
her actions were normal and expected in their context. Furthermore, from her title Lao-kuan niang we know that she already had
a reputation for special charismatic powers. The dancing sedan
chairs carrying divine images which preceded the sectarian army in
its march are further evidence of an authentic and highly pitched
sense of religious immediacy and expectancy, for the chair dances
because it is possessed by the god.[33]

As we have seen in later reports, Lo sect activity continued despite the reaction to the Fukien uprising, particularly in the south
China coastal provinces. DeGroot mentions a Lo chiao branch discovered in Szechwan, far to the west, in 1812, and a Hsien-t'ien
chiao in Shansi in 1835, while Huang Yü-p'ien recovered all five of
Lo Ch'ing's texts in Hopei in 1833. So, at least by the nineteenth
century, the Lo religion had reached a large part of China. Since
DeGroot's lengthy and detailed description of a late nineteenth cen-

tury Lo congregation called the Lung-hua hui is available in English, I will not discuss it here. Suffice it to say that this group was an excellent example of a lay Buddhist sect dedicated wholly to salvation and pious works. Its name, its veneration of Lo Huai, the use of the dharma name *p'u*, its use of the ranks *ta-sheng* and *hsiao-sheng*, and its location in Fukien all mark it clearly as the descendant of the eighteenth century Lo groups discussed above. The Amoy association, however, reached a much more complex level of development, which perhaps indicates orthodox Buddhist influence. This can be seen both in its general doctrinal sophistication and in its membership ritual, which was closely modeled on monastic upāsaka consecration.[34]

What was the relationship of the Lo sect to the White Lotus? Though scholars like Richard Chu have treated the Lo chiao as simply another offshoot of the better known tradition, the evidence available to us indicates otherwise.[35] It is significant that none of the records concerning the Lo sect mention the White Lotus, even though White Lotus activity was known and feared by Ch'ing officials.

This distinction is borne out by the contents of Lo sect *pao-chüan*. In the first place, as we have seen there is a "reformist" flavor in the titles of two of Lo Ch'ing's works, "The Key to Refuting Heresy and Making the Truth Manifest" and "The Precious Scroll Which Corrects Belief and Dispels Doubt, Standing by Itself, Not Needing Verification".

This somewhat exclusivist and self-righteous tone is reflected in the contents of these texts. For example, the *Cheng-hsin ch'u-i pao-chüan* says, "There are some who recklessly preach and transmit heretical teaching, [thus] confusing others. They fall into hell for an eternity."[36] This same *pao-chüan* also attacks a contemporary Taoist school which was well-known in Ming times, the Chin-tan p'ai, or School of the Golden Elixer, which practiced a variety of alchemical and breathing techniques. Of the Chin-tan p'ai Lo Ch'ing says in part, "There is a class of heretics (*hsieh jen*) who practice breathing exercises . . . They speak of the field of cinnabar, . . . the three apertures, . . . fate, and yin and yang . . . All that they teach is useless in times of danger."[37]

Another of Lo's books, the *T'an-shih wu-wei chüan*, contains a passage concerning defense of the dharma, which here might be taken to mean the teachings of the sect itself: "The merit of those who protect the dharma is very great. All the Buddhas rejoice [because of them] . . . But as to the sin of those who vilify the dharma (*pang-fa*), their guilt is limitless, and it is most difficult to save them."[38] However, what I take to be Lo chiao concern to define itself over against the White Lotus tradition is expressed most clearly in another passage from the scripture which deals with "correcting belief and dispelling doubt," in which we read that: "There are stupid folk who believe in heresy, burn paper and seek [aid from] the White Lotus religion, which is really evil. They fall into hell for an eternity never to be saved . . . The White Lotus . . . is a heretical school, which summons the devotion of multitudes for nothing."[39] The language used here is similar to that used by the Confucians themselves.

The distinction between the Lo and White Lotus traditions is further borne out by the absence of references to Maitreya and Lao-mu in early Lo texts, as noted above. There are no books related to either Maitreya or the Venerable Mother in either of the exhaustive lists of Lo sources compiled by Sakai Tadao. It is also significant that Chu-hung and Te-ch'ing fail to discuss Lao-mu. Surely these orthodox Buddhists would have been more offended by such a folk theme than they were by Lo's alleged misinterpretation of *wu-wei*. Furthermore, none of the extensive passages dealing with the Lo sect in the *Shih-liao hsün-k'an* refer to worship of the Eternal Mother of any of the associated White Lotus rituals, such as burning memorials to the deity on which were written the names of new members. Rather, the eighteenth century reports refer repeatedly to Lo images and scriptures (Lo hsiang and Lo ching) or simply to *fo-hsiang* (images of Buddhas).

However, all this is complicated by the fact that the Lo chiao texts in the *P'o-hsieh hsiang-pien* contain elements of the Native Land motif,[40] though the Lao-mu belief evidently did not appear in sectarian texts before P'iao Kao's work in 1594.[41] Huang Yü-p'ien was aware of this problem which he discussed as follows:

Lo Tsu, who wrote the *wu-pu* was born in the Cheng-te period; that is, more than fifty years before the appearance of the Wu-sheng cult . . . How is it then, that these texts all discuss the Eternal Mother? It is clear that because Lo Tsu was so venerated by the people, P'iao Kao then fabricated the story that the Chan-t'an fo [Chandana (Sandalwood) Buddha, here equated with Lo Huai] was reborn, and left the *wu-pu* scriptures. This was a false use of Lo Tsu's words, in order to honor and glorify [P'iao Kao's] religion.

Though Huang's date for Lo Huai is about forty years too late, his analysis here seems reasonable.[42]

I believe there may be corroboration for Huang's interpretation in a text entitled *Hun-yüan wu-shang ta-tao yüan-miao chen-ching* (The excellent and true scripture of the great *tao* without superior of primordial chaos), in which we read that;

The Most True Venerable Ancestor of Primordial Chaos (*Hun-yüan chih-chen lao-tsu*), was seated on the Golden Lotus Throne. He gathered a great group to discuss those who in the Eastern Land had forgotten their home, and instead clung to empty ornaments and floating shadows, who had so suddenly rushed into perdition. They discussed in what period all living beings might be lifted up and saved. [One of the gods] submitted a memorial to the Most True Venerable Ancestor that his fifth generation [descendant], P'iao Kao should prepare a sūtra, and earnestly preach to (*ch'üan*) the blind and confused.[43]

By the above chronology Lo Ch'ing was active about ninety years before P'iao Kao, which corresponds to three or four generations. Though Lo is not referred to directly in this passage, in the light of Huang Yü-p'ien's interpretation perhaps he is the Venerable Ancestor (Lao Tsu) referred to. It is also worth noting that the name P'iao Kao (He Who Soars on High) may be related to the legend in which Lo Ch'ing soars over the imperial palace while wearing 200 pounds of armor, in response to a test of his powers by Confucian enemies.[44] This again may indicate the extent to which the later sect leader sought to identify himself with Lo. Since the evidence is inconclusive, I can but suggest the hypothesis that by the end of the sixteenth century the Eternal Mother myth was edited into the originally more orthodox Lo Ch'ing texts by sect leaders such as P'iao Kao who were anxious to validate their own soteriology and mission.[45]

The integration of Lo Ch'ing into the three stage soteriological structure of the Maitreya-Native Land mythology can be seen in a Hsien-t'ien tao text collected by DeGroot in 1887 in which Lo himself appears as the savior of the third stage, thus taking Maitreya's place. In this text the Venerable Patriarch of the Limitless (Wu-chi lao-tsu) is the creator and prime mover.[46] It should be noted, however, that there is no reference to Lao-mu in this Hsien-t'ien tao text. Neither is there any such reference in scriptures of the Amoy Lung-hua sect, a sister congregation of the Hsien-t'ien group. Evidently, while Lo Ch'ing's scriptures were used by other sects, which edited them for their own purposes, the Lo tradition itself retained enough integrity to produce some groups which remained distinct from the White Lotus well into the nineteenth century.

In any case, by the late Ming the Lo/Wu-wei sect was considered by an uneasy government to be in the same category as the older proscribed sects and hence it too came to be prohibited. Sakai gives several memorials dated 1585, 1586, 1587, 1603, and 1615, all of which urge that the Wu-wei chiao be suppressed along with the White Lotus and other groups.[47] In 1618 the Nanking Board of Rites issued two orders to suppress this religion and its texts. The first reads:

> The Wu-wei chiao has recklessly produced vulgar books which they secretly call the "Five Mahāyāna Books" (*Ta-sheng wu-pu.* [These books] have never been a part of the great *Compendium* and their language is vulgar and crude. Therfore, they were prohibited earlier, but this prohibition was not enforced, so now [these texts] are again being printed. This is most reprehensible; therefore their printing blocks should be seized and burned.

The second order deals more directly with the sect itself, and begins,

> The Board of Rites of Nanking [wishes to] destroy heretical religions in order to correct the customs of the people. Whereas the Wu-wei sect has been confusing the world and misleading the people . . . [then follows a long list of indictments. The order concludes with these words:] It is not permitted to privately practice the Wu-wei and other similar religions. [Those who do] will bring punishment upon themselves. Those who have bookshops which

privately print small volumes shall be sought out by the officials, and all [illegal books] shall be burned.[48]

We have seen that despite such prohibition the Lo sects continued to flourish for the next three hundred years, and in fact, descendants of this tradition were still active in the twentieth century. For example, in 1902 a missionary in Hankow named George Miles described a "vegetarian sect," the Yao-ch'ih men, "Disciples of the Precious Pool," that is, of Hsi Wang-mu, the Mother Queen of the West. This group listed a man named Lo as its eighth patriarch and believed that at death the soul ascended to the paradise of Yao-ch'ih chin-mu, the "Golden Mother of the Precious Pool," which was equated with the Western Paradise. In its hierarchical structure the Hankow group resembled the Amoy Lung-hua hui, though it placed greater emphasis on breathing meditation than the earlier association. Buddhist influence is demonstrated by the inclusion of the "Three Refuges" and the "Five Prohibitions" in the membership ritual and by a genealogy of sect leaders which claimed to begin with Bodhidharma.[49]

Further evidence of Lo activity is unintentionally given by Henri Doré who in 1917 referred to "prayer formulas" used by "Taoist witches" which are "handed down in manuscript form from generation to generation." The quotes he gives from "a few specimens chosen at random" are from the *Wei-wei pu-tung chüan* and the *Cheng-hsin ch'u-i pao chüan*, both of which were written by Lo Ch'ing four centuries earlier. Unfortunately Doré does not describe the context in which these texts were found.[50]

Tsukamoto describes the report of a Japanese investigator in 1942 concerning a "vegetarian sect" he discovered in central China:

> Their members are strict vegetarians all their lives, so they are sometimes called "Perpetual Vegetarians." The names of the members are registered in each local branch. One man is in complete charge of activities of each group, supported by subordinate leaders. The various local branches are linked together . . .
>
> [Members say that] this sect was established in the T'ang dynasty by Chou Hung-jen and Lo Hui-neng both of whom were Buddhist monks . . . Hui-neng [actually] founded the religion.
>
> Each sect has a leader called Lao-kuan, under whom are twelve

classes of membership. The sect members desire a peaceful and happy life in this world, and hope for rebirth in the Western Pure Land after death . . . There are several subsects.[51]

The Singapore Hsien-t'ien tao groups investigated by Topley in 1955 claim to have been reorganized by a Lo Wei-ch'ün who was born in 1488, though of course the teachings of this group had long since blended together with those of the late Ming White Lotus tradition.

7
Patterns of Folk Buddhist Religion: Beliefs and Myths

Mao Tzu-yüan

Though there is no conclusive evidence that Mao Tzu-yüan founded an independent sect, such a sect did appear shortly after his death. This being the case, it would perhaps be worthwhile to look briefly at the teachings of this uniformly orthodox Pure Land master to learn if there is anything in them which might have encouraged the later development of a heterodox group. Sources for this discussion are three sections of the *Lien-tsung pao-chien*: the biography of *Tz'u-chao tsung-chu* translated above, the text of the *Yüan-jung ssu-t'u t'u*, chüan 2, and *Master Tz'u-chao's Gatha of Instructions for Reciting the Buddha's Name* [after first having] Vowed [to attain his Pure Land] (*T'zu-chao tsung-chu shih nien-fo fa-yüan chieh*) in chüan 7. In all this material the most one can elicit to assist in understanding later White Lotus development is a strong concern to make the way to salvation as simple and clear as possible through the use of rhymed lines, charts, and so on, a concern which of course had been present in the Ching-t'u tradition since at least the seventh century.

In Chapter 5 I have noted Mao's tendency toward popularization of Pure Land and T'ien-t'ai teachings, the first through urging that Amitābha's name be recited only five times (instead of the usual ten), the second through describing central philosophical themes in diagram form, the *Yüan-jung ssu-t'u t'u*. Soothill and Hodous define these terms as follows: "Yüan-jung [means] . . . the complete interpenetration of the absolute and the relative, the identity of apparent contraries. All things are of the same fundamental nature, *bhūtatathatā* . . . The universal realizes its true nature in the particular, and the particular derives its meaning from the universal." The *ssu-t'u* are defined as the four *Buddhaksetra* or Buddha realms of T'ien-t'ai, the first of which are realms where all classes dwell— men, *devas*, Buddhas, disciples, nondisciples; it has two divisions, the impure, for example, this world, and the pure, for example, the 'Western' pure land.[1] Shigematsu adds that: "seen vertically these four worlds differentiate between worldly and holy—ignorant and enlightened—, but seen horizontally, from the point of view of the Buddha of the [fourth] realm of eternal peace and light, the sacred and profane are fundamentally the same, and there is not difference in origin between Buddhas and sentient beings."[2]

The T'ien-t'ai masters approached this affirmation of unity by means of the doctrine of pure and impure natures in the absolute mind. *The Mahāyāna Method of Cessation and Contemplation*, (*Ta-sheng chih-kuan fa-men*) traditionally attributed to Hui-ssu (515-557), says:

> For this reason the storehouse of the Tathāgata has originally and for all time contained the two natures, the one impure, the other pure. Because of its impure nature, it is capable of manifesting the impure things pertaining to all sentient beings . . . But because it also contains the pure nature, it is capable of manifesting the pure attributes of all the Buddhas.[3]

Both pure and impure natures are fundamentally unified in the absolute mind.

Master Tz'u-chao makes the same point in the introduction to his *Ssu-t'u*: "Worldly and holy [follow] the same path, the four realms interpenetrate each other, the three [Buddha] bodies are as one; the Pure Land and Amitābha are everywhere." Commenting on the first realm, he adds "In this realm, [those who] only vow to recite the Buddha's name, without cutting themselves off from the hubbub of the world, without leaving the household life, without practicing meditation, when death comes will be welcomed by Amitābha, and all be reborn in the Pure Land. They will gain supernatural powers, never more to return to samsāra, and go straight on to enlightenment. This is the realm in which worldly and holy dwell together." He then goes on to describe the three higher realms.[4]

In his "Instructions for Reciting the Buddha's Name" Mao stresses that deliverance comes only to those who turn to Amitābha with proper understanding and intentions; all flows from the vow within: "When at the time of death one sees the Buddha, this is not something from the outside but is produced by consciousness only, just as a seed grows up by itself from within the ground . . . [so] the Pure Land and Amitābha . . . are produced from one's own mind." The first lines of this gatha read:

> The 10,000 dharmas all arise from the mind
> The 10,000 dharmas are all extinguished in the mind
> Our Buddha, the Great Srámana
> Taught this long ago
> If one lives a pure life but does not earnestly make a vow
> One will not attain rebirth in the Pure Land.[5]

I believe that the most that can be said about Master Tz'u-chao is that he popularized T'ien-t'ai and Pure Land teachings, but even at his most popular he did not abandon the epistemological perspective which is the hallmark of orthodox Mahāyāna thought. Perhaps his emphasis on the unity of worldly and holy led others to take him at his word and found a lay association based on this same premise.

The syncretic context

Though Mao himself remained firmly within the orthodox fold, the Sung White Lotus vegetarians did not, perhaps in part because of a tendency toward syncretism between Buddhism and popular cult which was developing around them. This syncretism should be understood against the background of the sinification of Buddhism, a long process which led to increasing amalgamation of Indian and Chinese themes at every level. The transformation of Buddhism in China is well known and need not be documented here. For our purposes it is sufficient to note that after the T'ang the pace of indigenization seems to have accelerated, no doubt encouraged by loss of regular contact with India through central Asia, the decline of most orthodox Buddhist schools after 845, and the Confucian renaissance.

In the Sung there were two syncretic traditions which provided the immediate context within which sectarian tendencies along these lines developed. The first was the willingness of some Pure Land leaders to canonize all deities as saviors in a Buddhist context. An excellent example of such doctrinal openness is provided by Wang Jih-hsiu, the Pure Land evangelist discussed above, who wrote:

> Looking up [pray to] all the Heavenly Emperors and Heavenly Men (*T'ien-jen*) in Heaven, the sun, moon, stars, the northern and southern poles, the Controller of Destiny, the gods of wind and rain and *all other saving deities* . . . Looking on earth below [pray to] all the deities among men who control blessings and misfortunes. *Honor and worship all of them together* . . . in order to save all the myriad sentient beings.[6]

Here in an orthodox Amitābhist devotional society we have a prayer to the entire pantheon of Chinese popular religion for the distinctly Buddhist purpose of universal salvation. Wang refers to these deities as *i-ch'ieh chu tsao-hua ling-shen* (all those holy gods who devote themselves to creation and transformation).

A second and perhaps more important influence toward syncretism was the "Cult of the Three Religions" with its slogan *San-chiao he-i* (the three religions (teachings) are one), the three being Buddhism, Confucianism, and Taoism.

Sakai says that while this *san-chiao* tradition goes back to the third century, not until the T'ang did it obtain public recognition. By Sung times it became so popular among the people that there were temples of the three religions (San-chiao t'ang) all over the land.[7] Many Buddhist clergy were also involved.

A detailed description of the "three religions" movement is of course a study in its own right, already introduced to the West by DeGroot, Liu Ts'un-yan, and others. Liu traces this tendency from early attempts to amalgamate Buddhism and Taoism, through the

Sung and Yüan dynasties to Wang Yang-ming (1472-1529) and Lin Chao-en (1517-1598) in the Ming. It was the latter who Liu says "was the first to promulgate formally the principle of the amalgamation of the Three Teachings as a single philosophical entity, in which the three of them could still exist." He adds that "Lin had many dozens of disciples, and tens of thousands of followers in several provinces . . . Temples to commemorate the Master of the *san-chiao* sprang up like mushrooms after his death." Liu goes on to point out that this movement continued to exist in the Ch'ing period.[8]

Buddhist scholars such as Tsung-hsiao and Tsung-pen discuss the *san-chiao* perspective at length, stressing that Confucianism, Buddhism, and Taoism are all necessary, all are different expressions of the same truth, "like the legs of a tripod, which cannot stand if one is missing."[9]

All this is at the level of the "Great Traditions," but it seems important that such blending was taking place already in the Sung and Yüan during the early period of White Lotus history and reached a peak during the late Ming, at the time of greatest sectarian literary activity.

When even the elite encouraged such syncretism it is understandable that folk sects with half educated lay leadership could develop their own myths and scriptures different from their Buddhist beginnings. Sectarian beliefs are a rich combination of background traditions, fused by charisma and hope. Such integration is well illustrated by the commentary on the *T'ai-shan pao-chüan* (a Lo-chiao text discussed above), in which we read:

> The three religions are Confucianism, Buddhism and Taoism. The saints of these religions, who have brought order and peace to the world, are like the legs of a tripod vessel; if one is missing, then it cannot stand. Unfortunately, among their followers, those who read Buddhist sūtras say that only the Buddhist dharma is all encompassing [and the Taoists and Confucians do the same] . . . This is truly rejecting other religions while promoting one's own and shows [that they] do not know that the three religions all came from the same root.[10]

Such thinking also influenced the fully developed White Lotus myths of creation and salvation preserved by Huang Yü-p'ien.

Creation and Salvation in Late Ming White Lotus Mythology

The *pao-chüan* which Huang says contains the most complete statement of sectarian doctrine is the *Precious Dragon-flower Scripture Examined and Corrected by the Heavenly Immortal Old Buddha (Ku-fo t'ien-chen k'ao-cheng lung-hua pao-ching)*. The chapter entitled "The First Division of Chaos" ("Hun-tun") says:

Before the beginning there was no heaven or earth, no sun or moon, no men, animals or plants. From the midst of the True Emptiness (*chen-k'ung*) there appeared [*hua-ch'u*, lit., "appeared by transformation"] the Limitless Divine Old Buddha . . . When the Old Buddha appeared he arranged (*an*) Heaven and Earth. The Unbegotten Venerable Mother (Wu-sheng lao-mu) established the Former Heaven [the period before the cosmos had its present form, when all being was potential].

The account is continued in another chapter:

The Eternal Mother gave birth to yin and yang, and to two children, male and female. She named the male child Fu-hsi and the girl Nü-kua . . . Fu-hsi was named Li, Nü-kua was named Chang. They were the original ancestors of man . . . They married . . . After the end of primeval chaos (*hun-yüan liao*), [they] gave birth to ninety-six *i* (960,000,000) of sons and daughters from the imperial womb (*huang-t'ai*), and also numberless auspicious stars . . . The Eternal Mother sent her children to the Eastern Land (*tung-t'u*) to live in the world. Here their heads were surrounded with light, [on] their bodies [they wore clothes] of five colors, and with their feet they rode on two [magic] wheels . . . [But after] they reached the Eastern Land they all became lost in the red dust world . . . and [the Mother sent] a letter summoning [them] to meet together again in the Dragon-flower assembly.

Huang summarizes here:

Since there was no one yet living in the Eastern Land, the Eternal Mother sent her children there, and gave them the Three Jewels [*san-pao*, that is, Buddhism]. But because they were all soiled by the red dust [a Buddhist term for the samsāra world], she wanted to call them all back to Heaven.[11]

Thus, in the Dragon-flower scripture there is a three-stage creation myth: chaos, the division of chaos and establishing of the

world by the Old Buddha, and the creation of man by Lao-mu and
her twin children.

Another text gives a somewhat more metaphysical account of
creation from chaos. In a chapter entitled "[The Time of] Emptiness
and Chaos before Heaven and Earth [Appeared]" ("Wu t'ien, wu ti,
hun-tun hsü-k'ung p'in"), of the *P'iao-kao Sūtra* says:

> Before Heaven and Earth appeared there was a formless mist
> (*hun meng*). Then this mist thickened, and after it had grown to
> great size, it coalesced to form the original egg (*yüan luan*), which
> was called the "Black and Yellow [Egg] of Heaven and Earth" (*t'ien-
> ti hsüan huang*). Then this egg split open, and Venerable Ancestor
> of Original Chaos (Hun-yüan lao-tsu) appeared and sat in the Land
> of the Arhats (A-lo kuo).[12]

This creation myth is closely related to ideas of paradise and a
three-stage eschatology. In the *Dragon-Flower Sūtra* we read:

> In the sacred precincts of the Native Land (*chia-hsiang*) there
> are Dragon-flower assemblies, held in the Great Imperial Palace of
> the Big Dipper. Here the Old Buddha and the Eternal [mother] are
> enthroned. [In this paradise] there are seven precious pools and
> eight "merit streams" (*kung-te shui*). The ground is of gold, and the
> roads are bordered with golden ropes. All the buildings, towers,
> halls and chambers are different . . . The first Dragon-flower as-
> sembly [was led by] the Lamplighter Buddha, the second by Śākya-
> muni Buddha, and the third [will be led by] Maitreya Buddha.[13]

Another version of this theme relates three time periods with
Taoist names to successive numbers of people saved: "There were
originally ninety-six *i* of the virtuous and good, of whom [in] the
Limitless [period] two *i* were saved, and in the Great Ultimate [peri-
od] two more, [leaving] only ninety-two *i* in the Imperial Ultimate
[era]."[14]

A text entitled *The Original Chaos Red Yang Sūtra which
Makes the True Nature Manifest and Leads to Fruition (Hun-yüan
hung-yang hsien-hsing chieh-kuo ching)* says:

> Original chaos was formed out of one material force (*Hun-
> yüan i-ch'i so hua*). Now Śākyamuni Buddha controls the religion
> (*chang chiao*). He is the leader of the Red Yang religion (*Hung-yang*

chiao-chu). The past [was the period of] the Green Yang; the present [is the time of] the Red Yang, the future [is the age of] the White Yang . . . In the Ming Wan-li period the Buddha established the Ancestral Religion of Primordial Chaos (*hun-yüan tsu-chiao*).[15]

The primary emphasis in these scriptures is on the promise of deliverance, for which the creation story appears as prelude. So we read in the *Hsiao-shih shou-yüan hsing-chüeh pao-chüan* (The precious scroll which explains the restoration of completeness and the perfecting of enlightenment):

The Eternal Mother in the Native Land weeps as she thinks of her children. She has sent messages and letters [urging them] to return home, and to stop devoting themselves solely to avarice in the sea of bitterness. [She calls them] to return to the Pure Land (Ching-t'u), to come back to Mount Ling [the Vulture Peak, so that] the mother and her children can meet again and sit together on the golden lotus.[16]

This theme of return to the Mother and to the Native Land is a constant refrain in sectarian texts. Huang quotes Lo Ch'ing's *T'ai-shan pao-chüan*: "[In contrast to repeated cycles of] birth and death and endless suffering, if one is able to ascend to the Native Land of one's true origin, [then for him] birth and death forever cease."[17]
Again, in another text:

The Yao-shih Bodhisattva [being unable to bear any longer the terrible suffering of mankind] out of his great compassion [decided to] save all classes of beings [enabling them] to leave their suffering behind and ascend to heaven . . . [So] in the Wan-li period he returned alone to the [Native] Land, and sent out Buddhist patriarchs from Ling-shan. [Thus] today, children [*ying-er*, lit. "baby," here, "disciple"] meet [their] Mother (*niang*), and confirm that [they are also] eternal, and will never again turn in the wheel of transmigration, will live forever, eternally realizing [their diamond] nature.
Since all sentient beings on earth are infatuated and lost they are not able to escape from repeated rebirth. But when they suddenly meet the Eternal Mother they are freed from their misery, and as children enter the Lotus Pool.[18]

The physical mother-child symbolism can be quite explicit:

"When he ascends to the eternal realm, as the boat drifts to the shore, the child sees his dear mother. When he enters the mother's womb . . . he eternally returns to peace and security."[19]

So, as Huang emphasizes, the meaning of the White Lotus "True Saying (Mantra) in Eight Characters (*pa tzu chen-yen*) 'The True Void Native Land and the Eternal Parents,' " is that "All sect members are children of the Eternal Parents. In the beginning they were all born in Heaven, so Heaven is their home."[20] Since all members are of one dharma-family (*fa-chüan*), "men and women were originally one, and all depend on the Eternal Mother."[21]

The concern for salvation can also be seen in *pao-chüan* titles and chapter headings. For example, the fourth text discussed by Huang is the *Hsia-sheng t'an shih pao-chüan* (The precious scroll of incarnation out of sorrow for the world). This scripture discusses eight forms of "release" (*chieh-t'o*—the Chinese Buddhist translation of *mukti*), including "Release by seeing one's true nature," "release by sweeping clean the mind," and "release by returning home" (*kuei-chia*).

Other titles are *The Precious Scroll of Returning Home and Responding to Mercy (Kuei-chia pao-en pao-chüan); Buddha Speaks of Penetrating to the Origin and Recovering the Source (Fo-shuo t'ung-yüan shou-yüan pao-chüan); A New Message of Universal Salvation and Rescue from Suffering (P'u-tu hsin-sheng chiu-k'u pao-chüan); An Explanation of Great Enlightenment and Perfect Knowledge (Hsiao-shih ta-hung chüeh-t'ung pao-chüan); The True Sūtra without Peer of the Origin in Chaos [sect, which speaks of] Universal Salvation and Divine Compassion (Hun-yüan wu-shang p'u-hua tz'u-pei chen-ching)*, and many others of similar import. Though the contents of these texts are all in the folk sectarian tradition, it can be seen that their message is based on Buddhist soteriology.[22]

What is the background of White Lotus creation mythology? Where did the Lao-mu motif come from? When did it become a part of sectarian belief? While there are no certain answers to these questions, some suggestions are possible. As to the origins of the Venerable Mother, Japanese scholars like Tsukamoto and Noguchi simply say that by Ch'ing times (1644-1912) her myth was a part of general popular religion.[23] There were, of course, earlier antecedents. In *pao-chüan* literature Lao-mu is considered superior to two other popular goddesses, Hsi Wang-mu (Mother Queen of the West) and the Bodhisattva Kuan-yin who manifests Amitābha's love on earth. Though both of these deities are made to appear as incarnations of the Venerable Mother,[24] it seems more probable that historically she herself is a later manifestation of Hsi Wang-mu, because this Mother Queen of the West is a very early figure in Chinese mythology. A Hsi mu (Western Mother) is mentioned on Shang dynasty (c. 1500-1050 B.C.) oracle bones. By the first century A.D. Hsi Wang-mu appears as a popular goddess who lived on top of the K'un-lun mountains. Here, the popular legends say, she presided over a huge palace built of precious stones, surrounded by a wall of solid gold. On the grounds there were an enchanted stream and a fountain made of gems. Here lived all the immortals, sustained by the peaches of immortality in the Mother Queen's garden. Once a year she entertained all the immortals at a great feast by the Yao-ch'ih pool in the garden. (One of her alternate titles is Yao-ch'ih chin-mu, The Golden Mother of the Jasper Pool.) She had a number of sons and daughters, all of whom were immortals. For our purposes it is also important that the *Shan-hai ching* refers to Hsi Wang-mu's paradise as "The Country of Satisfaction," and that as the keeper of the peaches of immortality she could offer immortality to her favorites, such as King Mu of the Chou dynasty.[25]

Thus, in the Hsi Wang-mu legends we see many elements of the Lao-mu mythology. The Eternal Mother also presided over a glorious paradise on the top of K'un-lun mountain. She also convened great assemblies of those saved by her grace, for which offering peaches of immortality was the Taoist equivalent in pre-Buddhist China. And, like the children of Hsi Wang-mu, those of Lao-mu also attained immortality, though in its Buddhist form, the cessation of birth and death.

Significant as well is the fact that by 3 B.C. Hsi Wang-mu had become the object of a popular ecstatic cult which promised immortality. Dubs has translated all the material relating to this movement from the *Han shu*. One passage describes processions involving thousands of people carrying the "wand of the goddess's edict" which passed through twenty-six commanderies and kingdoms. When the wand reached the imperial capital people began to sing and dance, sacrifice to the Mother and perform divination, all in the assurance that those who wore certain charms would not die. The eschatological fervor of this cult is indicated both by the frenzy of its devotees who "beat drums, and cried out, exciting and frightening each other," and by references to such signs as white hairs on the door hinges.[26]

So we see that Hsi Wang-mu could also serve as the deity of a popular, eschatologically oriented cult, which further indicates the possibility that Lao-mu was in fact one of *her* incarnations.[27]

It is also of interest that by the Ming dynasty female deities had a dominant role in popular vernacular novels such as the *Feng-shen yen-i* (Investiture of the gods), and *Shui-hu chuan* (Water margin).[28] This motif in universally available novels is important, for as T'ao Ch'eng-chang says of the White Lotus and T'ien-ti hui groups, "Those in the northern provinces all firmly believe in the novel *Feng-shen yen-i*, and all those in the southern province venerate the *Shui-hui chuan*."[29] So, while in a limited sense it is true, as Chesneaux says, that the Eternal Mother seems to have been created by the sects themselves,[30] in fact there was a rich tradition of female deities in the popular religious background.

Huang Yü-p'ien insists that the Lao-mu myth first appeared in the late Ming dynasty, an assertion based first of all on an inscription in a Wu-sheng temple in Ts'ang-chou city (in eastern Hopei). Huang says that this inscription, written during the Ming dynasty by an official, claimed that Wu-sheng lao-mu's self-revelation reached a peak in the Wan-li period. There is a more detailed account written by Tsung Wang-hua of An-hua county, Kansu (modern Ch'ing-yang county), which says that Lao-mu was the reincarnation of a white mule who first appeared in China at the end of the Ming Chia-ching period (1522-1566). In 1573, the first year of the Wan-li period, she was killed by lightning after having preached "heretical religion" together with P'iao Kao, whom Huang considers a central leader of the late Ming groups, founder of the Hung-yang chiao. They were active in the T'ai-hang mountains (a range which extends through parts of Shansi, Hopei and Honan). After Lao-mu died, P'iao Kao began to worship her as founder of the religion and wrote the texts exalting her as creator of mankind, and so on. Then sect leaders, like Huan-yüan, Kung Ch'ang, Ching K'ung, P'u-ming, and others, all accepted his teaching and began to worship Wu-sheng lao-mu. Huang says that the story of her inauspicious death by lightning was suppressed by the sects.[31]

In the *Hsü-k'an p'o-hsieh* Huang accepts the above account of Lao-mu's origin as definitive, because it came from outside sources. However, in an earlier chapter, he also reports that a member of an unnamed "heretical sect" told him that in

. . . the Ch'ing K'ang-hsi period (1662-1723), Wu-sheng lao-mu became incarnate in Ch'ing-yüan county [of Hopei province], and [after she grew up] was married and gave birth to a son. Later she was divorced by her husband and her son was killed by lightning. [After this] she taught disciples . . . in a monastery. After she died her disciples built a pagoda behind the monastery in which they placed her bones.[32]

These ambiguous accounts agree at least that Lao-mu began teaching after becoming incarnate as a human being, but the times and places mentioned are so disparate as to render the evidence meaningless. Furthermore, Tsung Wang-hua wrote to attack and discredit sectarian beliefs, so the value of his account would have to be questioned even if he didn't give it in legendary form. The rest I leave for the reader to judge.

The Buddhist background of White Lotus soteriology can be found in such popular and well-known sūtras as the *Lotus* and *Pure Land*, so I will not rehearse it here. Suffice it to say that some sectarian deities seem to have been influenced by the theme of the bodhisattva who turns back before entering Nirvāna to be born again in the world and save all living creatures. The oft-used term for salvation, *ch'eng-fo*, "become a Buddha," is found in the *Lotus Sūtra*, as is the emphasis that all creatures can reach enlightenment. This stress on universal deliverance is also found in the *Diamond Sūtra*, which was another very popular text, used, as we have seen, by such sects as the Ch'ang-sheng and Lo. It is also probable that Lao-mu and her Native Land were equivalent to, or influenced by, Amitābha Buddha and the Pure Land over which he ruled. The passage from the "Restoration of completeness" *pao-chüan* quoted above says that the Eternal Mother calls her children "to return to the Pure Land," which is here equated with the Native Land.

Another text, the *Explanation of True Emptiness* (*Hsiao-shih chen k'ung pao-chüan*), "praises Amitābha and proclaims the True Emptiness" thus holding together the orthodox and sectarian themes, though of course *chen-k'ung* is a Buddhist term as well.[33]

Wu-sheng lao-mu's usual function parallels Amitābha's as a saving being in paradise who sends down intermediaries, and to whom men pray for grace. However, as we have seen, the Eternal Mother was also believed to have appeared on earth herself, in this resembling more the Bodhisattva Kuan-yin, who manifests herself in many forms in order to rescue the lost.[34]

The background of the other distinctive structure of the Lao-mu myth, the propagation of mankind by her twin children, is more difficult to trace. It is possible that this primordial pair might be personifications of yin and yang, the two fundamental modes of creative energy, as has been suggested in the case of the Japanese Izanagi/Izanami story.[35] Representative statements of yin/yang theory can be found in the *Huai-nan Tzu* and in the writings of the Neo-Confucian scholar Chou Tun-i (1017-1073). In both accounts yin and yang emerge out of a primordial formless state, and through their interaction the world and mankind are produced. In the *Lung-hua ching* cosmogony translated above Lao-mu is described as creating both yin and yang and her two children. The word for daughter in this passage is *ch'a-nü*, which is a Taoist term designating a form of yin, so that a process of personification is not unlikely.[36]

As for Nü-kua and Fu-hsi, in orthodox mythology they were brother and sister culture heroes who ruled the world successively, with Fu-hsi serving as emperor first. Fu-hsi first taught mankind such arts as hunting, cooking, net making and writing; Nü-kua became known for her marital advice. In earlier accounts Nü-kua is also described as a superhuman figure who replaced broken pillars between heaven and earth and who created man out of yellow earth.[37]

So, other than the names themselves, there is little parallel in traditional accounts to the role of Fu-hsi and Nü-kua in *pao-chüan* myths.

Though the attempt to find the background of the Lao-mu Fu-hsi/Nü-kua structure in Han thought is not very satisfactory, there is a closer parallel in aboriginal mythology. Wolfram Eberhard writes that "female deities as such were typical for the Yao culture," and "Yao culture . . . spread in early times into Honan and parts of Shantung." He then goes on to discuss "a whole complex of [Liao] myths in which a brother and sister marry each other, this being the origin either of the whole of mankind or at least certain families. The first child of this couple is almost always a lump of flesh which falls into pieces, and from which emerge the ancestors."[38]

This myth is also prominent among the Miao tribes. We are told that two deities, the "Lord and Lady No . . . figure in a creation myth common to many Miao groups, wherein the incestuous union of a brother and sister . . . results in the peopling of the entire earth."[39]

David Graham says that the Ch'uan Miao "trace their ancestry to a female ancestor called Na Bo Hmo Ntse, or the Miao Mother named Ntse."[40] In his translation of a myth entitled "Opening the Road for the Soul to Travel to Paradise," we read that after a great flood "Two people, sister and brother, entered the demon drum, floating back and forth up to the land of Ndjü Nyong Leo's sky . . . [After the god had drained the water from the earth, there was still no human seed, so he sent down the brother and sister.] The two, sister and brother, came down to earth. They begat many earthly people in the world so they filled the entire sky."[41] Though we lack textual proof of direct aboriginal influence on sectarian thought, these parallels at least indicate its possibility.[42]

We see, then, that much of the White Lotus creation story was based on earlier mythologies. The sect leaders evidently combined traditional cosmologies with popular female deities and the aboriginal motif of the creation of man by a divine brother-sister couple to form the characteristic sectarian myth of origins.

The question "When did the Lao-mu myth become a part of sectarian theology?" can be answered a bit more positively on the basis of comments by Huang Yü-p'ien. A *pao-chüan* called *Hun-yüan hung-yang hsüeh-hu pao-ch'an* (The Lake of Blood Precious Confession of the Primordial Origin Red Yang [Sect]) says: "In the chia-wu year of the [Ming] Wan-li period [1594], the most honored P'iao Kao venerable ancestor, while living on the Great Tiger Mountain, opened wide a new means of salvation (*fang-pien*) to save the multitude of the lost." Huang Yü-p'ien confirms that the

Red Yang sect was founded by P'iao Kao and that it was this leader, along with Kung Ch'ang, the founder of the Huan Yüan (Return to the Origin) sect in 1588, who "first wrote concerning the Eternal Mother . . . These terms do not appear before this period."[43] All the Return to Origin/Red Yang scriptures are based on True Void Native Land paradise myth. These sects were recognized to be part of the White Lotus tradition.

However the union came about, by the late sixteenth century a segment of the popular mother-goddess cult had combined with Buddhist folk piety to produce what was to become the dominant theme of White Lotus mythology. Tsukamoto gives an example of this motif from a *pao-chüan* whose provenance he does not identify. This text is particularly valuable because in it we see clearly how the old Maitreya belief provided the salvation structure for Lao-mu. The passage provides its own date:

> Now I have heard that the *Precious Scroll of the Most Holy Savior Maitreya* (*Ta sheng Mi-le fo hua-tu pao-chüan*) appeared in the twenty-second year of the Ming Wan-li reign period [1594]. It is a work produced by imperial authority which has been [widely] circulated. Our Buddha [Wo fo—Maitreya?] mercifully took forty-eight vows to save all people [*huang-t'ai*, lit., "imperial children"] . . . Because all living beings were confused and lost in the red dust [world], had fallen and knew not how to return to their origin, our [Lord] Buddha established an expedient means [for entering] the dharma gate, [thereby] to save men and women everywhere, enabling them to take refuge in the way of long life and recovering completeness, to return home to see the Mother and sit together with her on the Lotus Tower (*lien-t'ai*).

Then follows a rhymed passage in eight lines of two sections each, with seven characters per section, as is common in *pao-chüan* literature:

> The imperial ultimate, great ultimate and limitless Mother, requested all the Buddhas to come to a dharma assembly.
> [She] transmitted [to them] this saving *pao-chüan* to which all pious men and women should listen clearly in silence.
> At present there are more than 60,000 of those who left [their] Native Land [to come to earth],
> But now [she] has ordered them to return home as soon as possible . . .

The Venerable Mother (Lao-mu) has given her imperial order
on a golden tablet, [and sent] the wise and the virtuous down to
this [world] of wind and dust.
The various Buddhas will save all the imperial children, for
[she] personally taught [them] a wonderful truth (*miao fa*) for rescuing the scattered and lost.[44]

So by 1594 Lao-mu was already Mistress of all the Buddhas.

Eschatology

Paradise in Chinese Thought. Before we discuss sectarian eschatology itself it is necessary to look briefly at the indigenous and
orthodox Buddhist backgrounds of this belief. The first point to
emphasize is that there was a long tradition of paradise belief in
Chinese thought and religion, some of it otherworldly in orientation, but most concerned with an ideal reordering of this world.
The antiquity of the paradise motif is perhaps indicated by its
presence in Miao mythology, which describes a "level land above
the sky," the realm of Ntse, the Miao female supreme deity. There
souls of the dead go to enjoy a life of ease forever.[45]
There are several parallels between this aboriginal vision of
paradise and a passage in the Taoist book *Lieh Tzu*, which also describes a distant land that is flat, naturally irrigated without rain-
fall, and full of rich natural resources that can be harvested without
effort. Here people live long lives at peace, without disease or social
distinctions, singing all day as they please.[46]
However, the more characteristic Chinese emphasis was on
achieving an ideal state of harmony and prosperity in this existence. The *Lieh Tzu* gives a convenient summary statement of this
pragmatically oriented longing:

The yin and yang are always in tune, the sun and moon always
shine, the four seasons are always regular, wind and rain are always temperate, breeding is always timely, the harvest is always
rich, and there are no plagues to ravage the land, no early death to
afflict men, animals have no diseases, and ghosts have no uncanny
echoes.[47]

There was also a somewhat more explicitly political utopian
strand in Confucian thought. Rolf Stein describes an ideal utopian

state in the Han period called Ta Ch'in. The capital of this state is
An Tu (Antioch), an idealization of vague rumors concerning the
Roman Empire. Here the king rotates his living quarters according
to the seasons in the four sections of the Hall of Light (*Ming T'ang*)
and rules through able sage-ministers.[48] Ta Ch'in of course should
be understood in the light of the implied utopianism in the charismatic role of the Confucian emperor himself. The thrust behind all
the imperial concern for cosmic/human regulation and tranquility
was the vision of a perfect world which was the apotheosis of the
existing sociopolitical system.[49]

In the second century the Taoist *Scripture of Great Peace*
(*T'ai-p'ing ching*), presented an eschatology of future harmony
which had great influence on the Yellow Turban movement in 184
and later. This text stresses that when heaven, earth and man operate in perfect concord, peace and long life will come.[50]

A more developed statement of Taoist eschatology can be
found in the *Tung-yüan shen-chou ching* of the Taoist Canon, a
scripture written before 420, which assures the faithful that in the
new age to come their illnesses will all be healed, their wishes will
come true and they will be high officials under the "Perfect Lord"
who is about to come (*tang-lai chen-chün*). There will be no suffering or punishments, and all will be gloriously happy. The coming
of the Perfect Lord is equated with setting up an ideal political state
on earth, in which sages, immortals and Taoist priests will serve as
government officials and advisers.[51] This concern for attaining an
ideal world through leaders who combine political and religious
roles is an important aspect of the background of sectarian eschatological thought. Even the "otherworldly" paradise texts noted
above from Miao mythology and the *Lieh Tzu* are concerned in
practical detail for food, water, and the absence of disease. The
other passages all deal in one way or another with the establishment of an ideal social order on earth. Though the sects often had
more immediate political and economic goals, they should also be
considered against this background, as a part of the Chinese *Wel-
tanshauung*.

Fate and the mandate of Heaven. Another important indigenous source of sectarian eschatology (and charismatic leadership)
was the all-pervading sense of fate, the Heaven-ordained nature of

things. My purpose here is not to discuss the complex origins of this concept but simply to give illustrations leading up to the popular understanding of destiny in the world of the folk religious movements.

The mandate of Heaven concept began in the early Chou period. Of it Creel writes:

> The fundamental theory of the Chinese state and governmental authority in China is that of the Decree of Heaven . . .
> The essence of the theory is simple. It holds that rulers are appointed by Heaven, that is, the supreme deity, for the purpose of ruling the world so as to bring about the welfare of men. The ruler may legitimately rule only so long as he does so in the interest of his subjects. The moment he ceases to bring about the welfare of the people, it is the right and duty of another to revolt and displace him, taking over the appointment of Heaven and administering the government for the public good . . . Heaven chooses the ruler, and Heaven chooses the man to displace him, [but] . . . the issue must be decided by war and bloodshed.[52]

Early statements of this idea in the *Shu ching* emphasize that an attack on a corrupt and repressive ruler is not a rebellion for one's private gain, but a divinely ordained punishment which must be carried out for the good of all.[53]

All Chinese monarchs tried in one way or another to justify their rule by the heavenly mandate. One of the most complete medieval restatements of this ancient doctrine was made by the first emperor of the Ming dynasty to justify his attack on the Mongol house. After a long statement listing the faults of Yüan emperors and officials, and the sufferings of the people, the new ruler says:

> Even though things have become so bad because of the actions of men, nonetheless, the true meaning of this is that now heaven is sick [of the Yüan] and has rejected them.
> . . . The ancients said, "No barbarians will enjoy one hundred years of Heaven's appointment" . . . When we look at the situation today, we see that this statement is quite correct. Now the destiny of Heaven has turned [changed] and the time is ripe for the descent of a sage (*sheng-jen*), who will drive out the barbarians, restore China, restore the ancient regulations and save (*chiu-chi*) this people, but to my knowledge, no such bearer of rescue and peace for the people has yet arisen . . . I have respectfully obtained a man-

date from Heaven, and dare not be at peace with myself, [so] I wish to send troops north to expel the barbarians.[54]

This statement, made in 1367 before T'ai-tsu launched another expedition against the Mongols, is noteworthy not only for its racial emphasis, but also because of its inclusion of the idea of a sage who descends to rescue the world. This concept was very popular in this period and much used by the sects.

The universal availability of the mandate of Heaven doctrine is illustrated by its constant use in such novels as the *Feng-shen yen-i*, which is a popularized account of the struggle between the Chou and Shang forces at the end of the Shang dynasty. In this novel, which might be called a Chinese *Iliad*, the forces of good (the Chou), both human and divine, battle against their evil counterparts who represent the Shang kingdom, which has clearly lost its mandate. Early in the novel an immortal prophesies that "the great destiny has already been established . . . The King of Shang will be destroyed and the House of Chou will flourish."

This prediction sets the stage for the rest of the book and leads to Chiang Tzu-ya being called to "descend from the mountain to aid the Lord of Light (the Chou king)." Chiang Tzu-ya is the key figure in the carrying out of Heaven's will, and he clearly states his rationale:

King Chou [of the Shang] does not have the Tao. He has destroyed the basic principles of human relationships; his royal charisma is dark and decayed (*wang-ch'i hei-jan*). But in the West [the Chou area] a benevolent ruler has already appeared, in perfect harmony with the time set by Heaven . . . [and] in response to the destiny which produces sages and worthies. It has always been the case that that which has the Tao subdues that which has not, the blessed topple those who lack blessing, the orthodox are able to defeat the heretical, and the heretical are unable to successfully resist the powers of order (*hsieh pu neng fan cheng*).[55]

All this traditional ideological support was available to any pretender to the throne, no matter how uncouth his origins. In addition, the Chinese concept of destiny was not limited to the king but covered all of life. It operated not as sanction for the status quo, but as sanction for what had already happened, including change and rebellion. So we find official memorials which counsel despair because the rebels themselves were fated to prevail. In 1800, during the Chia-ch'ing White Lotus uprising, Na-yen-ch'eng submitted a memorial which read in part:

[The fact that] the bandits are as numerous as insects means that putting them down is beyond human strength. How much more is this the case [when one considers that] this affair is predestined. If this fated calamity had already run its ordained course, then any useless soldier could kill more than ten bandits by himself. If it has not run its course, then even though the most excellent generals led picked troops, their efforts would still be of no avail. To supply additional troops is useless . . . All attempts to put down [the rebels] are useless. When government troops chase the bandits, the bandits simply fly even farther away, and the troops become even more exhausted. Nothing will be achieved by attacking . . . If [the rebels] want to enter Kansu from Szechwan, let them do as they please.

The emperor agreed with this memorial and thought it best to wait until destiny had run its course (*tai chieh chin*) in the hope that the rebels would destroy themselves.[56] If even the government could believe that rebels were divinely ordained, how much more might this sense of election have driven on the sectarian armies?

This sense of the predestined direction of political events was reinforced by the general fatalism in Chinese life. As C. K. Yang writes:

[The practices of divination and geomancy] . . . represented a well coordinated system of religious concepts containing the belief in the power of Heaven and Earth to predetermine the course of all events, large or small, by controlling the time and space within which they occurred. It was because the people believed in Heaven's power to control the fate of their personal lives that they came to embrace the idea of the Mandate of Heaven and the divine character of the supreme political power . . . In this sense the theology of Yin/Yang and the Five Elements served as a link between the supernatural basis of the affairs of state and the intimate life of the people.[57]

It is not my concern here to discuss the highly complex system of Chinese popular fatalism, which combined elements of astral determinism, the prescribed interaction of yin/yang and the Five Elements (agents), divine retribution, and karma. The imperial calendar and a variety of other almanacs gave long, detailed lists of lucky and unlucky days, and the actions which should be taken or avoided on them. Fortune tellers were always consulted both to prepare for important events in life and to ward off unexpected dangers. *Feng-shui* (geomantic) practitioners determined propitious sites for graves and houses. In traditional China all of life and every event within it were predetermined, and a great amount of effort was spent trying to discover what was in store.

This sense of the cosmic predestination of both political and personal events was of the utmost importance in sectarian eschatology. When further heightened by the conviction of Maitreya's imminent descent, proclaimed by inspiring and miracle working leaders, the sense of divine election could become powerful indeed. So Suzuki Chūsei maintains that the popular determinist view of history and sense of fate were basic to the effectiveness of leaders who preached that in eschatological warfare sect members would be impervious to injury by fire, water, and weapons and thus surely prevail. He states that this sort of preaching should not be seen merely as a trick to get members but as a part of the sense of destiny which was so powerful at the popular level.[58]

The orthodox Buddhist background. There was also much support for concrete, politically involved eschatology in orthodox Chinese Buddhism. Since I have already introduced the Maitreya belief and the popular sect in his name, I will here discuss only a few other aspects of the orthodox background. In the first place, though there is no specific evidence for sectarian use of orthodox Maitreya sūtras, the delightful, peasant oriented description of the world at the time of Maitreya's descent in the *Fo shuo Mi-le hsia-sheng ching* (The sūtra in which the Buddha speaks of Maitreya's descent to be reborn), translated by Chu Fa-hu (Dharmaraksha) between 265 and 275, might have added to the popular longing for paradise on earth.[59]

Though in Indian Buddhist tradition Maitreya's advent is as yet many thousands of years in the future, and he has no direct involvement in political life, the Chinese sectarians radically foreshortened the expectation of his coming, combined it with popular ideas of descending sages and charismatic leadership, and made it conform with indigenous theories of cyclic decay. Thus, in their view Maitreya appeared at the nadir of cosmic disintegration to establish an ideal world order in cooperation with a new emperor. The time of his descent was the present or the immediate future.

That this concretization of Maitreya was a part of the general movement of Chinese Buddhism not limited to the sects is illustrated by the fact that by Sung times Maitreya was popularly believed to have already appeared in the figure of a pot-bellied monk called Pu-tai (Cloth Bag). Pu-tai (d. 916) was a wandering cleric from Chekiang who carried all his belongings in a bag slung over his shoulder. He was said to be able to predict good and bad fortune, and to use a variety of strange actions to communicate his understanding of Buddhism. According to tradition, his dying words included this poem: "Maitreya, true Maitreya. His body takes myriad forms, but at the times he manifests himself to men, none of his contemporaries recognize [him]."[60]

The Pu-tai legend soon became very popular among the people, who made drawings and images of him used in worship. He came to be a symbol of prosperity and contentment, available to all. Before long Pu-tai was equated with Maitreya, so that to this day on Taiwan the image in a Maitreya temple is that of the jolly fat monk, his historical origins forgotten by the laity. This concept of a prosperity-bringing savior reincarnated many times was of course important to sectarian belief, though the sects retained more of the orthodox time scheme than did the Pu-tai cult.

The Maitreya belief was related to the Buddhist concept of world cycles and the rise and fall of the power of Buddhist teaching. Indian Buddhism adopted the Indian concept of the four *yugas* to develop its own theory of *mahā kalpas,* each divided into four periods of incalculable length; those of destruction, duration of destruction, renovation or revolution, and duration of the world renovated. During the progression of this cycle the length of human life moved from 80,000 years to 10 years, and from 10 years back to 80,000. Though the terms used clearly indicate that the length of these periods is impossible to determine, Buddhist writers tried to calculate their duration. However, Indian scholars generally did this by assigning hundreds of millions of years to each stage, in effect admitting its immeasurable length.[61]

For Chinese Buddhists, on the other hand, the theory of cyclic decay was quite definite and specific. Already by the period of the Northern and Southern Dynasties (420-589), a theory of the three periods of the dharma was popular. The three periods were those of the "true dharma, when the Master's teachings were strictly adhered to; the counterfeit dharma, when the true dharma was hidden but something resembling it practiced; and the decay of the dharma, when the dharma is in disrepute and about to disappear."[62]

There were many conflicting opinions concerning the duration of the first two periods, but the most prevalent view was that the "true" stage lasted 500 years and the "counterfeit" stage 1,000. The "decay" period would last 10,000 years. Since medieval Chinese Buddhists generally held that the Buddha had entered Nirvāna in 949 B.C., they believed that the "decay" period would begin in 550 A.D., 1,500 years later.

In the sixth century a monk named Hsin-hsing (d. 594) founded the Sect of the Three Stages (San-chieh chiao) based on this theory. He claimed that since the period of dharmic decay had already begun the people were ignorant of the true way, and none of the old traditional beliefs and practices would any longer suffice. This sect became very popular and its members built a great temple in the imperial capital of Ch'ang-an. Since it held that in the period of dissolution "no government was worthy of the respect of the people and that the present (T'ang) dynasty was incapable of restoring the religion or leading the people to salvation," the Three Stages sect was declared heretical and its organization dissolved in 721-725.[63]

The founders of the Pure Land movement, T'an-luan and Taoch'o, who were also active in this period, shared the belief that the period of decay had begun in 550 but proposed a less militant solution, namely, the chanting of Amitābha's name. Thus Amitābhism too, began as an eschatological movement.

It is quite natural that sect leaders would draw upon this dimension of the orthodox Buddhist tradition. It was an easy step to combine it with the Chinese theory of periodic dynastic decay and renewal which in turn was based on ancient theories of the immutability of change in the interaction of yin and yang.[64] Though, as we have seen, in canonical texts Maitreya appears at the beginning of a new cycle, a time of benevolent government and material plenty, in popular cult this sequence is transposed, a transposition which took place in Burmese Buddhism as well. As Sarkisyanz writes, "The next Buddha (Metteya), for whose advent the ideal Buddhist Cakkavatti was to prepare the way, was not expected to arise until progressive decline of Buddhist society shall have run its full course."[65]

However, the Buddhist background of sectarian politically involved eschatology was not limited to the Maitreya belief with its associated theory of cyclic decay and renewal. There was in addition a long tradition of applied Buddhist theology of kingship in China, which provided many models for rustic pretenders to the throne of the new world. While the prevalent royal ideology was Confucian, several emperors with Buddhist sympathies attempted to express in government the implications of their religious allegiance.

The rulers of the Northern Wei kingdom (386-534) often supported Buddhism, ordering that temples and images be built and monks housed. In 396-398 a monk named Fa-kuo, who had been appointed imperial adviser, propounded the doctrine that Wei T'ai-tsu, founder of the dynasty, was an incarnation of the Buddha. In 454 Emperor Wen-ch'eng had a stone image of the Buddha in his own likeness set up in the capital. He then commissioned five statues of Śākyamuni sixteen feet high, each representing one of his five predecessors on the Wei throne. These images "were worshipped as though they were the . . . emperors themselves."

Another Buddhist emperor was Wu of Liang who reigned from 502-549. Wu-ti took Aśoka as his model, built many temples, and frequently convened dharma assemblies at which attendance numbered in the many thousands, with no distinction between monks and laymen. The emperor "invited well-known monks to serve as his advisers and teachers," wrote commentaries on sūtras, and often lectured on Buddhist topics. He also ordered the abolition of all Taoist temples and the return of Taoist priests to the laity. As a result of these efforts, "Emperor Wu was sometimes called the Imperial Bodhisattva."[66]

Beginning in 581, Emperor Wen, the founder of the Sui dynasty, began to issue proclamations supporting Buddhism in the name of the Cakravartin king. He publicly took the layman's vows, including a title Bodhisattva Son of Heaven. In emulation of Aśoka, Wen-ti ordered that pagodas be built all over the realm, to which imperial envoys were sent bearing sacred relics.

Since Wen-ti was a northern emperor trying to conquer the south and thus reunite China, he needed a theoretical basis for unity. In T'ien-t'ai Buddhism he found the inclusive and universalist theology he needed. But the fact that Buddhism appeared to be ideally suited to his political purposes does not mean that Wen-ti's actions in support of the dharma were purely for the sake of propaganda. On the contrary, the emperor was born in a Buddhist temple and cared for by a nun until he was thirteen. He spent only a short time in Confucian studies before he began to work at the age of fourteen. Furthermore Wen-ti's wife, who had much influence on him, is described as a devout Buddhist.[67]

Though the Sui empire collapsed by 618, and I have not come across any specific evidence linking sectarian belief with Wen-ti's imperial theology, nonetheless his understanding of Buddhism might have provided yet another model for a charismatic leader seeking absolute justification for his thrust toward a new age. Since orthodox Chinese Buddhism could be quite at home with political power, it should cause no surprise to see the same combination at the popular level.[68]

A third source for sectarian "realized eschatology" is the Mahāyāna concern that the bodhisattva be reborn on earth in specific forms to work for the well-being of others. This theme appeared in Indian Buddhist texts, and was picked up by the Amitābha tradition in China and Japan. Winternitz writes of the *Ratnaloka-Dhāranī* that it expounds "the doctrine that a bodhisattva should not aspire to salvation immediately, but is to be reborn again and again in various professions and sects, for the welfare of the beings: a long list of these professions and sects is enumerated."[69]

In China the Sung Pure Land leader, Wang Jih-hsiu, in harmony with this approach, urged that the faithful be reborn as pious officials to turn this present world into Amitābha's paradise. In his *Lung-shu ching-t'u wen* we read that, with proper faith and devotion, as death approaches one will be welcomed by Buddhas and bodhisattvas, the western land will appear in space, and one will be taken to it, there to see the Buddha Amitābha and attain complete spiritual understanding. However, one should pray that before one has been in paradise a year he should "return to earth again to save all sentient beings, and gradually transform this land of Jambu, and all the limitless worlds of the ten directions, into the pure and quiet world of utmost bliss (*chien-chien pien tz'u nan-yen fou-t'i-chieh wei ch'ing-ching chi-le shih-chieh*)."

As for pious and compassionate officials, they too can attain salvation, but, "if they are deeply concerned about the people [that is, the lost] and cannot bear to abandon them, then after they have been reborn in the Western Paradise . . . they can come again into this world, appearing in the form of high ministers or officials, in order to bring great benefit and blessing to all. Why should this be impossible?"

Buddhas and bodhisattvas are also urged to manifest themselves in the world as court ministers and officials to support the ruler in administration and teaching. By means of these official positions "they are to convert all sentient beings, so that they devote themselves to the Buddha's way, and are released from the sea of suffering."[70] Suzuki Chūsei notes that this sort of thought and belief was very widespread among the people, and so they easily believed sect leaders who proclaimed the descent of Maitreya.[71]

Thus, concrete political involvement to save the world was not limited to Maitreyan eschatology but was present in the Pure Land tradition itself. Nothing could better illustrate the natural and easy relationship between administration and salvation in the Chinese mind.

We have seen that the Chinese context provided a rich and varied set of models and theoretical supports for politically related eschatological action. The oft-cited rebellious activities and ideologies of the more militant White Lotus groups should be viewed in the light of this context, of which they were a part.

Eschatology in sectarian belief. Though our references so far to folk sect eschatology have indicated its predominantly Maitreyan orientation, there were also such hopes not directly dependent on ideas about the future Buddha. Some of these folk beliefs appeared in almost "pure" form, while others were thoroughly mixed with Buddhist motifs. For example, Sun Tso-min reports a Shantung movement in 1837 led by a certain Ma Kang. Most of the members of this group were weavers. They believed that Ma Kang was an incarnation of the White Tiger star and that one of the female weavers was the Weaving Woman star (*Chih-nü hsing*) descended to earth. They were convinced their local uprising would succeed, not only because of this divine leadership but also because officers and troops from Heaven would come to their aid. After they had been suppressed, the "Weaving Woman Star," who was only nineteen, was condemned to death. But, "when she was about to be executed she still chanted '*chen-k'ung chia-hsiang, wu-sheng fu-mu*' and showed no sign of fear."[72] Despite the folk Taoist astral eschatology of Ma Kang's group with its emphasis on divinely sent armies, this mantra indicates at least some peripheral relationship with the White Lotus tradition. The incarnate star motif was a popular one as is evidenced by passages in the *Shui-hu chuan*, which identify Sung Chiang and all his followers as star gods.[73] The "heavenly troops" theme in the *Feng-shen yen-i* has already been referred to above and can still be found today in rural areas of Taiwan.[74] Thus, here again sect beliefs are rooted in the popular religious system.

Other groups, such as that led by Chou Tzu-wang and P'eng Ying-yü, based their hope for renewal on the indigenous concept of cyclical time. In the *Lung-hua ching* there is a passage in which cyclical time eschatology is blended with Eternal Mother mythology. Here the goddess predicts calamities at various times in the future and prescribes saving charms.[75] A sect which appeared in 1457 combined military plans and titles with hope for Amitābha's paradise. This group was led by a member of a prefectural garrison named Wang Pin, of whom we read that:

He cut off his hair, became a monk and took the name Wu-chen-ch'üan (Awakened to the truth completely), and fled to live in Shensi . . . He plotted to rebel with a T'ien-t'ai monk named Wei-neng, who falsely called himself Chen-ming Ti-wang, "Truly Enlightened Emperor," but their plans were discovered. [Wei]-neng was banished but [Wang] Pin escaped. He built a small temple [in the mountains], and with heretical teachings incited vagrants to rebel. They made battle-axes and halberds, and sun and moon banners of the Five Directions, calling where they lived Terrace of the Eight Treasures . . . They established a state called Chi-le (Perfect Bliss), taking the new reign title T'ien-hsiu (Ornamented by Heaven). They planned to . . . occupy Han-chung, and change its name to Lung-ch'eng (Dragon City). When they rebelled Wang gave [various followers] such official titles as Marquis Who Establishes Heaven (Ting T'ien Hou) and Commanders of the Left and Right. He chose a woman, [also] named Wang, with whom he was having illicit relations, as Empress and General of Heaven (T'ien-chiang). [The rebels said that Wang] Pin was the Tzu-wei star descended to earth and thus should reign as emperor.[76]

Here we see folk implementation of Wang Jih-hsiu's suggestion that Amitābha's Land of Perfect Bliss could be established on earth.

Indigenous eschatological symbolism was, as we have seen, also combined with the Maitreya belief, as in the case of a 1379 leader who proclaimed himself Maitreya and distributed paper symbols among the people. When troops captured him they confiscated over 100 ritual objects, such as a Dragon-Phoenix Sun-Moon Robe [imperial robe], wooden seals [imperial symbol], silk sashes, fans, banners, swords, and so on.[77]

The basic structure of mainline folk sect eschatology was Buddhist-Maitreyan, as has been noted in such clear-cut examples as Han Shan-tung's movement in the late Yüan and the Lo sect uprising of 1748. It was Maitreya who would come to usher in the third stage, sometimes assisted by another figure destined to be emperor. This emperor was usually believed to represent the reappearance of an earlier royal line. It will be remembered, for example, that Han's son Lin-er was believed to be both the King of Light and the ninth generation descendant of Emperor Hui-tsung of the Sung dynasty. Liu Fu-t'ung established Han Lin-er as ruler of a new Sung dynasty. In so doing he explained that at the time of the Mongol conquest, survivors of the Sung royal family had fled to Japan, where the line was continued. A variant of this story held that a loyal minister named Ch'en I-chung had taken a young Sung crown prince into hiding in the south China provinces of Fukien and Kwangtung, where he had been eagerly received by the people. In either case, the point was that Han Lin-er was a son of this long hidden royal line, now returned to reclaim his rightful place. So the banner inscription of Liu Fu-t'ung's army included the words, "Re-establish the Realm of the Great Sung (Ch'ung-k'ai ta-sung chih t'ien)."[78]

In the mid-Ch'ing period this form of doubly reinforced eschatological proclamation was continued. The Chia-ch'ing Emperor writes as follows concerning leaders of the 1796 White Lotus uprising: "[Liu Chih-hsieh] . . . bribed a certain Wang Shuang-hsi to assume the name of Niu-pa, which indicates a descendant of the Chu family [the Ming royal house]. He also proclaimed that Liu Sung's son, Lui Ssu-en, was the reincarnation of the Buddha Maitreya, and could assist the Niu-pa Emperor."[79] All this is reminiscent of popular medieval European expectations of the return of the Emperor of the Last Days who overthrows the oppressors and establishes a reign of peace. Though first identified with the last Roman emperors, this hope was later related to Charlemagne, who it was believed would return to lead a crusade and establish the age of bliss.[80]

This European version of the universal monarch was also known to the Italian Waldensians, who fervently hoped "that at the head of a great army a king of the Bohemians would come, belonging to their sect, subjugating the provinces, cities and villages, destroying the churches; that he would kill all clerics . . . abolishing tolls and all sorts of exploitation . . . introduce the community of goods, and make all conform to his law."[81] The Waldensians idealized Bohemia, land of the Hussite Reformation, much as the Chinese sectarians idealized the preceding dynasty.

The Münster Anabaptists, too, had a highly developed royal symbolism. John Beukels, who took control of the city in 1534, was crowned "king of righteousness over all." He was given a sword by the twelve ruling elders, anointed by a prophet in the Old Testament style, and proclaimed "King of the people of God in the New Temple . . . ruler of the new Zion." King John wore royal robes and "held a golden apple (*Reichsapfel*) in his hands, representing universal rule."[82] This comparison is both illuminating and dangerous: illuminating because it shows the transhistorical dimension of sectarian eschatological symbolism, dangerous because what was exceptional in Europe was quite common in China. Both Waldensian and Anabaptist royal imagery was a part of situations involving extreme danger and stress. It would be a mistake to attribute the same desperation to the Chinese groups. They, too, were often under stress, but the politically related imagery was always potentially present.[83]

The relationship between messiah and emperor is most clearly dealt with by Marjorie Topley in her study of Hsien-t'ien tao groups in twentieth-century Singapore. She writes that the Kuei-ken (Return to the Root) sect:

believes the third major cycle, that of Maitreya, has already begun and that its own present patriarch is Maitreya incarnate . . . [To avoid the end of the world in a great catastrophe] the patriarch must be given the opportunity for reaching the masses to teach them the Truth. This can be achieved only if there is a return to the dynastic system and the patriarch sits on the Dragon Throne as emperor . . .

Truth cannot reach the people, moreover, if the head of state does not hold Heaven's Mandate to rule. Ideally, Maitreya himself should head the earthly state as the Buddhas did in Tibet. Then he could easily reach all the people.[84]

Thus, changing the leadership of the country could be a necessary precondition for successfully carrying out the messiah's work. The intimate relationship between the dynastic and kalpic cycles is summed up in a passage from an unnamed text quoted by Huang Yü-p'ien: "Previously, Śākyamuni ruled the world (chang-shih); in the future Maitreya will rule the world. Since [the Buddha who] rules the world is different, therefore the Heaven determined destiny (T'ien-yun) [of the dynasties involved] is also different [italics added]."[85]

The messiah's coming meant more than enthroning a pious ruler and preaching the dharma; it also meant changes in the cosmos itself, changes in the categories of time. In the Precious Scroll of the Universal Enlightenment Tathāgata [which teaches the way of] No Artificial Action and Understanding the Principles [of doctrine] (P'u-ming ju-lai wu-wei liao-i pao-chüan), we read:

Eighteen kalpas have already been completed, and the form of all things is about to change. [In this new time] a year will have eighteen months, a day eighteen [Chinese] hours, . . . a month forty-five days, and a year eight hundred ten days. In heaven and earth there will be neither completeness nor deficiency, among men there will be neither youth nor old age, birth nor death, and there will be no distinction between men and women. This then is the Great Way of Long Life, in which all will live for 81,000 years. The time destined by Heaven has been fulfilled, and a new world is being established (yu-li ch'ien-k'un shih-chieh).[86]

Huang reports that another of the "heretical sects" (unnamed) increased the traditional eight trigrams to twelve, and the sixty-four hexagrams to one hundred and forty-four. He mentions another text which divided the day into eighteen hours instead of the usual twelve, giving names to the six new ones which corresponded to six new heavenly branches. Huang discusses in detail the fundamental importance of the twelve branches to the whole traditional system of time and space. There were twelve celestial regions (*shih-er kung*), twelve months, and twelve hours. The branches were also related to the five agents and produced twenty-four mountains, which in turn were related to the eight trigrams. Each trigram controlled three mountains, which constituted the points of the compass. He concludes: "The twelve periods of every day have a vitally important significance and a wide range of uses. This system of order (*li*) existed in high antiquity before the sages appeared, and since they appeared has been handed down for 10,000 generations. And now these heretics falsely say there are eighteen periods—how stupid, deceitful and reckless they are."[87]

The sectarian proposal to usher in a new universe, with new social relationships and categories of time, indicates that at the religious level, at least, they were certainly "revolutionary" and not simply "reformist" as is sometimes stated, though this debate is peripheral to my present concerns.

Texts of another group related to White Lotus tradition, the Religion of Completion (Yüan chiao), which was active in Kiangsu and Anhwei the first part of the nineteenth century, give further evidence of this same concern for renewing the cosmos. A scripture entitled *The Regulation of Time for 10,000 Years* (*Wan-nien shih-hsien*) says that in the time to come there will be forty-five days in a month, eighteen months in a year, and seven agents instead of five. A passage from another sect text reads: "When Maitreya comes to rule the universe there will be chaos for seventy-seven days . . . The sun and moon will alter their courses, the climate will change and only those who adhere to the Yüan chiao will be saved from the cataclysm."[88]

The relationship of this new order to the three-stage time scheme mentioned often above is borne out by other *pao-chüan* passages as well. "The age of the red yang has come to an end. The white yang will soon arise. Now the moon is full on the eighteenth day; when it is full on the twenty-third day, then the great kalpa (*ta-chieh, mahākalpa*) [will arrive]."[89] "In the past men lived thirty years. Now they live sixty years. In the future they will live ninety years."[90]

A Yüan chiao text called *The Book of Response to the Kalpas* (*Ying-chieh ts'e*), describes the three ages with their respective world rulers in relationship to sect names:

1. The Religion of the Limitless Green Yang (Wu-chi Ch'ing-yang Chiao) [in which] the Lamplighter Buddha rules the world, seated on a green lotus.
2. The Religion of the Great Ultimate Red Yang [in which] Śākyamuni rules the world, seated on a red lotus.
3. The present, in which Śākyamuni has resigned his throne and Maitreya rules, the time of the White Yang religion of the imperial ultimate. In this period, "the White Lotus rules the world" (Pai-lien chang-shih).[91]

Thus, the term White Lotus here refers to the messianic rule of Maitreya. This supports Topley's observation made in Singapore 140 years after the Religion of Completion was suppressed, that "White Lotus . . . is one of the terms for the cycle of Maitreya." This symbolism is a part of what Topley's sources called "work-names," that is, specific tasks carried out by the Buddhas of certain periods as directed by the Eternal Mother. White Lotus groups are those charged with carrying out the third type of "work," that of preparing the world for the advent of Maitreya. Unfortunately, Topley was unable to discover what the first two forms of "work" might involve, but her comments remain suggestive.[92] When the folk sects rebelled, it was at least in part because they believed they were doing the work their supreme deity had commissioned them to do.

8
Patterns of Folk Buddhist Religion: Leadership, Scriptures, Ritual

Background considerations

A discussion of sectarian leadership must begin with an understanding of the traditional Chinese view of man's integral role in the cosmos, for it is this role which made possible the wealth of charismatic and mediumistic phenomena.

Though there were some skeptics, like Hsün Tzu (died soon after 238 b.c.) who claimed that nature was indifferent to man, the average traditional Chinese assumed that what he did resonated with the cosmos and that natural phenomena in turn were fundamentally linked to the rhythms of his own life.

One of the most succinct statements of this understanding is found in the *Li chi:* "Man is the heart and mind of Heaven and Earth, and the visible embodiment of the Five Elements [agents]."[1] Other influential formulations of this view were by the Han philosopher Tung Chung-shu (c. 179-c. 104 b.c.) and the Neo-Confucian Chang Tsai (1020-1077). Tung wrote that:

The material force of Heaven is above, that of Earth below, and that of man between . . . Of all the creatures born from the refined essence of Heaven and Earth, none is more noble than man . . .
The agreement of Heaven and Earth and the correspondence

between Yin and Yang are ever found complete in the human body.
The body is like Heaven. Its numerical categories and those of
Heaven are interwoven, and therefore their lives are interlocked.
[Then follows a long list of such numerical correlations.] They are
all identical and correspond to Heaven. Thus [Heaven and Man]
are one.[2]

It follows from this understanding of man-in-the-cosmos,
which long preexisted Tung Chung-shu's formulation, that everything is related to everything else in one fundamentally sacred
whole. Since man and deities are in the same continuum of being,
most of the gods of popular religion were deified persons, from
Kuan Kung and Ma-tsu to the local city-god. This traditional an-
thropology dominated the popular consciousness until deep in the
twentieth century and is still a living force in the villages of Taiwan. Such an interpretation meant that communication between
different "levels" of being was considered to be relatively easy;
even death was but transition to another mode of existence. Hence
"miraculous" occurrences were common, and there was a variety of
mediumistic practices.[3]

The universal practice of ancestor worship added to this sense
of the intimate interrelationship of all levels of the world, for one's
own life was a bridge between that of his ancestors and descendants.

Put in another way, a man was in a sense the reincarnation of
his ancestors and he would continue to live in his sons.[4] This relationship, plus the fact that the ancestors had the role of concerned,
helpful spirits, made easy the acceptance of special claims to divine
favor and power.

Of course in addition to this general understanding of the essential unity of man and the divine there had always been those in
whom this relationship was particularly transparent: shamans,
exorcists, healers, mediums, and a variety of immortals or super-
men.

The character *wu* (shaman) appears both on Shang dynasty
oracle bones and in the *Shu ching* (Book of history).[5] In pre-Han
China there was a form of shamanic priesthood which was only
gradually pushed out of state circles by Confucianism. These *wu*
were both male and female, though in archaic times female sha-

mans probably predominated. The *wu* exorcised spirits of evil and illness, called down the spirits in sacrificial rituals, and danced and chanted to ward off rain and disasters. Usually the Chinese shaman was created through the descent of a *shen* and gained power by his ability to call down spirits, but examples of "magic flight" are also known.

The *wu* could penetrate the future, learn the wishes of the spirits, and interpret dreams. At the beginning of the Han dynasty the emperor decreed that *wu* from various parts of the realm should assist in all sacrifices at the capital. It was not until Confucianism was established as the state religion in the middle of the second century B.C. that the *wu* were forced out of the imperial cult and became the functioning "priesthood" of popular religion. As Needham writes: "[The] wu . . . played an important part in Chinese life as the representatives of a kind of chthonic religion and magic [basically shamanistic], closely connected with the masses of the people, and opposed to the ouranic State religion encouraged by the Confucians."[6] The antiquity of the *wu* is again suggested by the prominence of both male and female shamanic types among the Miao tribes, with the powers of exorcism, communication with spirits while in a trance, ascension up a ladder to the "level land of Ntse," and so on.[7]

The later development of this indigenous class of religious specialists has been described in detail by DeGroot under the title "The Priesthood of Animism." It is not my purpose to recapitulate this discussion here but only to indicate the rich heritage of charismatic leadership which underlay sectarian development. Spirit possession enabled the *wu* to act as mediums, to speak in ecstasy the words of the gods, and to represent the spirits of ancestors. *Wu* also served as priests in temples and officiated at mass sacrificial rituals. All this activity was still present in south China in the late nineteenth century under such names as *sai-kong* [Mandarin *shih-kung*], *wu-shih* (Wu Master), and female specialists (*shih-p'o*).[8]

This popular religious leadership continues on Taiwan today in the red-head (*hung-t'ou*) tradition of *shen-tao* (the Way of the Gods, as distinguished from orthodox Taoism, Tao-chiao). Gallin speaks of a folk shaman called a *t'iao-t'ung* (lit., "jumping boy") who is possessed by a local "ambassador god" and simulates trips to heaven and the underworld. The *t'iao-t'ung* has his power by spirit possession, while the more powerful *fa-shih* has his own supernatural abilities. For both ranks there are elaborate initiation rituals and ordeals, including purification, self-mutilation, ascent up a sword ladder, and walking through fire.[9]

The most important element in the theoretical background of sectarian leadership in addition to indigenous charismatic specialists was the widely held belief in reincarnate bodhisattvas, already mentioned above, who, in the familiar words of the *Lotus Sūtra*,

"must be held to perform the function of the Tathāgata, to be [deputies] of the Tathāgata . . . sent by the Lord of the world to convert men."[10]

Though there was a concept of saving beings in pre-Buddhist China,[11] by medieval times the popular understanding of such beings was dominated by this image of the bodhisattva with his marvelous "skill in means" and ability to manifest himself in the world in the form most conducive to the salvation of others.

The most popular such figure in China was Avalokiteśvara, who became the goddess Kuan-yin. The reason for this popularity is made clear by the *Lotus Sūtra* which describes his ability to rescue those who turn to him from all their difficulties.[12]

The widespread presence of Kuan-yin in home and temple worship and art and her role as general benefactor and bringer of children are too well known to need repeating here. The incarnational foundation of her role can also be seen in later religious literature. For example, in the *Precious Mirror of the Lotus School* we read: "The Bodhisattva Kuan-yin in her great compassion roams through all the five levels of existence, changing her form according to the types [of beings she is seeking to save] (*sui lei hua hsing*)."[13]

Cheng Chen-to gives an illustration of one of Kuan-yin's incarnations from *pao-chüan* literature, the *Precious Scroll of Kuan-yin the Fisherwoman* (*Yü-lan Kuan-yin pao-chüan*). This text describes Kuan-yin's descent to earth to save the evil and greedy inhabitants of a fishing village. The village chief was captivated by her beauty, fell in love, and asked her to marry him. She agreed, on the condition that he become a Buddhist. As a result the chief and his cohorts

put away their butcher knives and devoted themselves to constantly reciting the Buddha's name. Though Kuan-yin died on her wed-
ding night, "all the people of the village were transformed by her,
and in the end the village became a place of goodness."[14] In the
popular consciousness the incarnation principle of such saving beings as Kuan-yin and Maitreya was extended to all sorts of deities
fated to descend for particular purposes.

Leadership in the Sects

Leaders as incarnate deities. This rich background of saving
beings active on earth was directly assimilated by the sects in their
understanding of the role of founders and charismatic leaders. I
have already noted instances of sect leaders as incarnate gods in
Chapters 5 and 6. The thrust was always toward "emergent
deities," toward more immediate and direct contact with divine
power. Even such saviors as Maitreya and Amitābha at times appeared too distant and were replaced by more familiar and accessi-
ble figures.

One *pao-chüan* clearly states that sect members themselves are
to transmit the lamp of salvation. In a chapter titled "The Three
Buddhas Transmit the Lamp" we read:

Śākyamuni Buddha succeeded the Lamplighter Buddha [in the
task of] transmitting the lamp (*ch'uan teng*). After Śākyamuni,
Maitreya Buddha handed down the lamp. After Maitreya Buddha,
the True, Heavenly Venerable Ancestor (T'ien-chen lao-tsu) will in
his turn pass on the lamp. T'ien-chen asked who would succeed him
[and was told that his successors would be] the "three schools" (*san
tsung*) and the "five sections" (*wu p'ai*), the "nine stems" and the
"eighteen branches." The leader goes ahead, and teaches his disciples, so that they can all continue the transmission of the lamp.

Huang Yü-p'ien comments on this passage: "T'ien-chen is
Kung Ch'ang [a sect founder], who was a human being . . . [The
disciples referred to above] are Kung Ch'ang's own disciples . . .
[Such teaching] naturally causes the people to be fearless of difficulty and to happily follow [their leaders]."[15] Here the traditional
three-stage chronology has been extended to five so that sect members themselves can be directly involved in the continuing eschatological task.

In the Amoy Hsien-t'ien sect mythology Lo Huai takes Maitreya's place, as we have seen above. In another text he appears as the incarnation of Amitābha. Lo was thus seen as the representative of the two principal saviors of popular Buddhism: "The Eternal Mother sent Amitābha Buddha down to earth to become the Venerable Ancestor of Nonaction (Wu-wei lao-tsu). He concealed his [true] name, and saved all living beings."[16]

While folk Buddhist belief dominates the *pao-chüan*, there are also records of purely popular-Taoist theories of incarnational leadership. For example, an interrogated member of the Recover the Origin sect (Shou-yüan chiao) said that Han Te-jung, their leader, was "a star which descended to become the founder of the Shou-yüan religion."[17] Fang Jung-sheng, a leader of the Religion of Completion sect, claimed that he was a heavenly god (*t'ien shen*) and gave himself the title "The Eternal Venerable Patriarch of the [Island of Immortal Bliss] P'eng-lai" (P'eng-lai wu-chung lao-tsu). "He wrote the names of the 108,000 stars and constellations on paper, and claimed that by burning the paper he could cause stars to take possession of his body (*fu-t'i*), and his followers believed this." But even here the Maitreya-Eternal Mother structure is present. I have already noted the White Lotus elements in Yüan chiao eschatology. In addition, we read that Fang was joined by a woman named Li Yü-lien, who

. . . said that she was pregnant with Maitreya. As a result of this the sect's membership became very large. Fang Jung-sheng . . . gave her the title Holy Creator Mother (*k'ai-ch'uang sheng-mu*) . . . Because she lived near the Stone Kuan-yin monastery, he put in his writings that "The Imperial Ultimate Lord of True Destiny lives secretly at Stone Kuan-yin."[18]

At about the same time that the Yüan chiao was active, Lin Ch'ing, leader of the Eight Trigrams sect in 1813, combined the above two themes by claiming that he himself was the incarnation of both Maitreya and Venus.[19]

Incarnation in the sects was believed to be by divine command. Its purpose was the salvation of all beings, for which supernatural powers were bestowed. The *Lung-hua pao-chüan* gives further information concerning the sect leader Kung Ch'ang, who was considered an incarnation of the T'ien-chen Buddha. In a chapter titled "The Eternal [Mother] Issues a Decree" (*Wu-sheng ch'uan-ling*), we read that her decree was transmitted by the King of the Dharma (Fa-wang), and as a result: "The T'ien-chen Buddha came near to mankind and descended to be born in the Eastern [Land] . . . [He] was incarnate in China (chung-yüan ti) in Mulberry Garden (Sang-yüan) village south of Yen and North of Chao [and became] . . . the patriarch Kung Ch'ang."

In the chapter "Kung Ch'ang Receives the Dharma," the story continues:

> The Eternal Mother ordered Kung Ch'ang to personally come and receive the dharma. Her decree said, "I pass on to you the Religious Practice in Ten Stages (*shih-pu hsiu-hsing*) [a meditation text]" . . . [She further] presented him with the sacred jewel of the Yellow Emperor . . . and the ability to suddenly manifest the eye of wisdom (*hu-jan hsien hui-yen*).[20]

Another text called "*The Precious Scroll of Huan Yüan which Explains How to Become Enlightened*" (*Hsiao-shih wu-hsing huan-yüan pao-chüan*) describes the salvation and appointment of the founder of the Huan-yüan (Return to the Origin) sect:

> Huan Yüan was a man of the Tung-sheng station in Luan-chou, Yung-p'ing prefecture [in modern Hopei]. In the sixteenth year of the Ming Wan-li reign period (1588) his true nature returned home (*chen-hsing kuei-chia*). He cast away his false bodily form, and returned to the Purple Yang Hall and the Palace of Transforming Joy [*Hua-le kung*, that is, to the Native Land paradise]. There the Old Buddha gave him the eight holy precious gems, eight great bodhisattvas, arhats, and holy monks . . . With these [gifts] he returned to the Eastern Land and saved [all he met], both the evil and the good.[21]

This power of ascent and descent, which is rooted in Chinese folk shamanism, is further illustrated by Huang's report of a leader of the Pure River sect (Ch'ing-he chiao), who said that he was able to send out his spirit (*ch'u-shen*) and cause it to ascend to Heaven (*shang-t'ien*) where he could see the Eternal Mother. "He said that he was the 'Buddha of the Southern Yang.' "[22]

The basic structure of leaders as incarnate deities continued into the twentieth century. Of Singapore Hsien-t'ien Tao leadership Topley writes: "The patriarch is the human representation of the Mother of the Void. It was from her that yin and yang originated. The work under the patriarch's supervision is likewise divided into yin and yang affairs."

It follows that the title of the five sect leaders immediately below the patriarch in authority is Wu-kung (or Wu-hsing), the "Five Agents," which are produced by the transformation of yin and yang. Of the Wu-kung we read: "They can fly like Taoist sages of ancient times, and it is they who can build "Cloud Cities" as refuges from [cyclic] catastrophes. More important, they can become incarnate Buddhas or gods . . . When they are incarnate Buddhas or gods, these rank holders are said to be *hua-shen*, to have the 'Transformation Body' of such beings."[23]

In medieval Europe, too, we can see this folk concern for leaders who were direct manifestations of sacred power. For example, Aldebert (d. 746) claimed to be a living saint, and that "he was endowed with many mystical powers. While he was still in his mother's womb, he was filled with the grace of God." He dedicated churches only to himself, for he believed he was the equal of the apostles and said, "To me, all things that lie hidden are revealed." As was true with the Chinese groups, Aldebert's claims to charismatic power were verified by his followers. As Boniface wrote, "He led astray a multitude of the ignorant."[24]

Tanchelm (d. 1115) claimed to be the Holy Spirit and married the Virgin Mary represented by an image. He came to believe that he was equal to Christ and designated twelve of his followers as the twelve apostles. Of him Russell writes, "His appeal was enormous."[25]

Eudo (Eudes de l'Etoile, d. 1148), too, believed himself to be equal to the Trinity and said that he was the Son of God. His followers ended their prayers with the phrase, "Through Eudo, Jesus Christ Our Lord."[26]

This same sentiment was expressed in somewhat more orthodox fashion by many later Reformationist leaders with their powerful sense of personal vocation, among them Jacob Hutter (d. 1536), who wrote:

God . . . has given and entrusted to me his divine eternal word
. . . giving testimony thereto in the sharing and cooperation of the
Holy Spirit, evidenced in powerful miracles and signs [in me]
whom He has established as watchman, shepherd and guardian
over His holy people, over His elect, holy Christian congregation.[27]

Thus, claims by sect leaders to be the incarnations of divine
beings cannot be dismissed offhand as charlatanry, for they are
part of a structure of sectarian popular religion which is rooted in
turn in the folk thirst for divine immediacy. This is particularly true
in China with its tradition of the unity of man and the cosmos.[28]

Other Aspects of Sectarian Leadership. Writing of European
movements, Leff says, "There was frequent mention of priests in all
the main heretical sects." Tanchelm was a "renegade monk," and
one of his associates was a priest. Priests supported Theuda, the
leader of a religious movement near Mainz in 847-848. Eudo had
begun study for the priesthood before becoming a popular leader.[29]
Hans Böhm was "urged on by a priest who remained in the background."[30] The role of priests in the Protestant Reformation of the
sixteenth century and the movements preceding and following it is
too well known to need recounting.

We have already seen that Buddhist monks were active in the
Chinese groups as founders, leaders, or advisers. The White Cloud
sect was founded by such monks, who also led the first known
Maitreya movement and influenced the Sung Pure Land devotional
associations. We have seen in Chapter 6 that one third of the members of a Kiangsi Lo congregation investigated in 1729 were monks,
while DeGroot reports that the chief leaders of the Amoy Lung-hua
sect had "received full Buddhist ordination and live[d] in celibacy."
Other devout members of the sect also became priests devoted to
full-time work among the members after a period of training and
consecration in a monastery.[31]

This involvement of ordained clergy was characteristic of Chi-
nese sectarianism all through its history, from the time the first
"Buddhist bandits" appeared in 402. Many of these monks were as-
sociated with temples and led short-lived movements of their own.
For example, in 1264 a monk named Ch'ao-kuo of the Lung-ch'üan
(Dragon Spring) Monastery in Shensi "rebelled" (*tso-luan*). His be-

longings were confiscated and he was placed under restriction by the Office of Buddhist Affairs. In 1345 the abbot of the Ch'iao-shan Monastery in Kiangsu is also reported to have led an "uprising." He was soon captured and executed.[32]

As might be expected, some of these monk leaders had political aspirations. The *Yüan shih* records that "in [1327] a monk named Ch'en Ch'ing-an of P'u-ning county in Kwangsi province rebelled. He assumed the right to establish a state and changed the reign title."[33] In 1430 two monks from Shantung founded a movement whose slogan was "The Cakravartin King has appeared in the world (*Chuan-lun-wang ch'u-shih*)."[34]

Unfortunately, the violence-oriented state records do not give a complete picture of the more pastoral and supportive role of ordained clergy in the sects. At most these records note the religious stimulus given by such leaders but deplore the results. There is a good example of this approach in the *Ming shih-lu*, dated 1546:

> In recent years large groups of monks and laity have been gathering together in the T'ien-ning monastery, outside the Hsüan-wu gate [of Peking], frequently holding worship services to take vows of abstinence and preach the dharma. [The people] are jammed together, excited and stimulated, while from everywhere Buddhist clergy gather, [forming crowds of] up to 10,000. They reverently worship and obediently listen, gathering by day and dispersing at night, with men and women mixing together. There are very many escaped criminals in their midst. [These monks] initiate disciples by burning marks on their scalps and giving them tonsure, but they carry out criminal acts [on the grounds of] hidden karmic affinity. Therefore, from the fourth month [of this year] robbers and bandits have secretly flourished within and without the capital. Surely such activities should not be going on so close to the emperor!

A somewhat later account, dated 1615, gives us similar information about the relationship between clergy and sects: "The Board of Rites requests that heretical teachings be prohibited in order to rectify the minds of the people. Recently heretical Buddhist monks and vagrant Taoist priests have been gathering people together to talk of their scriptures, pool money for feasts, and conduct regular meetings." The memorial goes on to list a number of

sects by name.[35] For the mid-Ch'ing period, Suzuki Chūsei emphasizes that many professional Buddhist monks and Taoist priests
also participated in the sectarian movements. He notes Na-yen-
ch'eng's comment that White Lotus forces did not kill Buddhist and
Taoist clergy in the areas they captured and did not destroy temples
and monasteries and concludes that these professional clergy did
much to strengthen the life of the sects.[36]

However, the most characteristic sectarian leaders were laymen who came from what Muramatsu calls "a third or middle layer
of literate but originally powerless intellectuals: monks, priests,
jobless lower degree holders, and the like, including such pseudo-
intellectuals as fortunetellers and sorcerers."[37]

Huang Yü-p'ien would have agreed: "These sectarians pretend
to be doctors or fortunetellers, or act as merchants, and go to villages everywhere to recruit followers and collect money." In commenting on the origin of *pao-chüan*, he says, "Who wrote these
texts? Not the literati, who would never produce such trash, nor
the uneducated common people, who can't write." After a long discussion of the influence of popular plays and songs on sectarian
texts, he concludes that their writers must have first been actors.[38]
DeGroot notes that Li Wen-ch'eng, an Eight Trigrams sect leader in
1813, "was a proficient soothsayer, the son of a carpenter," and
was something of a "joiner," as he had been a member of three
other groups before rising to prominence in the Eight Trigrams.[39]

Suzuki Chūsei has made a detailed study of Chia-ch'ing White
Lotus leaders which confirms that they were not only from the
"third layer" but were also religious men who went through long
periods of training as the disciples of sect patriarchs such as Liu
Sung. Liu Sung himself had been banished to Kansu in 1775 as a result of his activities with the Origin in Chaos sect. In 1787 Liu Chih-
hsieh, the best known of the many Chia-ch'ing movement leaders,
traveled from Anhwei to Kansu to study with Liu Sung, and the
two discussed restoring the old Hun-yüan chiao and changing its
name to San-yang chiao (Three Yang sect).

Another leader in this period, Hsü T'ien-te, who came from a
very wealthy (merchant?) home, had held a county office for a
short time. We have seen that Wang San-huai was a shaman who
was not above supporting himself by salt smuggling and gambling.

An associate of Hsü T'ien-te named Leng T'ien-lu is described as a diviner and fortuneteller. Suzuki also discusses two sect leaders, Fan Ming-te and Ch'en Chin-yü, who were originally peasants. Fan was converted by a Hun-yüan sect member who healed him of an illness, and after a period of study became a leader himself. Among the leaders of this 1796 movement was also a woman named Ch'i Wang-shih (Ch'i, née Wang) who was the wife of a yamen runner. After her husband was arrested, she was made a sect leader and became an "extremely good and brave fighter, superior to all the other [White Lotus] leaders in the area."[40] Suzuki sums up his study of White Lotus leaders by saying: "They were all men who had extremely strong and ardent religious tendencies, so we cannot say that they merely utilized religion as a means to reach their political and social goals."[41]

I do not intend here a detailed socioeconomic investigation of sect leadership. Suffice it to say that while many came from poor backgrounds, there is enough evidence of economically well-off leaders to make one hesitate to interpret their origin as one of "social deprivation." For example Kuo Tzu-hsing at the end of the Yüan came from the home of a wealthy traveling fortuneteller. He was able to gather and equip an army of several thousand men with funds from his family's estate.[42] In his article "On the Economic Activities of Ming Religious Societies," Noguchi Tetsurō points out that in 1622 the White Lotus leader Hsü Hung-ju and his forces were well financed and equipped. His army had 260 cannon and 1,000 horses.

Another Ming leader named Liu Fu-ta (active in 1526), had enough money to purchase a government position, which gave him authority over 5,600 other officials. Of his many literati followers one was a captain in the army and another was a student. Noguchi goes on to describe the large amounts of property, grain, and money confiscated from various White Lotus leaders, as well as the expensive binding and excellent printing of many of the *pao-chüan* scriptures. He emphasizes that it was the more educated and wealthy villagers who formed and led the sects and composed their texts. After describing White Lotus physicians, fortunetellers, makers of charms, and traveling merchants, Noguchi goes on to discuss leaders who supported themselves by trading tea and horses with Central Asian tribes, by carpentry, and by coffin making. There were others who owned silver and copper mines, and some who owned substantial amounts of new farmland in border areas. Since most of these economic activities, particularly trading with "barbarians" and privately mining metals and salt, were illegal, what we see here is further evidence for the sect's ability to build up an economic "subculture" to support their religious life, as was the case with the Yüan dynasty White Lotus. Noguchi holds that this economic activity was rooted in sectarian eschatology—the leaders had to start delivering now on promises made of a better life in the future. Particularly in the poorly regulated and less congested frontier areas they moved directly toward physically creating an ideal world.[43]

I will not attempt to resolve here the thorny problem of the relationship of charisma to heredity in sectarian leadership succession. The general picture which emerges is of hereditary leadership at the top with master/disciple "spiritual succession" at the lower levels. But the hereditary status of sect founders and chiefs had first to be established charismatically and subsequently reaffirmed by the special powers of their successors. One thinks of a third option somewhere between Weber's categories of personal and institutionalized charisma.[44] As one might expect, the sects oscillated between the two models of the Chinese family line and monastic transmission of the dharma from master to disciple. One of the clearest examples of this is the Lo sect of Chekiang investigated in 1729. Here the sect chiefs were named Lo and traced their ancestry directly to Lo Ch'ing, while leaders of congregations received their office after being trained as the disciples of their predecessors. However, this pattern varied from sect to sect and even within one tradition in different periods or areas. We have seen that a Lo group investigated in 1753 traced its descent through men named Yao and Yin back to Lo, with Yao being considered a reincarnation of the founder.

We have also noted that Wang Sen was succeeded by his son Wang Hao-hsien, thus initiating the hereditary Wang family dynasty in Stone Buddha village which lasted two hundred years. When Kuo Tzu-hsing died his wife and son continued his leadership.[45] Huang Yü-p'ien speaks of a sect leader named Yin Tzu-yüan, who called himself the "Buddha of the Southern Yang" and who had several thousand followers in an organization covering three provinces. When he was caught and executed his son in Yin Ming-jen succeeded him. Huang comments, "This was really a means of continuing his [father's] evil on a hereditary basis."[46]

However, in the Chia-ch'ing White Lotus even the top leaders studied the books and charms of the sect with a master before achieving prominence. Many of them, like Ch'i Wang-shih, looked to Liu Sung as their "spiritual patriarch," even after he was executed early in the uprising. Liu Chih-hsieh also exerted a largely religious authority as the successor of Liu Sung, even though the two men were not related. But at the lower levels as well leadership could also be a family tradition. For example we read of a leader named Kao Chün-te that his father had been executed in the aftermath of a 1792 uprising, while his father's brother had joined the White Lotus two years before the younger Kao.[47]

Master/disciple succession was also the rule in a Honan Green Yang congregation discovered by officials in 1775. Their reports give long lists of leaders who passed their teachings on to disciples. However, in Han Te-jung's Return to the Origin group of 1748, at lower levels succession was from master to disciple, but the ideal for the position of sect chief was hereditary transmission. Thus, one informant said men who had been his father's disciples twenty years previously and whom he had not seen in all that time came and "paid obeisance to me as their master." He then gave them several *pao-chüan* left by his father.[48]

But whatever the exact form of succession, the role of the leader included that of religious guide and teacher. The relationship thus formed was evidently at times a close one which could withstand even the threat of death. Yang K'uan tells of official amazement at the courage of these leaders: "They fear nothing and look upon death as a return." Yang continues, "When Li Wen-ch'eng was defeated [in 1813] he set himself aflame and several scores of followers entered the flames and died with him. They called death 'Recovering the Origin' (*shou-yüan*) and believed they ascended straight to Heaven."[49]

This same sort of courage was evident in the Lo sect, of which we read, "As for all the arrested leaders, even when they were bound, roasted and their ears and muscles cut, they showed no fear at all."[50] In the eyes of the faithful such disregard for suffering and death must have been the ultimate seal of charismatic authority.

Scriptures

We have already noted that the use of vernacular scriptures is a prime characteristic of sectarian movements. This was true of Japanese Pure Land Buddhism in the thirteenth century and of bhakti movements in medieval India, where the Hymns of the Ālvārs were soon accepted as canonical scripture. Of the southern school of Rāmānuja's followers, the Tengalais, Eliot writes: "[They were] inclined to break away from the Sanskrit tradition, to ignore the Vedas in practice and to regard the Tamil *Nālāyiram* as an all-sufficient scripture." Rāmānand (f. c. 1400) wrote hymns and "his teaching is of great importance as marking the origin of a popular religious movement characterized by the use of the vernacular language instead of Sanskrit."[51]

Śaṅkara Deva (d. 1568) carried the popular Vaishnava tradition into Assam. He translated the *Bhāgavata Purāna* into simple verses adapted to music and wrote songs and religious dramas in the vernacular. His *Kīrtana,* and the *Nāma-Ghosā* of his disciple Mādhava Deva, became the principal scriptures of Assam Vaishnavism.[52] The European parallels to this vernacular emphasis in the work of the Waldensians, Lollards, Hussites, and the sixteenth-century Reformation are too well-known in our culture to bear repeating.

Chinese *pao-chüan* literature developed as part of the Mahāyāna practice of translating sūtras into a variety of languages without a strong sense of religious veneration for the Sanskrit of the original texts.[53] This practice was perhaps related to Mahāyāna missionary concern as well as to the conviction that the Buddha-cognition is an eternal, universal possibility which can be freshly revealed in different ways. In this context the movement from literary to colloquial Chinese was but a further step in a long process.

The direct impetus for this step was evangelistic preaching in ordinary speech which began in Buddhist monasteries by the first part of the eighth century. Such preaching in turn was related to a long tradition of popular story telling which is first mentioned in the *Mo Tzu* (fifth century B.C.). In the *Chou li* and in other books referring to the Chou period (twelfth to third century B.C.) there are references to blind musicians who chanted poems and told prose stories. That this tradition continued, probably carried on by families of storytellers, is further evidenced by the use of the terms *shuo-shu* and *shuo-hua* (to tell stories) in the Sui dynasty (581-618).[54]

In addition, by the Wei (220-265) and Chin (265-420) dynasties there was a form of preaching in monasteries called *chiang-ching* (to lecture on the sūtras). In this preaching one man, called a *tu-chiang*, chanted a portion of the text, while another called *fa-shih* (dharma-master) explained its meaning. The *tu-chiang* was usually the *fa-shih's* disciple, and sat in an inferior position. He and all other listeners had the right to ask questions, which the lecturer attempted to resolve in such a way as to lead to the enlightenment of his hearers. While the sūtras were in literary Chinese, the *fa-shih* must have been forced to use some colloquial forms in his explanations and response to questions. Furthermore, laymen were also invited to these lectures, which sometimes lasted deep into the night.[55]

In the T'ang dynasty these two traditions of popular story telling and monastic lectures came together in the first vernacular preaching directed primarily toward laymen of which we have record. This preaching dramatized its effect by employing the old Buddhist traditions of unison singing of gathas and chanting Amitābha's name. The sources call it *su-chiang* (expounding in the language of the common people).

The first well-known popular preacher was a monk named Wen-hsü, of the Hui-ch'ang monastery in Ch'ang-an, who Ennin reports in 841 was "the first priest to give lectures for laymen in the city."[56] Wen-hsü was called *su-chiang seng* (the preaching monk), one of many such monks whom contemporary sources describe as *hua-su fa-shih* (dharma-masters who convert the common people, that is, evangelists). Hsiang Chüeh-ming says that Wen-hsü's goal was to enlighten ordinary folk (*wu su*). He continues, "He preached on well-known sūtras such as the *Lotus*, and on doctrines such as being and non-being, emptiness, and the suffering of the world. He urged his lay hearers to become disciples, and other monks to become *hua-su fa-shih*."[57]

A contemporary source reports that "at Ch'ang-an, when the

preaching monk (*su-chiang seng*) Wen-hsü chanted the sūtras the tone of his voice was very pleasing and he had great influence on the villagers."[58]

Though for a time these sermons for laity were encouraged by the emperor, and Wen-hsü was appointed to the court by the Emperor Wen-tsung (827-841), Confucian hostility toward such popular preaching was soon evident. A scholar named Chao Lin (*chin-shih* 838) wrote:

The monk Wen-hsü preached publicly to multitudes gathered together. He pretended to rely on sūtra texts, but all he said concerned immoral and vulgar matters. Lawless types . . . ignorant dolts and bewitched women all loved to hear his words. His listeners filled the monastery hostel, and had the audacity to venerate him . . . [They] wrote songs in imitation of his tone of voice.[59]

In this comment we see both the movement away from sūtra texts to popular stories and illustrations, and Confucian association of such down-to-earth communication with lawlessness and ignorance.

When they preached, Wen-hsü and his predecessors used prompt books (*hua-pen*) filled with illustrations and points to remember. Before long, some of these prompt books were amplified and put into literary form. Thus developed the famous *pien-wen*, variously translated as changed texts or tales of marvelous events, which were the origin of Chinese popular literature. The *pien-wen* were written in the vernacular with alternating prose and verse sections. They were distinguished from the earliest vernacular explanations of sūtra texts by their adoption of the popular storytelling style. They were complete stories based on sūtra anecdotes, but having a new and independent form. Prusek tells us of a Vimalakīrti *pien-wen* in which "[an] original [sūtra] text of some one hundred words was transformed into a long epical composition containing no less than three thousand to four thousand words." The *pien-wen* did not quote sūtras directly.

Stories in the *pien-wen* style were soon developed around secular themes and historical events. In the Sung and Yüan periods several variations appeared, with such names as *tz'u-hua, ku-tzu tiao,* and *chu-kung tiao,* all of which employed in different ways the basic style of alternating sung verse with read or chanted prose sections, all aimed at dramatic presentation of stories in ordinary language. In addition, in the Sung there was a form called *t'an-ch'ang yin-yüan* (to pluck a musical instrument and chant about causation).[60]

During the reign of Emperor Chen-tsung (998-1023) of the early Sung dynasty Confucian hostility expressed by men such as Chao Lin took effect and popular preaching in the monasteries was prohibited. With its demise the production of *pien-wen* ceased.[61] However, the activities of secular storytellers were unaffected and continued to grow more popular. Traditions developed that certain types of tales were narrated at certain places in the cities. Since the prohibition was aimed at preaching within the temple grounds, it was not long before missionary-minded monks began to preach outside the monasteries in the market places. Their preaching was called *shuo-ching* (speaking about sūtras). These efforts, too, all had their *hua-pen* and thus contained the seeds of further literary development.[62]

The point of all this for our purposes is that the next step in the development of this vernacular literary tradition was the *pao-chüan* of the Ming dynasty. Thus, the *pao-chüan* were a continuation of the religious side of the literary movement begun by T'ang monk evangelists and the *pien-wen*. As Cheng Chen-to says, "*Pao-chüan* are the direct descendants of *pien-wen*."[63] Ch'en Ju-heng writes of the *pao-chüan*:

Their content and style differ little from that of the T'ang dynasty *pien-wen*. Their contents are taken both from Buddhist texts and folk traditions. They are definitely in the tradition of *pien-wen* and [other forms of] vernacular religious literature . . .

Preaching the *pao-chüan* (*shuo-ch'ang pao-chüan*) became a special means by which members of religious groups propagated their doctrines . . . They were produced by the secret sects as a means of stating and spreading their beliefs . . . The fact that many *pao-chüan* are called *ching* (sūtra) also indicates their close connection with the *shuo-ching* tradition. *Pao-chüan* was a later term.[64]

Cheng maintains that the *pao-chüan* can be roughly divided into two classes, Buddhist and non-Buddhist. In the Buddhist category are texts based on sūtra stories and those concerned with conversion of the world (*ch'üan-shih*), while the non-Buddhist precious scrolls consist of Taoist tales and secular stories intended for humor or general edification.[65]

Li Shih-yü says there are three types: 1. those which propagate the teachings of "secret religions"; 2. those which adopt Buddhist or Taoist stories in order to propagate secret religions; 3. miscellaneous texts based on folk tales, operas, and so on.

The third category is distinctly secondary in importance to the first two.[66] Li points out that many of the *pao-chüan* which Cheng lists as Buddhist in fact contain references to the Eternal Mother/ Native Land mythology, which he says is basic to the Precious Scroll literature. In this interpretation *pao-chüan* are different from *pien-wen* "primarily because *pien-wen* were at the service of ortho-dox Buddhist texts, whereas *pao-chüan* were a means of propagating the secret religions popular among the people." Li is concerned to stress that while the *pao-chüan* was a descendant of earlier types, "it was an independent form of folk literature, not just another variety of *pien-wen*."[67]

Sakai Tadao's interpretation is similar to that of Li Shih-yü. To Sakai, the *pao-chüan* are a form of *shan-shu*, popular morality books, which first came into general use during the Sung. These *shan-shu* are varied in content, but all use colloquial language to exhort the reader toward morally constructive behavior. Sakai says that *pao-chüan* are "vernacular scriptures . . . produced by popular Buddhist religious societies as a means of proclaiming their teachings." He adds that most of these texts, "which are basically Buddhist in structure," were used by "such heretical sects as the White Lotus."

However, Sakai goes on to demonstrate that the *pao-chüan* also show the influence of several other traditions, including Confucian historical legends, religious Taoism, the cult of the three religions, alchemy, and divination. What is the textual background of all these other elements? In discussing this question Sakai quotes a very interesting list of 125 "heretical" books compiled by the government in 1474 for distribution all over the empire as a warning to the people. While there are several titles on this list which show Buddhist influence, the majority deal with divination, the five elements, and other folk religious themes. As Sakai observes, none of the Buddhist sūtras and devotional texts used by Lo Ch'ing and his commentators appear in this compilation, even though most of the Lo sources were extant long before 1474. Evidently even the popular tracts they used were considered just Buddhist texts in the vernacular and hence were not proscribed. The Japanese scholar concludes that by the late Ming, folk Taoist texts such as those on the 1474 list were combined with the vernacular Buddhist tradition to form the *pao-chüan*, which were thus a new form of colloquial scripture.⁶⁸

While for the main body of *pao-chüan* literature the interpretations of Li Shih-yü and Sakai Tadao are certainly correct, perhaps neither scholar emphasizes enough that there are varieties of Buddhist-oriented *pao-chüan*, some being much more orthodox in general tone than others. One need only compare the accounts of Mu-lien (Moggallana) and the Buddha of Medicine in the texts discussed by Cheng Chen-to with the Red Yang sect *pao-chüan*, collected by Huang Yü-p'ien. While the Eternal Mother motif is mentioned in the *Yao-shih pao-chüan* and perhaps the *Mu-lien pao-chüan* as well, it is submerged in a generalized popular Buddhist concern for the salvation of all beings, virtuous behavior, avoiding "bad karma" and the judgments of hell, and filial piety as a means of rescuing one's parents, a sentiment well summed up in the following passage from the *Mu-lien chiu-mu ch'u-li ti-yü sheng-t'ien pao-chüan* (The precious scroll of Mu-lien, who by rescuing his mother [enabled her] to escape from hell and ascend to heaven):

All men should imitate the holy Mu-lien the Honored one in being filial to their parents, seeking out and questioning enlightened teachers, reciting the Buddha's name and maintaining a vegetarian diet. [So that] birth and death can forever be stopped (*sheng-ssu yung hsi*) [one should] with a determined heart cultivate the Tao and repay his parents for their loving care.⁶⁹

There is nothing here of the central importance of returning to the Native Land or of the eschatological urgency so characteristic of the *P'o-hsieh* texts. The *Mu-lien pao-chüan* seems to be the expression of a more general popular Buddhism.

While by the late Ming period sectarian scripture took the form of *pao-chüan*, the Ming sects themselves did not invent this form, since the earliest known *pao-chüan* appeared during the

Southern Sung. Cheng Chen-to says that the first book with the
term *pao-chüan* in its title is the *Hsiang-shan pao-chüan* (The
precious scroll of Incense Mountain), which was written by a Ch'an
monk named P'u-ming in 1103.[70] After a long discussion, Sakai
concludes that this date is incorrect, since the *Hsiang-shan* text in
fact first appeared in the Yüan or early Ming. He adds, however,
that there is another earlier scripture of the *pao-chüan* type, the
Hsiao-shih Chin-kang k'e-i (An explanation of the *Diamond Sūtra*
ritual), also known as the *Chin-kang k'e-i chüan*, which was written by a Ch'an monk in the Southern Sung.[71]

Given this dating, it is perhaps reasonable to suggest that the
pao-chüan grew out of the Sung *shuo-ching* tradition of sermons in
the marketplaces. The *pao-chüan* would thus be to *shuo-ching* as
the *pien-wen* were to T'ang monastic preaching in the vernacular.[72]
The increased use of rhyme, verse, vernacular forms, and non-
Buddhist themes might be related to this more "worldly" locus of
delivery. As preaching by monks was again cut off by official prohibition, perhaps the form they created was taken over by the lay
priesthood of the rapidly developing sects. In these groups the *pao-
chüan* form was then exposed to further influence from popular
beliefs, dramas, and legends, and Buddhist themes were combined
with those of folk religious texts, culminating in the development of
the characteristic sectarian scriptures of the late Ming.

Li Shih-yü gives the following account of the general
characteristics of *pao-chüan*:

1. They are usually divided into twenty-four chapters, though
some have fewer divisions and some none at all.
2. Most have gāthās and sacred verses at the beginning and
end. These chanted sections include rituals for burning incense.
3. There are *pai-wen*, "clear-text" prose passages, interspersed
with verse sections or those in other styles. (These passages are
spoken, not chanted, and state the meaning in simple terms.)
4. Chanted sections in seven-character lines of verse, with
four or eight lines per section, are found in a few texts.
5. Most of the verses are ten characters long, arranged three-
three-four. This ten-character verse form is always present.
6. There are sung sections, usually at the end of each chapter,
written to well-known popular tunes from folk songs or operas.[73]

The scriptures discussed by Cheng Chen-to largely bear out

Li's analysis. The *Yao-shih pen yüan kung-te pao-chüan* begins
with a "Hymn for Raising [offering] Incense" ("Chü hsiang tsan"),
which includes four lines of seven-character verse. There follows a
"Gāthā for Opening the Sūtra" ("K'ai-ching chieh"), also in seven-
character verse. The rest of the text consists of prose sections (*pai-
wen*) interspersed alternately with five- and seven-character lines of
verse. The *Mu-lien pao-chüan* follows the same form.[74]

Huang Yü-p'ien has some comments concerning the form and
style of the texts he collected:

> [The *pao-chüan*] are printed in large characters from wooden
> blocks. The scrolls are [carefully] bound and wrapped, and
> decorated with silver and satin. There are pictures of Buddhas on
> both front and back. All [the scrolls] are handsome in appearance,
> and look similar to orthodox Buddhist sūtras.
> [These scriptures] falsely change and supplement Buddhist
> sūtras in order to deceive the people.[75]

In the *Hsü-k'an p'o-hsieh* Huang adds that some of these
books "are similar to Buddhist sūtras, and must [have been written]
by monks who participated in heretical religion after first having
read orthodox texts. They inserted false teachings about Wu-sheng
into Buddhist sūtras, because they wanted to combine orthodoxy
and heresy into one."[76]

However, as we have noted above, Huang also emphasizes
that the background of many *pao-chüan* stories, terms, and
stylistic devices is in novels, such as the *Feng-shen yen-i* and *San-
kuo yen-i*, and tunes from popular operas. He goes on to point out
that *pao-chüan* use of two lines of three characters each followed
by one of four characters is based on the "Pang-tzu ch'iang-hsi," a
Shensi style of opera singing, and makes other similar compari-
sons.[77]

Pao-chüan use of musical and verse forms was due to the ritual
manner in which they were read. Chao Wei-pang says that "during
the reciting of canons and divine rolls musical instruments were
probably used. In the country districts in North China there are still
some similar organizations. They perform on musical instruments
when they recite their canons."[78]

Na-yen-ch'eng made a similar report more than a century
earlier: "In the villages they use wooden fish which they beat at

night while they preach and sing edifying sermons (*ch'ang-shuo hao-hua*)."[79] The *ts'ai-yu*, a Buddhist lay priesthood on Taiwan, still employs drums, cymbals, chimes, bells, and a form of piano-harp while reciting scriptures, alternating between chanting and singing. This use of drums and unison singing and chanting in sūtra-reading rituals began in the monasteries, as is illustrated by a "Ten-Stage Ritual for Vernacular Preaching," used in Sung times which begins with ringing bells to gather the congregation. Then follow: 1. taking refuge in the Three Treasures; 2. ascent by the preacher to his high seat; 3. beating of a drum to quiet the congregation; 4. singing of a hymn; 5. preaching the doctrine; 6. meditation, followed by a period of questions and answers; 7. the preacher turns around to face the altar; 8. singing of another hymn; 9. descent by the preacher and the end of the service.[80] In 1969 I observed very similar ritual in a preaching service conducted by the orthodox "Friends of the Lotus" upāsaka association in Taipei. The lecturer was a monk from a nearby monastery.

The opening section of the *Yao-shih pao-chüan* clearly demonstrates the ritual reverence with which the people approach the *pao-chüan*. The opening rite is in three sections: 1. *Act of praise for offering incense.* This includes a thrice-repeated prayer that Yao-shih Buddha and all other Buddhas and bodhisattvas draw near to receive worship. Then follow four lines of seven-character verse in praise of the Buddha and the dharma. This section ends with a threefold message venerating the Three Precious Jewels, the Buddha, dharma and sangha. 2. *Hymn for opening the sūtra.* This section consists of four seven-character lines of verse in praise of the dharma and includes a vow to clearly explain the true intention of the Tathāgata. 3. *An introduction to the Tathāgata Yao-shih.* This passage describes the sufferings and ignorance of the world before Yao-shih came, and the greatness of his compassion. It ends with an appeal to believe, venerate, and always dwell in the Three Precious Jewels and with another threefold statement, "[Now] all living creatures from the ten directions, take refuge in the Buddha, the dharma, and the sangha. The wheel of the dharma turns ceaselessly to save all sentient beings."[81]

Of course the sectarian faithful did not see their scriptures historically as inheritors of the *pien-wen* tradition. To them the *pao-chüan* were delivered by the gods through the agency of their

own founders and leaders. This concept was based on both Buddhist and folk Taoist ideas. Buddhist sūtras commonly speak of
themselves as being spoken by the Buddha himself,[82] while there
was a long popular tradition of letters and books sent from heaven
or delivered by immortals to elect leaders.[83] This concern to base
faith and conduct on directly revealed scriptures reached its culmination in the use of the planchette, which became very popular
at the end of the Ch'ing period and is still actively practiced by the
Taiwan Red Swastika society and the Religion of Compassion sect
today. There are various forms of this ritual, the most common
being the use of a stick to write on a tray of sand, with the stick
believed to be empowered by the revealing deity. Most of the scriptures of sects still active in the twentieth century were revealed via
planchette, though they retain many elements of *pao-chüan* style,
form, and content.[84]

I have already noted some references to the bestowal of sectarian scriptures by a deity. The *Lung-hua ching* makes a similar
reference to its own origin: "The T'ien-chen Old Buddha opened up
the precious storehouse of the Native Land (*ta-k'ai chia-hsiang
ts'ang-k'u*), took out the *Lung-hua ching* and handed it down to
later generations."[85]

This conviction of the divine origin of the *pao-chüan* is related
to the belief that sacred scriptures have a saving efficacy in their
own right. Many Buddhist sūtras extol themselves as all-sufficient
for salvation, and the reading, memorization, chanting, publication and distribution of such texts became independent meritorious
acts.[86] Of course all this is based on the fundamental missionary
concern of the Mahāyāna, with its exhortations to "proclaim" and
"fully explain to others" the scripture in question.

Such concern for propagation of the faith was concretely
expressed in China through the work of societies dedicated wholly
to the reading, copying, printing, and free distribution of scriptures. Some pious monks and laymen of the Sung period had sūtras
printed which were illustrated to make clear their meaning and to
which were added gathas and hymns of praise. Wang Jih-hsiu
argued that money spent for the distribution of scriptures was the
most effective form of contribution, for it resulted in salvation for
both readers and donor.[87]

All this orthodox veneration of scripture was taken up by the folk sects, doubly emphasized by China's traditional reverence for the written word. The opening passage of the *Precious Scroll which Explains the True Realm of Emptiness* says, "This . . . *pao-chüan* can open the door to liberation, contains marvelous hymns of merit, and leads [the reader] to enter the way of perfect wisdom."[88] The *Dragon-flower scripture* makes even greater claims, which again reflect folk influence on the lay-Buddhist tradition: "Chanting this scripture once will prolong one's life. By reading it twice one can regularly materialize the true origin. By reciting it three times, one can cause three generations of ancestors to be born in Heaven."[89] It is this scriptural tradition which perhaps more than anything else indicates the religious nature, continuity, and Buddhist origins of the Chinese folk sects.

Ritual

Unfortunately there are very few materials available for a discussion of sectarian ritual. I have mentioned aspects of worship in my treatment of the Ch'ang-sheng and Lo sects and of the orthodox Pure Land movement. From what data we do have it appears that sect ritual was quite simple and differed little from that of the temple cult of general popular religion.

I have noted that Mao Tzu-yüan carried the Pure Land tendency toward simplified worship a step further by substituting a "Fivefold Chanting of the Buddha's Name" for the tenfold repetition common in his day. In this he took a step towards further appropriation of salvation by grace similar to Shinran's later insistence that only one statement of the *Nembutsu* was sufficient. Chih-p'an reports, as we have seen, that Mao (or at least the sect which developed after his death) also used a "Ritual of Morning Penance" which was extracted from the "Sevenfold Penance" of the T'ien-t'ai monk Tz'u-yün. In addition he wrote "Hymns in Four Stanzas" which "were similar to woodcutters' songs."[90]

Thus, this earliest White Lotus ritual was deliberately simplified and even set to music in order to attract lay converts. Needless to say, this was a congregational cult which followed the long established practice of group worship in orthodox Buddhism, though its immediate context was the clerical-lay devotional societies of the T'ang and Sung period.[91] There was a conscious theory of collective worship in the devotional societies, because their basic goal was cooperative advancement in piety by means of *nien-fo*. Members believed that individual meditation and devotion were often very difficult because of laziness and resistance to concentration, so they developed a piety of mutual support and concern: "If one person falls back, then all unite their strength to lead him forward. When one forsakes the world they [join in] their care for one another."[92]

Suzuki lists the following names for types of devotional association worship: *chi-nien*, continuous recitation; *mo-nien*, silent recitation; *kuan-hsiang*, meditation; *kung-yang*, sacrificial offering (*pūjā*); *li-pai*, bowing before images; *sung-ching*, group chanting of sūtras; *t'ing-fa*, listening to the dharma (sermons); and *she-chai*, vegetarian feasts.[93] It seems reasonable to assume that all of these forms of popular Buddhist worship were employed in the sectarian tradition. For most of them there is evidence that this was the case.

The tendency toward simplicity was continued in later White Lotus tradition. We read in the *Scroll of Enlightenment through Ascetic Discipline* (*K'u-kung wu-tao chüan*) that "the work of contemplation consists of chanting the four characters, *A-mi-t'o-fo* ([Homage to] Amitābha Buddha). If one chants too slowly, Wu-sheng lao-mu in Heaven may not hear." Huang Yü-p'ien comments, "If all there is to meditation is chanting A-mi-t'o-fo, then anyone can meditate!"[94]

For ritual in sects related to the Ch'ing White Lotus tradition we have some useful comments. For example, in a 1775 report on the Green Yang sect in Honan we read that its members "worship the Mother (*feng mu-ch'in*) . . . Every first and fifteenth of the [lunar] month they burn incense, chant scriptures and sing songs . . . [The sect leader] gathers the people in his home on the fifteenth of the eighth month to chant sūtras and preach the religion (*ch'uan-chiao*)."[95]

In his discussion of Chia-ch'ing groups, Suzuki mentions reciting Buddha's name, burning incense, reading and chanting sūtras, chanting mantras, and maintaining a vegetarian diet. He also says there was a definite schedule of group services every month.[96] Na-yen-ch'eng provides more details. Of the Ch'ing-cha men of Shih-fo k'ou he writes that:

Its members take the "Three Refuges" and the "Five Prohibitions." The "Three Refuges" are the Buddha, the dharma, and the master. The "Five Prohibitions" are against killing living beings, stealing, adultery, eating meat or drinking wine, and lying. On each first and fifteenth of the month they burn incense morning and evening, and offer as well two kinds of tea. They call their preachers (*ch'uan-chiao che*) "Venerable Sirs" (*weng*), bow in obeisance to them, and give them silver and copper money.

In a report dated the next year, Na-yen-ch'eng gives us further information about ritual, this time of the San-yüan sect whose leader was also from Luan-chou. After noting the claim that those who practiced this religion for a long time could attain long life, he lists the three holy days of the sect as

. . . upper *yüan*, fifteenth of the first, middle *yüan*, fifteenth of the seventh, and lower *yüan*, fifteenth of the tenth. Each time they meet they offer sacrifices of food, burn incense, prostrate themselves (*k'e-t'ou*), recite mantras (*nien chou*) and circulate their *ch'i* while in seated meditation. [They say that] in all matters they follow the virtues of humanity, justice, propriety, wisdom and showing consideration, and may not commit evil. [Members of] the highest level [of attainment] study to become immortals and attain to the Tao. Those of the middle level study to avoid illness and lengthen life, while at the lowest level, [members] study to eliminate calamities and avoid difficulties . . .
They worship at night by burning incense, offering food and reciting mantras. When such worship is finished they separate to eat and meditate. [Some members] regularly meditate with [the sect leaders] in groups of three to five, while others practice the circulation of *ch'i* individually at home. Such matters are not fixed.[97]

For sectarian ritual later in the nineteenth century DeGroot gives a detailed description of Lung-hua sect observances in Amoy, which included a liturgical calendar, offerings of rice, vegetables, fruit, and tea, the chanting of sūtras accompanied by drums and bells, bowing to images, reciting Amitābha's name and a penance rite, all of which gives one a sense of what quite probably took place in the earlier groups for which our information is less complete.[98]

We have a bit more material concerning membership and meditation rituals. Huang summarizes the membership rite as follows:

These sects list the names of members in a memorial, which they present to the Eternal Parents so that they will know this man and in the future he can ascend to Heaven . . . The names of all new disciples are sent up to Heaven in memorial form each time they worship. Their names are registered in the [Heavenly] roster (*kua-hao piao-ming*).

His chief objection here is that the "heretics" make no moral selection—anyone can be registered in Heaven: "[They take in anyone], with no principles of selection (*pu-wen hsien-yü, pu-fen shan-e*)."

The *Lung-hua ching* says, "Only those whose names are registered can transcend the world (*ch'u-shih*). Those who are not registered are chased out of the City of the Clouds." According to Huang an offering was necessary before one's name could be entered on a memorial to the Eternal Mother. He says that the process was a three-step one: offering, sending up the memorial, registration (*shang-kung, sheng-piao, kua-hao*).[99] These memorials were written on yellow paper, in imitation of imperial usage. The sending of messages to the gods via burned paper is now a standard practice in popular religion, though in the Confucian view it was the prerogative of the emperor alone. After being properly registered the new member received a certificate called *yün-ch'eng shou-chüan*, which Chao translates as a "passport to heaven."[100]

In 1813 a captured member of the Pa-kua chiao said that the first steps in entering the sect were to kneel with incense and prostrate oneself, after which one was taught the eight-character mantra, *chen-k'ung chia-hsiang, wu-sheng fu-mu*. One then contributed to the local sect master 200 cash as "foundation money." Other contributions were made annually at the Ch'ing-ming and Chung-ch'iu festivals. Other informants added that becoming a member could also involve being taught how to meditate.[101]

Registration in the heavenly roster was continued into the twentieth century. Topley reports of the Singapore group that "when a new member wants to join a sect, a petition is burnt to Mother informing her of the name, age, sex and place of birth of the candidate."[102]

DeGroot gives the entire Lung-hua initiation rite in the first volume of his *Sectarianism*. It includes taking the Three Refuges, hearing the sect's five commandments, repeating a scripture in twenty-eight characters and vowing to keep the commandments and "not to turn from the Patriarch" (Lo Huai). The whole ritual is based on Buddhist models, with the addition of some folk Taoist and Confucian elements, such as an injunction to "assimilate with the five elements (agents)," and obey the "six prescriptions of the [Imperial] Sage Edict."

The White Lotus sects had a fairly complex meditation ritual, basically Taoist, which was based on a correspondence between raising one's "vital force" to the top of the head and ascending to paradise, both of which are referred to as the "K'un-lun mountain."

In his discussion of the late sixteenth century Lo sect, T'ao-k'ai wrote:

At midnight in the still of the night they recite imprecations and swear oaths of brotherhood in order to transmit their oral tradition in secret. They tightly close the six bodily openings, clenching their fists and putting their tongues in the roofs of their mouths. [Then] they quietly chant [scriptures] and give oral instruction, [resolving] to save and lift up all people to enable them to escape from the bitter sufferings of life.[103]

The meditation terms here indicate influence from the Taoist tradition of "embryonic meditation" and "circulation of the breaths," the origins of which can be seen as early as the time of Chuang Tzu. Though it is not my purpose here to describe this long and complex tradition, it is important to note that its goal was immortality. Immortality was attained by a form of internal rebirth, the nourishing of an embryo-body within the old body. The circulation of the breaths caused the yang essence to return, which formed the embryo of the immortal body, causing it to grow little by little. By the mid-T'ang period this form of breathing ritual was well known. In the twelfth century Ch'üan-chen sect "embryonic breathing" became the meditative basis of a form of Taoist monasticism. At the popular level such a quest for immortality was easily correlated with the hope for rebirth in paradise.

There are several short passages indicating the nature of White Lotus meditation. In discussing the San-yüan, Na-yen-ch'eng says, "Their method of circulating the breaths (*yün-ch'i*) is to first rub the face with the hand, shutting the eyes and closing the mouth. The *ch'i* is sent down from the stomach, and then let out through the nose."[104]

The soteriological goal of the meditation is indicated by Huang: "These sects hold that by means of seated meditation and circulation of the breath, one can penetrate to the truth, see the immortals, and neither enter hell nor meet with disaster." Huang says that White Lotus meditation was called the Meditative Attainment in Ten Steps (*shih-pu kung-fu*). The correlation of such meditation with Native Land mythology is revealed by a passage from an unnamed *pao-chüan*: "Rise out of the sea into the light, penetrate through to K'un-lun mountain, and see the immortals (*tang-jen*); manifest [your true self as a] child [of Lao-mu], and ascend directly into Heaven, not entering hell."

Another text makes completely explicit the identical results of salvation by meditation and salvation by grace: "The result of completing the work of the ten steps is to ascend to K'un-lun mountain from the bottom of the sea. That is, to ascend directly to Heaven, meet together with the Eternal Mother, and never again return to this world."[105] In Taoist meditation the Lower Red Field, that is, the lower abdomen, is also known as the Sea of Breath (*ch'i-hai*). In this text the Sea of Breath is correlated with the Buddhist Sea of Bitterness (*k'u-hai*), that is, this samsara world. This correlation corresponds to that between K'un-lun as the crown of the head and K'un-lun as paradise. In both cases the movement upward means salvation.[106]

Chao Wei-pang gives a summary of White Lotus meditation:

There were ten steps of development. The first step was "to take up the brilliance from the bottom of the sea." The brilliance was the soul substance, which was imagined to be a brilliant ball and was therefore also called the round light. The beginning of self-cultivation was to try to find it in the abdomen. The last step of self-cultivation was when it passed through the K'un-lun. K'un-lun was the crown of the head. As the result of self-cultivation by sitting in meditation, the soul substance was supposed to be able to come out through the crown of the head and to go up to the heavenly palace.[107]

Collective meditation appeared with the rise of congregational

Taoism near the end of the second century. It was developed further by Taoist monasticism, which in turn interacted with collective dhyāna exercises in Buddhism. The folk sects helped make this practice widely available to the laity, among whom it can still be observed in the ritual of such groups as the Taiwan Red Swastika society.[108]

9
Concluding Observations

Typological Considerations

What has been said so far should make it possible to distinguish folk Buddhist sects from the great variety of popular resistance movements which beset imperial China all through its history. Such movements ranged from local riots in reaction to oppressive laws or corrupt county officials to full-scale rebellions led by "middle layer" gentry, literati, or merchants openly ambitious to take over imperial power. Though official sources usually labeled all such movements as *tsei* or *k'ou* (bandits), the majority of them were sporadic reactions to intolerable conditions, which should be distinguished from organized bandit gangs which at times also moved toward direct acquisition of political power. While the preponderance of peasants in the Chinese population made it inevitable that they would be in the majority in any large-scale popular movement, it is not accurate to call all such movements peasant rebellions or peasant wars. As John Dardess has demonstrated in his studies of late Yüan rebellions, the larger uprisings were usually led by discontented elements surrounded by a group of like-minded followers. Only if the circumstances were right were such leaders able to attract the support of the peasants who formed the "outer ring" of participants.[1] We have seen that in the sects there was a similar movement from "middle layer" charismatic leaders to the general population. This is not to deny that local uprisings directed against relatively specific grievances could be instigated and led by peasants themselves.

At the local level there were outbreaks by "tenant bandits" against unfair interest rates or lending practices by landlords. These outbreaks involved anything from refusal to pay rent to killing landowners and burning their homes, but as K. C. Hsiao points out, such violent opposition by tenant farmers in the Ch'ing period was "usually unorganized and on a small scale." While Hsiao says that conflicts between tenants and landlords were the most important source of local uprisings he also describes several different types of riots by "local inhabitants against local officials." These riots were directed not against government authority itself but against abuses of that authority and included outbreaks against extortion and tax collection and protest against the lack of food reserves or their distribution during famines. "Hunger riots" could also involve simple plundering of the granaries of wealthy families. The fundamentally economic intention of these riots is demonstrated by the fact that they were usually preceded by petitions against corrupt practices by local officials and began only when these petitions were ignored by higher authorities. Hsiao emphasizes the circumstantial and "loosely organized" character of such expressions of local discontent.[2]

There were also outbreaks against laws restricting economic activity in areas in which the government sought to impose a monopoly in production or distribution. In the Sung dynasty, for example, there were violent protest movements led by tea merchants, dubbed "tea bandits" (*ch'a k'ou*) in the official records. In 1175 an army financed and led by tea merchants moved from Hupei south to Hunan and Kiangsi, and from there all the way to Kwangtung. In 1217 there was another such uprising in Hupei which involved a force called the "tea merchant army" (*ch'a-sheng chün*).

Government monopoly of salt production was a perennial source of discontent, because salt prices were often maintained at an artificial level so high that common people had to go without. The result was private mining and smuggling of salt supported by the majority of the population. Such activity necessitated tight organization and secrecy, and as a consequence salt smugglers often fought effectively for their own survival. Their experience enabled them to provide leadership in times of general uprising.

There were also resistance movements by miners (*k'uang-k'ou*, "miner bandits") in reaction to government seizure of private silver mines and the prohibition of private mining and smelting. For example, in 1181 an iron miner named Wang Ke led a rebellion in Anhwei. In none of these mercantile uprisings does there appear to have been any religious motivation.[3]

There were some groups to which the official term "bandit" was quite rightly applied, though in popular tradition some bandits were more "righteous" than others, depending on the extent to which they were said to dispossess the rich and oppose corrupt officials in favor of the poor. The best known of such "righteous bandits" was Sung Chiang of Shantung, whose exploits became the historical core of the novel *Shui-hu chuan*. Sung, active between 1085 and 1130, was in fact just one of a long line of bandit leaders who fortified themselves in the swamps of Liang-shan-p'o. Such bandit groups were composed of refugees, beggars, and other rootless elements at the edges of the established social system. Hsiao distinguishes between "professional" and "occasional" bandits, the professional form sometimes being a hereditary occupation.[4] Though the goal of all these organized bands was plunder, they used a variety of means according to the nature of their environment. The Liang-shan-p'o bandits on occasion used small boats for mobility; in addition, there were sea pirates, lake pirates, and river pirates. The membership of many of these latter groups consisted of discontented fishermen, like the group led by Shao Ch'ing in the area between the Yangtze and Huai Rivers from 1129 to 1131, which built large boats the government troops were long unable to attack successfully.[5]

It is true that in periods of unusual social disintegration and unrest all sorts of oppressed peasants, angry merchants, and bandit gangs might join forces with a sectarian eschatological movement and thereby sublimate their more limited goals into that of replacing the existing dynasty. In fact, in such periods the situation could become quite confused, with sect members plundering for food and bands of raiders developing imperial pretensions. But the intentional distinctions remain clear; only the sects moved out of preexisting scriptural and cultic traditions, inspired by eschatological hope.[6]

This same essential distinction is true in the case of the many full-scale political rebellions which regularly challenged the existing government. The first well-known such uprising was led by Ch'en She (Ch'en Sheng) and Wu Kuang against the Ch'in dictatorship in 209 B.C. Though Ssu-ma Ch'ien reports that one of Ch'en's first acts after deciding to rebel was to "consult a diviner, who urged them to seek the help of the spirits," and that he proclaimed a new mandate for the vanquished state of Ch'u, it is clear that this rebellion began as a desperate reaction to Ch'in cruelty. Wu and Ch'en were part of a detachment of 900 military conscripts who all faced certain execution because they were late for their destination. That they consulted a diviner, swore an oath of mutual loyalty, sacrificed the heads of their slain officers on an improvised altar, and shouted "Great Ch'u"[7] does not make them a sectarian movement. Such an appeal for divine support and justification was very common in Chinese resistance movements, but here and in many other cases it did not involve the cultic tradition and congregational life that were central to the sects.

What I have written above concerning the concept of man-in-the-cosmos should not be construed to mean that the Chinese were somehow incapable of straightforward political ambition and military power plays. In fact, traditional China seethed almost constantly with plots to usurp the throne, coups d'état by high officials or imperial relatives, revolts by warlords or local officials trying to become warlords, invasions by "barbarian" forces supported by Chinese dissidents, and uprisings by disgruntled military units. T'ao lists 119 military-based outbreaks between 1127 and 1161 alone.[8] Whatever their use of religious symbols, whether out of sincere desire for divine support or for propaganda purposes, political motivations were central for most of these rebellions.

This can be clearly seen in the several anti-Sui political uprisings which led to the founding of the T'ang dynasty. One of the important rebel leaders, Tou Chien-te, began as an army officer but soon took to banditry as a means to build up his strength for a try at the "great enterprise." In 613 Yang Hsüan-kan, president of the Board of Rites, revolted in Honan against the weakening control of the Sui kingdom in a direct attempt to take over political power.

The eventually successful plots by Liu Wen-ching and Li Shih-min were completely within the ancient tradition of struggling for the Mandate of Heaven by intrigue and force of arms. These were only a few of the best known revolts among the scores that occurred between 613-617.[9] The fact that a few eschatological uprisings occurred in this tumultuous period, led by the Maitreya sect and by Taoist groups looking forward to the long expected arrival of Li Hung,[10] only accents the distinction that must be drawn between such fundamentally religious movements and those of obvious and unabashed political motivation.

This distinction holds as well for other uprisings with popular bases of support. For example, at the end of the Western Chin kingdom (265-316), a time of terrible famines with resulting hordes of starving refugees, there were at least ten different rebellions between 299 and 311, supported by displaced peasants, aboriginal Man tribesmen and slaves. Their leaders took such titles as "Emperor of the Han," "Great General," or "Magistrate," none of which can be said to have any strong eschatological content, since the Han dynasty had fallen only 80 years earlier and was the best available model of imperial unity and prosperity. Though the records note that in 299 Chang Ch'eng-chi used "*yao-yen* (heretical words) to gather several thousand followers and start a disturbance," this probably means no more than certain folk prophecies concerning his divinely bestowed right to lead a rebellion and does not imply that his movement was fundamentally cultic and eschatological in orientation. Other leaders in this period included Man tribesmen, a knight-errant (*yu-hsia*), and a first degree scholar; to none of whom are attributed any charismatic powers.[11]

In 875 a bandit leader named Wang Hsien-chih rebelled against the T'ang government at the head of 3,000 men and gave himself the title "Grand General" (Ta chiang-chun). His revolt was soon echoed by Huang Ch'ao, the son of a wealthy salt merchant family, who decided to become a knight-errant after failing several times in the civil service examinations. After Wang was defeated and killed, the remnants of his forces joined Huang, who soon became very powerful. After winning repeated victories the rebel armies captured Ch'ang-an, the capital, in 881, and Huang took such titles as "Great General Who Contends with Heaven" and "Grand General of the National Terrain" and attempted to prove by analysis of the contemporary T'ang reign title, coupled with the progression of the five agents, that his reign was foreordained by Heaven. However, all this is but the traditional claim to the Mandate of Heaven. There is nothing further in the records to indicate concern with divine justification or religious belief. Huang was constantly occupied with economic and military problems and, after taking power, with setting up a mildly reformed administration. Much of his support probably grew out of the intensive suffering of the time, which the *Hsin T'ang shu* says was characterized by "starvation for successive years"[12] in which the people were reduced to eating weed seeds and bark.

This same general lack of concern with religious matters can be seen in the "roving bandit" (*liu-k'ou*) movements of the late Ming period, led by Li Tzu-ch'eng and Chang Hsien-chung. Parsons' research establishes that Chang (d. 1647) was essentially the leader of a force of horse-mounted marauders who tried and failed to make the transition to a stable government on the imperial model. Though Chang believed that he had been given a divine commission to kill by a Taoist deity, which may partially explain his bloodthirsty activities, his other recorded religious beliefs were strictly conventional: casting lots, belief in *feng-shui*, and the slaughter of a horse and ox after a military planning session. There is nothing resembling sectarian evangelistic activity in his work, which was more characterized by mass slaughter of scholars and others who opposed him.[13]

Vincent Shih makes it clear that what ideology Li Tzu-ch'eng employed was traditional and Confucian, involving little more than the Mandate of Heaven belief fortified by divination. When he established his own state in the present Hupei province in 1644, Li took the title Feng-t'ien ch'ang-i ta yüan-shuai, the Great Commander Who Rose in Righteous Movement in the Name of Heaven. When he gave the state examination, the first subject was *T'ien yü chih* (Heaven gave it [the empire] to him).[14] There is nothing here of salvation or anticipation of a messiah.

I have already discussed the difference between "peasant rebellions" and sects and have noted Shao Hsün-cheng's position that "there were a great many large scale peasant wars in Chinese history that had no relation whatsoever to religion." While Shao's position may be an improvement over that of his colleagues, the issue is not between the presence or absence of religion, but between types and degrees of importance. Generalized piety seeking divine assistance for what one believes to be necessary social or political reforms is not the same as specific commitment to a saving deity and seeking to implement its paradise on earth.

The Problem of Secrecy

The term "secret society" was introduced into discussions of Chinese history by modern European and Japanese scholars. As Chesneaux has written, "The Chinese, until the nineteenth century, did not feel the need to underline the secret character of these organizations."[15] Nonetheless, as has been indicated above, this term has become so well entrenched that it has been necessary to deal in some detail with the perspective it represents. Even though the word "secrecy" may not have been used by Chinese officials, it is clear that to them many sectarian activities appeared clandestine. Since these groups were often declared illegal they were understandably concerned to stay away from the authorities. However, it is also possible that the loose structure of imperial authority at the local level in some cases allowed nonviolent popular movements to flourish for years, unknown to officials but widespread among the people. For example, the Ch'ien-lung Emperor commented as follows in 1777, after receiving a report on sectarian activity in Kansu: "The people of the interior presume to establish sects, assemble large groups, set up leaders and plant flags, and [when they] have taken over a whole village, all those who join the sect use white cloth as a symbol [of their allegiance]."[16]

An official report of 1839 states that after first discovering a Wu-sheng lao-mu temple in Chi county of Honan, officials went on to uncover a total of thirty-nine such temples in every county of the province, all of them established in the Ming dynasty, which ended about 200 years before this report was made. Crowds of people were gathered at these temples to offer incense, even though such groups had frequently been prosecuted in Honan before.[17]

In such instances what appeared clandestine to the government was a function of its own lack of information.

This problem is rooted in the absence of central government structure below the county level, coupled with laws prohibiting magistrates from serving in their home districts. As Brian McKnight notes for the Sung, "Local administration [was] spread like a thin film across the surface of rural life."[18] During the Ch'ing at the village level there were local constables, headmen, and gentry families, and even government units for purposes of taxation, but "no formal government of any sort existed below the *chou* [department] and *hsien* [county, district] levels."[19] In this period average county population was 100,000-250,000, a number very difficult to keep under close surveillance.[20] To be sure the district magistrate had subordinates charged with collecting taxes and information, but they could be bribed or intimidated by powerful local interests, including the sects themselves.[21]

Other difficulties of county officials described by Chang Chung-li included insufficient staff, lack of funds, and short terms in office, all of which in some situations could lead to unfamiliarity with local conditions.[22] Though by Ch'ing times there was an elaborate system of local control including monthly village lectures by magistrates and organization of the population into mutual responsibility groups, in many areas this system was not regularly enforced. As a result, information concerning village life could be inadequate, so that some officials perceived the sects as undercover operations, despite the fact that these groups often made no attempt to conceal their activities.[23]

Marjorie Topley has a comment which bears directly on the problem of secrecy in modern scholarly studies of the sects:

The terms "sect" and [secret] "society" are often used interchangeably in the literature. I think it less confusing if the term sect is reserved for groupings which attempt their own ideological synthesis, which are oriented directly to spiritual ends (although they may have intermediary ends which are secular), and have their own priesthood, and the term society is reserved for other types of groupings which may use religious elements, but do not attempt a new synthesis of ideas, have no priesthood and are not directly oriented to religious ends. These differences are brought out clearly if we compare the Triad society with the Great Way sects.[24]

There is no need to rehearse here the evidence for open membership and propagation in the sects. Nevertheless, there are indications that during the nineteenth century some White Lotus related sects were influenced by the Triad society emphasis on secrecy and code characters. For example, the Religion of Completion group distributed sealed rolls of scriptures which contemporary sources indicate were written in code characters impossible for an outsider to understand. This code was formed by putting several characters together to make one conglomerate. These texts were evidently deciphered by use of another, titled *Tzu-mu*, a glossary or vocabulary of the coded characters. The *Tzu-mu* contained some 1,030 characters which were all written in a complex esoteric style.[25] This concern for secrecy is also found in at least some branches of the I-kuan tao, in which Kubo reports, "It is strictly forbidden to divulge secrets of the sect to outsiders. If one does so the god of thunder will smash him to pieces."[26]

However, we have seen that such secrecy and deliberate obscurity are not characteristic and in fact are antithetical to the long sectarian tradition of simplified doctrine and ritual in the vernacular. Despite some amalgamation in the nineteenth century, the sectarian and secret society traditions remained distinct into the mid-twentieth century. In the I-kuan tao, which Kubo and Grootaers call a "secret society," the only membership requirements are to pay a membership fee (*tu-fei*, lit., "salvation fee") and be examined by the sect master. The ritual consists of the Master Evangelist (*tien ch'uan shih* or *pu-chiao shih*) pressing the "dark aperture" (*hsüan-kuan*) of the applicant with his finger,[27] the applicant learning the Five Word Mantra, *Wu-t'ai fo mi-le*, and the making of a mark on his forehead (*yin t'ou*).[28]

Grootaers says that one of the three basic characteristics of the I-kuan tao is "soliciting revelations via the planchette and then propagating their contents," and in all the thirty-one I-kuan tao texts he describes there is not one word enjoining secrecy, not even amid detailed regulations for ritual, administrative responsibilities, and the duties of members. Rather, the faithful are instructed to exhort their parents and families to enter the Way, the rich to aid in propagation, "since the end of the world approaches," and the literate to assist the illiterate in understanding the doctrine. This spirit is summed up in a verse which appears on the cover of most of the scriptures Grootaers collected, after the phrase "not for sale" (*fei mai p'in*): "To widely circulate [this scripture] so that all can see it brings immeasurable merit. There is no greater sin than profaning it or keeping it secret."[29] There is nothing here which enjoins preserving esoteric doctrine from the eyes of the uninitiated. The same can be said for the Hsien-t'ien tao groups studied by Topley. The stress on pious discipline and training in scripture and meditation as one moves up the ranks is no different in essence from the discipline required by any religious body conscious of the integrity of its tradition.

There is little resemblance in all this to the oft-repeated Triad theme "overthrow the Ch'ing and restore the Ming," to "reinstate the Master of Ming upon his throne," or "to avenge ourselves of the wrong done to us."[30] While there are certainly echoes of concern for rebirth and salvation in the Triad initiation ritual, expressed primarily by the transition from Ch'ing (darkness) to Ming (light), the context of this concern is the establishing of a revolutionary brotherhood bound together with thirty-six elaborate oaths, each sanctioned by a painful form of death. Thus, the Master addresses the initiate:

> For what purpose have you come hither?
> To worship the T'ien-ti hui.
> Why do you wish to worship the T'ien-ti hui?
> In order to drive out Ch'ing and restore Ming . . . The people of Ch'ing usurped our patrimony. We desire to restore the Empire and obey the instructions of our leaders. Rising by this clear moon we will raise the banner of patriotism.

The Triad stress on absolute loyalty and secrecy is also distinctive. The initiate vows:

> I . . . will use my best endeavor to overthrow Ch'ing and restore Ming. I also promise to obey the thirty-six laws . . . If I fail to carry out each and every particular of this my solemn obligation, may I perish utterly, and my life be extinguished, even as now I extinguish this incense stick . . .
> Having performed the [initiation] ceremonies, on returning home a brother must not sell the signs and secrets of the Hung brotherhood. If any brother is so shameless, may he be killed by a tiger, or have his eyes bitten out by a snake.[31]

All this ritual is set in an elaborate scenario of death and rebirth, including passing through arches and under crossed swords. Along the way the initiate and all the members present drink a solution containing his blood. He is shown esoteric symbols and taught a variety of secret hand signs and passwords.[32] Though both sects and secret societies were involved in rebellions, and both at times operated openly, it should be clear that they moved in different intentional worlds.

Much work needs to be done before our understanding of Chinese folk Buddhist sects is complete. We need intensive studies of particular groups, studies sensitive to every dimension of the phenomenon, rooted in local history.[33] In addition, there is room for research in those Ming and Ch'ing sectarian *pao-chüan* such as Lo Ch'ing's *wu-pu*, which are still extant in China and Japan. With this and other research perhaps we can eventually develop a thoroughgoing history of the White Lotus tradition in all its aspects. In the meantime we can further explore connections between contemporary groups, such as the various Eternal Mother sects on Taiwan, and earlier manifestations of this type.[34]

Beyond the sects themselves there is the problem of their relationship to the history of orthodox Buddhism and Taoism. De-Groot argues that popular religious associations grew as government intervention cut the people off from means of salvation based in monasteries.[35] Surely this position is oversimplified, but before the issue can be decided we need to know more about how much enforcement of official prohibitions of contact between clergy and laity there actually was. In addition we need more information concerning what orthodox monasteries in the Ming and Ch'ing did to promote the spread of Buddhism among the common people.

We also need to understand more clearly how self-consciously organized sects were related to general popular religion. Were these groups agents of religious change for those beyond the circle of their own members? Did their rituals and mythologies influence nonsectarian cult? Or did such influence move primarily in the opposite direction, as Huang Yü-p'ien maintains?

At a more abstract level sectarian thought needs to be seen as an important dimension of popular intellectual history. What does the Lao-mu myth imply about the situation of man in the world? What does the use of healing charms or hope for Maitreya tell us about the self-understanding of the Chinese peasant? How might such self-understanding have shaped popular response to the impact of Western ideas and technology? There is material here as well for the history of Christian missions in nineteenth century China. How did teachings about Jesus and the church look to one raised in a belief context of mother goddesses, charismatic leaders, and hope for a future savior? More important, how did such a context shape popular interpretation of revolutionary ideas and personalities in the twentieth century? Was the old quest for deliverance imposed on the images of new heroes?

In sum, popular beliefs such as those espoused by folk sects need to be dealt with in a sustained and serious fashion to understand their role in Chinese history and their contribution to world culture. Perhaps in this way we can better understand the inner dynamics of developments now taking place.

Notes
Bibliography
Glossary
Index

Notes

1. Ch'üan Heng (f. 1340-1370), *Keng-shen wai-shih*, 1369 (Shanghai, 1922), pp. 5b-6b. Yüan-chou was in modern I-ch'un county, Kiangsi. P'eng fled north to Ma-ch'eng in Hupei, where he helped launch another uprising in 1351, during the tumultuous last years of the Yüan dynasty. In *Yüan shih* 39:13b a description of this uprising says that Chou Tzu-wang gave himself the title "King of the Chou." For the transcription of Chinese to Western dates in this book I have considered it sufficient to list just years, not months and days.

2. Li Shih-yü, *Hsien-tsai Hua-pei pi-mi tsung-chiao* (Chengtu, 1948), p. 2. However, some Ming dynasty sectarian scriptures have been preserved in Japan and the China mainland.

In romanization of Chinese I have used the modified Wade-Giles system except in the cases of *he* for *ho*, *ke* (*k'e*) for *ko* (*k'o*), and *er* for *erh*, etc., following H. G. Creel in his *Literary Chinese by the Inductive Method*, 3 vols. (Chicago, 1938-1952).

1. Introduction

Issues and Perspective

1. The sectarian tradition devoted primarily to Maitreya was active from approximately 600 to 1800, the White Lotus from the mid-twelfth to the early nineteenth century, the White Cloud for about 200 years after its founding in 1108, and the Lo sect from about 1509 until the twentieth century.

2. C. K. Yang, *Religion in Chinese Society* (Berkeley, 1967), pp. 301, 231.

2. A Case in Point

The Ch'ang-sheng chiao

1. This report appears in the *Shih-liao hsün-k'an*, a thematically organized collection of memorials to the throne in the Ch'ing dynasty (1644-1912) (Peking, 1930-1931), *t'ien* 527-531. Chüeh-lo designates a member of the Manchu imperial clan.

2. From this passage it appears that the sect was named Ch'ang-sheng (lit., "long-life") out of a concern for longevity as well as in honor of its founder. Hsi-an was in western Chekiang, in modern Ch'ü-hsien, while Chia-hsing and Hsiu-shui are both in the northern part of the province, in modern Chia-hsing county.

3. That is, in 1727, forty-two years previous to this report.

4. Wei-t'o, Sanskrit Veda, is a deity of Indian origin responsible for protecting Buddhist teaching and temples.

5. Kuan Kung—a popular god of many functions, chiefly symbolizing loyalty—to the state, army, business, religious associations, etc.

6. The above four phrases are all taken almost verbatim from the Ch'ing law code, itself based on Ming law, and represent a stereotyped official tradition for describing almost any sect. For the Ming code on which this language is based, see *Ming lü chi-chieh fu-li*, "Li lü" (1908 reprint), 11:9b. If the Ch'ang-sheng chiao were to be legally suppressed the reporting official of course had to describe it in terms indicating activities proscribed by law.

7. It is possible, however, that the Ch'ang-sheng chiao was influenced by the Lo-chiao, which was also active in Chekiang and Kiangsu, even though the Lo sect and its texts are not mentioned in this report. One minor indication of this possibility is that the founder's religious name, Wang P'u-shan (lit., "Universal Goodness") is similar to such names in the Lo sect tradition in which *p'u* was also the first element. Sawada Mizuho, in his *Kōchu haja shoben* (Tōkyō, 1972), p. 219, maintains that the Ch'ang-sheng sect was related to the Huang-t'ien tao (Way of Yellow Heaven) which began in the late Ming and continued to flourish in Hopei in the mid-twentieth century. However, in Li Shih-yü's detailed discussion of the Huang-t'ien tao I find no reference to Wang Ch'ang-sheng or the sect in his name, nor to the name P'u-shan. See Li's *Hsien-tsai Hua-pei pi-mi tsung-chiao*, pp. 10-31.

3. History of Interpretation

Rebels, Evangelists, or Both?

1. Pierre Thevenaz, *What Is Phenomenology?* ed. James M. Edie,

trans. James M. Edie, Paul Brockelman and Charles Courtney (Chicago, 1962), pp. 19-29, 50-51.

2. Norman Cohn, *The Pursuit of the Millennium* (London, 1957), pp. 22-29. On pp. 281-286 of the revised and expanded edition of this book (London, 1970), Cohn presents essentially this same perspective in modified language.

3. E.J.Hobsbawm, *Primitive Rebels* (Manchester, 1959), pp. 4-6, 24.

4. Yonina Talmon, "Pursuit of the Millennium: The Relation between Religious and Social Change," quoted in William A. Lessa and Evon Z. Vogt, eds., *Reader in Comparative Religion* (New York, 1965), pp. 523-524, 530-534. It is curious that both Hobsbawm and Talmon deny that millenarian movements appear in Hinduism or Buddhism. See Hobsbawm, *Primitive Rebels*, pp. 57-58, and Talmon, "Pursuit of the Millennium," p. 531. This presumably is due to an uncritical reading of Max Weber.

5. Byron R. Wilson, *Sects and Society* (Berkeley, 1961), pp. 325, 342-343, 4, 353-354. For a recent and more sophisticated treatment by Wilson, see his *Magic and Millennium: A Sociological Study of Religious Movements of Protest among Tribal and Third-world Peoples* (London, 1973). Unfortunately, except for brief mentions of the Taiping and twentieth century groups in Singapore, this important study does not discuss Chinese phenomena.

Werner Stark gives an interesting summary of the class and economic backgrounds of Christian sects in his *Sociology of Religion, II, Sectarian Religion* (London, 1967), pp. 5-37. This book is a detailed presentation of sectarian typology, including causes, leadership, forms of political relationship, organization, etc.

6. Talmon, "Pursuit of the Millennium," p. 536.

7. Joachim Wach, *Sociology of Religion* (Chicago, 1944), p. 203.

8. For a representative statement of Eliade's position, see his "Quest for the Origins of Religion," *History of Religions*, 4:168 (1964).

9. Wach, *Sociology*, pp. 109-111.

10. George H. Williams, *The Radical Reformation* (Philadelphia, 1962), p. 857.

11. Gordon Leff, *Heresy in the Later Middle Ages* (Manchester, 1967), I, 6-11; II, 598.

12. Jeffrey B. Russell, *Dissent and Reform in the Early Middle Ages* (Berkeley, 1965), pp. 232, 231, 102-107, 232-239. In a more recent work Russell continues this methodological discussion and includes long passages from recent European Marxist and idealist students of medieval religious dissent. The book is, Jeffrey B. Russell, ed., *Religious Dissent in the Middle Ages* (New York, 1971), pp. 143-150.

13. Suzuki Chūsei, *Shinchō chūkishi kenkyū* (Tokyo, 1952), pp. 102-103, 116.

14. Tao Hsi-sheng, "Sung-tai te ke chung pao-tung," *Chung-shan wen-hua chiao-yü kuan chi-k'an*, 1:676-679 (Winter 1934).

15. James Legge, trans., "Confucian Analects," bk. 2, ch. 16, in his *The Chinese Classics* (London, 1893-1895), I, 150. Translation modified by me.

16. Legge, trans., "The Works of Mencius," bk. 3, pt. 2, ch. 9, in his *The Chinese Classics*, II, 284.

17. *Li chi*, pt. 3 of the *Texts of Confucianism*, ed. James Legge, in *Sacred Books of the East*, XXVII, ed. F. Max Müller (London, 1885), p. 237. In all this the influence of Legalism and Hsün Tzu should also be kept in mind, the Legalists because of their rigorous proscription of all opinions other than their own in Ch'in, and Hsün Tzu (f. 250 B.C.) because of his overriding concern for rationality and order, which came to influence the *Li chi*. For Hsün Tzu's perspective on nonconforming views, read his fierce attack on those who "recklessly make up new names" in *Hsün Tzu: Basic Writings*, trans. Burton Watson (New York, 1963), pp. 140-141.

18. See for example Hsiao Kung-ch'üan, *Rural China: Imperial Control in the Nineteenth Century* (Seattle, 1960), p. 230, and C. K. Yang, *Religion*, pp. 192-204.

19. C. K. Yang, *Religion*, pp. 197-198.

20. See Marcel Granet, *La Pensée chinoise* (Paris, 1950), pp. 389-418, and W. E. Soothill, *The Hall of Light: A Study of Early Chinese Kingship*, ed. Lady Hosie and G. F. Hudson (London, 1951).

21. For a good summary of official cult functions, see Laurence G. Thompson, *Chinese Religion: An Introduction* (Belmont, California, 1969), pp. 65-77. See also K. C. Hsiao, *Rural China*, pp. 220-223, and Ch'ü T'ung-tsu, *Law and Society in Traditional China* (Paris, 1961), pp. 207-225.

22. *Li chi*, ed. and trans. James Legge, *Sacred Books of the East*, XXVII, ed. F. Max Müller, pp. 116, 225-227.

23. *Ming-lü*, 11:6a-6b, 11b.

24. *Ch'in-ting ta Ch'ing hui-tien shih-li* (1899 ed.), 399:26b.

25. Erik Zürcher, *The Buddhist Conquest of China* (Leiden, 1959), I, 52.

26. Kenneth K. S. Ch'en, *Buddhism in China* (Princeton, 1964), pp. 147-151, 190-194, 226-233; C. K. Yang, *Religion*, p. 122. The usual punishment for monks was defrocking and enforced return to lay life.

27. See, for example, Kenneth K. S. Ch'en, "The Economic Background of the Hui-ch'ang Suppression of Buddhism," *Harvard Journal of Asiatic Studies*, 19:67-105 (June 1956).

28. Zürcher, *Conquest*, I, 256-257; see also Han Yü's (d. 824) "An

Inquiry on the Way," in Wing-tsit Chan, ed., *A Sourcebook in Chinese Philosophy* (Princeton, 1963), pp. 454-455, where he says of the Buddhists and Taoists, "They destroy the natural principles of human relations . . . [and] take the ways of barbarism and elevate them above the teachings of our ancient kings."

29. In actual practice there were, of course, some factors which tended to mitigate the distinction between official and popular cult. In the first place, the local landed gentry participated in both popular and Confucian traditions at the same time, with the same leader perhaps cooperating with the district magistrate in tax collection and also serving as director of a village temple. These gentry, together with the whole middle level of merchants, artisans, and rich peasants made Chinese society and religion more interrelated than the above quotes indicate.

In addition, Confucianism itself was rarely as rational and secular in its concerns as the view from classical texts might suggest. Not only did officials perform a variety of required public religious rituals, but they also believed in fate, practiced divination and geomancy, and prayed to Wench'ang, the God of Literature, for success in civil service examinations. C. K. Yang has stressed that the Confucians shared many ideas about Heaven and fate with the common people, and that there was constant interchange through such activities as the collecting of folk tales by members of the elite. On this see his *Religion*, pp. 244-277.

However, though some Confucian-oriented officials were personally open to aspects of popular religious thought and practice, they rarely approved of groups organized around particular deities, especially those with messianic propensities. The combination of messianism and new organization implied an alternative sociocosmic order which could not be accepted by those with official responsibility for the existing arrangement, centered on family, village, and state.

30. *Ta Yüan t'ung-chih t'iao-ke* (Taipei, 1968), 29: 16b. Reprint of early Ming manuscript edition.

31. *Ta Ch'ing hui-tien*, 399: 5a-5b. This passage is dated 1739.

32. *Ming-lü*, "Li lü," 11:9b. This section goes on to prohibit adorning images of the gods and carrying them in processions. *Ming-lü*, 18:6a-6b, also prohibits heretical books: "All those are to be beheaded who write heretical prognostication books and heretical teachings, using them to confuse the people. If there are those who possess and conceal [such] heretical books, and do not deliver them to the officials, they are to be given 100 strokes and banished three years."

33. *Ming T'ai-tsu shih-lu*, ed. Yao Kuang-hsiao (1335-1419), (Nankang, 1962-1968), 53:3b.

34. *Ta Ch'ing hui-tien*, 399:24b.

35. *San-kuo chih*, ed. Ch'en Shou (233-297), and others, (Peking,

1960), 8:264, biography of Chang Lu. The comment in question was written by P'ei Sung-chih (372-451) in his commentary on the San-kuo chih.

36. Sung Min-ch'iu (1019-1079), ed., T'ang ta chao-ling chi, chüan 113, K'ai-yüan 3, 11th month, 17th day.

37. Yüan shih, ed. Sung Lien (1310-1381), (Taipei, 1966-1967), vol. 1, chüan, 39, p. 329; Ming T'ai-tsung shih-lu, ed. Yao Kuang-hsiao (Nan-kang, 1962-1968), 94:6; Ming ta-cheng tsuan-yao, ed. T'an Hsi-ssu (1895), 60:24b. See also Ming Ying-tsung shih-lu, ed. Yao Kuang-hsiao (Nankang, 1962-1968), 277:15a, for a similar reference to "coercion," dated 1457.

38. Lien Tzu-ning, Lien Chung-ch'eng chin ch'uan chi, in P'an Hsi-en, ed., Ch'ien-k'un cheng ch'i chi (1848), 186:22a. See also Li Shou-k'ung, "Ming-tai Pai-lien chiao k'ao lüeh," in Pao Tsun-p'eng, ed., Ming-tai tsung-chiao, in Pao Tsun-p'eng, ed., Ming-shih lun-ts'ung (Taipei, 1968), 10:18.

39. Ming T'ai-tsu shih-lu, 81:1b. This report is dated 1373. Lo-t'ien county is in the eastern end of Hupei province. See also Li Shou-k'ung, "Ming-tai Pai-lien chiao," p. 31.

40. Ming lü, "Li lü," 11:9b-10a. The first Ming prohibition of these sects came in 1370, two years after the founding of the dynasty. Here Ming law goes back to the words of T'ai-tsu himself, including the terms "White Lotus society," "White Cloud school," "writing charms," etc. See: Ming T'ai-tsu shih-lu, 53:3a-3b. The laws against overt rebellion were more severe. See Ming lü, 18:1a-1b.

41. Ta Ch'ing lü-li hui-chi pien-lan (Hupei, 1872), "Li lü," 16:13a, 14a. For extensive English translations of relevant sections of the Ch'ing code, see J. J. M. DeGroot, Sectarianism and Religious Persecution in China (Amsterdam, 1903), I, 137-148.

42. Ming shih, ed. Chang T'ing-yü and others, 1739 (Taipei, 1962), vol. 4, chüan 226, pp. 2605-2606. Another dimension of official awareness of legitimate reasons for popular protest can be found in criticisms of cruel and corrupt administrators which appear in authorized historical records. On this see Sawada Mizuho, Kōchu haja shōben, "Introduction," p. 25, and K. C. Hsiao, Rural China, pp. 434-444, 466-470.

43. T'ao Hsi-sheng describes several such incidents in his "Ming-tai Mi-le Pai-lien chiao chi ch'i-t'a te yao-tsei," Shih huo, 1.9:48-50 (1935). Examples of cases in which followers were released will be cited below. Advocacy of this practice goes back at least as far as Hsün Tzu, who wrote, "In carrying out punitive expeditions, [the king's army] does not punish the common people; it punishes those who lead the common people astray," in Hsün Tzu, trans. Burton Watson, p. 67.

44. Li Shou-k'ung, "Ming-tai Pai-lien chiao," p. 33.

45. The standard treatments of Chinese historiography in English are Charles S. Gardner, Chinese Traditional Historiography (Cambridge, Mass, 1938), and W. G. Beasley and E. G. Pulleyblank, eds., Historians of

China and Japan (London, 1961). For a recent summary of pre-Republican attitudes toward peasant rebellions, see James P. Harrison, *The Communists and Chinese Peasant Rebellions* (New York, 1969), chap. 4, "Pre-1949 Interpretations," pp. 62-80.

46. Huang Yü-p'ien, *P'o-hsieh hsiang-pien* (1883 reprint), preface to 1834 edition, pp. 1b-2. Huang collected these texts in the three Hopei districts which he served as magistrate between 1830-1842, Ch'ing-he, Chü-lu and Ts'ang-chou (modern Ts'ang county). The four books, which total 6 chüan, are titled *P'o-hsieh hsiang-pien* (1834); *Hsü-k'an p'o-hsieh hsiang-pien* (1839; A continuation . . .); *Yu-hsü p'o-hsieh hsiang-pien* (1841; A further continuation . . .); and *San-hsü p'o-hsieh hsiang-pien* (1841; A third continuation . . .). The first contains three chüan, the latter three one chüan each. The complete text of all six chüan can be found in Sawada Mizuho, *Kōchu haja shōben*. Huang himself was from Kansu and as an administrator was noted for his support of education and his destruction of heretical temples. For a brief but detailed biography see Sawada, *Kōchu haja shōben*, "Introduction," pp. 18-22. Huang published and distributed his books at his own expense.

47. Huang Yü-p'ien, *Hsu-k'an p'o-hsieh hsiang-pien* (1883 reprint), 1:10b, 34b-35a. The work Huang cites is Tsung Wan-hua, *Hsieh-chiao yin-pao lu* (A record of heretical religion being requited in hell), written in 1825. Tsung's father, a member of an unnamed sect, had been executed in 1777, after which Wan-hua himself proceeded to urge people everywhere to turn away from heresy.

48. Huang Yü-p'ien, *P'o-hsieh*, 1:8b, 2:9. *Pao-chüan* is a general name for folk sect scriptures, discussed below.

49. Ibid., 1:12b, 22. The Eternal Mother (Wu-sheng lao-mu), who presides over a paradise called the "Native Land," was the chief deity of the Ming and Ch'ing White Lotus tradition. Her children were Fu-hsi and Nü-kua, who in turn gave birth to mankind.

50. Ibid., 1:2, 3:21-24b. The quoted passage is on p. 24b.

51. Ibid., 2:10a-11b.

52. Their position will be discussed below under "dualist" approaches.

53. Harrison, in his *Communists and Chinese Peasant Rebellions*, pp. 80-85, attributes this shift in Republican historiography to consolidation of the Kuomintang position after 1928.

54. T'ao Hsi-sheng, "Ming-tai Mi-le Pai-lien chiao," pp. 46-52.

55. Ibid., p. 46.

56. T'ao Hsi-sheng, "Sung-tai te ke-chung pao-tung," p. 671.

57. T'ao Hsi-sheng, "Yüan-tai Mi-le Pai-lien chiao-hui te pao-tung," *Shih huo*, 1.4:36 (1935).

58. Li Shou-k'ung, "Ming-tai Pai-lien chiao," p. 18.

59. Chan is now at the University of Washington in Seattle, and formerly taught at Auckland and Columbia; he was earlier on the faculty

of the University of Hong Kong. This background, plus his treatment of the subject, led to his being discussed here as a "non-Marxist Chinese."

60. Tai Hsüan-chih, "Pai-lien chiao te pen-chih," *Shih-ta hsüeh-pao*, 12:119, 122, 123, 125 (June 1967).

61. Chan Hok-lam, "The White Lotus-Maitreya Doctrine and Popular Uprisings in Ming and Ch'ing China," *Sinologica*, 10:211-233 (1969).

62. Liang Ch'i-ch'ao, *Fo-hsüeh yen-chui shih-pa p'ien* (Taipei, 1966), p. 12. (First published in Shanghai in 1936) and Ch'en, *Buddhism*, p. 76.

63. Shan-tao, "Lin-chung wang-sheng cheng-nien wen," in Wang Jih-hsiu (d. 1173), ed., *Lung-shu Ching-t'u wen*, chüan 12, "Appendix," *Taishō shinshū Daizōkyō* (Tōkyō, 1929), 47, 287.

64. Tsung-chien, *Shih-men cheng-t'ung* (1237), "P'ai wei," in *Hsü tsang-ching* (Hongkong, 1946), 130, 413a. The title of this section means "rejecting falsehood."

Yu-t'an P'u-tu (f. 1300-1312), in his *Lien-tsung pao-chien*, chüan 4, also discusses a number of heterodox tendencies: "Ignorant and benighted people all fall into heretical teachings even though the orthodox path is available to them. [Thus, heterodox] associations arise . . . each attacking the other." P'u-tu's list of such groups includes "those who pretend they can communicate with gods and spirits" and those who say that the Pure Land school is only for the laity, while the Śākyamuni school is for those who have left the household life. He also complains about the use of such orthodox terms as *p'u* (universal) and *tao* in heterodox teaching. *Taishō*, 47, 320. (This P'u-tu should not be confused with Ching-shan Hsü-chou P'u-tu, whose dates are 1199-1280.)

65. Cited in P'u-tu, *Lien-tsung pao-chien*, chüan 7 in *Taishō*, 47 336. The problem of Mao's relationship to the White Lotus tradition will be discussed in Chapter 5.

66. Tsung-pen (f. 1550), *Kuei-yüan chih-chih chi* (1553), chüan 1, in *Hsü tsang-ching*, 108, 119a-120a. Tsung-pen was from a monastery on Mount Ssu-ming near Ningpo in Chekiang province. He should not be confused with the Northern Sung monk of the same name who lived between 1020-1099 in what is now Kiangsu province.

67. Chu-hung, *Chu ch'uang er pi*, "Lien-she," p. 23a, in *Yün-ch'i fa-hui* (Chin-ling, 1897), vol. 4. Chu-hung was right. There is no historical connection between the orthodox meditation society founded by Hui-yüan in 402 and the twelfth-century Lotus sect. However, there is an indirect typological connection in that Mao Tzu-yüan took the name Pai-lien heshang (White Lotus monk) in imitation of the Mount Lu model. In this he was part of a general Sung rediscovery and admiration of the earlier group. This will be discussed further below. See also T'ao Hsi-sheng, "Yüan-tai Mi-le Pai-lien chiao-hui," p. 39.

68. Chu-hung, *Cheng e chi*, "Wu-wei chüan," pp. 19a-19b, in *Yün-ch'i fa-hui*, vol. 4. See also Tsukamoto Zenryū, "Rakyō no seiritsu to

ryūden ni tsuite," *Tōhō gakuhō*, 17:28 (November 1949).

69. Kitagawa makes a similar distinction between orthodox Buddhists and the *ubasoku* in Japan: "The problem was not so much a question of orthodoxy versus unorthodoxy . . . as of two diametrically opposed ways of understanding the nature of charisma, soteriology and eschatology." See Joseph M. Kitagawa, *Religion in Japanese History* (New York, 1966), p. 41.

70. *Ming shih*, vol. 3, chüan 149, p. 1833, and chüan 183, p. 2149. Li Tao-ming is also discussed in T'ao Hsi-sheng, "Ming-tai Mi-le Pai-lien chiao," p. 48.

71. *Ta Ch'ing shih-ch'ao sheng-hsün, Jen-tsung*, (1879), 98:4a-b. These comments are very similar to the emperor's "Hsieh-chiao shuo," in Shih Ssu, ed., *K'an-ching chiao-fei shu-pien* (1880), "Introduction," pp. 1-2b. See also DeGroot, *Sectarianism*, II, 368-369. The term "Niu-pa" was considered subversive because the two characters together form "Chu," the surname of the Ming royal house.

72. The Chia-ch'ing Emperor, "Hsieh-chiao shuo," in Shih Ssu, ed., *K'an-ching chiao-fei shu-pien*, "Introduction," p. 2.

73. For Susan Naquin's comments on this issue see her excellent and detailed doctoral dissertation, "Millenarian Rebellion in China: The Eight Trigrams Uprising of 1813" (Yale, 1974), pp. 25, 44, 284-285. This dissertation is to be published by Yale University Press, with the same title.

On general characteristics of charismatic leadership, see Max Weber, "Religious Rejections of the World and Their Directions," in H. H. Gerth and C. Wright Mills, eds., *From Max Weber* (New York, 1946), pp. 246-249, where he writes, "[The charismatic leader] . . . demands obedience and a following by virtue of his mission. His success determines whether he finds them. His charismatic claim breaks down if his mission is not recognized . . . His power rests upon this purely factual recognition [of his mission and power] and springs from faithful devotion." I have seen the validity of this interpretation in the Taiwan Religion of Compassion sect, in which the members of a Taipei branch fervently affirm the healing power of their leader. This trust he accepts in a modest and matter of fact way.

74. Suzuki, *Shinchō*, pp. 109, 113.

75. Chia-ch'ing Emperor, "Hsieh-chiao shuo," in Shih Ssu, ed., *K'an-ching chiao-fei shu-pien*, "Introduction," p. 1.

76. This will be discussed in Chapter 7.

77. Suzuki, *Shinchō*, p. 122.

78. T'ao Ch'eng-chang, "Chiao-hui yüan-liu k'ao" (Canton, 1910), in Hsiao I-shan, ed., *Chin-tai pi-mi she-hui shih-liao* (Peking, 1935), chüan 2, appendix, pp. 2, 3b, 7b.

79. Hsiao I-shan, "Tien-ti hui ch'i-yüan k'ao," in Hsiao I-shan, ed., *Chin-tai pi-mi she-hui* (Peking, 1935), chüan *shou*, pp. 1b, 3.

80. Tai Hsüan-chih, "Pai-lien chiao te pen-chih," pp. 119-121. The

point concerning Manichaean influence is a bit ambiguous, for while there is no doubt that in 1351 Han Lin-er's title Hsiao Ming-wang (Lesser King of Light) was eschatological, by Ch'ing times there was the whole Ming dynasty to look back on. Tai neglects to point out that in 1813 Li Wen-ch'eng's chosen title, Ta Ming t'ien-shun (Ruler of the Great Ming Heavenly Harmony), incorporated a Ming dynasty reign title, T'ien-shun, which indicates to me, at least, some conscious appropriation of the Ming as a political model. I am gratified that Susan Naquin confirms this by pointing out that Li deliberately appropriated T'ien-shun, the reign title of the Ming emperor Ying-tsung, but at the same time also claimed to be a reincarnation of the late Ming rebel leader Li Tzu-ch'eng. On this, see her "Eight Trigrams," pp. 117, 262.

81. On this point it is instructive to note that in his *Chin-tai pi-mi she-hui,* 1:4a, Hsiao I-shan indicates that his purpose in writing this article was to strengthen China's sense of national consciousness in a time of turmoil.

82. For a detailed discussion of Marxist interpretations, see Harrison, *The Communists and Chinese Peasant Rebellions,* esp. pp. 140-189.

83. Sun Tso-min, "Chung-kuo nung-min chan-cheng he tsung-chiao te kuan-hsi," in Sun Tso-min, ed., *Chung-kuo nung-min chan-cheng wen-ti t'an-so* (Shanghai, 1956), pp. 73, 76, 79-88. The last quote here is from p. 88.

84. Yang K'uan, "Lun Chung-kuo nung-min chan-cheng chung ke-ming ssu-hsiang te tso-yung chi ch'i yü tsung-chiao te kuan-hsi," in Shih Shao-pin, ed., *Chung-kuo feng-chien she-hui nung-min chan-cheng wen-t'i t'ao-lun chi* (Peking, 1962), pp. 329-330, 321-323, 330-332, 334.

85. Shao Hsün-cheng, "Pi-mi she-hui, tsung-chiao he nung-min chan-cheng," in Shih Shao-pin, ed., *Chung-kuo feng-chien she-hui,* pp. 369-378. The last quote here is from p. 378.

86. Shigematsu Shunshō, "Ch'u-ch'i te Pai-lien chiao-hui," trans. T'ao Hsi-sheng, *Shih huo,* 1:143 (1935).

87. Shigematsu Shunshō, "Sō Gen jidai no Byakuun shūmon," *Shien,* 2:54 (1930).

88. Suzuki Chūsei, "Sōdai Bukkyō kessha no kenkyū," *Shigaku zasshi,* 52:309, 312 (1941).

89. Richard Yung-deh Chu, "An Introductory Study of the White Lotus Sect in Chinese History," Ph. D. diss., Columbia University, 1967, pp. 176-178, "Abstract," and p. 1.

90. Chan, Hok-lam, "White Lotus," p. 220.

91. Richard Chu, "White Lotus Sect," pp. 200, 192, 113, 199, 14-25, 35-47.

92. Quoted in DeGroot, *Sectarianism,* I, 256-257.

93. Joseph Edkins, *Chinese Buddhism* (London, 1893), p. 379. See also his article, "Religious Sects in North China," *Chinese Recorder,*

17.7:251 (July 1886), where he writes, "The White Lily sect still exists as a religion without any political importance whatever. The followers of this religion, once so famous, live quietly without proselytizing, two or three families together. They may be found in the neighborhood of Te-cheu in Shantung."

94. DeGroot, *Sectarianism*, I, 169, 90, 121, 175, 161, 252-253.

95. Max Weber has an insightful discussion of the relationship between official and popular religion and of sects and persecution in his *The Religion of China*, ed. and trans. Hans H. Gerth (New York, 1951), pp. 173-174, 213-255. However, a discussion of Weber's interpretation would necessarily involve his whole approach to Chinese religion, which is beyond the scope of this study. Suffice it to mention that Weber, partly due to the sources available to him, consistently overemphasizes the actual impact of Confucian rationalism on Chinese life. Such statements as "the emergence of prophetic religiosity was completely inhibited" (p. 209) cannot be supported.

96. DeGroot, *Sectarianism*, I, 14-15; II, 335-336.

97. Tsukamoto Zenryū, "Rakyō no seiritsu to ryūden ni tsuite," *Tōho gakuhō*, 17:28, 31, 33, 14 (1949).

98. Suzuki, *Shinchō*, pp. 98-103.

99. Yano Jinichi, "Kuan-yü Pai-lien chiao chih luan," trans. Yang T'ieh-fu, *Jen-wen yüeh-k'an*, 6:1-20 (February-March 1935).

100. Suzuki, *Shinchō*, pp. 104-105, 116, 119, 121, 123. On p. 121 Suzuki states that religious belief was the central cohesive factor among sect members, but that mutual economic aid was also important.

101. C.K. Yang, *Religion*, pp. 112, 230, 240, 231, 144-217, 224-227.

4. Cross-Cultural Perspectives

1. Chan Wing-tsit, *Religious Trends in Modern China* (New York, 1953), pp. 158-159, and Jean Chesneaux, *Secret Societies in China*, trans. Gillian Nettle (Ann Arbor, 1971), p. 36. For similar recent statements see Ch'en, *Buddhism*, pp. 426-427, and Wilfred Blythe, *The Impact of Chinese Secret Societies in Malaya* (London, 1969), pp. 19-21.

2. It is perhaps instructive to note that the interpretations of Chan, Chesneaux and Blythe all date back to the early twentieth century. They reflect very closely the language of T'ao Ch'eng-chang (d. 1911) in his "Chiao-hui yüan-liu k'ao" (cited above).

3. Edwin M. Loeb, "Tribal Initiations and Secret Societies," *University of California, Publications in American Archaeology and Ethnology* (1929), 25:250.

4. Hutton Webster, *Primitive Secret Societies* (New York, 1908), pp. 16-43.

5. While women did not hold office in the Triad society, there is

some evidence that they were admitted as members in a separate, private ceremony. J. S. M. Ward and W. G. Stirling, *The Hung Society or Society of Heaven and Earth* (London, 1925), III, 128-129.

6. Shih Ssu, *K'an-ching chiao-fei shu-pien*, 11:12b. Here we read that several hundred men with their whole families joined Hsü T'ien-te's movement in Szechwan between 1796 and 1802.

7. Loeb, "Tribal Initiations," p. 249. See also Mircea Eliade, *Birth and Rebirth: Rites and Symbols of Initiation*, trans. Willard R. Trask (New York, 1958), pp. 72-79.

8. Webster, *Primitive Secret Societies*, pp. 40-42, 95, 78.

9. Wach, *Sociology*, p. 114.

10. Ward and Stirling, *The Hung Society*, I, 53-107, 108-131. In what I say throughout concerning differences between the Triad or T'ien-ti hui tradition and the sects it should be understood that the category of secrecy applies only to ritual and myth, and in some cases to membership, not to the existence or public activities of the group. Philip Kuhn has demonstrated that in the mid-ninteenth century some Triad associations operated openly as systems of local order, alongside those established by the government. In addition, there were times when so-called secret societies launched full-scale military attacks several thousand strong, captured towns, and carried out mass initiations in broad daylight. Of course, in both sects and societies, local groups were concerned with local issues as well as with more general theoretical concerns expressed in their texts, and individuals might join for a variety of personal reasons.

On public activities of Triad groups, see Philip A. Kuhn, *Rebellion and Its Enemies in Late Imperial China* (Cambridge, Mass., 1970), pp. 165-180, and Frederic Wakeman, Jr., "The Secret Societies of Kwangtung, 1800-1856," in Jean Chesneaux, ed., *Popular Movements and Secret Societies in China* (Stanford, 1972), pp. 32, 38.

11. Webster, *Primitive Secret Societies*, p. 27.

12. R. F. Fortune, *Omaha Secret Societies* (New York, 1932), pp. 46-47.

13. Norman MacKenzie, *Secret Societies* (New York, 1967), p. 14.

14. Georg Simmel, "The Sociology of Secrecy," *American Journal of Sociology* (January 1906), 11:470-490.

15. MacKenzie, *Secret Societies*, pp. 15-18.

16. B. Favre, *Les Sociétés Secrètes en Chine* (Paris, 1933), p. 24. See also Yang, *Religion*, p. 213, "The severest political blow was aimed at the heterodox religious societies . . . By legal threats and actual persecutions, popular religious organizations and movements were driven underground. To this day these organizations carry a degree of secrecy, regarding legal authorities as a natural enemy."

17. Wach, *Sociology*, pp. 120-121.

18. W. K. C. Guthrie, *The Greeks and Their Gods* (Boston, 1950),

pp. 267-268, and Franz Cumont, *Oriental Religions in Roman Paganism* (New York, 1956, reprint of 1911 ed.), pp. 27-28.

19. Simmel, "The Sociology of Secrecy," pp. 471, 483-484.

20. Wach, *Sociology*, p. 126.

21. Franz Cumont, *The Mysteries of Mithra*, trans. Thomas J. McCormack (New York, 1956, reprint of 1902 ed.), pp. 152-161.

22. Apuleius, *Metamorphosis*, Book 11, v. 1-25, in Frederick C. Grant, *Hellenistic Religions* (Indianapolis, 1953), pp. 141-142.

23. Cumont, *Oriental Religions*, p. 100.

24. Plutarch, *On the Soul*, Book 2, in Grant, *Hellenistic Religions*, p. 148.

25. Chan Wing-tsit, *A Sourcebook in Chinese Philosophy* (Princeton, 1963), p. 397.

26. Ch'en, *Buddhism*, p. 312.

27. Grant, *Hellenistic Religions*, pp. xxxiii, xxvii.

28. Paul Ricoeur, *The Symbolism of Evil*, trans. Emerson Buchanan (New York, 1967), p. 11.

29. However, I have come across some discussions of unnamed pre-Triad groups which were concerned with ritual secrecy, and there may be others. The first is mentioned by P'u-tu in his *Lien-tsung pao-chien* (1305), in *Taishō*, 47, 348-349, section titled "Pien fo-fa yin-ts'ang" (Disputing that the Buddhist dharma is hidden in secret). The second reference is in Tsung-pen's *Kuei-yüan chih-chih chi*, chüan 1, in *Hsü tsang ching*, 108, 118-119.

P'u-tu writes: "[While] the Buddhist dharma is a teaching which has appeared [openly] in the midst of the world . . . there are some confused people who do not understand [this] and say that it is hidden in secret . . . There are ignorant folk who recklessly say that . . . there are hidden Buddhist scriptures. They falsely employ scattered heretical teachings, which they transmit behind closed doors, calling them 'the mysterious classics of life and death,' thus deluding and confusing others." In chüan 4, p. 320, of *Taishō*, vol. 47, P'u-tu also berates those who "speak of secret mysteries which are transmitted in hidden ways."

Tsung-pen, another Pure Land scholar, continues this attack on un-specified heretics who "gather at night and disperse during the day, treacherously claiming that . . . the Buddhist dharma is hidden in secret, and that one should blow out the candles and teach its wonderful truths in the dark. They say that, 'If you follow our teachings, in seven days you will become enlightened.' They instruct those who enter their groups to swear an oath which is presented to the Emperor of Heaven by being burned, saying that only thus do they achieve salvation. But outsiders are not permitted to know of this 'sublime and excellent matter.' [The disciples] are told that if they reveal Heaven's secrets they will certainly fall into hell. Before this ceremony they make sure the coast is clear in front and back of the house, for they are afraid the neighbors might see or hear what is going on."

Suzuki Chūsei in his "Sōdai Bukkyō," p. 315, says of these passages
that they are part of a general influence on the White Lotus by the concern
for a close relationship between master and disciple which characterizes
Ch'an Buddhism and some aspects of Taoism. Both of these traditions
stressed personal transmission of esoteric material, whether of Ch'an wisdom or Taoist magical techniques.

In the *Na Wen-i-kung ch'u-jen Chih-li tsung-tu tsou-i* by Na-Yen-
ch'eng (1764-1833), ed. Jung An (b. 1788) (Taipei, 1968), 41:43b, there is a
brief reference to secrecy in a description of the meditation ritual of the
San-yüan chiao in Hopei, Luan-chou (modern Luan-hsien) dated 1816:
"Sect members are warned that while they are worshipping and meditating
they should not let others watch them." However, since no details are
given, we cannot be sure if this was ritual secrecy or simply fear of discovery.

There is also a reference to secrecy in an initiation ritual of the nine-
teenth-century Lung-hua sect in Amoy as described by DeGroot in his *Sectarianism*, I, 213. Here, however, secrecy refers not to the rite itself, but to
not revealing the name of the sect leader to outsiders. Since private religious consecration had long been illegal, this stress on caution is perhaps
related to the ever-present threat of police action.

See also the comments about secrecy in Lo sect meditation ritual in
Chapter 8.

30. H. R. Niebuhr, *The Social Sources of Denominationalism* (New
York, 1929), p. 17, and Ernst Troeltsch, *The Social Teaching of the Chris-
tian Churches*, I, 331-343, in Louis Schneider, ed., *Religion, Culture and
Society* (New York, 1964), pp. 457-461.

31. Wach, *Sociology*, p. 197.

32. Many interesting similarities can also be found in Burmese
gaings, esoteric sects combining Buddhist and folk beliefs, led by charismatic figures sometimes considered to be incarnations of the Universal Emperor or of the Future Buddha. *Gaing* parallels to Chinese groups will be
mentioned in Chapter 7.

33. Kitagawa, *Religion in Japanese History*, pp. 131-132. Of course
there was political division in Chinese history as well, but the imperial
ideal and its supporting institutions, once formulated in the Han dynasty,
were never forgotten. This ideal included unification of thought as well as
society, guided by a literate elite. Even states governing only a fragment of
the empire aspired to maintain imperial traditions, including opposition to
nonrecognized religions.

34. Sir Charles Eliot, *Japanese Buddhism* (London, 1935), p. 306.

35. Leff, *Heresy*, II, 456-459.

36. Eliot, *Japanese Buddhism*, pp. 376-379.

37. Thomas A. Lindsay, *A History of the Reformation* (New York,
1906), I, 135, 100.

38. Russell, *Dissent and Reform*, p. 62.

39. Leff, *Heresy*, II, 463. It should be said, however, that the Waldensians generally rejected saint worship as superfluous.

40. Hsieh Jung-chih, "Lo chiao yü Ch'ing-pang kuan-hsi chih yen-chiu," *Shih yün*, 132:5 (1968).

41. For an interesting discussion of the relationship of religion and warfare among the English Puritans of the seventeenth century see Michael Walzer, *The Revolution of the Saints* (Cambridge, Mass., 1965). Here all of life was seen as a battle for God and against Satan, the army disciplined after the pattern of the church, and warfare carried out as an expression of divine will. As Walzer writes on p. 12, "The Puritan cleric insisted that political activity was a creative endeavor in which the saints were privileged as well as obliged to participate. Their enthusiastic and purposive activity was part of their religious life, not something distinct and separate: they acted out their saintliness in debates, elections, administration and warfare. Only some sensitivity to religious zeal can make the behavior of the English in the sixteen-forties and fifties explicable."

Puritanism was led by sophisticated organizers and intellectuals, and hence reached levels of articulation beyond that attainable by folk movements. Nevertheless, in seeking to understand the Chinese sects it is perhaps useful to recall this synthesis of faith, politics, and violence, so recent in European history. I am indebted to Ellen Frost (née Ojha) for first telling me of Walzer's book and its perspective.

42. Eliot, *Japanese Buddhism*, p. 295.

43. *Mahāvastu*, I, 52-53, quoted in Emanuel Sarkisyanz, *Buddhist Backgrounds of the Burmese Revolution* (The Hague, 1965), p. 45. The most important Pali source of this theme is the *Cakkavati-sihanada Suttanta* of the *Dīgha-Nikāya*. For the Mahāyāna scriptural background see Edward Conze, trans., *Buddhist Scriptures* (Harmondsworth, 1959), pp. 237-242 (selections for the *Maitreyavyākarana*). This sūtra was translated into Chinese by Chu Fa-hu (Dharmaraksha) between 265 and 275 as the *Fo-shuo Mi-le hsia-sheng ching*, *Taishō*, 14, 421-423.

44. Sarkisyanz, *Buddhist Backgrounds*, pp. 45, 31.

45. Ch'en, *Buddhism*, pp. 124, 150-152. Emperor Wu reigned from 502 to 549. For Sui Wen-ti see Arthur F. Wright, "The Formation of Sui Ideology, 581-604," in John K. Fairbank, ed., *Chinese Thought and Institutions* (Chicago, 1957), pp. 71-104.

46. Ibid., p. 168.

47. Marjorie Topley, "The Great Way of Former Heaven: A Group of Chinese Secret Religious Sects," *Bulletin of the School of Oriental and African Studies*, 26.2:372, 387 (1963).

48. Leff, *Heresy*, I, 13.

49. Williams, *Radical Reformation*, p. 362.

50. For discussions of the relative roles of economic and eschatological factors in Japanese peasant uprisings of the Tokugawa and Meiji periods, see Hugh Borton, *Peasant Uprisings in Japan of the Tokugawa*

Period, 2nd ed. (New York, 1968), and Irwin Scheiner, "The Mindful Peasant: Sketches for a Study of Rebellion," *Journal of Asian Studies* 32: 579-591 (1973). Borton stresses economic deprivation, while Scheiner discusses as well "world renewal" movements, whose members believed that they were "active agents of Maitreya."

51. On this see Lindsay, *Reformation*, I, 334, and Williams, *Radical Reformation*, p. 81.

52. T'ao Ch'eng-chang, "Chiao-hui," p. 86.

53. For Böhm see Lindsay, *Reformation*, I, 99-102, and Leff, *Heresy*, pp. 474-475; for Sun Ta-yu see *Shih-liao hsün-k'an*, t'ien 201-204, 250-254. Sun was from Ching-men in central Hupei.

5. An Outline History of the White Lotus Tradition

1. For Western language summaries, see: Max Kaltenmark, *Lao Tzu and Taoism*, trans. Roger Greaves (Stanford, 1969); Henri Maspero, *Le Taoisme: Mélanges posthumes sur les religions et l'histoire de la Chine*, vol. II (Paris, 1950); Paul M. Michaud, "The Yellow Turbans," *Monumenta Serica*, 17:14-127 (1958); Anna K. Seidel, "The Image of the Perfect Ruler in Early Taoist Messianism: Lao Tzu and Li Hung," *History of Religions*, 9:216-247 (November 1969-February 1970); Michael R. Saso, "The Taoist Tradition in Taiwan," *The China Quarterly*, 41:83-101 (January-March 1970); R. A. Stein, "Remarques sur les mouvements du Taoisme politico-religieux au IIe Siècle ap. J.-C.," *T'oung Pao*, 50.1-3:1-78 (1963); and Holmes Welch, *Taoism: The Parting of the Way* (Boston, 1957).

For a useful Chinese summary, see Wang Tan-ts'en, *Hou Han nung-min ch'i-i* (Shanghai, 1952). Important primary sources are *Hou Han shu*, chüan 71, "Biographies of Huang-fu Sung and Chu Chün," for the Yellow Turbans and *San-kuo chih*, chüan 8, "Biography of Chang Lu," for the Heavenly Master sect. The chief scripture text of the Yellow Turbans was the *T'ai-ping ching* (c. 150 A.D.) which is preserved in part in the *Cheng-t'ung Tao-tsang* (1444-1447), vols. 746-755, in the T'ai-p'ing section. See also Wang Ming, *T'ai-p'ing ching he-chiao* (Peking, 1960) for a modern reconstruction of the early text.

2. Stein, "Mouvements du Taoisme," p. 6.

3. See Stein's article cited above.

4. The distinction between liturgical Taoism and popular religion has been made by K. M. Schipper in Holmes Welch, "The Bellagio Conference on Taoist Studies," *History of Religions*, 9.2 and 3:123-127 (November 1969-February 1970). See also Michael R. Saso, *Taoism and the Rite of Cosmic Renewal* (Pullman, Washington, 1972).

5. It is interesting that for Chinese writers the Yellow Turbans were the fountainhead of all later heretical movements, not only Taoist, but

Manichaean and White Lotus as well. Thus, Chih-p'an (f. 1260-1270) in his *Fo tsu t'ung-chi* calls sectarian Manichaeans "Descendants of the Yellow Turbans" (chüan 48, *Taishō*, 49, 431), and Huang Yü-p'ien writes, "The Yellow Turbans were originators of all the evil of all those who have practiced heresy since antiquity." *Hsü-k'an p'o-hsieh* 1:1b. Thus, for these writers the late Han sect began a specific type of organized dissent.

    6. Jacques Gernet, *Daily Life In China*, trans. H. M. Wright (New York, 1962), pp. 208-210. While Gernet's translation of the character *mo* here as "demon" is literally correct, it is theoretically confusing, since Manichaeans oppose the devil, not worship him. Perhaps the character *mo* for devil was substituted by hostile writers for the *mo* which was the first of two characters used to transliterate Mani into Chinese (*mo-ni*). On this point see Vincent Y. C. Shih, *The Taiping Ideology* (Seattle, 1967), p. 348.

    7. Edouard Chavannes and Paul Pelliot, "Un Traité manichéen retrouvé en Chine," pt. 2, *Journal Asiatique*, 2.1:147, 171, 261, 284, 303 (1913). The Manichaeans were proscribed at the same time that Buddhism was suppressed in 841-845.

    Tsung-chien, in his *Shih-men cheng-t'ung*, chüan 4, gives a long and detailed summary of Manichaean beliefs and activities, including the names of texts and leaders, a discussion of Persian origins, and an account of progress and suppression in China. After noting that during the Hui-ch'ang period many Manichaean temples were destroyed and their clergy killed or returned to lay life, he adds, "However, they were not completely wiped out, and in time divided up and spread everywhere." *Hsü tsang-ching*, 130, 412b. For a recent treatment of this topic, see Antonio Forte, "Deux Études sur le Manichéisme chinois," *T'oung Pao*, 59:220-253 (1973).

    8. Chih-p'an, *Fo tsu*, chüan 54, *Taishō*, 49, 474-475. This passage is translated in French in Chavannes and Pelliot, "Un Traité manichéen," pp. 320-321. Ch'en-chou was in modern Hsiang-ch'eng county in central Honan.

    9. Fang Ch'ing-ying, "Pai-lien chiao te yüan-liu chi ch'i he Mo-ni chiao te kuan-hsi," *Li-shih chiao-hsüeh wen-t'i*, 5:34-38 (1959).

    10. Wu Han, "Ming chiao yü ta Ming ti-kuo," in his *Tu shih tsa-chi* (Peking, 1956), pp. 268-269. Wu Han makes it clear that the term Ming chiao (Religion of Light) refers to Manichaeism (p. 237). Wen-chou was in modern Yung-chia county of Chekiang; Ch'üan-chou in Min-hou county of Fukien.

    11. For discussions of Manichaeism in English, see A. V. Williams Jackson, *Researches in Manichaeism* (New York, 1932) and George Widengren, *Mani and Manichaeism*, trans. Charles Kessler (London, 1965).

    12. Chih-p'an, *Fo tsu*, chüan 48, *Taishō*, 49, 431.

    13. See Edwin O. Reischauer, *Ennin's Travels in T'ang China* (New York, 1955), section on "Maigre Feasts," pp. 177-183.

    14. Hsing Yüeh, "Sung-tai te Ming chiao yü nung-min ch'i-i," *Li-shih chiao-hsüeh*, 6:41 (June 1959).

15. The Manichaean sects were evidently well organized. Despite numerous official prohibitions, in the twelfth century there were over forty Manichaean temples (Ming-chiao chai-t'ang) in one prefecture alone in what is now Chekiang province. In 1134 an official reported that, despite severe prosecution following the defeat of a Manichaean uprising led by Fang-la in 1120, "[We] have still not been able to completely prevent the common people from becoming Manichaeans . . . I have heard that in each village there are two or three crafty types who are called Manichaean chiefs (Mo t'ou). These men record the names of all the villagers, who then take oaths to form associations. None of these Manichaeans eat meat, and when one of their families has trouble, all the other members join together to help them." Li Hsin-ch'uan, *Chien-yen i-lai hsi-nien yao-lu*, chüan 76, pp. 1248-1249, in the Peking 1956 reprint, cited in Tai Hsüan-chih, "Pai-lien chiao te yüan-lui," *Chung-kuo hsüeh-chih*, 5:311 (1969). The reference to Manichaean temples can be found on the same page of this article by Professor Tai.

16. Chih-p'an, *Fo tsu*, chüan 48, in *Taishō*, 49, 431. The *Lao Tzu hua hu ching* is in *Taishō*, 54, 1267-1270. I have not been able to find these references in Hung Mai's extant writings.

17. *Taishō*, 54, 1279-1280. See also the study of this text by G. Haloun and W. B. Henning, "The Compendium of the Doctrines and Styles of the Teaching of Mani, the Buddha of Light," *Asia Major*, 3:184-212 (1953).

18. Jackson, *Manichaeism*, p. 13. On this see also Paul Pelliot, "Les Traditions manichéennes au Fou-kien," *T'oung Pao*, 22:193-208 (1923). On p. 196 Pelliot quotes a Ming description of Manichaeism which says, "Their religion is called 'Luminous' (*Ming*); they wear white clothing; in the morning they worship the sun and in the evening worship the moon."

19. *Shih-liao*, t'ien 991.

20. T'o Chin and others, eds., *Ch'in-ting p'ing-ting chiao-fei chi-lüeh* (n.p., 1816), 26:24. There is another reference to sun worship, dated 1815 in the *Na Wen-i kung tsou-i*, 38:73b, where we are told that sectarians who recited the White Lotus mantra also "kowtow facing the sun, every morning to the east, noon to the south and evening toward the west." This group was active in Fu-ch'eng county in southeastern Hopei.

Henri Doré, in his *Researches into Chinese Superstitions*, trans. M. Kennelly (Shanghai, 1914), V, 518-523, provides more details of such worship a century later: "Members of Vegetarian Sects are frequently devout worshippers of the sun." He describes a daily morning ritual, including a prayer which begins: "Oh, Buddha, thou resplendent and glorious orb. Whosoever shall circulate this prayer to the Sun, old or young in the household need not fear any malignant star . . . Oh, Buddha . . . may thy worship be practiced by all righteous men and believing women . . . Whosoever shall recite seven times every morning the above prayer will never enter the dark abode of Hades. After his death he will be transported to the Pure Land of bliss."

21. *Li chi,* bks. 9 and 21, *Sacred Books of the East,* SBE XXVII, 218-219. There may be Taoist influence present here as well. In his "Taoist Self-Cultivation in Ming Thought," in Wm. Theodore deBary, ed., *Self and Society in Ming Thought* (New York, 1970), pp. 303-304, Liu Ts'un-yan points out that Taoist priests inhaled air facing the sun in the morning and the moon at night, to "benefit from the essences emitted from the heavenly bodies."

22. Some scholars, DeGroot and Chan Hok-lam, leave the character *yang* untranslated, thus reading "three yang" or "red yang," as I have here, while Richard Chu, on the other hand, translates *yang* as "sun." Since the sun is the cosmic source of *yang* influence the distinction in this context is difficult to draw. However, whatever the translation, the sources make it clear that the sun was a primary cult object in some of the sects. On this point see DeGroot, *Sectarianism,* I, 152; Chang Hok-lam, "White Lotus," p. 217; and Chu, "White Lotus," pp. 70-72. The translation problem is complicated by the fact that in some cases the character *hung* "red" is replaced by *hung* meaning, "wide, extensive" in either of two forms. Furthermore the character *yang* is occasionally transcribed as *yang* for "ocean."

23. Chih-p'an, *Fo tsu,* chüan 48 (translated above). *Ming* is also the character used in a Manichaean text translated by Chavannes and Pelliot, "Un Traité manichéen," p. 106.

24. Wu Han, "Ming chiao," pp. 236-237, 239.

25. Tai Hsüan-chih, "Pai-lien chiao te yüan-liu," p. 312.

26. Wu Han, "Ming chiao," p. 254.

27. Fang Ch'ing-ying, "Pai-lien chiao," p. 35.

28. Tsukamoto Zenryū, *Shina Bukkyō-shi kenkyū* (Tōkyō, 1942), pp. 248, 256, 259, 260.

29. *Wei shu,* chüan 47, "Lu Yüan chuan," quoted in ibid., p. 261. The Red Eyebrows were a rebel movement of 25 A.D.

30. *Wei shu,* "Shih-tsung chi," quoted in Tsukamoto, *Shina Bukkyō,* pp. 265-266.

31. Liang Ch'i-ch'ao, *Fo-hsüeh,* p. 11.

32. *Maitreyavyākarana,* trans. Edward Conze in his *Buddhist Scriptures,* pp. 238-242.

33. Chiang Wei-ch'iao, *Chung-kuo fo-chiao shih* (Shanghai, 1933), II, 7-8.

34. Ch'en, *Buddhism,* pp. 177-178.

35. William E. Soothill and Lewis Hodous, *A Dictionary of Chinese Buddhist Terms* (London, 1937), pp. 156-157; Zürcher, *Conquest,* I, 315.

36. Shigematsu Shunshō, "Tō Sō jidai no Mirokukyō-hi," *Shien,* 3:74-75 (1931). Fa-ch'ing's movement presents a historical problem, for while the dualistic language used is an innovation which implies Manichaean influence, the first recorded entry of Manichaeism into China was in 694. Shigematsu on p. 85, n. 3, notes that a part of Fa-ch'ing's hostility to the sangha may be explained by the fact that he had been rejected by his own disciples. This movement was called the *ta-sheng tsei* (Mahāyāna ban-

dits) by its contemporaries, but by the Sung period it had blended with popular Manichaeism. Fa-ch'ing was from Chi-hsien in Hopei. The "tenth abode" indicates a bodhisattva who has reached the highest level of one of several forms of attainment in ten steps.

37. *Sui shu*, ed. Wei Cheng (580-643) and Ch'ang-sun Wu-chi (d. 659) (Shanghai, 1936), 3:8b.

38. Ssu-ma Kuang (1019-1089), *Tzu-chih t'ung-chien pu*, commentary by Hu San-hsing (1230-1302), supp. by Yen Yen (1575-1645), (Taipei, 1967), 182:15a. Sung Tzu-hsien was from Kao-yang county in Hopei, Hsiang Hai-ming from Fu-feng county in Shensi.

The intimate relationship of Maitreyan eschatology to political concerns is further revealed in the fact that the Empress Wu Tse-t'ien of the T'ang proclaimed herself an incarnation of Maitreya in 695 and ruled her own Chou dynasty in his name between 690-705. I will not describe the complex political setting and court intrigues surrounding this event. For our purposes it is sufficient to note that the empress and a group of her monk supporters had a partially forged scripture, the *Great Cloud Sūtra* (*Ta-yün ching*), distributed and read all over the empire. In this text the Buddha predicts to a female divinity that because of her great merit she will be born as a universal monarch. In addition, Wu Tse-t'ien ordered that Great Cloud monasteries be built in every district of the realm, with 1,000 monks ordained in each, and that Taoism, heretofore favored by the T'ang rulers, be proscribed.

Since the Empress Wu had been raised by a pious Buddhist mother, had long supported the carving of sacred sculptures at Lung-men, and had become a nun after her husband's death in 683, there may have been an element of sincere belief in her devotion to Maitreya, despite the palace intrigues and assassinations in which she was involved. Perhaps her public embrace of this tradition served to encourage popular adherence to Maitreya as well, but this has yet to be demonstrated. Shigematsu devotes pp. 75-81 of his "Mirokukyō-hi" to a discussion of this experiment with Maitreyan Buddhism as imperial ideology. Ch'en, *Buddhism*, gives an English summary of these events on pp. 219-222. Empress Wu was forced to abdicate in 705, and the T'ang house of the Li family was restored to power. The standard account of her life and activities in English is C. P. Fitzgerald, *The Empress Wu* (Melbourne, 1955).

39. Shigematsu, "Mirokukyō-hi," p. 81. Does the "House of Liu" here refer to a hoped for revival of the Han dynasty (the ruling clan of which was named Liu)? Pei-chou was in Ch'ing-he county of modern Hopei, somewhat south of where Fa-ch'ing and Sung Tzu-hsien had been active earlier.

40. Li T'ao (1115-1184) *Hsü tzu-chih t'ung-chien ch'ang-pien* (reprinted in Taipei, 1961), 161:8a-b; Li Yu (f. 1134) *Sung-ch'ao shih-shih* (reprinted in Peking, 1955), chüan 16, pp. 248-249 in this edition. Wang Tse's rebellion is discussed at some length in both these sources. For a detailed modern treatment see Shigematsu, "Mirokukyō-hi," pp. 92-94, and

his note on sources, p. 102. In response to Wang Tse's revolt the Emperor Jen-tsung issued strict orders that heterodox sect activity in any form was prohibited. Thus, it was such radical outbreaks by the Maitreya sect that indirectly led to suppression of more peaceful groups.

41. *Yüan shih,* vol. 1, chüan 29, pp. 259-260.

42. *Yüan shih,* vol. 1, chüan 29, p. 329. Pang Hu's forces captured two towns before being suppressed in the same month they were discovered. Officials also confiscated orders and seals in the imperial style.

43. Li Shou-k'ung in his "Ming-tai Pai-lien chiao," pp. 32, 40, describes uprisings in 1379 and 1515 which do not seem to have been White Lotus related. Noguchi Tetsurō's whole article, "Byakuren kyō sha no henyō o megutte," *Yamazaki sensei taikan kinen tōyōshi-gakū ronshū* (Tōkyō, 1967), pp. 353-365, is devoted to describing the change in the White Lotus after it absorbed Maitreyan messianism. He states that before the fourteenth century the White Lotus had no revolutionary emphasis but rather was an association of pious laymen no different from any other recognized religious groups of the time. Noguchi stresses that the Maitreya group was never granted official recognition.

44. *Smaller Sukhāvatī-vyūha Sūtra,* chap. 17, trans. F. Max Müller in *Buddhist Mahāyāna Texts in Sacred Books of the East,* XLIX, ed. F. Max Müller (Oxford, 1894), pt. 2, p. 101. A Chinese translation of this text, by Kumārajīva (344-413, var. 409), can be found in *Taishō* 12, 347-348, entitled *Fo shuo A-mi-t'o ching.*

45. Ch'en, *Buddhism,* pp. 342-343.

46. Though Hui-yüan never left Mount Lu to preach among the people, and his group retained an aristocratic flavor with an emphasis on meditation, tradition nevertheless called him the first patriarch of the Chinese Pure Land School. For several hundred years his devotional fellowship was a model for similar groups. The tradition also developed that the name of Hui-yüan's association was Pai-lien she, and thus that this was the origin of the White Lotus sect. DeGroot follows this interpretation in his *Sectarianism,* I, 162-163.

However, since an article by Paul Pelliot in 1903 ("La secte du Lotus Blanc et secte du Nuage Blanc," *Bulletin de l'École Française de'Extreme-Orient,* II, 304-317), scholars have questioned the supposed connection between the fifth and twelfth century groups, and by now it has been disproven. Most recently Fang Ch'ing-ying has argued that the popularity of the Pai-lien she idea in the T'ang and Sung periods began with poems extolling Hui-yüan's association written by the late T'ang poets Po Chü-i (772-846) and others after they visited Mount Lu. There is no historical foundation for the legend that the Lu-shan group was called White Lotus, because this term was first applied in the ninth century. Nonetheless the *idea* of the fifth century association had great influence. See Fang Ch'ing-ying, "Pai-lien chiao te yüan-lui chi-ch'i he Mo-ni chiao te kuan-hsi," 5:37 (1959); Suzuki, "Sōdai Bukkyō," pp. 69-71; Ch'en, *Buddhism,* pp. 106-108, and Zürcher, *Buddhist Conquest,* I, 204-253.

47. Kitagawa, *Religion in Japanese History*, pp. 76-78.

48. It should be mentioned that the involvement of literati and gentry in Buddhism had a history going back to the beginnings of the religion in China. One of the earliest references to Buddhism in China notes the activities of a royal convert, Prince Liu Ying (d. 71 A.D.) in 65 A.D. Erik Zürcher, in his *The Buddhist Conquest of China* (Leiden, 1959), I, 73, emphasizes that after 300 it was "the penetration of the doctrine to the highest gentry circles which paved the way to the later Buddhist 'conquest of China.' " On this see also Richard B. Mather, "Vimalakīrti and Gentry Buddhism," *History of Religions*, 8:60-73 (August 1968).

49. Tsung-hsiao (1151-1214), *Le pang wen lei*, chüan 3, in *Taishō*, 47, 187.

50. Ta-yu, *Ching-t'u chih-kuei chi* (colophon dated 1394), chüan 2, in *Hsü tsang-ching*, 108, 79a. This group was formed in the Sung Ch'un-hua reign period (990-995).

51. Suzuki, "Sōdai Bukkyō," pp. 83-87.

52. Tsung-hsiao, *Le pang i kao*, chüan 2, in *Taishō*, 47, 242-243. Wang Chung was active in the Cheng-he reign period of the Northern Sung (1111-1118), at Hsi-hu in Chekiang.

53. Tsung-hsiao, *Ssu-ming chiao-hsing lu* (1202), chüan 1, in *Hsü tsang-ching*, 100, 446. This text says "prosperity for army and people" (*chün min*), but perhaps *chün* should be read as *chung* (multitude), as Suzuki suggests in his "Sōdai Bukkyō," p. 215. This group was located in a monastery on Ssu-ming shan in modern Yin-hsien.

54. Many of the literati associated with Sung Pure Land groups wrote books, pamphlets, and charts to popularize their views.

55. Tsung-hsiao, *Ssu-ming chiao-hsing lu*, chüan 1, in *Hsü tsang-ching*, 100, 446b.

56. Wang Jih-hsiu, *Lung-shu Ching-t'u wen*, chüan 6, in *Taishō*, 47, 269.

57. For Western language studies of social change in the Sung see: Gernet, *Daily Life* · E. A. Kracke Jr., "Sung Society: Change Within Tradition," *Far Eastern Quarterly*, 14:479-488 (1954-1955); James T. C. Lui and Peter J. Golas, eds., *Change in Sung China* (Lexington, Mass., 1969); Laurence J. C. Ma, *Commercial Development and Urban Change in Sung China* (Ann Arbor, Mich., 1971); and Shiba Yoshinobu, *Commerce and Society in Sung China*, trans. Mark Elvin (Ann Arbor, Mich., 1970).

58. See, for example, Gernet, *Daily Life*, pp. 87-88.

59. Shiba, *Commerce and Society*, p. 208.

60. Shigematsu, "Ch'u-ch'i," p. 144.

61. P'u-tu, *Lien-tsung pao-chien*, chüan 4, in *Taishō*, 47, 326-327. The *Cheng-tao ke* was written by the T'ang monk, Yung-chia Hsüan-

chüeh. I have not been able to find more information concerning the *Mi-t'o chieh-yao*.

62. Wang Jih-hsiu, *Lung-shu Ching-t'u wen*, chüan 12, in *Taishō*, 47, 287.

63. I-nien, *Hsi-fang chih-chih* (colophon dated 1606), chüan 2, in *Hsü tsang-ching*, 108, 319b. There are also quotes from Tz'u-chao tsung-chu's writings in Tsung-pen's, *Kuei-yüan chih-chih chi*, chüan 1, in *Hsü tsang-ching*, 108, 121a-b, and in Li Chih, *Ching-t'u chüeh*, in *Hsü tsang-ching*, 108, 185b-186b.

64. Chih-p'an, *Fo tsu*, chüan 47, in *Taishō*, 49, 425.

65. Tsung-chien, *Shih-men cheng-t'ung*, chüan 4, in *Hsü tsang-ching*, 130, 412b.

66. Ibid. The other four prohibitions relevant to a lay sect are against stealing, adultery, lying, and the use of intoxicating liquors. Of course, for clergy no sexual relations were permitted. In the biography of Mao Tzu-yüan he is quoted as urging all to adhere to these prohibitions.

67. Chih-p'an, *Fo tsu*, chüan 47, in *Taishō*, 49, 425.

68. *Sung shih* (Shanghai, 1937, reprint of Yüan Chih-cheng, ed.), 44:9a, 46:24b. Trad. ed. T'o T'o (1313-1355). Both these notices from the *Sung History* are mentioned by Shigematsu in his "Ch'u-ch'i," p. 148.

69. *Ta Yüan t'ung-chih t'iao-ke*, 28:30. The *T'ui pei t'u* was an illustrated book describing the rise and fall of dynasties, used to foretell the future. Though there were earlier forms of such texts, the first to be called *T'ui-pei t'u* (illustrated inferences concerning the future), evidently appeared during the T'ang dynasty in 643 and remained popular into the Republican period, despite the fact that their use was prohibited by imperial edict from the reign of Sung T'ai-tsu (960-976) on. The *T'ui-pei t'u* inferred the future with the help of hexagrams from the *I Ching*. For a detailed study see Nakano Torū, "Suihaizu shotan," *Tōhō Shūkyō*, 36:20-37 (October 1970). I am grateful to Nathan Sivin of M.I.T. for referring me to the Nakano article. The government was naturally disturbed by such politically oriented prognostication texts in the hands of commoners. For other references to sectarian use of *T'ui-pei t'u*, see Sakai Tadao, *Chūgoku zensho no kenkyū* (Tokyo, 1960), pp. 444, 461, 465. Michael Saso of the University of Hawaii informs me that the *Wu-kung fu* is a popular Taoist version of the *Wu-ying kung fu* charms or talismans used to protect territory from attacks by evil spirits or to ward off injury or defeat in battle. Such charms were derived from esoteric orthodox forms first popularized in the early twelfth century.

70. *Yüan shih*, vol. 1, chüan 22, p. 195. See also Shigematsu, "Ch'u-ch'i," p. 149.

71. *Ta Yüan t'ung-chih t'iao-ke*, 29:17a-17b.

72. Topley, "Great Way," p. 362.

73. *Ta Yüan sheng-cheng kuo-ch'ao tien-chang* (Taipei, 1964, reprint of 1908 ed.), 33:12a, section on "Pai-lien chiao." This is the same group as that referred to in the 1308 edict, located in Chien-ning lu, Fukien. Shigematsu demonstrates that this passage must be dated 1313; "Ch'u-ch'i," p. 150.

74. *Yüan shih*, vol. 1, chüan 28, p. 244.

75. *Yüan shih*, vol. 1, chüan 42, p. 349. This took place in Ying-chou (modern Fu-yang county, Anhwei) in 1351. Han was from Luan-ch'eng county in Hopei.

76. *Ming shih*, vol. 3, chüan 122, pp. 1560-1561. See also the biography of Kuo Tzu-hsing in this same chüan.

77. John W. Dardess, "The Transformation of Messianic Revolt and the Founding of the Ming Dynasty," *Journal of Asian Studies*, 29.3:557 (May 1970).

78. Ch'üan Heng, *Keng-shen wai-shih*, p. 21a.

79. Kao Tai, *Hung yu lu*, chüan 7, "Sung shih shih mo," quoted in Wu Han, "Ming chiao," p. 260.

80. He Ch'iao-yüan (*chin-shih* 1586), *Ming shan ts'ang*, chüan 43, "T'ien-yin chi," quoted in Wu Han, "Ming chiao," p. 260.

81. Chu, "White Lotus," pp. 97-98; Li Shou-k'ung, "Ming-tai Pai-lien chiao," p. 31; T'ao Hsi-sheng, "Pai-lien chiao," p. 6. For a detailed account of Hsü Shou-hui (Hsü Chen) and his T'ien-wan state, see *Yüan shih*, vol. 1, chüan 42, p. 349.

82. Li Shou-k'ung, "Ming-tai Pai-lien chiao," pp. 32-33.

83. Ch'en *Buddhism*, pp. 168-169.

84. Li Shou-k'ung, "Ming-tai Pai-lien chiao," pp. 35-36, 39, 36. Dardess corroborates this continuity in his "Transformations of Messianic Revolt," p. 558.

85. *Ming shih*, vol. 4, chüan 206, p. 2390. Li Fu-ta was from Kuo-shan county in Shansi (modern Hun-yüan county). T'ao Hsi-sheng discusses his complex involvement with gentry and officials in his "Pai-lien chiao," p. 12.

86. *Ming ta-cheng tsuan-yao*, 60:24b. This group was led by a man named Chang Ch'ao-yung. See also Li Shou-k'ung, "Ming-tai Pai-lien chiao," p. 43.

87. *Ming shih*, vol. 4, chüan 226, p. 2606. See also Tsukamoto, "Rakyō," pp. 23-24.

88. See DeGroot, *Sectarianism*, II, 277-566, for a running account of sectarian activities from 1736 to 1861, and Chu, "White Lotus," pp. 109-174, for a description of such activities from 1622 to 1813.

89. Huang Yü-p'ien, *P'o-hsieh*, 1:1.

90. Chu, "White Lotus," p. 109. For a more detailed description of this period and two of its best known rebellions, see: James Bunyan Parsons, *Peasant Rebellions of the Late Ming Dynasty* (Tucson, 1970).

91. *Ming shih*, vol. 4, chüan 257, pp. 2902-2903. See also T'ao Hsi-sheng, "Ming-tai Mi-le Pai-lien chiao," p. 52.

92. Huang Yü-p'ien, *P'o-hsieh*, 1:7b.

93. *Na Wen-i kung tsou-i*, 42:32b. There is another account of this report, with comments by the Chia-ch'ing Emperor in the *Ta-Ch'ing shih-ch'ao sheng-hsün, Jen-tsung*, 101:8b (Chia-ch'ing 20, 8 mo.). The whole of *Na Wen-i kung tsou-i*, chüan 42, is a detailed account of the Wang family and its connections in different parts of China. Na-yen-ch'eng started unraveling the situation with the arrest of a sect leader in Kiangsu who was from Shih-fo k'ou.

94. *Na Wen-i kung tsou-i*, 42:18a-19a.

95. Kubo Noritada, "Ikkandō hōkō," *Tōyō bunka kenkyūjo kiyō*, 11:180-182 (November 1956). For a recent summary of I-kuan tao activities see Lev Deliusin, "The I-kuan Tao Society," in Jean Chesneaux, ed., *Popular Movements and Secret Societies in China, 1840-1950* (Stanford, 1972), pp. 225-233. The most comprehensive study is Li Shih-yü, *Hsien-tsai Hua-pei pi-mi tsung-chiao* (Chengtu, 1948), pp. 1-9, 32-130.

96. "I-kuan tao i-wen hsiang-ta," ms. (Taiwan, n.d.), p. 12. Li Shih-yü describes this text on pp. 104-105 of his *Pi-mi tsung-chiao*.

97. Ibid., pp. 5a-5b.

98. Kubo, "Ikkandō hōkō," pp. 182-183, 187. This article is based on reports in Chinese newspapers.

99. William A. Grootaers, "Une Société secrète moderne, I-kuan tao; Bibliographie annotée," *Folklore Studies*, 5:318-323 (1946).

100. Topley, "Great Way," pp. 362, 372.

101. Li Shih-yü maintains that there was a continuous tradition of sect leadership from the Wang family at Shih-fo k'ou in the Ming to Wang Chüeh-i of the I-kuan tao. See his *Pi-mi tsung-chiao*, pp. 36-37.

6. Other Groups:
An Introduction to the White Cloud and Lo Sects

1. Suzuki, "Sōdai Bukkyō," pp. 90-92.

2. Topley, "Great Way," p. 367.

3. DeGroot, *Sectarianism*, I, 170-241.

4. In the *Tao-te ching*, *wu-wei* is better translated as "no artificial action" or as "spontaneous action in accord with Tao," but this issue need not concern us here.

5. Chüeh-an, *Shih-shih chi-ku lüeh* (1355), chüan 4, in *Taishō*, 49, 886.

6. It is interesting that the Jōdo Shinshū cult also originated at Shinran's tomb. See Kitagawa, *Religion*, p. 116. We have seen that this was true of the Ch'ang-sheng sect.

7. Chih-p'an, *Fo tsu*, chüan 54, in *Taishō*, 49, 475. For a discussion

of the "ten stages" see Leon Hurvitz, *Chih-i (538-597) An Introduction to the Life and Ideas of a Chinese Buddhist Monk* (Bruges, 1963), pp. 366-367.

8. Shigematsu Shunshō, "Sō Gen jidai no Byakuun shūmon," *Shien*, 2:43 (1930). For details see Tsung-chien, in his *Shih-men cheng-t'ung*, chüan 4, *Hsü tsang-chiṅg*, 130, 413a, who adds that because of their emphasis on daily worship of the Buddha they were not the same as Manichaeans.

9. Cited in Chih-p'an, *Fo tsu*, chüan 48, *Taishō*, 49, 431. Shen was banished and the White Cloud temple destroyed. Tsung-chien's version of this same memorial adds that the White Cloud "were neither Buddhist nor Taoist." The temple was located at Nan-shan in Yü-hang county of Chekiang, north of Hangchow. Shigematsu describes all this in his "Byakuun shūmon," pp. 50-52.

10. These events in the early fourteenth century White Cloud are discussed in *Yüan shih* 25:10a, and 26:3b, 17b, 19b. The Shen family evidently maintained hereditary leadership for over 100 years. The title Ssuk'ung can be translated as Minister of Works, one of the Six Ministries of the Han but in the Yüan a purely honorary position. In modern dictionaries a *ch'ing* is defined as 15.13 acres.

11. Shigematsu, "Byakuun shūmon," p. 44.

12. Edkins, *Chinese Buddhism*, p. 377.

13. Li Shih-yü, "Pao-chüan hsin-yen," *Wen-hsüeh i-ch'an tseng-k'an*, no. 4 (Peking, 1957), pp. 173-174.

14. Li Shih-yü, *Pao-chüan tsung-lu* (Shanghai, 1961), "Introduction." In his *Chūgoku zensho*, p. 440, Sakai Tadao says that all the Lo texts were written in 1509.

The names of Lo's books are as follows: *T'an shih wu-wei chüan* (The scroll of nonaction and pity for the world), *P'o-hsieh hsien cheng yao-shih chüan* (The key to refuting heresy and making the truth manifest), *Cheng-hsin ch'u-i wu hsiu cheng tzu tsai pao-chüan* (The precious scroll which corrects belief and dispels doubt, standing by itself, not needing verification), *K'u-kung wu-tao chüan* (The scroll of enlightenment through asceticism), *Wei-wei pu-tung T'ai-shan shen-ken chieh-kuo pao-chüan* (The scroll of deeply rooted fruition, which like Mount T'ai of the lofty peaks never moves). These texts are collectively called the *Wu-pu liu-ts'e* (Five books in six volumes) because the *P'o-hsieh hsien cheng chüan* is in two chüan. For additional discussion of these texts, see Sawada Mizuho, *Hōkan no kenkyū* (Nagoya, 1963), pp. 15-16, 81-84.

15. Tsukamoto, "Rakyō," pp. 29-30.

16. Topley, "Great Way," pp. 366-368. Lo is referred to here as Lo Wei-ch'un. Ch'en Chung-hsi, in his *Chung-hsi pao-chüan*, first published in 1840, gives Lo Tsu's dates as 1442-1527. On Ch'en's book, which gives brief descriptions of seventy Ming and Ch'ing sects, see Sawada Mizuho, *Kōchu haja shōben*, pp. 219-235. The Wu-wei chiao is discussed on p. 222.

17. Lo Ch'ing, *Cheng-hsin pao-chüan*, p. 65b; *T'ai-shan pao-chüan*, chap. 24, and Sakai, *Chūgoku zensho*, pp. 469-471.

18. Mi-tsang Tao-k'ai, *Tsang i ching shu* (1597), in the *Sung-lin ts'ung-shu* (1918), 3, 10-12b. Tsukamoto's discussion of this evidence is on pp. 29-31 of his "Rakyō."

19. Lo Ch'ing must have made quite an impression on his orthodox Buddhist contemporaries, for we find criticisms of his teaching in the writings of both Chu-hung and a famous Ch'an master of the time, Han-shan Te-ch'ing (1546-1623). On this see: Chu-hung, *Cheng-e chi*, "Wu-wei chüan" section, p. 19b in *Yün-ch'i fa-hui*, vol. 4; and Han-shan Te-ch'ing *Han-shan ta-shih nien-p'u shu chu*, ed. Fu-cheng (f. 1624-1651) (Taipei, 1967), 1:52. Te-ch'ing had built a convent for meditation on Lao-shan in 1583, so he was familiar with the area. In his chronological biography we find an entry dated 1585 which reads, "The heretic (*wai-tao*) Lo Ch'ing, who is still spoken of today, was a man from [the village of] Ch'eng-yang at the foot of the mountain . . . His teachings are widespread in the east." It is also interesting that Lo Ch'ing is the subject of a story in the *Liao-chai chih-i*, written in 1679 by P'u Sung-ling (1630-1715). This story, in chüan 9, is titled Lo Tsu and describes Lo as a man from Chi-mo county of Shantung who became a Taoist hermit living in a cave, venerated by the local populace. No date is mentioned in this story; neither is there any discussion of Lo as sect founder.

20. I am presently translating the five Lo Ch'ing texts, kindly made available to me in 1975 by Professor Sakai. These comments are based on my preliminary work with this material.

21. See, for example, a memorial of 1729 where all five titles are listed, *Shih-liao*, t'ien 48.

22. DeGroot, *Sectarianism*, I, 183. The sect name used in Amoy was Hsien-t'ien chiao, "The Religion of Former Heaven." This is one of several alternative names in the Lo tradition.

23. Sakai, *Chugokū zensho*, p. 451.

24. Ibid., pp. 452-454.

25. Tsukamoto, "Rakyō," p. 30; DeGroot, *Sectarianism*, I, 184.

26. *Shih liao*, t'ien 408. This memorial is dated 1768. On t'ien 405 it is mentioned that before the renewed prohibition in 1727 more than seventy Lo temples had been discovered.

27. Ibid., t'ien 404-405, 406, 408, 525-528, 49-50. The Lo sect had been officially proscribed in 1618.

28. The character *p'u* means "universal" and was possibly derived here from the common Buddhist phrase, *p'u-tu chung-sheng*, literally, "universally save all living creatures." Lung-hua hui is the same name as that of the second Lo group investigated by DeGroot in Amoy 130 years later. Lung-hua, which refers to three great eschatological assemblies called by Maitreya, is a common term in later sectarian theology. The name Lao-kuan comes from the Lo sect practice of members calling each other "venerable official" as a term of respect.

29. *Shih-liao*, t'ien 861-862.

30. *Shih-liao*, t'ien 964. The other Lo related movement inclined to

violence which I have encountered also had a number of eschatological titles and symbols, some related to Maitreya. This group, which was located in Anhwei, was led by Liu T'ien-hsü, who evidently planned an uprising in 1606. He was arrested that same year. Liu was a member of the Wu-wei chiao who called himself both Wu-wei chiao-chu (Chief of the Wu-wei religion) and Lung-hua ti-wang (Dragon-flower Emperor). Liu wrote several pamphlets and at least one *pao-chüan*, gathered his people together to "chant sūtras and preach the dharma," and gave some of his followers military titles. His wife he named both queen and the Bodhisattva Kuan-yin. Liu planned to rebel at the winter solstice, not only to raid storehouses and attack imperial tombs but perhaps also to welcome his version of the Buddha of the future, the Tang-yang huang chi fo (the Buddha of the Imperial Ultimate, in Harmony with Yang). The forces of *yang* are revived at the winter solstice, while desecrating imperial tombs destroys their beneficent influence on the ruling house, thus paving the way for a successor. Liu's use of mutually reinforcing double titles and symbols is an old White Lotus-Maitreya characteristic. His movement is discussed in detail in Sakai, *Chūgoku zensho*, pp. 473-474.

31. *Mi-le t'uan*. This title seems more appropriate to a group than to an individual. Perhaps Chu was the leader of a Maitreya Club.

32. *Shih-liao*, t'ien 963-967. There are also lengthy memorials concerning the aftermath of these events in ti 25-36 and ti 61-62. This local uprising was obviously a matter of great concern to the government. The location of these events was in modern Chien-ou county in north-central Fukien.

33. I have had several conversations with a "red-head" priest of popular religion on Taiwan who himself was once carried in such a procession as an incarnate deity. DeGroot also describes the use of sedan chairs in ritual and divination in his *Religious System of China* (Leiden, 1910), VI, 1316-1322.

34. Of course, it is possible that the earlier Lo groups were also more complex than öfficial sources indicate. DeGroot's account of the Lung-hua hui is in his *Sectarianism*, I, 197-241. To my knowledge, this is the most complete description of a folk Buddhist congregation available in the literature, east or west.

35. Chu, "White Lotus," pp. 128, 138.

36. *Cheng-hsin pao-chüan*, p. 53b. At several other points in this text Lo roundly condemns those who do evil or lack proper belief to "remain eternally in samsāra never to escape."

37. *Cheng-hsin pao-chüan*, p. 58. The passage goes on to attack others who claim supernatural powers that enable them to pass unharmed through water and fire and gain help for the spirits. This whole text is a vigorous and self-conscious defense of a particular position against all sorts of folk practices and beliefs.

38. Huang Yü-p'ien, *P'o-hsieh*, 2:7.

39. *Cheng-hsin pao-chüan*, p. 46b. Lo goes on to attack the Maitreya sect (Mi-le chiao) in similar terms. "Burning paper" probably refers to the White Lotus practice of burning memorials to Lao-mu.

40. Li Shih-yü, *Hsin yen*, p. 173.

41. *P'o-hsieh*, 2:3. This problem is discussed below. Huang says that P'iao Kao, founder of the Red Yang sect, was a man named Kao Yang from Shansi. On this see Sawada, *Kōchu haja shōben*, p. 136.

42. Huang Yü-p'ien, *San-hsü p'o-hsieh*, in Sawada, *Kōchu haja shōben*, p. 158.

Li Shih-yü in his *Hsin-yen*, p. 174, has doubts about Huang's interpretation and holds out the possibility that the Eternal Mother cult began in the Cheng-te period, because we have *pao-chüan* texts which clearly say "printed in the Cheng-te year." However, this is related to Li's general position that the Lao-mu myth is constitutive of *pao-chüan* literature per se, which he carries to the point of questioning whether any true *pao-chüan* appeared before the Ming. While I greatly sympathize with Li's attempt to relate all *pao-chüan* to sectarian cultic activity, I am not prepared to limit this relationship to that existing between the Lao-mu mythology and the later White Lotus tradition. The *pao-chüan* is a literary form related to a specific sociological context but not necessarily to a specific doctrinal content.

43. Huang Yü-p'ien, *P'o-hsieh*, 2:4.

44. DeGroot, *Sectarianism*, I, 182.

45. However, Lo Ch'ing in his *Cheng-hsin pao-chüan*, p. 37b, published eighty-five years before P'iao Kao's texts, attacks those who equate *wu-sheng fu-mu* (eternal parents) with Amitābha. He also criticizes use of the phrase *Ying-er chien-niang* (the child sees its mother). The term *wu-sheng lao-mu* is not mentioned. Since Lo provides no details or contexts for these terms, their interpretation remains problematic. All one can suggest at this point is that P'iao Kao did not invent such terms, though he may have interpreted them differently.

46. DeGroot, *Sectarianism*, I, 181-184.

47. Sakai, *Chūgokū zensho*, p. 478.

48. *Nan-kung shu-tu*, chüan 4, Wan-li 46, third month, cited in Sakai, *Chūgoku zensho*, p. 479. I have not been able to locate this source.

49. George Miles, "Vegetarian Sects," *The Chinese Recorder*, 33:1-10 (January 1902).

50. Doré, *Researches*, V, 554-556.

51. Tsukamoto, "Rakyō," p. 21.

7. Patterns of Folk Buddhist Religion: Beliefs and Myths

1. Soothill and Hodous, *Dictionary*, pp. 397, 172. See also Hurvitz, *Chih-i*, pp. 305-306.

2. Shigematsu, "Ch'u-ch'i," p. 146.

3. Quoted in Fung Yu-lan, *History of Chinese Philosophy*, trans. Derk Bodde (Princeton, 1953), II, 362. Originally published in 1937. The Chinese text of this passage is in *Taishō*, 46, 647.

4. P'u-tu, *Lien-tsung pao-chien*, chüan 4, in *Taishō*, 47, 313.

5. Ibid., chüan 7, in *Taishō*, 47, 336. "Vow" here refers to inner resolve to attain rebirth in paradise.

6. Wang Jih-hsiu, *Lung-shu Ching-t'u wen*, chüan 4, *Taishō*, 47, 262. Italics added.

7. Sakai, *Chūgoku zensho*, p. 226. For an interesting imperial prohibition of an evidently widespread cult of the "three religions" in 1106, see Chih-p'an, *Fo tsu*, chüan 46, in *Taishō*, 49, 419. This is translated in De-Groot, *Sectarianism*, I, 79.

8. Liu Ts'un-yan, "Lin Chao-en (1517-1598), The Master of the Three Teachings," *T'oung Pao*, 53:260-261, 276-277 (1967). DeGroot in his *Sectarianism*, I, 108-109, discusses an edict of 1744 which indicates 590 "Temples of the Three Religions" in Honan alone.

9. Tsung-pen, *Kuei-yüan chih-chih chi*, chüan 1, in *Hsü tsang-ching*, 108, 130a. See pp. 129-157b of this same volume for several other *san-chiao* discussions collected by Tsung-pen. Tsung-hsiao's treatment of this theme is in *Hsü tsang-ching*, 101, 205-208a. There is a rich collection of essays on the unity and differences of the three teachings in *Ku-chin t'u-shu chi-ch'eng*, ed. Ch'en Meng-lei (1725), (Shanghai, 1934 reprint), vol. 494, section "Shen-i," chüan 57, pp. 20-30a.

Of course, there were other Buddhists who remained committed to the supremacy of Buddhism. Chu-hung, for example, has this to say on the subject: "There are Buddhists who say that the 10,000 teachings all return to one, Taoists who talk about 'embracing the origin and protecting the one,' and Confucians who 'unite them all with one [principle], for all [teachings] are the same.' This is erroneous . . . If the 10,000 teachings all return to one, then there is only one, certainly not 10,000 . . . [Whatever] 'one' the [other] two teachings may exalt, Buddhism still transcends it."

Elsewhere in response to the saying *san-chiao i-chia* (the three teachings form one household), he says that if this is the case, then just as there are positions with differing status in a household, so are there superior and inferior among religions: "Buddhism . . . is senior . . . and most honored." See his "Cheng e chi," pp. 22a-b, in *Yün-ch'i fa-hui*, vol. 4.

10. Quoted in Sakai, *Chūgoku zensho*, p. 226. For an interesting discussion of the leaders of the "three religions" as culture heroes, see the *Hun-yüan hung-yang lin-fan P'iao Kao ching* (The scripture of the descent to earth in the Red Yang period of P'iao Kao), as quoted in Huang Yü-p'ien, *Yu-hsü p'o-hsieh*. Cf. Sawada, *Kōchu haja shōben*, p. 128. Here we are told among other things that Śākyamuni left behind the Buddhist *Compendium*, and Lao Tzu the Five Agents (metal, wood, water, fire, earth) and the *Tao-te ching*, while Confucius bequeathed the Confucian classics and ethical principles.

11. Huang Yü-p'ien, *P'o-hsieh*, 1:1-3a. Huang points out that the words *er-lun* (two mountains named Lun) in this text should be read *er-lun* (two wheels), which enable their wearer to fly, as the deity No-cha in the *Feng-shen yen-i*, chap. 14.

12. Huang Yü-p'ien, *Yu-hsü p'o-hsieh*, in Sawada, *Kōchu haja shōben*, pp. 122-123.

13. Huang Yü-p'ien, *P'o-hsieh*, 1:1b. For another sectarian description of paradise see the *P'iao Kao ching* as quoted by Huang Yü-p'ien in his *Yu-hsü p'o-hsieh*, in Sawada, *Kōchu haja shōben*, p. 131. A common general designation for paradise in sectarian texts is Yün-ch'eng, "City of the Clouds." The words "seven precious pools and eight merit streams" are found in the description of Amitabha's paradise in the *Fo-shuo A-mi-t'o ching* in *Taishō*, 12, 346-347.

14. Huang Yü-p'ien, *Hsü-k'an p'o-hsieh*, p. 26b. Various values are assigned to *i*, the most common being 100,000,000. This scheme represents an interesting inversion of orthodox Buddhist teaching, in which Maitreya first converts ninety-six *i*, then ninety-four, then ninety-two, in three great preaching assemblies during his lifetime on earth. On this see *Fo-shuo Mi-le hsia-sheng ching*, in *Taishō*, 14, 442. In orthodox Taoism "Limitless" (*wu-chi*) refers to the primordial state before the world appeared, and the "Great Ultimate" (*t'ai-chi*) to the beginnings of light and form. As for Imperial Ultimate (*huang-chi*) there is a Confucian usage which might be translated as "the epitome of imperial ethical spirit," but no orthodox Taoist reference that I know of. Perhaps the sects invented the meaning of *huang-chi* referring to a third and later time period. It would help in such matters to have available a good and comprehensive dictionary of Taoist terms.

15. Huang Yü-p'ien, *Hsü-k'an p'o-hsieh*, 2:1.

16. Huang Yü-p'ien *San-hsü p'o-hsieh*, in Sawada, *Kōchu haja shōben*, p. 160. There is a similar passage on p. 162 in which all are urged to recite the Buddha's name and practice the ten stages of meditation, for the Eternal Mother has long waited for her children to return, etc.

17. Huang Yü-p'ien, *P'o-hsieh*, 2:6b.

18. *Yao-shih Ju-lai pao-chüan* (The precious scroll of the Buddha of medicine); quoted in Cheng Chen-to, *Su-wen hsüeh*, II, 314. This text is dated 1543. Ling-shan technically refers to Ling-chiu shan, "Spirit vulture peak" (Sanskrit, Grdhrakūta), the place in India where the Buddha is said to have preached the *Lotus Sutra*. However, for the sects Ling-shan was another term for paradise, so that in this context perhaps it should be understood in its literal Chinese meaning, "divine mountain." In canonical Taoism the term *ying-er* is "the esoteric name for long-life . . . the little red child . . . which is formed in the body of the adept, thus providing him rebirth." Saso, *Taoism*, pp. 78, 80.

19. *Chin-kang k'e-i* (The diamond ritual), quoted in Li Shih-yü, *Pao-chüan hsin-yen*, p. 178. This scripture is also described in Huang Yü-p'ien,

Hsü-k'an p'o-hsieh, p. 19. *Ke-i* here refers to a liturgy explaining the sūtra.

20. Huang Yü-p'ien, *P'o-hsieh,* 3:1b. There is some ambiguity concerning the Eternal Parents (*wu-sheng fu-mu*). I have taken *fu-mu* to refer to Fu-hsi and Nü-kua as in the myth quoted above. However, as noted in Chapter 6, Lo Ch'ing in his *Cheng-hsin pao-chüan* attacks those who equate *wu-sheng fu-mu* with Amitābha. In addition, in this same text, p. 49b, he criticizes a Hsüan-ku chiao (Mysterious Drum sect) for "worshiping the sun and moon as father and mother," thus indicating the possibility of a connection between *fu-mu* and the sun and moon cult. Susan Naquin translates *wu-sheng fu-mu* as "eternal progenitor" in Chapter 1 of her forthcoming *Millenarian Rebellion in China: The Eight Trigrams Uprising of 1813* (New Haven, Yale University Press).

21. *Hsü-k'an p'o-hsieh,* p. 9b. This is from the *Chiu-k'u chung-hsiao Yao-wang pao-chüan* (The precious scroll of the loyal and filial King of Medicine who rescues from suffering).

22. All the sixty-eight titles Huang collected are listed in Hsiang Chüeh-ming, "Ming Ch'ing chih chi chih pao-chüan wen-hsüeh yü Pai-lien chiao," *Wen-hsüeh,* 2:1218-1225 (June 1934). See also Sawada, *Kōchu haja shōben.*

23. Tsukamoto, "Rakyō," p. 23; Tetsurō Noguchi, private conversation in Tōkyō, December 1969.

24. Hsiang Chüeh-ming, "Pao-chüan wen-hsüeh," pp. 1222-1223. In his *Hsü-k'an p'o-hsieh,* pp. 5b-6a, Huang discusses a *Hu-kuo wei-ling Hsi Wang-mu pao-chüan* (The precious scroll of the majestic Mother Queen of the West, who protects the nation), which says that Hsi Wang-mu is a reincarnation of Wu-sheng lao-mu.

25. Homer H. Dubs, "An Ancient Chinese Mystery Cult," *Harvard Theological Review,* 35:223-225 (October 1942), and Doré, *Researches,* IX, 31-34.

26. *Han shu,* 11:6b and 27:22a, cited in Dubs, "Mystery Cult," p. 235.

27. George Miles in his "Vegetarian Sects," *The Chinese Recorder,* 33:1-10 (January 1902) indicates that Hsi Wang-mu was still worshiped by Lo-related vegetarian sects at the beginning of this century, where she was called Yao-ch'ih chin-mu, the keeper of paradise. Hsi Wang-mu is also the chief deity of the Taiwan Religion of Compassion sect, (Tz'u-hui t'ang).

28. Lu Hsi-hsing (c. 1520-1601), *Feng-shen yen-i,* chap. 1. Here Nü-kua niang-niang or Shang-ti shen-nü (The Divine Woman, God on High) decrees the end of the corrupt Shang dynasty. She is the supreme being of this novel. In Shih Nai-an (c. 1290-1365) *Shui-hu chuan,* chap. 31, we find an account of Sung Chiang's rescue by Chiu-t'ien hsüan-nü, the Mysterious Goddess of the Ninth Heaven. She appears in a brilliant theophany to give him his divine commission as Lord of the Stars to carry out the will of Heaven (*t'i t'ien hsing tao*). Here again a female deity dominates

the supernatural dimension of the novel. Of course Hsi Wang-mu, or Yao-ch'ih Wang-mu, is also discussed in Chapters 5 and 6 of the *Hsi-yu chi* (Journey to the West) by Wu Ch'eng-en (c. 1500-1580). However, her role is peripheral to that of the hero, Sun Hou-tzu. There is nothing resembling sectarian Lao-mu myth in the Hsi Wang-mu of the *Hsi-yu chi*, whose activities are entirely traditional. I give the traditional "authors" and dates for these novels, concerning which there are differences of scholarly opinion.

29. T'ao Ch'eng-chang, "Chiao hui," p. 1b.

30. Chesneaux, *Les Sociétés secrètes*, p. 97.

31. Huang Yü-p'ien, *Hsü-k'an p'o-hsieh*, pp. 5a-b. In the Hopei *Luan-chou chih* (1898 ed.), 18:28b-30, there is a different version of this same account. Here we are told that "Wu-sheng lao-mu and P'iao Kao were husband and wife. Taking advantage of the disorder at the end of the Yüan, they gathered their followers in the T'ai-hang mountains, dividing the more able among them as the 'twenty-eight patriarchs.' The [ancestral] patriarch of [the branch at] Shih-fo [village] was one of them. They deceived several thousand men and women [into joining with them]." This passage goes on to describe sectarian mythology in somewhat garbled fashion, including the statement that because she longed for her confused and suffering children, "Lao-mu descended to earth to save those who had been beheaded, those who had been sliced to pieces because they were registered on red [pieces of paper] to ascend to heaven, and those who had put on the great red robe [of martyrdom], who of all those who had ascended to Heaven were the most honored."

32. Huang Yü-p'ien, *P'o-hsieh*, 3:26a-b.

33. Hsiang Chüeh-ming, "Pao-chüan wen-hsüeh," p. 1225. In his texts Lo Ch'ing repeatedly equates *chia-hsiang* (native place) with *ching-t'u* (Amitābha's Pure Land), and "returning home" with going to be reborn in Amitābha's paradise. See for example his *Cheng-hsin pao-chüan*, p. 7b.

34. *Wu-sheng* itself is a Buddhist term which Soothill and Hodous define as "Not born . . . uncreated, no rebirth . . . an immortal life, a *nir-mānakāya* or transformation appearance of a Buddha in the world." They also give a term, Wu-sheng pao-kuo, which means "The precious country beyond birth and death, the immortal paradise of Amitābha" (*Dictionary*, pp. 380-381).

In the *Hsü-k'an p'o-hsieh*, p. 8b, Huang describes a *Fo-shuo Mi-t'o pao-chüan* (Amitābha *pao-chüan*), which speaks of members "together entering the Heaven of Utmost Bliss of the Eternal [Mother] (Wu-sheng chi-le t'ien)" and urges people to *nien-fo wu wu-sheng* (realize their eternal natures by reciting the Buddha's name).

35. Masaharu Anesaki, *History of Japanese Religion* (London, 1930), pp. 24-25, discusses this myth and notes that Aston "thinks that the [Japanese] primal triad is but an adoption of the Chinese triad of the ultimate reality and its two principles, Yin and Yang."

36. For the *Huai-nan tzu* and Chou Tun-i, see Chan, *Sourcebook*, pp. 306-308 and pp. 463-465. For this meaning of *ch'a-nü* (which can also mean just "young daughter") see Tai Yüan-ch'ang, *Hsien-hsüeh tz'u-tien* (Taipei, 1962), p. 112.

37. On Fu-hsi and Nü-kua, see Derk Bodde, "Myths of Ancient China," in Samuel Noah Kramer, ed., *Mythologies of the Ancient World* (Chicago, 1961), pp. 386-389, E. T. C. Werner, *A Dictionary of Chinese Mythology* (New York, 1961), pp. 334-335, and Zürcher, *Conquest*, I, 318.

38. Wolfram Eberhard, *The Local Cultures of South and East China*, trans. Alide Eberhard (Leiden, 1968), pp. 141, 144, 444-445. Honan and Shantung were primary areas of White Lotus activity. Eberhard also says, "Since at least T'ang times on the sources again and again mention cults of female deities as typical traits of Chekiang and Fukien" (p. 40), and, "In early China there were indeed female deities who were worshipped not only as deified ancestresses, but also as creator-goddesses . . . comparable to goddesses among the Yao" (p. 115). He also mentions two accounts of Fu-hsi uniting with his sister Nü-kua in "later Chinese mythology," but both seem to be influenced by aboriginal models.

39. Frank M. Lebar, Gerald C. Hickey, and John K. Musgrave, *Ethnic Groups of Mainland Southeast Asia* (New Haven, 1964), pp. 68-70.

40. David Crockett Graham, "The Customs of the Ch'uan Miao," *Journal of the West China Border Research Society*, 9:18 (1937).

41. David Crockett Graham, *Songs and Stories of the Ch'uan Miao* (Washington, 1954), pp. 72-73. The myth continues to describe the fate of the dead: "Gone, dead, thinking of your nine generations of ancestors assembled at the Hua T'an (flowery altar) ceremony, and the altar of the ceremonial drum, and returning to the level land of Ntzi Nyong Leo in the sky." This return to paradise motif is also parallel to sectarian mythology and could have made it easier for a Pure Land sect to accept a divine-couple creation story.

42. In the *Ming shih* there is an account dated 1515 of an aborigine named P'u Fa-e, who could speak Chinese and knew how to write charms and who proclaimed that Maitreya had appeared in the world and that he himself was King of the Man (tribe). He was supported in his uprising by Chinese *liu-min*. Li Shou-k'ung discusses other Maitreya-related outbreaks among "mountain people," and among Miao and I tribespeople in Szechwan and Kweichow, earlier than P'u Fa-e, in 1392 and 1475. Since this demonstrates sectarian influence on aboriginal groups, perhaps it is not too much to suggest that influence might have moved the other way as well. On this see *Ming shih*, vol. 3, chüan 187, p. 2192; T'ao Hsi-sheng, "Ming-tai Mi-le Pai-lien chiao," p. 48; and Li Shou-k'ung, "Ming-tai Pai-lien chiao," pp. 34, 39-40. P'u Fa-e was from the area of modern Chen-hsiung county in Yünnan.

43. Huang Yü-p'ien, *P'o-hsieh*, 2:3, 2:1, 1:3b-4. We have seen,

however, that the Lao-mu myth is mentioned in the *Yao-shih pao-chüan*, which Cheng Chen-to dates forty-five years earlier than this.

44. Given in Tsukamoto, "Rakyō," pp. 23, 24.

45. Graham, *Ch'uan Miao*, pp. 57-58.

46. *The Book of Lieh Tzu*, trans. A. C. Graham (London, 1960), pp. 102-103. Graham says that while this book "certainly contains material" from as early as the third century B.C., it was not written in its present form until the third century A.D. (p. 1).

47. Ibid., p. 35. For some other expressions of Chinese utopian thought see the *Li chi*, bk. 7, sec. 1, and Pao Ching-yen's essay quoted in Ko Hung, *Pao P'u-tzu, wai-p'ien*, sec. 48, trans. in Etienne Balazs "Nihilistic Revolt or Mystical Escapism," trans. H. M. Wright, in Arthur F. Wright, ed., *Chinese Civilization and Bureaucracy* (New Haven, 1964). For a detailed study of Chinese utopian thought from the Chou period to Mao Tse-tung see Wolfgang Bauer, *China und die Hoffnung auf Glück* (München, 1971). His discussion of secret societies can be found on pp. 311-323.

48. Rolf Stein, "Remarques sur les mouvements du Taoisme," pp. 3-12. G. F. Hudson in his *Europe and China* (London, 1931), p. 97, says, "Politically Ta Ts'in was the Roman Empire, geographically it was Egypt and Syria . . . Most of the descriptions apply only to Syria, and An-tu was supposed to be the capital of Ta Ts'in."

49. For a classic statement of the utopian concern built into the world view of the Confucian state, see the *Li chi*, bk. 7, sec. 4, in the Legge translation, *Sacred Books of the East*, XXVII, 391. After describing the harmony between classes which comes from all living according to *li* the passage concludes, "All under Heaven is in good condition. All this produces what we call [the state of] great mutual consideration [and harmony] . . . This would be the perfection of . . . a state of mutual harmony."

Such hopes were expressed in direct relationship to the pacification of dissenting sects. For example, in the *Ming Shen-tsung shih-lu*, 533:19a, we read after a long description of how to suppress heresy: "If all this is done, then the hearts of the people can be returned to orthodoxy, and the world will be in perfect peace for countless generations." This comment was written in 1615, near the end of the Ming dynasty.

50. Quoted in Fan Yeh (398-445), ed., *Hou Han shu* (Peking, 1965) chüan 30, *hsia*, pp. 19a-b. This passage is translated in Vincent Shih, *Taiping Ideology*, pp. 339-340.

51. This passage concerning the True Ruler is in the *Tung-yüan ching*, 1:11-12b, in *Cheng-t'ung Tao-tsang*, box 21, vol. 170, and is translated on pp. 238-239 of Seidel, "Perfect Ruler."

52. H. G. Creel, *The Birth of China* (New York, 1937), p. 367. See also Creel's more recent discussion of *t'ien-ming* in his *Origins of Statecraft in China*, vol. 1, *The Western Chou Empire* (Chicago, 1970), 81-100.

53. See for example Bernard Karlgren, trans., *The Book of Documents* (Stockholm, 1950), p. 20.

54. *Ming T'ai-tsu shih-lu*, 26:10b-11a. See also Li Shou-k'ung, "Ming-tai Pai-lien chiao," pp. 28-29.

55. *Feng-shen yen-i*, chaps. 6, 15, 43.

56. *Shih-er ch'ao tung-hua lu*, ed. Chiang Liang-ch'i (1722-1789), (Taipei, 1963), *Chia-ch'ing ch'ao*, 3:22b.

57. Yang, *Religion*, p. 136. See also Daniel H. Kulp, *Country Life in South China* (New York, 1925), I, 171.

58. Suzuki, *Shinchō*, p. 110. Of course, the other side of this fatalism was the conviction that with proper knowledge, faith or ritual action one could influence the course of fate or at least mitigate its results. So emperors proclaimed general amnesties and the people prayed to the gods or had grave sites changed, all in the hope of avoiding what appeared to be determined. In sectarian belief the power of fate could ultimately be transcended by salvation and return to paradise after death. So we read in the *Hun-yüan hung-yang t'an-shih chüan* (The origin in chaos Red Yang scroll of sorrow for the world), "Human wealth and honor, poverty and low station all are determined by fate; one should not energetically strive [after what is so fated], but rather should only develop in piety, attain enlightenment, [and thus] return to one's origin and native land." Huang Yü-p'ien, *Yu-hsü p'o hsieh*, in Sawada, *Kōchu haja shōben*, p. 133.

59. Chu Fa-hu, trans., *Fo-shuo Mi-le hsia-sheng ching, Taishō*, 14, 421. The setting given this sūtra is a prediction of Maitreya's coming in the very distant future made by Śākyamuni to Ānanda. After a detailed description of how wonderful the world will be in that time, the text continues with an account of a Brahman named Subrāhamana who will serve as chief minister of a king of the dharma. Maitreya will be born to Subrāhamana's wife, Brahmavatī. After entering the homeless life he will become (the next) Buddha following an earth-shaking enlightenment experience, and then proceed to convert tens of thousands by his preaching. Maitreya will live 84,000 years, and after his *parinirvāna* his teachings will remain among men for another 84,000. At the end of the sūtra all those listening to Śākyamani's sermon are told that if they wish to be reborn on earth during Maitreya's advent they should earnestly strive to progress in worship and service.

There are four other sūtras describing Maitreya's future Buddhahood in this volume of the *Taishō Compendium*. Their accounts of paradisal conditions on earth at that time are much the same as that summarized above, though with differences in detail.

Orthodox descriptions of Amitābha's Pure Land also contributed to sectarian visions of paradise. On this see *The Smaller Sukhāvatī-vyūha*, trans. F. Max Müller, in *Sacred Books of the East*, vol. 49, part 2, pp. 91-98; and the *Fo-shuo A-mi-t'o ching in Taishō*, 12, 346-348.

60. Chih-p'an, *Fo tsu*, chüan 42, *Taishō*, 49, 390-391. Pu-tai is dis-

cussed in Helen B. Chapin, "The Ch'an Master Pu-Tai," *Journal of the American Oriental Society*, 53.1:47-52 (1933), in Ch'en *Buddhism*, pp. 405-408, and at more length by Ferdinand D. Lessing, *Yung-Ho-Kung: An Iconography of the Lamaist Cathedral in Peking* (Stockholm, 1942), I, 15-35.

61. L. de Vallée Poussin, "Ages of the World-Buddhist," *Encyclopedia of Religion and Ethics*, I, 187-190.

62. Ch'en, *Buddhism*, pp. 297-298. This theory of three periods of the dharma was first developed in such Indian Mahāyāna texts as the *Lotus Sūtra*. On this see Yamada Ryūjō, *Daijō Bukkyō seiritsuron josetsu* (Kyōto, 1965), I, 568, 580-581, 591. For this reference I am indebted to Professor Shotaro Iida of the University of British Columbia.

63. Ibid., pp. 298-300.

64. For a good statement of the relationship of yin and yang to cosmic cycles, see the summary of Chu Hsi's views in Fung, *Chinese Philosophy*, II, 549-550. One of the best known statements of the concept of dynastic cycles occurs in the opening lines of the popular medieval novel, *The Romance of the Three Kingdoms*, which describe alternate periods of unification and civil war in Chinese history, up to the Han. Then follows a long passage detailing signs of the decline of the Han dynasty, including dissolute emperors, power-grabbing eunuchs, sycophant officials, and a variety of such evil omens as a flying green serpent coiled on the throne, a black cloud in the palace, terrible earthquakes and storms, and the transformation of hens into roosters. This symbolism of regression into chaos points toward the need for the restoration of cosmic order through the establishing of a benevolent emperor on the throne, all of which was easy to relate to the image of the Buddhist Universal Monarch. See Lo Kuan-chung (c. 1330-1400), *San-kuo yen-i*, chap. 1.

65. Sarkisyanz, *Buddhist Backgrounds*, pp. 103, 151.

66. Ch'en, *Buddhism*, pp. 146, 152, 124-127.

67. Arthur F. Wright, "The Formation of Sui Ideology, 581-604," in John K. Fairbank, ed., *Chinese Thought and Institutions* (Chicago, 1957), pp. 101, 78.

68. It is interesting that in 581 Wen-ti used the T'ien-t'ai theory of the interpenetration of this world and the Pure Land to proclaim a Buddhist doctrine of holy war. C. F. Wright, "Sui Ideology," p. 97.

69. Moriz Winternitz, *A History of Indian Literature* (Calcutta, 1927), II, 382-383.

70. Wang Jih-hsiu, *Lung-shu Ching-t'u wen*, chüans 4 and 6, in *Taishō*, 47, 262, 263, 270. In Japan, Honen also supported the idea that "one who has obtained ōjō, or birth in paradise, can return to the world and work for the salvation of others." See Eliot, *Japanese Buddhism*, p. 367. Jambu is *jambudvīpa*, the earth, one of four great continents in every world system.

71. Suzuki, "Sōdai Bukkyō," p. 240.

72. Sun Tso-min, "Nung-min chan-cheng," p. 84.

73. In Chapter 41 of the *Shui-hu chuan* Sung Chiang is called Sung Master of the Stars (*Sung hsing-chu*) by Chiu-t'ien hsüan-nü's messengers. The goddess explains to him that when his task on earth is done he will be able to resume his position in the heavens. His rough and ready follower Lu Ta is finally admitted to a monastery after the abbot, in a trance, learns that he was in fact a Star of Heaven (Chapter 3). In Chapter 70 there is a complete list of the stars corresponding to all 108 of these "righteous bandits."

74. Bernard Gallin, *Hsin Hsing, Taiwan: A Chinese Village in Change* (Berkeley, 1966), p. 236.

75. Huang Yü-p'ien, *P'o-hsieh*, 1:9b-10b. One of the earliest recorded uses of such cyclical time period eschatology by a popular religious movement was by the Yellow Turbans in 184 who proclaimed: "The Azure Heaven is already dead, and the Yellow Heaven is about to be established. In the year *chia-tzu* there will be great prosperity in the empire. Using chalk [the Yellow Turbans] wrote the characters *chia-tzu* on the walls and office gates at the capital." *Hou Han shu*, 101:1-2, quoted in Paul M. Michaud, "The Yellow Turbans," *Monumenta Serica*, 17:76 (1958).

76. *Ming Ying-tsung shih-lu*, 277:14b-15a. Wang Pin was active in Pao-ch'eng county of Shensi province (in modern Han-chung district). In popular belief every emperor was considered the incarnation of the Tzu-wei star (Weiger, *Dictionary*, p. 536). Though Wang raised an army of several thousand, he was soon defeated by government troops and executed, along with four associates. Other followers arrested were released.

77. *Ming T'ai-tsu shih-lu*, 182:4b-5a. This was Li Mou of I-ch'un county in Kiangsi.

78. Wang Ch'ung-wu, "Lun Ming T'ai-tsu ch'i-ping chi ch'i cheng-ts'e chih chuan-pien," *Li-shih yü-yen yen-chiu so chi-k'an*, 10:60 (1948).

79. *Shih-ch'ao sheng-hsün, Jen-tsung*, 98:4a. This comment is dated 1800. We see here another interesting folk transposition of Maitreyan thought, for in this account the Buddha helps the emperor, instead of the other way around. Yano Jinichi in his "Pai-lien chiao," p. 8, indicates that the theme of Maitreya assisting the emperor occurred in other groups of this same period as well.

80. Cohn, *Pursuit*, revised and expanded edition, pp. 71-74.

81. Williams, *Radical Reformation*, p. 520.

82. Ibid., pp. 373-374.

83. A closer parallel to the Chinese pattern can be found in Burmese *gaings*, which also institutionalized a politically related eschatology. There are over one hundred of these groups in Burma, some of which have elaborate temples. *Gaing* members believe that their leaders are reincarnations of famous folk heros of the past (*weikza*), and also are, or soon will be, manifestations of the righteous monarch who is to prepare the way for the coming of Arimadeya (Sanskrit, Maitreya). Melford Spiro, in his *Bud-*

dhism and Society (New York, 1970), pp. 173-174, describes this Future King: "He will be a pious Buddhist, turning the Wheel of the Law—indeed, his Burmese title is derived from the Sanskrit Cakravarti (Pali, Cakkavatti)—but more important, he will be the king of Burma, restoring law and order to that country, driving out the foreigners, and bringing prosperity and wealth to the Burmese people . . . Millennial Buddhism combines two additional features. First, on the belief level it stresses that the Future King, or at least the herald of the Future King, is already here. Second, on the social level, it entails membership in an esoteric sect (gaing) which is devoted to him and to his alleged powers . . ."

Spiro goes on to describe the persons and "palaces" of two putative Future Kings living in Mandalay at the time of his investigations (1965). Gaing temples include such eschatological symbolism as the thrones which both Bo Min Gaung and Arimadeya will occupy. In some groups the distinction between Future King and Future Buddha is blurred, so that gaing leaders are identified with Arimadeya himself. On this see also E. Michael Mendelson, "A Messianic Buddhist Association in Upper Burma," Bulletin of the School of Oriental and African Studies, 24.3:560-580 (1961) and his earlier article, "Religion and Authority in Modern Burma," The World Today, 16.3:110-118 (March 1960). Several of these sects actively rebelled against British rule in order to reestablish a Buddhist monarch who could prepare the way for Arimadeya.

84. Topley, "Great Way," pp. 372, 387. As is noted above, Burmese gaings also believe that a righteous ruler must cooperate with the messiah.

85. Huang Yü-p'ien, P'o-hsieh, 3:17b. The grammatical structure here is chi (since) . . . ku (therefore) . . . i (also).

86. Ibid., 2:10b. This text may have been related to the Wang family of Shih-fo k'ou. Na-yen-ch'eng tells us that in one of their texts, the San-chiao ying-chieh tsung-kuan t'ung-shu, there was the following passage: "In the past, when the Lamplighter Buddha (Dīpamkara) ruled the religion (chang-chiao), each year had six months and each day six hours. Now Sā-kyamuni controls the religion, and each year has twelve months, with twelve hours per day. In the future the Buddha Who is Yet to Come (Wei-lai fo), that is, Maitreya, will rule the religion. [Then] each year will have eighteen months, and each day eighteen hours. The Buddha Who is Yet to Come will be reborn in the Wang family of Shih-fo k'ou." Na Wen-i kung tsou-i, 42:18b-19, dated 1815. One could scarcely ask for a better example of the relationship of eschatology to leadership in sectarian thought. Note that here the successive Buddhas are said to control the religion rather than the world.

87. Huang Yü-p'ien, P'o-hsieh, 3:12-17. The quoted passage is on p. 17a.

88. Wu Chih-ying, "Yüan-chiao shih-mo chi-ch'i ching-chüan," Jen-wen yüeh-k'an, 8:4-5 (June 15, 1937). Wu makes it clear that the character yüan, sometimes translated as "round," here had the Buddhist meaning of

"completion," taken from the *Sūtra of Complete Awakening* (*Yüan-chüeh ching*). The leader of this sect was Fang Jung-sheng, who was executed in Chiang-ning county of Kiangsu after an abortive uprising in 1815.

89. Unnamed text in Huang Yü-p'ien, *P'o-hsieh*, 3:10b.

90. *P'u-ching Ju-lai yao-shih t'ung-t'ien pao-chüan* (Precious scroll of the Tathāgata of universal stillness, whose wisdom penetrates to Heaven), quotes in ibid., 2:10a. This is an interesting folk echo of the old Buddhist doctrine of the lengthening of life in the third Period of Restoration.

91. Wu, "Yüan chiao," p. 5.

92. Topley, "Great Way," pp. 373, 384-387.

8. Patterns of Folk Buddhist Religion:
Leadership, Scriptures, Ritual.

1. James Legge, trans., *Li chi*, in *Sacred Books of the East*, XXVII, 382.

2. Chan, *Sourcebook*, pp. 280-282. Chang Tsai's somewhat more poetic statement can be found on p. 497.

3. For a succinct statement see Kristopher Schipper, "On Chinese Folk Religion," ms. (Taipei, 1968), pp. 8-9.

4. Gallin quotes a story told by Taoist priests as a part of funeral ritual in modern Taiwan: "People must marry, since the parents have given us our bodies and we must give the parents another body—a descendant" (*Hsin Hsing, Taiwan*, p. 227). The intention of this form of "incarnation" is of course different from that in the bodhisattva belief. For a good discussion of the implications of ancestral cult for an understanding of man, see: Francis L. K. Hsü, *Under the Ancestor's Shadow* (New York, 1948), pp. 224, 8, 245, 167.

5. Needham, *Science and Civilization*, II, 139.

6. Ibid., II, 33-34.

7. Lebar, Frank, and Hickey, *Ethnic Groups*, pp. 70-71; Graham, *Ch'uan Miao*, p. 58.

8. DeGroot, *Religious System*, VI, 1187-1341. See also Needham, *Science and Civilization*, II, 32-35, 132-139; David Hawkes, ed. and trans., *Ch'u Tz'u, The Songs of the South* (Oxford, 1959), pp. 10, 21-22, 28-29, 81-87, 101-104; Eberhard, *Local Cultures*, pp. 304-315; Shih, *Taiping Ideology*, pp. 320-328.

9. Gallin, *Hsin Hsing, Taiwan*, pp. 209, 241-246. See also Alan J. A. Elliott, *Chinese Spirit-Medium Cults in Singapore* (London, 1955), for a detailed discussion of contemporary *dang-ki* (Mandarin, *t'ung-chi*, divining youth), young men believed to speak for the deities while possessed by them. For the distinction between *shen-tao* and *tao-chiao* I am indebted to conversations with Kristopher Schipper in 1969. On this point

see also, Saso, *Taoism*, pp. 84-85, for the differences between five forms of Taoist priesthood.

10. *Saddharma-Pundarīka* (The Lotus of the True Law), trans. Hendrik Kern, *Sacred Books of the East*, XXI, F. Max Müller, ed. (Oxford, 1884), Chap. 10, pp. 216, 217. For Kumārajīva's Chinese translation of these passages, see the *Miao-fa lien-hua ching*, chüan 4, Chap. 10, in *Taishō*, 9, 30-31.

11. The helpful role of ancestors was mentioned above. For examples from the Chou period of prayers of thanks to legendary ancestors for their aid, see Arthur Waley, trans., *The Book of Songs* (Boston, 1937), pp. 160, 227, 250-251.

In the *Chuang Tzu* there are some passages which indicate that Taoist immortals could also be concerned to help others. On this see, for example, Burton Watson, trans., *The Complete Works of Chuang Tzu* (New York, 1968), p. 33.

Seidel, in her "Perfect Ruler," refers to several Han and post-Han instances of divine assistance by Taoist sages and immortals. While it is certain that the theme of the descent of a sage from his mountain vigil to assist the ruler is of indigenous origin, other more inclusive references to saving activity in these Taoist texts may reflect Buddhist influence.

12. *Lotus Sūtra*, trans. Kern, chap. 24, pp. 406-418, and the *Miao-fa lien-hua ching*, chüan 7, chap. 25, in *Taishō*, 9, 56-58.

13. P'u-tu, *Lien-tsung pao-chien*, chüan 7, in *Taisho*, 47, 338.

14. Cheng Chen-to, *Su wen-hsüeh*, II, 328.

15. *Lung-hua ching*, quoted in ibid., 1:7b-8a. Huang Yü-p'ien quotes an unnamed sectarian text which claimed that *all* members, male and female, were reincarnations of Buddhas. See his *Yu-hsü p'o-hsieh*, in Sawada, *Kōchu haja shōben*, p. 130.

16. Huang Yü-p'ien, *Hsü-k'an p'o-hsieh*, p. 23b. In another text, the *Hung-yang chung-hua pao-ching*, we are told that Lo Ch'ing was a manifestation of yet a third deity, Shang-ku sheng-jen, the Ancient Sage, in which form he revealed his five scriptures. This text tells us that, "Now he is coming again to save all sentient beings." Quoted in Sakai, *Chūgoku zenshō*, p. 450.

17. *Shih-liao*, ti 100. A 1748 memorial from Shansi.

18. Wu Chih-ying, "Yüan chiao," pp. 1-2.

19. S. Naquin, "Eight Trigrams," pp. 117-118.

20. Huang Yü-p'ien, *P'o-hsieh*, 1:3b-4b. The text adds that it was the Jade Emperor who *asked* Lao-mu to summon Kung Ch'ang, the two characters for which form the surname Chang. I have not been able to locate this Sang-yüan village, assuming that it actually existed, but the text would put it somewhere between Chao-ch'eng county in Shansi and Peking in Hopei.

21. Ibid., 1:16. I take *chen-hsing kuei-chia* here to mean a return of his spirit while he was in a trance state. However, in other contexts it can mean "to die."

22. Ibid., 1:21a-21b. Huang adds that when this man was taken to court, he was terrified, wept for mercy, and admitted that he could not ascend to Heaven, and that just before he was to be slowly sliced to pieces he cried out piteously but was still unable to ascend. So, such claims by sectarians "cannot be believed."

23. Topley, "Great Way," pp. 376-378.

24. Russell, *Dissent and Reform*, pp. 102-106.

25. Ibid., pp. 56-57; Cohn, *Pursuit*, revised and expanded edition, pp. 46-50.

26. Russell, *Dissent and Reform*, p. 123. Cohn, *Pursuit*, revised and expanded edition, pp. 44-46. Cohn gives the name as Eon.

27. Williams, *Radical Reformation*, p. 425.

28. One must admit, however, that charlatanry evidently was present in some Chinese groups. Let me give three examples, the first (to me) ambiguous, the second two less so.

In discussing the various White Lotus related sects connected with the Wang family in Shih-fo k'ou, Na-yen-ch'eng several times mentions that members were expected to contribute "foundation money" (*ken-chi ch'ien*), which was really a form of investment in the new age to come: "Those who enter the sect in the first and twelfth months of each year contribute 'foundation money,' [and are told that] they will be rewarded when the Future Buddha appears. Because of this the people all believe." *Na Wen-i kung tsou-i*, 42:19a. There are of course many other references in the literature to regular contributions of food and money by members to leaders. Such contributions on the one hand are the economic lifeblood of voluntary associations, but on the other hand do provide opportunities for the unscrupulous, perhaps particularly when related to eschatological promises. Surely in some of the sects there was ground for the oft-repeated official complaint that leaders were merely trying to cheat people out of their money.

Two descriptions which indicate more clear-cut rapacity are given in Shih Ssu's *K'an-ching chiao-fei*, 11:12b-14a. While Shih Ssu was no lover of dissenters, his comments here go beyond the usual stereotyped accusations to a level of detail which appears authentic. The first description is of Hsü T'ien-te, a Szechwan leader of the 1796 White Lotus rebellion. When the uprising began, Shih tells us that Hsü proclaimed: "Now the empire is in great disorder, and Shang-ti on such and such a date will send down terrible calamities in which large numbers of people will certainly die. Only [members of] our religion will be spared, so why don't you invite each other to come [and join us] with your whole families? I will ask a [religious] teacher to preach and recite scriptures, so that we may be saved together."

Shih continues: "Before long, several hundred families came from far and near. [Then] T'ien-te [with his brother and eight other leaders] said that since they had already gathered such a multitude of supporters they could start a rebellion [which they did].

"[Hsü] commanded his people, saying, 'Now we are going to rebel; those who do not support us will be beheaded.' Those sect members who had not known of [Hsü's] plans for rebellion, having already joined with their whole families, had no choice but to obey." This rebellion lasted seven years, ending with Hsü's execution in 1802.

The second account is of another rebel leader in the same period, Wang San-huai of Tung-hsiang (modern Hsüan-han county), of whom Shih Ssu tells us that he was a "shaman" (*wu-chu*) who prayed for blessings for others [who consulted him], privately sold salt, [and with other] gamblers and vagrants practiced the White Lotus religion." At the time of the uprising "he used heretical teachings to confuse the people, saying that his master, a divine man (*shen-jen*), had said that a terrible disaster would occur very soon, earth and sky would be plunged into darkness, and the sun and moon would not shine. [He claimed that in this time] those who did not die by knives, weapons, flood or fire would contract strange illnesses, and their wives and daughters would be violated, saying, 'The world is about to go through a great transformation, and only those who join our religion can hope to escape.' " Shih concludes this account by saying, "Though his words were completely wild and false, ignorant folk believed in him and became his followers. They chanted scriptures in worship, and in time became extremely numerous."

It is possible that bias against folk leaders is involved here as elsewhere, but it was not common for literate reporters to invent such material at this level of detail. It is also possible that Wang San-huai believed his own teachings, but the opportunity for propaganda was certainly present.

On this point see also S. Naquin's detailed study of the Pa-kua chiao leader Lin Ch'ing who seems to have been largely an opportunist intent on increasing his own wealth and prestige, though he was also believed to have healing powers. Yet even in this most blatant case one hesitates simply to apply the word charlatan. He convinced many others, some of whom were willing to risk death on his behalf. Who knows; perhaps he convinced himself as well. "Eight Trigrams," pp. 89-105.

29. Leff, *Heresy*, I, 28, and Russell, *Disent and Reform*, pp. 56, 62, 108, 119. In their *Heresies of the High Middle Ages* (New York, 1969), p. 96, Walter L. Wakefield and Austin P. Evans write, "As a result of revisionist studies, Tanchelm is now presented as probably a monk and priest, one of the wandering preachers whose activities were so prominent in the twelfth century; his theme, the furthering of Gregorian reforms."

30. Leff, *Heresy*, p. 475.

31. DeGroot, *Sectarianism*, I, 201, 219.

32. T'ao Hsi-sheng, "Yüan-tai Mi-le Pai-lien chiao-hui," p. 155. Un-

fortunately the official records often devote no more than a few characters to such incidents. The Lung-ch'üan monastery was in modern Feng-hsiang county of Shensi. Ch'iao-shan is in Chen-chiang, Kiangsu.

33. *Yüan shih*, vol. 2, chüan 30, p. 270. See also Li Shou-k'ung, "Ming-tai Pai-lien chiao," p. 18.

34. Wu Han, "Ming-chiao," p. 270. It should be noted that T'ang Sai-er, who led a powerful uprising in 1420, is described as a nun. The *Ming shih*, vol. 3, chüan 158, p. 1911, states: "At that time, in the urgent search for T'ang Sai-er, several tens of thousands of Buddhist nuns in Shantung, Peking and elsewhere in the realm were arrested. However, the people were very sympathetic toward them, so they were pardoned, after which the people calmed down." But see also Fu Wei-lin, *Ming shu* (Changsha, 1937), vol. 29, chüan 160, p. 3174, where we are told that a large number of Buddhist and Taoist nuns were killed during this investigation. T'ang Sai-er was never captured.

35. *Ming Shih-tsung shih-lu*, 313:4a and *Ming Shen-tsung shih-lu*, 533:18b.

36. Suzuki, *Shinchō*, p. 117. One may wonder, of course, just how "professional" some of these clergy were, at least by orthodox monastic standards. On this see Chu-hung, *Chu-ch'uang san-pi*, pp. 16b-17, in *Yün-ch'i fa-hui*, vol. 4, where there is a brief essay entitled "Seng wu tsa shu" (On monks who devote themselves to miscellaneous arts). Here he describes Buddhist clergy of the Ming period who specialized in geomancy, prognostication, medicine, the preparation of charms, and so on. No doubt many of the clergy involved with sects were of this "miscellaneous" sort, a type which goes back at least to the T'ang dynasty. For T'ang prohibitions of healing and divination by monks and nuns, see Kenneth Ch'en, *The Chinese Transformation of Buddhism* (Princeton, 1973) pp. 101-103.

37. Yuji Muramatsu, "Some Themes in Chinese Rebel Ideologies," in Arthur F. Wright, ed., *The Confucian Persuasion* (Stanford, 1960), p. 255.

38. Huang Yü-p'ien, *P'o-hsieh*, 3:28.

39. DeGroot, *Sectarianism*, II, 429.

40. Suzuki, *Shinchō*, p. 101. This discussion is based on pp. 98-102 of Suzuki's book. For the relationship of Liu Sung and Liu Chih-hsieh, see Shih Ssu, *K'an-ching chiao-fei shu-pien*, 11:10a-10b. We have already discussed the treatment of Hsü T'ien-te and Wang San-huai in this source.

41. Ibid., p. 113.

42. *Ming shih*, vol. 3, chüan 122, p. 1559.

43. Noguchi Tetsurō, "Min-dai shūkyō kessha no keizai katsudō," *Yokohama Kokuritsu Daigaku jimbun kiyō*, 1:12-15, 27 (December 1968). For details on Hsü Hung-ju see *Ming shih*, vol. 4, chüan 257, pp. 2902-2903. We have referred above to the detailed discussion of Liu Fu-ta in *Ming shih*, vol. 3, chüan 206, pp. 2388-2390. There are also a few general statements in Ming records indicating that the sects appealed to an economic cross-section of the population. For example, in the 1546 report describing sects in the capital area which we have discussed above we

read: "Moreover, wealthy people and members of well-known families are joining together in associations, which they say is for self-protection. These ignorant and unlearned folk spend all their wealth, and exhaust their resources, competing with each other in bestowing charity." *Ming Shih-tsung shih-lu,* 313:4a.

A report dated fourteen years later from the same source laments: "The people's minds are all poisoned by heretical teaching, which they then proceed to follow; the ignorant hope to obtain blessings and prosperity, and the educated to seek for protection, while the rich overturn their homes [i.e., give all they own] to join, and the poor offer themselves as slaves." *Ming Shih-tsung shih-lu,* 486:3a, dated Chia-ching 39 (1560).

Of course, it could also be shown that the membership of many groups was from the lowest levels of society, as for example Wu Chih-ying's statement in his "Yüan chiao," p. 2, that most Yüan chiao members around Mao-shan in Kiangsu were sweet potato growers. I seek here only to illustrate the complexity of relationships between economics and religion in these associations. On this point see also S. Naquin's very helpful and detailed discussion of the socioeconomic backgrounds of Pa-kua chiao members and leaders in 1813, in her "Eight Trigrams," p. 47-48, 396-401. They came from a great variety of backgrounds, occupations, and levels of social status.

44. Such charisma, however, could be measured in very pragmatic terms. As Huang Yü-p'ien writes in his *P'o-hsieh,* 3:5, "[Status in the sects] depends upon seniority, amount of monetary contribution, loyalty, and how many disciples recruited."

45. *Ming shih,* vol. 3, chüan 122, p. 1559. One should add, however, that Kuo's sons faced fierce competition for leadership in the person of Chu Yüan-chang. See also Li Shou-k'ung, "Ming-tai Pai-lien chiao," p. 26.

46. Huang Yü-p'ien, *P'o-hsieh,* "Introduction," pp. 10b-11.

47. Suzuki, *Shinchō,* p. 101.

48. *Shih-liao,* t'ien 993, ti 100-102. The oft-repeated sentence structure is "(A master) *chuan-shou* (another person) *wei t'u*—he in turn received so and so as his disciple." There is ample material on the interconnections of sectarian leadership, which could be a study in its own right. Government officials were most of all interested in the names of rebel leaders, their activities and relationships to each other, some of which were tracked down in some detail through concurrent investigations in different areas. As is mentioned above, one of the best sources for such a study is chüan 42 of the *Na Wen-i kung tsou-i,* which begins with the arrest of a leader named Wang Tien-k'uei in I-cheng county, Kiangsu, in 1815. I cannot resist summarizing a part of his fascinating confession as recorded as pp. 2b-3b of this chapter.

Wang begins by admitting that his family was originally from Shih-fo k'ou in Hopei, having moved south in 1650. From then on they had for generations transmitted the Pure Tea sect, "urging others to become vegetarians and recite scriptures." His father and grandfather had been arrested in 1771 for sectarian activity, with the result that his father was executed and his grandfather banished. At that time he was only seven *sui* of age. Later two of his uncles as well were arrested for preaching (*ch'uan-chiao*), but he himself did not begin to do religious work until 1792. When he did, sect members in areas where he went became his disciples because their fathers had been followers of his father. The account continues with long lists of interrelated names and places, which are being sorted out by Susan Naquin.

49. Yang K'uan, "Pai-lien chiao te t'e-tien," p. 4. DeGroot describes this event in his *Sectarianism*, II, 436: The last of the sectaries were besieged in a house. At the end, "they themselves set fire to the house and about forty or fifty perished in the place, locked in each other's arms. Not one escaped."

50. *Shih-liao*, t'ien 50.

51. Eliot, *Hinduism and Buddhism*, II, 231, 236, 243.

52. Raj Mahon Nath, "Śankara Deva and the Assam Vaishnavite Movement," in Haridas Bhattacharya, ed., *The Cultural Heritage of India*, vol. IV, *The Religions* (Calcutta, 1956), pp. 203, 209.

53. Except for *dhāraṇīs*, spells, which remain efficacious only if the order of Sanskrit syllables is retained.

54. Ch'en Ju-heng, *Shuo-shu shih-hua* (Peking, 1958), pp. 7-10. In his "Narrators of Buddhist Scriptures and Religious Tales in the Sung Period," *Archiv Orientalni*, 10:377 (1938), Jaroslav Prusek writes: "The storytelling profession was hereditary, like other professions in ancient China . . . This led to long preservation of oral tradition."

55. Sun K'ai-ti, "T'ang-tai su-chiang kuei-fan yü ch'i pen chih t'its'ai," in his *Lun Chung-kuo tuan-p'ien pai-hua hsiao-shuo* (Shanghai, 1953), pp. 105-115. See Edwin O. Reischauer, *Ennin's Travels in T'ang China* (New York, 1955), pp. 183-187 for a detailed discussion of monastic lectures on sūtras in the T'ang dynasty. A recent summary of modern scholarship on this topic is provided by Kenneth Ch'en, *Chinese Transformation*, pp. 240-255.

56. Ennin, *Ennin's Diary*, trans. Edwin O. Reischauer (New York, 1955), p. 299. However, Ennin also says that, "since the ninth year of T'aiho (835) they have held no lectures, but the new Emperor has started them again," so this custom evidently began earlier. In the *Hsü kao-seng chuan* (665) Tao-hsüan discusses a popular preaching monk in Ch'ang-an named Pao-yen who died in 627. Of him we read that, "he stimulated his listeners [and said that] by a clap of the hands they could attain immediate enlightenment. All those [who heard them] cut off their hair and took off their [ordinary] clothes [i.e., resolved to become monks or nuns]" chüan 30, in *Taishō*, 50, 705.

57. Hsiang Chüeh-ming, "T'ang-tai su-chiang k'ao," *Wen-shih tsa-chih* (May 1944), 3:42-43.

58. Tuan An-chieh, *Yüeh-fu tsa-lu*, p. 24, Wen-hsü section, quoted in ibid., p. 19.

59. *Yin-hua lu*, 4:3a, quoted in Ch'en, *Shuo-shu*, p. 19.

60. Prusek, "Narrators of Buddhist Scriptures," p. 378.

61. Cheng Chen-to, *Su wen-hsüeh*, I, 252.

62. Ibid., II, 306-307. For recent discussions of Chinese vernacular literature see Jaroslav Prusek, *Chinese History and Literature* (Dordrecht, Holland, 1970), and Tadao Sakai, "Confucianism and Popular Educational Works," in Wm. Theodore DeBary, ed., *Self and Society in Ming Thought* (New York, 1970).

63. Cheng Chen-to, *Su wen-hsüeh*, II, 307. See also Sun K'ai-ti, "Tz'u-hua k'ao," in his *Lun Chung-kuo tuan-p'ien pai-hua hsiao-shuo* (Shanghai, 1953), p. 54, for a summary list of six basic steps in the development of Chinese popular literature, leading to the novels of the Ming period. The *pao-chüan* are the fourth step.

64. Ch'en Ju-heng, *Shuo-shu*, pp. 124-126. In his *Chūgoku zensho*, pp. 441, Sakai gives the names of two Ming *pao-chüan* which can be traced directly to T'ang *pien-wen*, the *Ti-yü chüan* (Scroll of Hell) and the *Mu-lien chüan* (Scroll of Mu-lien; Sanskrit, Moggallana). He also lists a number of titles based on sūtras in which *ching* has been changed to *chüan*, such as the *Mi-t'o chüan* (Amitābha), *Chin-kang chüan* (Diamond), and the *Fa-hua chüan* (Lotus). For additional discussion of Ming and Ch'ing *pao-chüan* see Sawada Mizuho, *Hōkan no kenkyū*.

65. Cheng Chen-to, *Su wen-hsüeh*, II, 311.

66. Li's observation here is corroborated by the fact that only one of the sixty-eight texts collected by Huang Yü-p'ien is based on a secular theme. See Sakai, *Chūgoku zensho*, p. 448.

67. Li Shih-yü, *Hsin-yen*, pp. 170-171, 165.

68. Sakai, *Chūgoku zensho*, pp. 437-438, 442-445. Eighty-eight of these texts titles are listed in Chu Kuo-chen, *Yung ch'uang hsiao-p'in*, 32:6b-7a, all collected from one Shansi sect during the Ming Ch'eng-hua period (1465-1488). Sect leaders, both of whom studied under a Pure Land monk, claimed that these scriptures had been revealed to them by the Buddha in their dreams. This group was suppressed after staging an abortive uprising. One of the arresting officials received imperial permission to distribute a list of their texts as a warning to the common people. None of these texts have the same names as those collected by Huang Yü-p'ien 350 years later.

69. Cheng Chen-to, *Su wen-hsüeh*, II, 325.

70. Ibid., p. 308.

71. Sakai, *Chūgoku zensho*, p. 439.

72. Yang K'uan, in his "Pai-lien chiao te t'e-tien," p. 4, comments, "White Lotus scriptures originated as notes and prompt books for their sermons."

73. Li Shih-yü, Hsin-yen, pp. 169-170. Lo Ch'ing's texts show all these characteristics except the sixth.

74. Cheng Chen-to, Su wen-hsüeh, II, 312-327.

75. Huang Yü-p'ien, P'o-hsieh, Preface, pp. 1b, 1:7a. Huang Yü-p'ien says that the elegant appearance of some late Ming pao-chüan was due to the support of eunuchs at court, for, " . . . in this time all the eunuchs believed in heretical religion." Yu-hsü p'o-hsieh, in Sawada, Kōchu haja shōben, p. 122. See also pp. 31, 127 and 150 of Sawada's edition for similar comments, including a text in which a eunuch is enshrined in scripture as "Lord of the Eighth Heaven," met by P'iao Kao when the latter reached the "City of Clouds," sectarian paradise.

76. Huang Yü-p'ien, Hsü-k'an p'o-hsieh, p. 8b.

77. Huang Yü-p'ien, P'o-hsieh, 3:28a.

78. Chao Wei-pang, "Secret Religious Societies in North China in the Ming Dynasty," Folklore Studies (1948), 7:112.

79. Na Wen-i kung tsou-i, 41:18a.

80. This ritual is described by Hsiang Chüeh-ming in his "T'ang-tai su-chiang k'ao," Wen shih tsa-chih (May 1944), 3:44. Detailed descriptions of similar rituals can be found in Ennin, Ennin's Diary, pp. 183-187.

81. Cheng Chen-to, Su wen-hsüeh, pp. 312-313. The text proper begins with a prose section immediately following the three-stage introductory rite.

82. See, for example, Lotus Sūtra, chap. 7, sec. 82 of Kern translation. The tradition that scripture comes from divine beings can be found in the Pali texts as well. For example, the Jana-Vasabha Suttanta of the Dīgha-Nikāya attributes its origin to a revelation from Brahma.

83. See Doré, Researches, V, 510-517. The receipt of divine messages was a common claim of Taoist-oriented sect leaders such as Sun Ta-yu and T'ang Sai-er. This phenomenon was also known in Europe. Aldebert claimed to have received a letter directly from Jesus Christ, "which fell from Heaven in Jerusalem." Russell says that this was "part of a long tradition of letters falling from Heaven." See his Dissent and Reform, p. 105.

84. For further information on planchette writing see Eberhard, Local Cultures, pp. 300-303; DeGroot, Religious System, VI, 1295-1322; Hsü, Ancestor's Shadow, pp. 136-137, 167-179, and Chao Wei-pang, "The Origin and Growth of the Fu-chi," Folklore Studies 1:9-27 (1942).

85. Huang Yü-p'ien, P'o hsieh, 1:1.

86. See for example the Lotus Sūtra, chap. 10, pp. 214-215 of Kern translation. Other Mahāyāna sūtras, such as the Diamond and Pure Land, make similar claims.

87. Wang Jih-hsiu, Lung-shu Ching-t'u wen, chüan 6, in Taishō, 47, 270-271.

88. Cheng Chen-to, Su wen-hsüeh, p. 311.

89. Huang Yü-p'ien, *P'o hsieh*, 2:4. For other assurances that scripture recitation saves ancestors, self and one's whole family, and that those who simply listen to *pao-chüan* being read will have good fortune, live long, etc., see Sawada, *Kōchu haja shoben*, pp. 137-138, 145 (*Yu-hsü p'o hsieh*). Sakai notes that expenses for printing *pao-chüan* were covered by voluntary contributions, which then permitted their free distribution. A passage in the *Hsiao-shih wu-hsing huan-yüan pao-chüan* (Precious scroll which explains realizing [one's true] nature and returning to the origin) urges its readers to "carve printing blocks, contribute money, and believe in the scriptures." Quoted in Sakai, *Chūgoku zensho*, p. 450.

90. Chih-p'an, *Fo tsu*, chüan 47, in *Taishō*, 49, 425.

91. We have seen that there was group ritual in Taoism as early as the Yellow Turban and Five Pecks of Rice movements near the end of the second century. For a description of T'ang congregational worship in monasteries see Reischauer, *Ennin's Travels*, pp. 187-190.

92. P'u-tu, *Lien-tsung pao-chien*, chüan 1, in *Taishō*, 47, 309.

93. Suzuki, "Sōdai Bukkyō," p. 222.

94. Huang Yü-p'ien, *P'o-hsieh*, 2:4a-4b. Originally a Lo text.

95. *Shih-liao*, t'ien 991. The first and fifteenth are still the primary worship days in Chinese popular religion. There is no mention of Green Yang temples here, only group worship in private homes.

96. Suzuki, *Shinchō*, p. 120.

97. *Na Wen-i kung tsou-i*, 42:17a; 41:43, 44b. These reports are dated 1815-1816. Huang Yü-p'ien once asked some sect members what was the means of obtaining release, and they said it was just "making offerings and reciting scriptures." He also comments that they "at any time worship the Eternal Mother and daily offer incense." Huang Yü-p'ien, *P'o-hsieh*, 2:5; 3:3. See also 1:6 where Huang quotes a related passage from the *Lung-hua ching*: "We burn true incense, and when we raise this incense, all the Buddhas from Ling-shan draw near."

98. DeGroot, *Sectarianism*, I, 220-231. He also describes a Lung-hua funeral ritual on pp. 231-241.

99. Huang Yü-p'ien, *P'o-hsieh*, 3:3b; 1:5b; 1:12a; 1:5a.

100. Chao, "Secret Religious Societies," p. 104. Chao also says of this "passport" that, "It was believed that his soul would go to the Eternal Mother with it when he died." There was a similar burning of a long "document for the journey home" (*kuei-chia wen-tan*) in Lung-hua funeral ritual. DeGroot gives a complete translation in his *Sectarianism*, I, 233-237.

There were evidently four types of ritual involving *piao*, memorials to the Native Land. The first, also sent every month, was called *k'ai-huang chen-piao*, the True Memorial Concerning the Opening Up of New Fields. In it the sect leaders reported their success in recruiting new members. The second was the membership ritual *piao*, already discussed, which was called the *kuei-chia sheng-piao*, the Holy Memorial Concerning Those Who Have Taken Refuge in the Native Land. The third type was named the *pa-huang chen-piao*, which *hsiao tsui-an* (gives remittance to sins);

that is, it was part of a penance ritual. The fourth *piao* was called *san-yüan sheng-piao*, Holy Memorial of the Three Origins, which develops good karma (*hsiu lai-yin*). Huang Yü-p'ien, *P'o hsieh*, 1:5a.

101. *Ch'in-ting p'ing-ting chiao-fei*, 1:23; 16:32b.

102. Topley, "Great Way," p. 375, no. 1. However, in these later groups members had to take written examinations before they were admitted to the higher ranks.

103. Tao-k'ai, *Tsang i ching shu*, p. 12. This passage is a good example of the sectarian combination of folk religion, Taoist self-cultivation, and the Buddhist concern for universal salvation.

104. *Na Wen-i kung tsou-i*, 41:43b. See also S. Naquin's discussion of meditation in the 1813 Pa-kua chiao in her "Eight Trigrams," pp. 32-35.

105. Huang Yü-p'ien, *P'o-hsieh*, 1:19, 3:17b, 1:21. Huang's comment of this last passage is instructive: "These heterodox sects make getting to heaven very easy to attract the faith of the people."

106. For a succinct description of Taoist meditation and its vision of human anatomy, see Chung-yüan Chang, "An Introduction to Taoist Yoga," *Review of Religion* (November, 1965), 20:131-148. Liu Ts'un-yan discusses the active practice of such meditation by Ming literati in his "Taoist Self-Cultivation in Ming Thought," pp. 291-330.

107. Chao, "Secret Religious Societies," p. 100.

108. The Red Swastika society (Shih-chieh hung-wan tzu hui), traces its origin to planchette revelations received by local officials and gentry in Pin *hsien* of Shantung province in 1916. The society was officially established in Peking in 1922, developed 600 centers on the mainland, and came to Taiwan in 1949. It has voluminous scripture, congregational ritual and well-organized charitable and educational activities. Its chief deity, however, is not the Venerable Mother but Chih-sheng hsien-t'ien lao-tsu, the Most Holy Venerable Patriarch of Primordial Times. It is instructive to note that while the sects of folk origin worship a mother goddess, this gentry counterpart does not. There is a strong emphasis on disciplined meditation and study in the Red Swastika society. This information I obtained through Red Swastika materials given me in Taiwan, discussions with sect leaders, and observing rituals. See also Paul DeWitt Twinem, "Modern Syncretic Religious Societies in China, Part I," *The Journal of Religion*, 5:472-482 (1925).

9. Concluding Observations

1. Dardess, "Messianic Revolt," pp. 540-544, and "The Late Ming Rebellions: Peasants and Problems of Interpretation," *The Journal of Interdisciplinary History*, 3.1:103-105, 115.

2. K.C. Hsiao, *Rural China*, pp. 427-431, 433-447.

3. T'ao Hsi-sheng, "Sung-tai," pp. 680-681.

4. K.C. Hsiao, *Rural China*, pp. 462-463. On the role of such bandits as criminal gangs, sometimes coinciding with secret societies, see

Thomas A. Metzger, "Chinese Bandits: The Traditional Perception Re-evaluated," *Journal of Asian Studies*, 33:455-458 (1974).

5. T'ao Hsi-sheng, "Sung-tai," pp. 679-680.

6. This is not to deny that there were elements in other associations of more limited scope which resembled those in the sects. Thus, there were eschatological overtones in such "Equalization of poverty and riches" (*chün p'in fu*) movements as that led by Wang Hsiao-po in Szechwan between 990-995, who proclaimed, "Our problem is the inequality of poverty and riches . . . Now I will equalize them for you," (*Sung shih*, 276:12b). In addition, the stress on "horizontal" relationships and morality in some of the bandit-groups, with their emphasis that "all within the four seas are brothers," is reminiscent of the White Lotus doctrine of the equality of all children of Lao-mu. The well-known rebel slogan *t'i t'ien hsing-tao* (act [i.e., overthrow the dynasty] on behalf of Heaven) rooted in the Mandate of Heaven concept, also served as divine justification for eschatological warfare.

7. Ssu-ma Ch'ien, *Records of the Grand Historian of China*, trans. Burton Watson (New York, 1961), I, 20-22.

8. T'ao Hsi-sheng, "Sung-tai," pp. 676-679. These risings mostly involved local militia.

9. Woodbridge Bingham, *The Founding of the T'ang Dynasty* (Baltimore, 1941), pp. 40-41, 43-45, 83-94; Bingham lists ninety-five uprisings in this four year period, led by assorted bandits, military commanders, local and court officials, and members of noble families.

10. Seidel, "Perfect Ruler," p. 244.

11. Wu Hsien-ch'ing, "Hsi Chin mo te liu-min chih luan," *Shih huo* 1.6:3-7 (1935).

12. *Hsin T'ang shu*, chüan 225, "Biography of Huang Ch'ao," p. 1a, in Howard S. Levy, trans., *Chinese Dynastic Histories Translations*, no. 5 (Berkeley, 1955), p. 8. My comments on Huang Ch'ao's movement are based on this Levy translation, pp. 1-45, coupled with Teng Kuang-ming, "Shih-t'an wan T'ang te nung-min ch'i-i," in Li Kuang-pi, ed., *Nung-min ch'i-i*, pp. 52-57.

13. James B. Parsons, "Overtones of Religion and Superstition in the Rebellion of Chang Hsien-chung," *Sinologica*, 4:170-176 (1956), and "The Culmination of a Chinese Peasant Rebellion: Chang Hsien-chung in Szechuan, 1644-1646," *The Journal of Asian Studies*, 16:387-399 (May 1957). In his *The Peasant Rebellions of the Late Ming Dynasty* (Tucson, 1970), p. 189, Parsons notes that: "Unlike some of the earlier peasant rebellions in Chinese history, and the subsequent Taiping movement, the late Ming uprisings did not manifest any fundamental religious orientation revolving around a popular cult."

14. Vincent Shih, *Taiping Ideology*, pp. 375-376. A more literal translation of this title might be Great Commander Who Advocates Justice in Obedience to Heaven.

15. Chesneaux, *Les Sociétés secrètes*, p. 269.

16. *Ta Ch'ing shih-ch'ao sheng-hsün*, 257:4a (Ch'ien-lung 42, 11 mo.).

17. *Ta-Ch'ing shih-ch'ao sheng-hsün, Hsüan-tsung*, 78:5b (Tao-kuang 19, 3 mo.). DeGroot discusses this report in his *Sectarianism*, I, 22. The temples were destroyed as they were found.

18. Brian E. McKnight, *Village and Bureaucracy in Southern Sung China* (Chicago, 1971), p. 8.

19. Ch'ü T'ung-tsu, *Local Government in China under the Ch'ing* (Cambridge, Mass., 1962), p. 1.

20. K. C. Hsiao, *Rural China*, p. 5.

21. Suzuki in his *Shinchō*, p. 117, gives an example of such influence during the late eighteenth century White Lotus uprising. When a district magistrate in Hupei ordered yamen officials to arrest White Lotus members, they turned on him instead and beat him to death.

22. Chang Chung-li, *The Chinese Gentry* (Seattle, 1955), pp. 52-53.

23. On this see also K. C. Hsiao, *Rural China*, pp. 261-264, 320-322, 413-416, and John R. Watt, *The District Magistrate in Late Imperial China* (New York, 1972), pp. 16-17, 232-233.

However, S. Naquin, in her "Eight Trigrams," pp. 156, 202, 214-215, notes that in the case of the 1813 uprising the problem was not lack of contact with the people, but the slowness of government reaction to information that was available. Sect members and members of the local elite "lived in the same villages, worked in the same places [e.g., the hsien *yamen*], and were sometimes relatives. In the vicinity of Peking, the membership of Chinese Bannermen, Chinese bondservants and Manchus themselves in the sect created even more links between the would-be rebels and the government. Information about their plans filtered upward in many different ways." However, though in a few instances official investigations were carried out, they did not interrupt Eight Trigrams activities, partly because a number of those responsible for surveillance were sect members themselves. One suspects that another factor in such communication problems may have been the reluctance of some officials to admit that heretical activities were taking place in their own districts.

24. Topley, "Great Way," p. 388.

25. Wu Chih-ying, Yüan chiao," pp. 2, 4.

26. Kubo, "Ikkandō Hōkō," p. 189.

27. *Hsüan-kuan* refers to the "entrance to the mysterious meaning of the excellent Way." It also means "entrance" or "narrow door." The general meaning of the term refers to enlightenment, though here it refers more specifically to the nasal septum between the eyes, the place through which the soul leaves that body at death; Grootaers, "I-kuan tao," p. 319.

28. Kubo, "Ikkandō," p. 185. Of Hsien-t'ien tao membership ritual Topley writes, "At death the soul can become a Buddha if it leaves the space between the eyes, called the Hsüan-kuan, 'Dark Pass.' If it leaves by other openings of the body it is destined for rebirth . . . Initiation into a sect

includes dotting the 'Dark Pass' with Chinese ink." See her "Great Way,"
pp. 375-376.

29. Grootaers, "I-kuan tao," pp. 318, 334-339, 319.

30. Ward and Stirling, *Hung Society*, I, 48, 51-52. For a more recent
treatment of the political orientation of secret societies see Boris Novikov,
"The Anti-Manchu Propaganda of the Triads," in Jean Chesneaux, ed.,
Popular Movements and Secret Societies in China, 1840-1950 (Stanford,
1972), pp. 49-63.

31. Ward and Stirling, *Hung Society*, pp. 54, 57, 60, 67, 71. The
characters for the Ch'ing and Ming dynasties also mean, respectively,
darkness and light. The symbolic double meaning of these terms in the initiation rite is best shown in the injunction, "Wash the filth of Ch'ing from
off your faces, that your true countenances may appear, and your mouths
be closed." For Chinese texts of T'ien-ti hui initiation oaths, see Hsiao
I-shan, *Pi-mi she-hui*, chüan 3.

32. Ibid., pp. 53-107. On secret societies see also Frederic Wakeman,
Jr., "The Secret Societies of Kwangtung," in his *Nothing Concealed:
Essays in Honor of Liu Yü-yün* (Taipei, 1970), pp. 129-160. On p. 129
Wakeman says, "Throughout, however, the Triads were a distinctly
modern phenomenon, different from what came before, and presaging
what came after."

33. I have in mind such studies as those by Susan Naquin, mentioned several times above. I understand that Richard L. K. Jung of Harvard University is working on Wang Lun's movement in the late eighteenth
century. No doubt there are others as well.

34. For one preliminary attempt to look at a recently founded sect in
the light of sectarian history, see Daniel L. Overmyer, "The Tz'u-hui
t'ang: A Contemporary Religious Sect on Taiwan" (paper delivered at the
annual meeting of the Canadian Society for Asian Studies, June 2, 1974).
Though the Tz'u-hui t'ang (Religion of Compassion) was founded in
Taiwan in 1949, its belief system is very similar to that discussed in late
Ming *pao-chüan*, including a supreme Mother Goddess, three stage
chronology and so on.

35. For a summary of DeGroot's views on this point, see his *Sectarianism*, I, 120, 156.

Bibliography

Anesaki, Masaharu. *History of Japanese Religion*. London, Kegan Paul, Trench, Trubner, 1930.

Barber, Bernard. "Acculturation and Messianic Movements," in William A. Lessa and Evon Z. Vogt., eds. *Reader in Comparative Religion*. 2nd ed. New York, Harper and Row, 1965.

Bauer, Wolfgang. *China und die Hoffnung auf Glück*. München, Carl Hanser Verlag, 1971.

Bhattacharya, Haridas, ed. *The Cultural Heritage of India*. Vol. IV. *The Religions*. Calcutta, Ramakrishna Mission, 1956.

Bingham, Woodbridge. *The Founding of the T'ang Dynasty*. Baltimore, Waverly Press, 1941.

Blythe, Wilfred. *The Impact of Chinese Secret Societies in Malaya*. London, Oxford University Press, 1969.

Bodde, Derk. "Myths of Ancient China." In Samuel Noah Kramer, ed., *Mythologies of the Ancient World*. Chicago, Quadrangle Books, 1961.

Borton, Hugh. *Peasant Uprisings in Japan of the Tokugawa Period*. 2nd ed. New York, Paragon Reprint, 1968. Originally published in 1938.

Chan Hok-lam. "The White Lotus–Maitreya Doctrine and Popular Uprisings in Ming and Ch'ing China," *Sinologica*, 10: 211–233 (1969).

Chan Wing-tsit. *Religious Trends in Modern China*. New York, Columbia University Press, 1953.

———, ed. and trans. *A Sourcebook in Chinese Philosophy*. Princeton, Princeton University Press, 1963.

Chang Chung-li. *The Chinese Gentry*. Seattle, University of Washington Press, 1955.

Chang Chung-yüan. "An Introduction to Taoist Yoga," *Review of Religion*, 20: 131–148 (November 1955).

Chao Wei-pang. "The Origin and Growth of the Fu-chi," *Folklore Studies*, 1: 9–27 (1942).

—— "Secret Religious Societies in North China in the Ming Dynasty," *Folklore Studies*, 7: 95–115 (1948).

Chapin, Helen B. "The Ch'an Master Pu-tai," *Journal of the American Oriental Society*, 53: 47–52 (1933).

Chavannes, Édouard, and Paul Pelliot. "Un Traité manichéen retrouvé en Chine," pt. 2, *Journal Asiatique*, 11: 99–199, 261–394 (1913).

Ch'en Ju-heng 陳汝衡. *Shuo-shu shih hua* 說書史話 (A history of storytelling). Shanghai, 1958.

Ch'en, Kenneth K. S. "The Economic Background of the Hui-ch'ang Suppression of Buddhism," *Harvard Journal of Asiatic Studies*, 19: 67–105 (June 1956).

—— *Buddhism in China*. Princeton, Princeton University Press, 1964.

—— *The Chinese Transformation of Buddhism*. Princeton, Princeton University Press, 1973.

Cheng Chen-to 鄭振鐸. *Chung-kuo su wen-hsüeh shih* 中國俗文學史 (History of Chinese vernacular literature). 2 vols. Peking, 1959. First pub. in 1938.

Chesneaux, Jean. *Les Sociétés secrètes en Chine*. Paris, Julliard, 1965.

—— *Secret Societies in China in the Nineteenth and Twentieth Centuries*, trans. Gillian Nettle. Ann Arbor, University of Michigan Press, 1971.

——, ed. *Popular Movements and Secret Societies in China, 1840–1950*. Stanford, Stanford University Press, 1972.

Chiang Hsien-teng 姜憲燈, ed. *Tz'u-hui t'ang shih* 慈惠堂史 (A history of the Religion of Compassion). Hualien, Taiwan, 1969.

Chiang Siang-tseh. *The Nien Rebellion*. Seattle, University of Washington Press, 1954.

Chiang Wei-ch'iao 蔣維喬. *Chung-kuo Fo-chiao shih* 中國佛教史 (History of Chinese Buddhism). 3 vols. Shanghai, 1933.

Chih-p'an 志磐 (f. 1260–1270). *Fo tsu t'ung chi* 佛祖統記 (A comprehensive record of the Buddha and Buddhist patriarchs). 54 chüan. In *Taishō shinshū Daizōkyō* 大正新修大藏經 (Taishō Compendium of Buddhist Texts). Eds. Takakusu Junjirō 高楠順次郎 and Watanabe Kaigyoku 渡邊海旭. 85 vols. Tokyo, 1914–1932, vol. 49.

(*Ch'in-ting*) *Ta Ch'ing hui-tien shih-li* 欽定大清會典事例 (Laws and regulations of the Ch'ing dynasty, with supplementary precedents). 1,220 chüan in 24 vols. Taipei, 1963. Photo reprint of 1899 edition. Shorter edition published in 1818.

Chou Tso-jen 周作人. *Chih t'ang i yu wen pien* 知堂乙酉文編 (Essays from the Hall of Wisdom). Hongkong, 1961.

Chu-hung 袾宏 (1535–1615). *Cheng-e chi* 正訛集 (Records of Truth and Error). In his *Yün-ch'i fa-hui* 雲棲法彙 (Collected Works of Chu-hung), 34 vols. in 4 cases, vol. 4. Taipei, 1973. Photo-reproduction of 1897 edition. Taipei edition titled *Lien-ch'ih ta-shih ch'üan-chi* 蓮池大師全集 (Complete writings of Master Lien-ch'ih).

—— *Chu-ch'uang er-pi* 竹窗二筆 (Later writings from a bamboo window), in his *Yün-ch'i fa-hui*, vol. 4.

———— *Chu-ch'uang san-pi* 竹窗三筆 (Writings from a bamboo window, third series), in his *Yün-ch'i fa-hui*, vol. 4.

Chu Kuo-chen 朱國禎. *Yung-ch'uang hsiao-p'in* 涌幢小品 (Short essays from the Yung-ch'uang studio). 32 chüan. In *Pi-chi hsiao-shuo ta-kuan* 筆記小說大觀 (A collection of stories and miscellaneous writings). 6 vols. Taipei, 1962.

Chu Yung-deh R. "An Introductory Study of the White Lotus Sect in Chinese History." Ph.D. diss., Columbia University, 1967.

Chuang Tzu (c. 369–286 B.C.). *The Complete Works of Chuang Tzu*, trans. Burton Watson. New York, Columbia University Press, 1968.

Ch'ü T'ung-tsu. "Chinese Class Structure and Its Ideology." In John K. Fairbank, ed., *Chinese Thought and Institutions*. Chicago, University of Chicago Press, 1957.

———— *Local Government in China under the Ch'ing*. Cambridge, Mass., Harvard University Press, 1962.

Ch'üan Heng 權衡 (f. 1340–1370). *Keng-shen wai-shih* 庚申外史 (Unofficial history of the reign of Emperor Shun [r. 1333–1368] of the Yüan dynasty). In Chang Hai-p'eng 張海鵬 (1755–1816), comp. *Hsüeh-chin t'ao-yüan* 學津討原 (Seeking the source of the stream of scholarship). 200 vols. Shanghai, 1922.

Chüeh-an 覺岸, ed. *Shih-shih chi-ku lüeh* 釋氏稽古略 (Outlines of historical studies of Buddhism). 4 chüan. 1355. In *Taishō shinshū Daizōkyō*, vol. 49.

Cohen, Paul A. *China and Christianity*. Cambridge, Mass., Harvard University Press, 1963.

Cohn, Norman. *The Pursuit of the Millennium*. London, Secker and Warburg, 1957.

———— *The Pursuit of the Millennium*. Revised and expanded edition. London, Temple Smith, 1970.

Collingwood, R. G. *The Idea of History*. Oxford, Clarendon Press, 1946.

Comber, Leon. *The Traditional Mysteries of the Chinese Secret Societies in Malaya*. Singapore, Eastern Universities Press, 1961.

Conze, Edward, ed. and tr. *Buddhist Scriptures*. Baltimore, Penguin Books, 1959.

Conze, Edward, I. B. Horner, D. Snellgrove, and A. Waley, eds. and trans. *Buddhist Texts through the Ages*. New York, Harper and Row, 1964.

Creel, Herlee Glessner. *Sinism*. Chicago, Open Court Publishing Co., 1929.

———— *The Birth of China*. New York, F. Ungar, 1937.

———— *The Origins of Statecraft in China*. Vol. I. *The Western Chou Empire*. Chicago, University of Chicago Press, 1970.

Cumont, Franz. *The Mysteries of Mithra*, trans. Thomas J. McCormack. New York, Dover Publications, 1956. Originally published in 1902.

———— *Oriental Religions in Roman Paganism*. New York, Dover Publications, 1956. Originally published in 1906.

Dardess, John W. "The Transformations of Messianic Revolt and the Founding of the Ming Dynasty," *The Journal of Asian Studies*, 29: 539–558 (1970).

———— "The Late Ming Rebellions: Peasants and Problems of Interpretation,"

Bibliography

The Journal of Interdisciplinary History, 3: 103–117 (1972).

Deliusin, Lev. "The I-kuan Tao Society." In Jean Chesneaux, ed., *Popular Movements and Secret Societies in China, 1840–1950*. Stanford, Stanford University Press, 1972.

D'Enjoy, Paul. "Associations, congregations et sociétés secrétes chinoises," *Bulletins et Mémoires de la Société d'Anthropologie de Paris*, 5: 373–386 (1904).

DeGroot, J. J. M. *The Religious System of China*. 6 vols. Leiden, E. J. Brill, 1892–1910.

―――― *Sectarianism and Religious Persecution in China*. 2 vols. Amsterdam, Johannes Muller, 1903.

Dilthey, Wilhelm. *Meaning in History*, trans. and ed., H. P. Rickman. London, George Allen and Unwin, 1961.

Dobson, W. A. C. H., trans. *Mencius*. Toronto, University of Toronto Press, 1963.

Doré, Henri. *Researches into Chinese Superstitions*. 13 vols., trans. M. Kennelly. Shanghai, T'usewei Printing Press, 1914–1938.

Dubs, Homer A. "An Ancient Chinese Mystery Cult," *Harvard Theological Review*, 35: 221–240 (1942).

Durkheim, Emile. *The Elementary Forms of the Religious Life*, trans. Joseph Ward Swain. New York, Macmillan, 1915.

Dyck, Cornelius. "Anabaptism and the Social Order." In Quirinius Breen, ed., *The Impact of the Church upon Its Culture*. Vol. II. *Essays in Divinity*. Chicago, University of Chicago Press, 1968.

Eberhard, Wolfram. *Conquerors and Rulers*. Leiden, E. J. Brill, 1952.

―――― *The Local Cultures of South and East China*, trans. Alide Eberhard. Leiden, E. J. Brill, 1968.

Edkins, Joseph. *Chinese Buddhism*. London, Kegan Paul, Trench, Trubner, 1893.

Eichhorn, Werner. "Description of the Rebellion of Sun En and Earlier Taoist Rebellions," *Deutsche Akademie der Wissenschaften zu Berlin Mitteilungen des Instituts für Orient-forschung*, 2: 325–352 (1954).

Eliade, Mircea. *Birth and Rebirth: Rites and Symbols of Initiation*. Trans. Willard R. Trask. New York, Harper and Row, 1958.

―――― and Joseph M. Kitagawa, eds. *The History of Religions: Essays in Methodology*. Chicago, University of Chicago Press, 1959.

―――― *Shamanism: Archaic Techniques of Ecstasy*. New York, Pantheon Books, 1964.

―――― "The Quest for the Origins of Religion," *History of Religions*, 4: 154–169 (1964).

――――, ed. *From Primitives to Zen: A Thematic Sourcebook in the History of Religions*. New York, Harper and Row, 1967.

Eliot, Sir Charles. *Hinduism and Buddhism*. 3 vols. London, Edward Arnold, 1921.

―――― *Japanese Buddhism*. London, Edward Arnold, 1935.

Elliott, Alan J. A. *Chinese Spirit Medium Cults in Singapore*. London, London School of Economics and Political Science, 1955.

Ennin (793–864). *Ennin's Diary*, trans. Edwin O. Reischauer. New York, Ronald Press Co., 1955.

Fang Ch'ing-ying 方慶瑛. "Pai-lien chiao te yüan-liu chi ch'i he Mo-ni chiao te kuan-hsi" 白蓮教的源流及其和摩尼教的關係 (The origins of the White Lotus Society and its relationship to Manichaeism). *Li-shih chiao-hsüeh wen-t'i* 歷史教學問題 (Issues in historical study), 5: 34–38 (1959).

Favre, B. *Les sociétés secrètes en Chine*. Paris, G. P. Maisonneuve, 1933.

Fei Hsiao-t'ung. *Peasant Life in China*. London, Routledge and Kegan Paul, 1939.

—— *China's Gentry*, ed. and rev. Margaret Park Redfield. Chicago, University of Chicago Press, 1953.

Filliozat, Jean. "Maitreya l'invaincu," *Journal Asiatique*, 238: 145–149 (1950).

Fitzgerald, C. P. *The Empress Wu*. Melbourne, F. W. Cheshire, 1955.

Fo shuo A-mi-t'o ching 佛說阿彌陀經 (Amitābha sūtra). Trans. Kumārajīva (344–413, var. 409), in *Taishō shinshū Daizōkyō*, vol. 12.

Fo shuo Mi-le hsia-sheng ching 佛說彌勒下生經 (Sūtra of Maitreya's Rebirth), trans. Chu Fa-hu 竺法護 (f. 266–308), in *Taishō shinshū Daizōkyō*. Vol. 14.

Forte, Antonino. "Deux études sur le manichéisme chinois," *T'oung Pao*, 59: 220–253 (1973).

Fortune, R. F. *Omaha Secret Societies*. New York, Columbia University Press, 1932.

Fu Wei-lin 傅維鱗. *Ming shu* 明書 (On Ming history). 171 chüan in 30 vols. Ch'angsha, 1937.

Fuchs, Stephen. *Rebellious Prophets*. Bombay, Asia Publishing House, 1965.

Fung, Yu-lan. *History of Chinese Philosophy*. 2 vols. Trans. Derk Bodde. Princeton, Princeton University Press, 1952–1953. Originally published in 1937.

Gallin, Bernard. *Hsin Hsing, Taiwan: A Chinese Village in Change*. Berkeley, University of California Press, 1966.

Gardner, Charles S. *Chinese Traditional Historiography*. Cambridge, Mass., Harvard University Press, 1938.

Gernet, Jacques. *Daily Life in China on the Eve of the Mongol Invasion, 1250–1276*. Trans. H. M. Wright. New York, Macmillan, 1962.

Graham, David Crockett. "The Customs of the Ch'uan Miao," *Journal of the West China Border Research Society*, 9: 13–70 (1937).

—— *Songs and Stories of the Ch'uan Miao*. Washington, Smithsonian Institution, 1954.

Granet, Marcel. *La Pensée chinoise*. Paris, Editions Albin Michel, 1950.

Grant, Frederick C., ed. *Hellenistic Religions*. Indianapolis, Bobbs-Merrill, 1953.

Grootaers, Willem A. "Une Société secrète moderne, I Kuan Tao: Bibliographie annotée," *Folklore Studies*, 5: 316–352 (1946).

Guthrie, W. K. C. *The Greeks and Their Gods*. Boston, Beacon Press, 1950.

Haloun, G., and W. B. Henning, "The Compendium of the Doctrines and Styles of the Teaching of Mani, the Buddha of Light," *Asia Major*, 3: 184–212 (1953).

Han-shan Te-ch'ing 憨山德清 (1546–1623). *Han-shan ta-shih nien-p'u shu-cheng* 憨山大師年譜疏證 (Chronological biography of Master Han-shan). Ed. Fu-cheng 福徵 (f. 1624–1651). 2 chüan. Taipei, 1967.

Hanan, Patrick. "The Early Chinese Short Story: A Critical Theory in Outline," *Harvard Journal of Asiatic Studies*, 27: 168–207 (1967).

Harrison, James P. *The Communists and Chinese Peasant Rebellions*. New York, Atheneum, 1969.

Hawkes, David, ed. and trans. *Ch'u Tz'u: The Songs of the South; An Ancient Chinese Anthology*. Oxford, Clarendon Press, 1959.

Hirayama Shū 平山周. *Chung-kuo pi-mi she-hui shih* 中國秘密社會史 (A history of Chinese secret societies). Shanghai, 1934. First published in Japanese in 1911. Chinese trans.,.1912.

Hobsbawm, E. J. *Primitive Rebels*. Manchester, Manchester University Press, 1959.

Hou Han shu 後漢書 (History of the Latter Han Dynasty). Ed. Fan Yeh 范曄 (398–445). 120 chüan. Peking, 1965.

Hsiang Chüeh-ming (Hsiang Ta) 向覺明 (向達). "Ming Ch'ing chih chi chih pao-chüan wen-hsüeh yü Pai-lien chiao" 明清之際之寶卷文學與白蓮教 (The precious scroll literature of the Ming and Ch'ing periods and the White Lotus Society), *Wen Hsüeh* 文學 (Literature), 2: 1218–1225 (1934).

——— "T'ang tai su-chiang k'ao" 唐代俗講考 (A study of T'ang dynasty vernacular sermons), *Wen shih tsa-chih* 文史雜誌 (Journal of literature and history), 3: 40–60 (1944).

Hsiao I-shan 蕭一山. "T'ien-ti hui ch'i-yüan k'ao" 天地會起源考 (A study of the origins of the Heaven and Earth Society). In his *Chin-tai pi-mi she-hui shih-liao* 近代秘密社會史料 (Historical materials on modern secret societies), 7 chüan. Peking, 1935. Reprinted in Taipei, 1965.

Hsiao Kung-ch'üan. *Rural China: Imperial Control in the Nineteenth Centruy*. Seattle, University of Washington Press, 1960.

Hsieh Jung-chih 謝榮治. "Lo chiao yü Ch'ing pang kuan-hsi chih yen-chiu" 羅教與清幫關係之研究 (A study of the relationship between the Lo Sect and the Green Spear Society), *Shih yün* 史耘 (Winnow of history), 132: 3–11 (June 1968).

Hsing Yüeh 星月. "Sung tai te Ming chiao yü nung-min ch'i-i" 宋代的明教與農民起義 (The Sung Dynasty Religion of Light and peasant rebellions). *Li-shih chiao hsüeh* 歷史教學 (Historical studies), 6: 39–42 (1959).

Hsü, Francis L. K. *Under the Ancestors' Shadow*. New York, Columbia University Press, 1948.

Hsü kao-seng chuan 續高僧傳 (A continuation of "Biographies of Eminent Monks"). Ed. Tao-hsüan 道宣 (d. 667). 30 chüan. 665 A. D. In *Taishō shinshū Daizōkyō*, vol. 50.

Hsün Tzu. *Hsün Tzu: Basic Writings*. Trans. Burton Watson. New York, Columbia University Press, 1963.

Hu Hsien-chin. *The Common Descent Group in China and Its Functions*. New York, Viking Fund, 1948.

Huang Yü-p'ien 黃育楩 (f. 1830–1840). *P'o-hsieh hsiang-pien* 破邪詳辯 (A detailed refutation of heresies). Ching-chou chiang-chün shu k'e-pen 荊州將

軍署刻本, 1883. First published in 1834.

—— *Hsü-k'an p'o-hsieh hsiang-pien* 續刻破邪詳辯 (Continued detailed refutation of heresies). 1883. First published in 1839.

Hucker, Charles O. *The Traditional Chinese State in Ming Times*. Tucson, University of Arizona Press, 1961.

Hudson, G. F. *Europe and China*. London, Edward Arnold and Co., 1931.

Hurvitz, Leon. "Chu-hung's One Mind of Pure Land and Ch'an Buddhism." In Wm. Theodore de Bary, ed., *Self and Society in Ming Thought*. New York, Columbia University Press, 1970.

—— *Chih-i (538–597): An Introduction to the Life and Ideas of a Chinese Buddhist Monk*. Bruges, Imprimerie Sainte-Catherine, 1963. Extracted from *Mélanges Chinois et Bouddhiques*, vol. 12.

"I-kuan tao i wen hsiang ta" 一貫道疑問詳答 (Detailed answers to doubts and questions concerning the I-kuan tao). Ms., Taiwan, n.p., n.d.

I-nien 一念, ed. *Hsi-fang chih-chih* 西方直指 (Pointing directly to the Western Land). 3 chüan. Colophon dated 1606, in *Hsü Tsang-ching* 續藏經 (A continuation of the Buddhist Compendium). 150 vols. Hongkong, 1946. Photo-reproduction of Kyōto edition, published 1905–1912, vol. 108.

Jackson, A. V. Williams. *Researches in Manichaeism*. New York, Columbia University Press, 1932.

Jung Sheng 戎笙, Lung Sheng-yün 尤盛运, and Ho Ling-hsiu 何齡修. "Shih-lun Chung-kuo nung-min chan-cheng he tsung-chiao te kuan-hsi" 試論中國農民戰爭和宗敎的關係 (A tentative discussion of the relationship between Chinese peasant wars and religion). In Shih Shao-pin 史紹賓, ed., *Chung-kuo feng-chien she-hui nung-min chan-cheng wen-t'i t'ao-lun chi* 中國封建社會農民戰爭問題討論集 (Collected discussions concerning problems of peasant wars in Chinese feudal society). Peking, 1962.

Kao Yu-kung. "A Study of the Fang La Rebellion," *Harvard Journal of Asiatic Studies*, 24: 17–63 (1962–1963).

Kaplan, Abraham. "Purpose, Function and Motivation." In Nicholas J. Demerath and Richard A. Peterson, eds., *System, Change and Conflict*. New York, Free Press, 1967.

Karlgren, Bernard, trans. *The Book of Documents*. Stockholm, Museum of Far Eastern Antiquities, 1950.

Kitagawa, Joseph M. *Religion in Japanese History*. New York. Columbia University Press, 1966.

Kracke, E. A., Jr. *Civil Service in Early Sung China*. Cambridge, Harvard University Press, 1966.

Ku-chin t'u-shu chi-ch'eng 古今圖書集成 (A complete collection of books and illustrations from antiquity to the present). Ed. Ch'en Meng-lei 陳夢雷 and others. 10,040 chüan in 800 vols. Shanghai, 1934. Photo-reproduction of 1725 edition. First presented to the throne by Chiang T'ing-hsi 蔣廷錫.

Kubo Noritada 洼德忠. "Ikkandō hokō" 一貫道補考 (A supplementary study of the I-kuan tao). *Tōyō bunka kenkyūjo kiyō* 東洋文化研究所紀要 (Journal of the Institute of Eastern Culture), 11: 179–212 (1956).

Kuhn, Philip. Review of *I-ho-t'uan yen-chiu* (A study of the Boxers) by Tai Hsüan-chih. *Journal of Asian Studies*, 25: 760–761 (1966).

Kuhn, Philip A. *Rebellion and Its Enemies in Late Imperial China.* Cambridge, Mass., Harvard University Press. 1970.

Kulp, Daniel Harrison II. *Country Life in South China. The Sociology of Familism.* Vol. I. *Phenix Village, Kwangtung, China.* New York, Teachers College, Columbia University, 1925.

Lai Chia-tu 賴家度. "Nan-chao T'ang Yü-chih so ling-tao te nung-min ch'i-i" 南朝唐寓之所領導的農民起義 (The peasant rebellion led by T'ang Yü-chih in the southern dynasties period). In Li Kuang-pi 李光璧, ed. *Chung-kuo nung min ch'i-i lun-chi* 中國農民起義論集 (Collected essays concerning Chinese peasant rebellions). Peking, 1954.

Lamotte, Etienne, trans. *Le Traité de la grande vertu de sagesse de Nagarjuna.* Vol. I. Louvain, Bureaux du Muséon, 1944.

Lancashire, Douglas. "Anti-Christian Polemics in Seventeenth Century China," *Church History,* 38: 218–241 (1969).

Lebar, Frank M., Gerald C. Hickey, and John K. Musgrave. *Ethnic Groups of Mainland Southeast Asia.* New Haven, Human Relations Area Files, 1964.

Leff, Gordon. *Heresy in the Later Middle Ages.* 2 vols. Manchester, Manchester University Press, 1967.

Legge, James, trans. *The Chinese Classics.* 4 vols. London, Oxford University Press, 1893–1895. First published 1865–1872.

Lessing, Ferdinand B. *Yung-Ho Kung: An Iconography of the Lamaist Cathedral in Peking.* Stockholm, The Sino-Swedish Expedition Publications, 1942.

Lévi, Sylvain. "Maitreya le Consolateur," *Études d'Orientalisme Publiées par le Musée Guimet à la Mémoire de Raymonde Linossier.* Vol. 2. Paris, Libraire Ernest Leroux, 1932. Preface by René Grousset.

Levy, Howard S. trans. "Biography of Huang Ch'ao," *Chinese Dynastic Histories Translations.* No. 5. Berkeley, University of California Press, 1955.

―――― "Yellow Turban Religion and Rebellion at the End of the Han," *Journal of the American Oriental Society,* 76: 214–227 (1956).

Li chi, in James Legge, trans. *The Texts of Confucianism.* Pt. 3. In F. Max Müller, ed. *Sacred Books of the East.* Vols. XXVII and XXVIII. London, Oxford University Press, 1885.

Li Chih 李贄, comp. *Ching-t'u chüeh* 淨土決 (Certainty about the Pure Land). 1 chüan. n.d. In *Hsü Tsang-ching,* vol. 108.

Li Hsin-ch'uan 李心傳 (1166–1243). *Chien-yen i-lai hsi-nien yao-lu* 建炎以來繫年要錄 (A continuous record of important events from the Sung Chien-yen reign period, 1127–1131, on). 200 chüan in 10 vols. Peking, 1956.

Li Shih-yü 李世瑜. *Hsien-tsai Hua-pei pi-mi tsung-chiao* 現在華北秘密宗教 (Secret religions in contemporary North China). Chengtu, 1948.

―――― *Pao-chüan hsin-yen* 寶卷新研 (A new study of *pao-chüan*). *Wen-hsüeh i-ch'an tseng-k'an* 文學遺產增刊 (Literary heritage). No. 4. Peking, 1957.

———— *Pao-chüan tsung lu* 寶卷綜錄 (A general bibliography of *pao-chüan*). Shanghai, 1961.

Li Shou-k'ung 李守孔. "Ming-tai Pai-lien chiao k'ao-lüeh 明代白蓮敎考略 (A brief study of the Ming dynasty White Lotus sect). In Pao Tsun-p'eng 包遵彭, ed., *Ming-tai tsung-chiao* 明代宗敎 (Ming dynasty religion). In Pao Tsun-p'eng, ed., *Ming-shih lun-ts'ung* 明史論叢 (Collected essays on Ming history). Vol. 10. Taipei, 1968.

Li T'ao 李燾 (1115–1184). *Hsü tzu-chih t'ung-chien ch'ang-pien* 續資治通鑑長編 (Long draft of a continuation of the "Comprehensive mirror for aid in government"). 600 chüan in 15 vols. Taipei, 1961. Completed manuscript submitted to the throne in 1182.

Li Yu 李攸 (f. 1134). *Sung-ch'ao shih-shih* 宋朝事實 (A true [record] of events in the Sung dynasty). 20 chüan. Shanghai, 1955. Based on 1776 edition prepared by Lu Hsi-hsiung 陸錫熊 and others.

Liang Ch'i-ch'ao 梁啟超 (1873–1929). *Fo-hsüeh yen-chiu shih-pa p'ien* 佛學研究十八篇 (Eighteen essays of Buddhist studies). Taipei, 1966. First published in 1936.

Liang Yü-kao. *Village and Town Life in China.* London, George Allen and Unwin, 1915.

Lieh Tzu. *The Book of Lieh Tzu.* Trans. A. C. Graham. London, J. Murray, 1960.

Lien Tzu-ning 練子寧. *Lien Chung-ch'eng chin ch'uan chi* 練中丞金川集 (Lien Chung-ch'eng's golden stream collection). 1 chüan. First entry dated 1385. In P'an Hsi-en 潘錫恩, ed. *Ch'ien-k'un cheng-ch'i chi* 乾坤正氣集 (Essays in the orthodox spirit). 574 chüan. Taipei, 1966. First published in 1848.

Lindsay, Thomas A. *A History of the Reformation.* 2 vols. New York, Charles Scribner's Sons, 1906–1907.

Liu, James J. Y. *The Chinese Knight-Errant.* London, Routledge and Kegan Paul, 1967.

Liu, James T. C., and Peter J. Golas, eds. *Change in Sung China.* Lexington, Mass., D. C. Heath, 1969.

Liu Ts'un-yan. *Buddhist and Taoist Influences on Chinese Novels.* Wiesbaden, Kommissionsverlag, Otto Harrassowitz, 1962.

———— "Lin Chao-en (1517–1598): The Master of the Three Teachings," *T'oung Pao*, 53: 253–278 (1967).

———— "Taoist Self-cultivation in Ming Thought." In Wm. Theodore DeBary, ed., *Self and Society in Ming Thought.* New York, Columbia University Press, 1970.

Liu Wu-chi. *An Introduction to Chinese Literature.* Bloomington, Indiana University Press, 1966.

Lo Kuan-chung 羅貫中 (c. 1330–1400). *San-kuo yen-i* 三國演義 (The romance of the Three Kingdoms). 3 ts'e. Hongkong, n.d.

Loeb, Edwin M. "Tribal Initiations and Secret Societies," *University of California Publications in American Archaeology and Ethnology*, 25: 249–288 (1929).

Lowie, Robert H. *Primitive Society.* New York, Liveright, 1920.

Bibliography

Lu Hsi-hsing 陸西星 (c. 1520–1601). *Feng-shen yen-i* 封神演義 (Investiture of the Gods). Shanghai, 1936.

Luan-chou chih 灤州志 (Gazetteer of Luan-chou, Hopei Province). Ed. Yang Wen-ting 楊文鼎, Wang Ta-pen 王大本 and others. 18 chüan in 2 vols. Taipei, 1969. Photo-reproduction of 1898 edition.

Ma, Laurence, J. C. *Commercial Development and Urban Change in Sung China.* Ann Arbor, Mich., Department of Geography, University of Michigan, 1971.

Mackenzie, Norman Ian, ed. *Secret Societies.* New York, Holt, Rinehart and Winston, 1967.

McKnight, Brian E. *Village and Bureauocracy in Southern Sung China.* Chicago, University of Chicago Press, 1971.

Mannheim, Karl. *Ideology and Utopia.* New York, Harcourt, Brace, 1936.

Maspero, Henri. *Le Taoisme. Mélanges Posthumes sur les Religions et l'Histoire de la Chine.* Vol. II. Paris, Civilizations du Sud, 1950.

Mather, Richard B. "Vimalakirti and Gentry Buddhism," *History of Religions,* 8: 60–73 (1968).

Meadows, Thomas T. *The Chinese and Their Rebellions.* N. p., 1856. Reprinted by Academic Reprints, Stanford, Calif., 1953.

Mendelson, E. Michael. "Religion and Authority in Modern Burma," *The World Today,* 16: 110–118 (1960).

——— "A Messianic Buddhist Association in Upper Burma," *Bulletin of the School of Oriental and African Studies, University of London,* 24: 560–580 (1961).

Meng Sen 孟森 (1867–1937). *Ming-tai shih* 明代史 (A history of the Ming dynasty). Taipei, 1957.

Merton, Robert K. *On Theoretical Sociology.* New York, Free Press, 1967.

Meskill, John. "Academies and Politics in the Ming Dynasty." In Charles O. Hucker, ed., *Chinese Government in Ming Times.* New York, Columbia University Press, 1969.

Metzger, Thomas A. "Chinese Bandits: The Traditional Perception Re-evaluated," *Journal of Asian Studies,* 33: 455–458 (1974).

Mi-tsang Tao-k'ai 密藏道開. *Tsang i ching shu* 藏逸經書 (Texts not included in the Buddhist canon), in the *Sung-lin ts'ung-shu* 松鄰叢書 (The Sung-lin Collectanea). Vol. III. 1918. First published in 1597.

Michaud, Paul M. "The Yellow Turbans," *Monumenta Serica,* 17: 47–127 (1958).

Miles, George. "Vegetarian Sects," *The Chinese Recorder,* 33: 1–10 (1902).

Miller, Nathan. "Secret Societies," *Encyclopedia of the Social Sciences.* 1st ed. XIII, 621–623.

Ming-lu chi-chieh fu-li 明律集解附例 (The Ming law code, with commentary and appended precedents). 30 chüan in 10 vols. 1908 reprint of an edition published in 1610.

Ming shih 明史 (History of the Ming dynasty). Ed. Chang T'ing-yü 張廷玉 (1672–1755) and others. Taipei, Kuo-fang yen-chiu yüan 國防研究院. 1963. First published in 1739.

Ming shih-lu 明實錄 (Veritable records of the Ming dynasty). Comp. Yao Kuang-hsiao 姚廣孝 (1335–1419) and others. 183 vols. Nankang, Taiwan, 1962–1968. Based on manuscript edition of Peking National Library. Organized chronologically by reign periods of emperors.

Ming ta-cheng tsuan-yao 明大政纂要 (Important documents of Ming administration). 63 chüan. Ed. T'an Hsi-ssu 譚希思. Hunan, 1895.

Miao-fa lien-hua ching 妙法蓮華經 (The lotus sūtra of the wonderful dharma), 28 chapters in 7 chüan. Trans. Kumārajīva (344–413, var. 409), in *Taishō shinshū Daizōkyō*. Vol. 9.

Mo-ni kuang fo chiao fa i lüeh 摩尼光佛教法儀略 (An outline of the teachings of the Manichaean Buddha of Light). Trans. 731. 1 chüan. In *Taishō shinshū Daizōkyō*, vol. 54.

Mochizuki Shinkō 望月信享. *Mochizuki Bukkyō Daijiten* 望月佛教大辭典 (Mochizuki's dictionary of Buddhism). 10 vols. Rev. ed. Kyōto, 1954–1971.

Muramatsu Yuji. "Some Themes in Chinese Rebel Ideologies." In Arthur F. Wright, ed., *The Confucian Persuasion*. Stanford, Stanford University Press, 1960.

Na-yen-ch'eng 那彥成 (1764–1833). *Na Wen-i kung ch'u-jen Chih-li tsung-tu tsou-i* 那文毅公初任直隸總督奏議 (Memorials of Na-yen-ch'eng submitted during his first term as Governor-General of Chihli). Ed. Jung An 容安 (b. 1788). 52 chüan in 4 vols. Taipei, 1968.

Nakano Tōru 中野達. "Suihaizu shotan" 推背圖初探 (A preliminary investigation of the "T'ui-pei t'u"). *Tōhō Shūkyō* 東方宗教 (The journal of eastern religions), 36: 20–37 (October 1970).

Nan Huai-chin 南懷瑾. *Er-shih shih-chi chih Tao-chiao* 二十世紀之道教 (Twentieth century Taoism). In Yen Ling-feng 嚴靈峯, ed., *Er-shih shih-chi chih tsung-chiao* 二十世紀之宗教 (Twentieth century religion). *Er-shih shih-chi chih jen-wen k'e-hsüeh* 二十世紀之人文科學 (Twentieth century humanities). Taipei, 1968.

Nath, Raj Mohan. *Śankara Deva and the Assam Vaishnavite Movement*. In Haridass Bhattacherya, ed., *The Cultural Heritage of India*. Vol. IV. Calcutta, Ramakrishna Mission, 1956.

Naquin, Susan. "Millenarian Rebellion in China: The Eight Trigrams Uprising of 1813." Ph.D. diss., Yale University, 1974.

Needham, Joseph. *Science and Civilization in China*. Vol. II. Cambridge, Cambridge University Press, 1956.

Niebuhr, H. R. *The Social Sources of Denominationalism*. New York, Henry Holt and Co., Inc. 1929.

Noguchi Tetsurō 野口鐵郎. "Byakuren kyō sha no henyō o megutte" 白蓮教社の變容をめぐって (On the modification of the White Lotus society). *Yamazaki sensei taikan kinen Tōyōshi-gaku ronshū* 山崎先生退官記念東洋史學論集 (Studies on oriental history presented to Hiroshi Yamazaki). Tōkyō, 1967.

——— "Min-dai shūkyō kessha no keizai katsudō" 明代宗教結社の經濟活動 (Economic activities of Ming dynasty religious sects). *Yokohama Kokuritsu Daigaku jimbun kiyō* 横浜國立大學人文紀要 (The Humanities: Journal of

Yokohama National University), 1: 10–28 (December 1968).

Novikov, Boris. "The Anti-Manchu Propaganda of the Triads." In Jean Chesneaux, ed. *Popular Movements and Secret Societies in China, 1840–1950.* Stanford, Stanford University Press, 1972.

Osgood, Cornelius. *Village Life in Old China.* New York, Ronald Press, 1963.

Overmyer, Daniel L. "Folk-Buddhist Religion: Creation and Eschatology in Medieval China," *History of Religions,* 12: 42–70 (1972).

—— "The Tz'u-hui t'ang: A Contemporary Religious Sect on Taiwan." Paper at Toronto, Canadian Society for Asian Studies, June 2, 1974.

Parsons, James B. "A Case History of Revolt in China—The Late Ming Rebellion of Chang Hsien-chung," *Oriens Extremus,* 3: 81–93 (1956).

—— "Overtones of Religion and Superstition in the Rebellion of Chang Hsien-chung." *Sinologica,* 4: 170–176 (1956).

—— "The Culmination of a Chinese Peasant Rebellion: Chang Hsien-chung in Szechwan, 1644–46," *The Journal of Asian Studies,* 16: 387–399 (1957).

—— "Attitudes toward Late Ming Rebellions," *Oriens Extremus,* 2: 177–209 (1959).

—— *The Peasant Rebellions of the Late Ming Dynasty.* Tucson, University of Arizona Press, 1970.

Pelliot, Paul. "La Secte du Lotus Blanc et la secte du Nuage Blanc," *Bulletin de l'École Francaise d'Extrême-Orient,* 2: 304–317 (1903).

—— "Les Traditions manichéennes au Fou-kien," *T'oung Pao,* 22: 193–208 (1923).

Petzold, Bruno. "The Chinese Tendai Teaching," *Eastern Buddhist,* 4: 299–347 (1928).

Porter, D. H. "Secret Sects in Shantung," *The Chinese Recorder,* 17: 1–10, 64–73 (1886).

Poussin, L. de Vallée. "Ages of the World-Buddhist," *Encyclopedia of Religion and Ethics.* I, 187–190.

Průšek, Jaroslav. "The Narrators of Buddhist Scriptures and Religious Tales in the Sung Period," *Archiv Orientalni,* 10: 375–389 (1938).

—— *Chinese History and Literature.* Dordrecht, Holland, D. Reidel, 1970.

P'u Sung-ling 蒲松齡 (1630–1705). *Liao-chai chih-i* 聊齋誌異 (Records of strange matters from the Liao studio). First published in 1679.

P'u-tu 普度. *Lien-tsung pao-chien* 蓮宗寶鑑 (An account of the Lotus school). 10 chüan. 1305. In *Taishō shinshū Daizōkyō.* Vol. 47.

Purcell, Victor. *The Boxer Uprising.* Cambridge, Cambridge University Press, 1963.

Reischauer, Edwin O. *Ennin's Travels in T'ang China.* New York, Ronald Press, 1955.

Richard, Timothy. "Sects—Chinese," *Encyclopedia of Religion and Ethics.* XI, 309–315.

Ricoeur, Paul. *The Symbolism of Evil.* Trans. Emerson Buchanan. New York, Harper and Row, 1967.

Rivers, W. H. R. *Social Organization*. New York, Alfred A. Knopf, Inc., 1924.

Ruhlmann, Robert. "Traditional Heroes in Chinese Popular Fiction." In Arthur F. Wright, ed., *The Confucian Persuasion*. Stanford, Stanford University Press, 1960.

Russell, Jeffrey Burton. *Dissent and Reform in the Early Middle Ages*. Berkeley, University of California Press, 1965.

———, ed. *Religious Dissent in the Middle Ages*. New York, John Wiley and Sons, 1971.

Saddharma-Puṇḍarīka (The Lotus of the True Law). Trans. Hendrik Kern. In F. Max Muller, ed., *Sacred Books of the East*. Vol. XXI. Oxford, Clarendon Press, 1884.

Sakai Tadao 酒井忠夫. *Chūgoku zensho no kenkyū* 中國善書の研究 (A study of Chinese morality books). Tōkyō, 1960.

——— "Confucianism and Popular Educational Works." In William Theodore de Bary, ed., *Self and Society in Ming Thought*. New York, Columbia University Press, 1970.

San-kuo chih 三國志 (History of the Three Kingdoms). Comp. by Ch'en Shou 陳壽 (233–297) and others. Commentary by P'ei Sung-chih 裴松之 (372–451). Peking, 1960.

Sarkisyanz, E. *Buddhist Backgrounds of the Burmese Revolution*. The Hague, M. Nijhoff, 1965.

——— "Messianic Folk-Buddhism as Ideology of Peasant Revolts in Nineteenth and Early Twentieth Century Burma," *Review of Religious Research*, 10: 32–38 (1968).

Saso, Michael R. "The Taoist Tradition in Taiwan," *The China Quarterly*, 41: 83–101 (1970).

——— *Taoism and the Rite of Cosmic Renewal*. Pullman, Washington, Washington State University Press, 1972.

Sawada Mizuho 澤田瑞穗 *Hōkan no kenkyū* 寶卷の研究 (A study of "precious scroll" literature). Nagoya, 1963.

——— *Kōchu haja shōben* 校注破邪詳弁 ("A detailed refutation of heresies," with corrections and commentary), Tōkyō, 1972.

Scheiner, Irwin. "The Mindful Peasant: Sketches for a Study of Rebellion," *Journal of Asian Studies*, 32: 579–591 (1973).

Schneider, Louis, ed. *Religion, Culture and Society: A Reader in the Sociology of Religion*. New York, Wiley, 1964.

Schurmann, H. F. "On Social Themes in Sung Tales," *Harvard Journal of Asiatic Studies*, 20: 239–261 (1957).

Seidel, Anna. "The Image of the Perfect Ruler in Early Taoist Messianism," *History of Religions*, 9: 216–247 (1969–1970).

Shao Hsün-cheng 邵循正. "Pi-mi she-hui, tsung-chiao he nung-min chan-cheng" 秘密社會, 宗教和農民戰爭 (Secret societies, religion and peasant wars). In Shih Shao-pin 史紹賓, ed., *Chung-kuo feng-chien she-hui nung-min chan-cheng wen-t'i t'ao-lun chi* 中國封建社會農民戰爭問題討論集 (Collected discussions of problems concerning peasant wars in Chinese feudal society). Peking, 1962.

Shiba Yoshinobu. *Commerce and Society in Sung China*. Trans. Mark Elvin. Ann Arbor, Michigan, Center for Chinese Studies, University of Michigan, 1970.

Shigematsu Shunshō 重松俊章. "Sō Gen jidai no Byakuun shūmon" 宋元時代 の白雲宗門 (The White Cloud sect of the Sung and Yüan dynasties). *Shien* 史淵 (Depths of history), 2: 39–55 (1930).

―――― "Tō Sō jidai no Mirokukyō-hi" 唐宋時代の彌勒教匪 (The Maitreya religious bandits of the T'ang and Sung). *Shien*, 3: 68–103 (1931).

―――― "Ch'u-ch'i te Pai-lien chiao-hui" 初期的白蓮教會 (The early White Lotus society). Trans. T'ao Hsi-sheng 陶希聖. *Shih huo* 食貨, 1: 143–151 (1935).

―――― "Sō Gen jidai no kō-kin-gun to Gem-matsu no Miroku Byakurenkyō-hi ni tsuite" 宋元時代の紅巾軍と元末の彌勒白蓮教匪に就いて (Concerning the Red Turbans of the Sung and Yüan and the Maitreya and White Lotus religious bandits). *Shien*, 24: 79–90 (1940).

Shih-er ch'ao tung-hua lu 十二朝東華錄 (A record of twelve [Manchu] reigns). First ed. Chiang Liang-ch'i 蔣良騏 (1722–1789). 509 chüan. Taipei, 1963. Record of first six reigns published in 1770. This is a reprint of 1884 edition, covering eleven reigns. Ed. Wang Hsien-ch'ien 王先謙, with later additions.

Shih liao hsün-k'an 史料旬刊 (Historical materials published every ten days). Taipei, 1963. First published in Peking in 1930–1931.

Shih Ssu 石俟. *K'an-ching chiao-fei shu-pien* 戡靖教匪述編 (An account of the pacification of religious bandits). 12 chüan. Taipei, 1968. Reprint of 1880 edition. Preface dated 1826.

Shih Nai-an 施耐菴 (c. 1290–1365). *Shui-hu chuan* 水滸傳 (The Water Margin). 71 chapters. Peking, 1953.

Shih, Vincent Y. C. "Some Chinese Rebel Ideologies," *T'oung Pao*, 44: 151–226 (1956).

―――― *The Taiping Ideology*. Seattle, University of Washington Press, 1967.

Simmel, Georg. "The Sociology of Secrecy and of Secret Societies," *American Journal of Sociology*, 11: 441–498 (1906).

Smaller Sukhāvati-vyūha Sūtra. Trans. in F. Max Müller, ed., *Sacred Books of the East*. Vol. XLIX. Oxford, Clarendon Press, 1894.

Soothill, W. E., and Lewis Hodous. *A Dictionary of Chinese Buddhist Terms*. London, Kegan Paul, Trench, Trubner, 1937.

―――― *The Hall of Light: A Story of Early Chinese Kingship*. Ed. Lady Hosie and G. F. Hudson. London, Lutterworth Press, 1951.

Spiro, Melford E. *Buddhism and Society*. New York, Harper and Row, 1970.

Ssu-ma Ch'ien. *Records of the Grand Historian of China*. 2 vols. Trans. Burton Watson. New York, Columbia University Press, 1961.

Ssu-ma Kuang 司馬光 (1019–1089). *Tzu-chih t'ung-chien pu* 資治通鑑補 ("A comprehensive mirror for aid in government," with supplement). Comm. by Hu San-hsing 胡三省 (1230–1302). Supp. by Yen Yen 嚴衍 (1575–1645). 294 chüan. Taipei, 1967. Photoreprint of 1876 edition. First presented to the throne in 1084.

Stark, Werner, *The Sociology of Religion*. Vol. II. Sectarian Religion. London, Routledge and Kegan Paul, 1967.

Stein, Rolf A. "Remarques sur les mouvements du taoisme politico religieux au IIe siécle ap. J. C.," *T'oung Pao*, 50: 1–78 (1963).

Sui shu 隋書 (History of the Sui dynasty). Ed. Wei Cheng 魏徵 (580–643) and Ch'ang-sun Wu-chi 長孫無忌 (d. 659). 85 chüan in 12 vols. Shanghai, 1936. Wei Cheng's ed. published in 629.

Sun K'ai-ti 孫楷第. *Lun Chung-kuo tuan-p'ien pai-hua hsiao-shuo* 論中國短篇白話小說 (A discussion of Chinese short vernacular novels). Shanghai, 1953.

Sun Tso-min 孫祚民. *Chung-kuo nung-min chan-cheng wen-ti t'an-so* 中國農民戰爭問題探索 (An investigation of problems concerning Chinese peasant wars). Shanghai, 1956.

Sung Min-ch'iu 宋敏求 (1014–1074), ed. *T'ang ta chao-ling chi* 唐大詔令集 (A collection of T'ang edicts). 130 chüan. Taipei, 1968. First compiled in 1070.

Sung shih 宋史 (History of the Sung dynasty). Trad. ed. T'o-t'o 托托 (1313–1355). 499 chüan. Shanghai, 1937. Reprint of Yüan Chih-cheng (1341–1368) edition.

Suzuki Chūsei 鈴木中正. "Sōdai Bukkyō kessha no kenkyū" 宋代佛教結社の研究 (Buddhist religious societies of the Sung dynasty). *Shigaku zasshi* 史學雜誌 (Historical miscellany), 52: 65–98, 205–241, 303–333 (1941).

——— *Shinchō chūkishi kenkyū* 清朝中期史研究 (A study of mid-Ch'ing history). Tōkyō, 1952.

Ta Ch'ing lü-li hui-chi pien-lan 大清律例彙輯便覽 (Laws and regulations of the Ch'ing dynasty, collected for convenient reference). 40 chüan in 32 vols. Hupei, 1872.

Ta Ch'ing shih-ch'ao sheng-hsün 大清十朝聖訓 (Imperial instructions of the ten reigns of the Ch'ing dynasty). 922 chüan in 20 vols. Taipei, 1965. First published in 1880 (?).

Ta-yu 大佑 (1334–1407). *Ching-t'u chih-kuei chi* 淨土指歸集 (Collected writings on returning to the Pure Land). 2 chüan. Colophon dated 1394, in *Hsü Tsang-ching*, vol. 108.

Ta Yüan sheng-cheng kuo-ch'ao tien-chang 大元聖正國朝典章 (Statutes of the Yüan dynasty). Ed. Shen Chia-pen 沈家本 (1840–1913). 60 chüan in 2 vols. Taipei, 1964. Photo-reproduction of 1908 edition. First published in 1322.

Ta Yüan t'ung-chih t'iao-ke 大元通制條格 (Records of Yüan administration). Taipei, 1968. Photo-reproduction of early Ming manuscript edition.

Tai Hsüan-chih 戴玄之. "I-he t'uan yü Pai-lien chiao wu kuan k'ao" 義和團与白蓮教無關考 (A study of the absence of relationship between the Boxers and the White Lotus). *Ta-lu tsa-chih* 大陸雜誌 (Mainland magazine), 25: 7–12 (August 1962).

——— *I-he t'uan yen-chiu* 義和團研究 (A study of the Boxer movement). Taipei, 1963.

——— "Pai-lien chiao te pen-chih" 白蓮教的本質 (The true nature of the White Lotus sect), *Shih-ta hsüeh-pao* 師大學報 (Journal of Taiwan Normal University), 12: 119–128 (1967).

———— "T'ien-ti hui yüan-liu k'ao" 天地會源流考 (A study of the origins of the Heaven and Earth society), *Ta-lu tsa-chih*, 36: 1–9 (June 15, 1968).

———— "Pai-lien chiao te yüan-liu" 白蓮教的源流 (The origin of the White Lotus sect), *Chung-kuo hsüeh-chih* 中國學誌 (Journal of Chinese scholarship), 5: 303–318 (1969).

Takakusu Junjirō. *Essentials of Buddhist Philosophy.* Ed. W. T. Chan and Charles A. Moore. Honolulu, University of Hawaii Press, 1947.

Tai Yüan-ch'ang 戴源長. *Hsien-hsüeh tz'u-tien* 仙學辭典 (A dictionary of Taoist terms). Taipei, 1962.

T'ao Ch'eng-chang 陶成章 (d. 1911). "Chiao-hui yüan-liu k'ao" 教會源流考 (A study of the origins of sects and societies) (Canton, 1910). In Hsiao I-shan 蕭一山, ed., *Chin-tai pi-mi she-hui shih-liao* 近代秘密社會史料 (Historical materials on modern secret societies). Peking, 1935. Reprinted in Taipei, 1965.

T'ao Hsi-sheng 陶希聖. "Sung-tai te ke-chung pao-tung" 宋代的各種暴動 (Various violent movements in the Sung dynasty), *Chung-shan wen-hua chiao-yü kuan chi-k'an* 中山文化教育館季刊 (Journal of the Sun Yat-sen Cultural and Educational Center), 1: 671–681 (1934).

———— "Yüan-tai Mi-le Pai-lien chiao-hui te pao-tung" 元代彌勒白蓮教會的暴動 (Violent activities of the Maitreya and White Lotus societies in the Yüan dynasty), *Shih huo* 食貨 (Economics), 1.4: 36–39 (1935).

———— "Ming-tai Mi-le Pai-lien chiao chi ch'i-t'a yao-tsei" 明大彌勒白蓮教及其他妖賊 (The Maitreya and White Lotus sects of the Ming dynasty and other religious bandits), *Shih huo*, 1.9: 46–52 (1935).

Taylor, Romeyn. "Social Origins of the Ming Dynasty, 1351–1360," *Monumenta Serica*, 21: 1–78 (1962).

Teng Kuang-ming 鄧廣銘. "Shih-t'an wan T'ang te nung-min ch'i-i" 試談晚唐的農民起義 (A tentative discussion of late T'ang peasant rebellions). In Li Kuang-pi, ed., *Chung-kuo nung-min ch'i-i lun chi*. Peking, 1954.

———— "T'an Chung Hsiang Yang Yao te ch'i-i" 談鐘相楊么的起義 (A discussion of the Chung Hsiang and Yang Yao rebellions). In Li Kuang-pi, ed., *Chung-kuo nung-min ch'i-i lun-chi*. Peking, 1954.

Thevenaz, Pierre. *What Is Phenomenology? And Other Essays.* Ed. James M. Edie, trans. James M. Edie, Paul Brockelman, and Charles Courtney. Chicago, Quadrangle Books, 1962.

Thompson, Laurence G. *Chinese Religion: An Introduction.* Belmont, California, Dickenson, 1969.

Thrupp, Sylvia L., ed. *Millennial Dreams in Action.* The Hague, Mouton, 1962.

Ting Tse-liang 丁則良. "Kuan-yü Pei Sung ch'u nien Wang Hsiao-po yü Li Shun ch'i-i te chi-ke wen-t'i" 關於北宋初年王小波与李順起義的幾個問題 (A few problems concerning the rebellions of Wang Hsiao-po and Li Shun in the Northern Sung). In Li Kuang-pi, ed., *Chung-kuo nung-min ch'i-i lun-chi*. Peking, 1954.

T'o Chin 托津 et al., eds. (*Ch'in-ting*) *P'ing-ting chiao-fei chi-lüeh* 欽定平定教匪紀

略 (An account of the pacification of religious bandits). 42 chüan in 8 vols. Taipei, 1971. First published in 1816.

Topley, Marjorie. "The Great Way of Former Heaven: A Group of Chinese Secret Religious Sects," *Bulletin of the School of Oriental and African Studies,* 26: 362–392 (1963).

Tsukamoto Zenryū 塚本善隆. *Shina Bukkyō-shi kenkyū* 支那佛敎史研究 (A study of Chinese Buddhist history). Tōkyō, 1942.

——— "Rakyō no seiritsu to ryūden ni tsuite" 羅敎の成立之流傳について (On the founding and spread of the Lo Tsu chiao or Wu-wei sect in the Ming era), *Tōhō gakuhō* 東方學報 (Journal of Eastern Studies), 17: 11–34 (November 1949).

Tsung-chien 宗鑑. *Shih-men cheng-t'ung* 釋門正統 (Buddhist orthodoxy). 8 chüan. Preface dated 1237. In *Hsü Tsang-ching.* Vol. 130.

Tsung-hsiao 宗曉 (1151–1214), ed. *Le-pang i kao* 樂邦遺稿 (A supplementary collection of writings concerning the Land of Bliss). 2 chüan. Colophon dated 1205. In *Taishō shinshū Daizōkyō.* Vol. 47.

———, ed. *Le-pang wen-lei* 樂邦文類 (Writings concerning the Land of Bliss). 5 chüan. Colophon dated 1200. In *Taishō shinshū Daizōkyō.* Vol. 47.

———, ed. *Ssu-ming chiao-hsing lu* 四明敎行錄 (A record of teaching and practice at Ssu-ming). 7 chüan. Preface dated 1202. In *Hsü Tsang-ching.* Vol. 100.

Tsung-pen 宗本, comp. *Kuei-yüan chih-chih chi* 歸元直指集 (A collection of instructions for returning to the origin). 2 chüan. 1553. In *Hsü Tsang-ching.* Vol. 108.

Tung yüan shen chou ching 洞淵神咒經 (The profound and deep divine mantra scripture). *Cheng-t'ung Tao-tsang* 正統道藏 (The Taoist canon of the [Ming] Cheng-t'ung reign period). Box 21, vol. 170. Shanghai, 1924–1926, reprinted in Taipei, 1962. Reprint of the Peking Pai-yün 白雲 Monastery edition. First published 1444–1447.

Twinem, Paul De Witt. "Modern Syncretic Religious Societies in China," *The Journal of Religion,* 5: 463–482, 595–606 (1925).

Vajracchedikā-prajñāpāramitā-sūtra (Diamond Cutter Sūtra). Trans. F. Max Müller. In F. Max Müller, ed., *Sacred Books of the East.* Vol. XLIX. Oxford, Clarendon Press, 1894.

Wach, Joachim. *Sociology of Religion.* Chicago, University of Chicago Press, 1944.

Wakefield, Walter L., and Austin P. Evans, eds. *Heresies of the High Middle Ages.* New York, Columbia University Press, 1969.

Wakeman, Frederic, Jr. *Strangers at the Gate: Social Disorders in South China, 1839–1861.* Berkeley, University of California Press, 1966.

———, ed. *Nothing Concealed: Essays in Honor of Liu Yü-yün.* Taipei, Chinese Materials and Research Aids Service Center, Inc., 1970.

——— "The Secret Societies of Kwangtung, 1800–1856." In Jean Chesneaux, ed., *Popular Movements and Secret Societies in China, 1840–1950.* Stanford, Stanford University Press, 1972.

Waley, Arthur, trans. *The Book of Songs*. Boston, Houghton Mifflin Co., 1937.

Wallace, Anthony F. C. "Revitalization Movements," *American Anthropologist*, 58: 264–281 (1956).

Walzer, Michael. *The Revolution of the Saints*. Cambridge, Mass., Harvard University Press, 1965.

Wang Ch'ung-wu 王崇武. "Lun Ming T'ai-tsu ch'i-ping chi ch'i cheng-ts'e chih chuan-pien" 論明太祖起兵及其政策之轉變 (On the rebellion of Emperor T'ai-tsu of the Ming and the change in his policy). *Li-shih yü-yen yen-chiu so chi-k'an* 歷史語言研究所集刊 (Journal of the Institute of History and Philology), 10: 57–71 (1948).

Wang Jih-hsiu 王日休 (d. 1173), comp. *Lung-shu Ching-t'u wen* 龍舒淨土文 (Wang Jih-hsiu's collection of Pure Land writings). 12 chüan. Earliest preface dated 1161. In *Taishō shihshū Daizōkyō*. Vol. 47.

Wang Ming 王明. *T'ai-p'ing ching he-chiao* 太平經合校 (A reconstructed edition of the scripture of great peace). Peking, 1960.

Wang Tan-ts'en 王丹岑. *Hou Han nung-min ch'i-i* 後漢農民起義 (Peasant rebellions of the latter Han dynasty). Shanghai, 1952.

Ward, J. S. M., and W. G. Stirling. *The Hung Society or Society of Heaven and Earth*. 3 vols. London, Baskerville Press, Ltd., 1925.

Watt, John R. *The District Magistrate in Late Imperial China*. New York, Columbia University Press, 1972.

Weber, Max. "Religious Rejections of the World and Their Directions." In Hans H. Gerth and C. Wright Mills, eds., *From Max Weber*. New York, Oxford University Press, 1946.

———— *The Religion of China*. Ed. and trans. Hans H. Gerth. New York, Free Press, 1951.

Webster, Hutton. *Primitive Secret Societies*. New York, Macmillan, 1908.

Weckman, George A. "The Rites of Entrance into Closed Religious Communities." Ph.D. diss., University of Chicago, 1969.

Wedgwood, Camilla. "The Nature and Function of Secret Societies," *Oceania*, 1: 129–145 (1930).

Wei Chien-yu 魏建猷. "Pa-kua chiao ts'an-yü ching-tien shu lüeh" 八卦教殘餘經典述略 (A brief account of extant scriptures of the Eight Trigrams sect). *I Ching* 逸經 (Folk texts), 10: 539–541 (1936).

Weiger, L. *Moral Tenets and Customs in China*. Trans. L. Davrout. Ho-Kien-fu, Catholic Mission Press, 1913.

Welch, Holmes. *Taoism: The Parting of the Way*. Boston, Beacon Press, 1957.

———— *The Practice of Chinese Buddhism, 1900–1950*. Cambridge, Mass., Harvard University Press, 1967.

Werner, E. T. C. *A Dictionary of Chinese Mythology*. New York, Julian Press, 1961. First published in 1932.

Widengren, Geo. *Mani and Manichaeism*. Trans. Charles Kessler. London, Weidenfeld and Nicolson, 1965.

Williams, George H. *The Radical Reformation*. Philadelphia, Westminster Press, 1962.

Wilson, Byron R. *Sects and Society*. Berkeley, University of California Press, 1961.

———— *Magic and the Millennium: A Sociological Study of Religious Movements of Protest among Tribal and Third-world Peoples*. London, Heinemann Educational Books, Ltd., 1973.

Winternitz, Moriz. *A History of Indian Literature*. 2 vols. Calcutta, University of Calcutta, 1927.

Wright, Arthur F. "The Formation of Sui Ideology, 581–604." In John K. Fairbank, ed., *Chinese Thought and Institutions*. Chicago, University of Chicago Press, 1957.

Wu Chih-ying 吳之英. "Yüan chiao shih-mo chi ch'i ching chüan" 圓教始末及其經卷 (The rise and fall of the Religion of Completion sect and its scriptures). *Jen-wen yüeh-k'an* 人文月刊 (Humanities monthly), 8: 1–6 (June 1937).

Wu Ching-tzu (b. 1701). *The Scholars*. Peking, Foreign Languages Press, 1957.

Wu Han 吳晗. "Ming chiao yü ta Ming ti-kuo" 明教與大明帝國 (The Religion of Light and the Ming dynasty). In his *Tu shih tsa chi* 讀史襍記 (Miscellaneous notes from studying history). Peking, 1956.

Wu Hsien-ch'ing 武仙卿. "Hsi Chin mo te liu-min chih luan" 西晉末的流民之亂 (Refugee uprisings at the end of the Western Chin). *Shih huo*, 1: 3–7 (February 1935).

Yamada Ryūjō 山田龍城. *Daijō Bukkyō seiritsuron josetsu* 大乘佛教成立論序説 (Prolegomena to a theory of the formation of Mahāyāna Buddhism), 2 vols. (Kyōto, 1965).

Yamamoto Hideo 山本秀夫. "Chūgoku ni okeru itan shisō no tenkai" 中國における異端思想の展開 (The development of heterodox thought in China). *Tōyō bunka* 東洋文化 (Oriental culture), 9: 41–75 (June 1952).

Yang, C. K. *Religion in Chinese Society*. Berkeley, University of California Press, 1961.

Yang K'uan 楊寛. "Shih-lun Pai-lien chiao te t'e-tien" 試論白蓮教的特點 (A tentative discussion of special characteristics of the White Lotus sect). *Kuang ming jih pao* 光明日報 (Bright light daily), March 15, 1961.

———— "Lun Chung-kuo nung-min chan-cheng chung ke-ming ssu-hsiang te tso-yung chi ch'i yü tsung-chiao te kuan-hsi 論中國農民戰爭中革命思想的作用及其与宗教的關係 (A discussion of the function of the revolutionary thought of Chinese peasant wars and the relation to this thought to religion). In Shih Shao-pin, ed., *Chung-kuo feng-chien she-hui nung-min chan-cheng wen-t'i t'ao-lun chi*. Peking, 1962.

Yang Lien-sheng. "The Organization of Chinese Official Historiography." In W. G. Beasley and E. G. Pulleyblank, eds., *Historians of China and Japan*. London, Oxford University Press, 1961.

———— "Ming Local Administration," in Charles O. Hucker, ed., *Chinese*

Government in Ming Times. New York, Columbia University Press, 1969.

Yano Jin'ichi 矢野仁一. "Kuan-yü Pai-lien chiao chih luan" 關於白蓮教之亂 (Concerning the White Lotus rebellion). Trans. Yang T'ieh-fu 楊鐵夫, *Jen-wen yüeh-k'an,* 6: 1–20 (February–March 1935).

Yüan shih 元史 (History of the Yüan dynasty). Ed. Sung Lien 宋濂 (1310–1381) and others. 210 chüan in 4 vols. Taipei, Kuo-fang yen-chiu yüan, 1966–1967. Based on the Ming Hung-wu (1368–1399) edition.

Zürcher, Erik. *The Buddhist Conquest of China.* 2 vols. Leiden, E. J. Brill, 1959.

Glossary

A-lo kuo 阿羅國
an 安
An-hua 安化
An-pan shou-i ching 安般守意經
An-tu 安都
ch'a-k'ou 茶寇
ch'a-nü 姹女
ch'a-sheng chün 茶生軍
chai-t'ang 齋堂
Chan-t'an fo 旃檀佛
Ch'an 禪
ch'an-ting 禪定
Chang 張
Chang Ch'ao-yung 張朝用
Chang Ch'eng-chi 張承基
chang chiao 掌教
Chang-ch'iao 張翹
Chang Ch'iu 張求
Chang Hsien-chung 張献忠
Chang Lu 張魯
Chang Lun 張倫
chang shih 掌世
Chang Tsai 張載
Ch'ang-an 長安
Ch'ang-sheng chiao 長生教
ch'ang-shuo hao-hua 唱說好話

Chao-ch'eng 趙城
Chao Ch'ing 昭慶
Chao Ch'ou-ssu 趙丑廝
Chao Ku-yüan 趙古元
Chao Lin 趙璘
Ch'ao-kuo 超過
ch'ao-sheng 超升
chen-cheng 眞正
Chen-chiang 鎮江
chen-hsing kuei-chia 眞性歸家
Chen-hsiung 鎮雄
chen-jen 眞人
Chen-ming ti-wang 眞明帝王
Chen-tsung 眞宗
chen-k'ung chia-hsiang, wu-sheng lao-
    mu (wu-sheng fu-mu) 眞空家鄉
    無生老母(無生父母)
Ch'en-chao li-ch'an wen 晨朝禮懺文
Ch'en Chin-yü 陳金玉
Ch'en-chou 陳州
Ch'en Ch'ing-an 陳慶安
Ch'en Chung-hsi 陳衆喜
Ch'en I-chung 陳宜中
Ch'en Kuang-yao 陳光耀
Ch'en She 陳涉
Ch'en Yu-liang 陳友諒

281

Cheng-e chi 正訛集
Cheng-he 政和
Cheng-hsin ch'u-i wu hsiu-cheng tzu-tsai pao-chüan 正信除疑無修証自在寶卷
Cheng-tao ke 證道歌
Cheng-te 正德
Cheng-t'ung 正統
ch'eng-fo 成佛
ch'eng-hsien 成仙
Ch'eng-yang 成陽
chi 既
Chi hsien 冀縣
Chi-mo 即墨
chi-nien 繼念
ch'i 氣
Ch'i-ch'un 蘄春
ch'i-hai 氣海
Ch'i Wang-shih 齊王氏
chia-chieh 假借
Chia-ch'ing 嘉慶
Chia-hsiang hsin-shu 家鄉信書
Chia-hsing 嘉興
chia-tzu 甲子
chia-wu 甲午
chiang-ching 講經
Chiang-chou 江州
Chiang-ning 江寧
Chiang Tzu-ya 姜子牙
chiao-chu 教主
chiao-t'ang 教堂
chiao yü liu-su 教於流俗
Chiao-shan 焦山
chieh-shu 刧數
chieh-tien k'u 解典庫
chieh-t'o 解脫
chien-chien pien tz'u nan-yen-fou-t'i chin shih-chieh chieh wei ch'ing-ching chi-le shih-chieh 漸漸變此南閻浮提盡世界皆爲清淨極世界
Chien-ning 建寧
Chien-ou 建甌
Ch'ien-lung 乾隆
Chih-he 致和

Chih-i 智顗
Chih-li 智禮
Chih-nü hsing 織女星
Chih-sheng hsien-t'ien lao-tsu 至聖先天老祖
Chih-ta 至大
chih tsai pi sheng 志在必勝
Chih-tun 支遁
Chin 晋
Chin-kang Nu 金剛奴
Chin kuang-ming ching 金光明經
chin Pai-lien fo-shih 禁白蓮佛事
chin-shih 進士
Chin-tan p'ai 金丹派
Ch'in 秦
ching 經
Ching-chou 荊州
Ching-chü kuo-ming fa-wang 淨居國明法王
Ching-hsing she 淨行社
Ching-men 荊門
Ching-shan Hsü-chou P'u-tu 徑山虛舟普渡
Ching-t'u 淨土
Ching-t'u wen 淨土文
ching-yeh 淨業
Ch'ing 清
Ch'ing-ch'a men 清茶門
Ch'ing-he 清河
Ch'ing-he chiao 清河教
Ch'ing-li 慶歷
Ch'ing-ming 清明
Ch'ing-yang 慶陽
Ch'ing-yang chiao 青陽教
Ch'ing-yüan 慶元
Ch'ing-yüan t'iao-fa shih-lei 慶元條法事類
chiu-chi 救濟
Chiu-k'u chung-hsiao Yao-wang pao-chüan 救苦忠孝藥王寶卷
Chiu T'ang shu 舊唐書
Chiu-t'ien hsüan-nü 九天玄女
Chiu Ting-kuo 咎定國
Chou 紂

chou 州

Chou Hung-jen 周宏忍

Chou li 周禮

Chou Tun-i 周敦頤

Chou Tzu-wang 周子旺

Chu 朱

Chu-ch'i 竹谿

chu-ch'ih 主持

Chu Chün 朱儁

Chu Fa-hu 竺法護

chu-kung tiao 諸宮調

Chu Yüan-chang 朱元璋

Ch'u 楚

ch'u-lu 出路

ch'u-shen 出神

ch'u-shih 出世

ch'u tz'u k'u-hai er teng pi-an 出此苦海而登彼岸

chuan-fan ch'eng-sheng 轉凡成聖

Chuan-lun-wang ch'u-shih 轉輪王出世

chuan-shih 轉世

chuan-shou wei-t'u 轉收爲徒

ch'uan-chiao 傳教

ch'uan-tao 傳道

ch'uan-teng 傳燈

ch'uan-t'ou 傳頭

Ch'un-ch'iu 春秋

Ch'un-hua 淳化

chung-chih 中支

Chung-ch'iu 中秋

Chung-hsi pao-chüan 衆喜寶卷

Chung-hsing fu-lieh ti 中興福烈帝

chung-min 衆民

chung-yüan ti 中原地

Ch'ung-chen 崇禎

ch'ung-k'ai ta Sung chih t'ien 重開大宋之天

Chü chih ta ming-shih 舉智大明使

chü chung fan 聚衆反

Chü-lu 鉅鹿

chü-shih 居士

Chü-hsiang tsan 舉香讚

Ch'ü hsien 衢縣

chüan 卷

Ch'üan-chen 全眞

Ch'üan-chou 泉州

ch'üan-chu 勸主

ch'üan fu chi p'in 勸富濟貧

ch'üan-shan 勸善

ch'üan-shou 勸首

"Ch'üan yü san-shih-ch'i pien" 勸諭三十七編

Chüeh-lo Yung-te 覺羅永德

Ch'üeh Kung-tse 闕公則

chün-min 軍民

chün p'in-fu 均貧富

Er-lun 二崙，二輪 (wheel)

Er-tsung san-chi ching 二宗三際經

Fa-ch'ing 法慶

fa-chüan 法眷

Fa-ch'üan 法權

Fa-hsiu 法秀

Fa-hua chüan 法華卷

Fa-kuo 法果

fa-ming 法名

fa-shih 法師

Fan Ming-te 樊明德

fan-pen huan-yüan 返本還源

Fang Jung-sheng 方榮升

Fang La 方臘

fang-pien 方便

fei mai p'in 非賣品

fei seng fei tao 非僧非道

Feng-hsiang 鳳翔

feng fo hsin-nü 奉佛信女

feng mu-ch'in 奉母親

feng-shui 風水

Feng-t'ien ch'ang-i ta yüan-shuai 奉天倡義大元帥

Feng-yang 鳳陽

fo-lai 佛來

fo-pao 佛寶

fo-shih 佛事

Fo-shuo Mi-t'o pao-chüan 佛說彌陀寶卷

Fo-shuo t'ung-yüan shou-yüan pao-chüan 佛說通元收源寶卷

Fu-ch'eng 阜城
fu-chiang 副將
Fu-feng 扶風
Fu-hsi 伏羲
Fu-shan 浮山
fu-t'i 附體
Fu-yang 阜陽
Hai-hui 海慧
Han 漢
Han-chung 漢中
Han Lin-er 韓林兒
Han Shan-t'ung 韓山童
Han Te-jung 韓德榮
Han wang 漢王
Hao-chou 濠州
Hao-hua ke-tz'u 好話歌詞
He Ch'iao-yüan 何喬遠
Hsi-an 西安
Hsi-chou 息州
Hsi-hu 西湖
Hsi-hua 西華
Hsi-hsing chi 西行集
Hsi-kuei she 西歸社
Hsi-ning 熙寧
Hsi-tsung shih-lu 熹宗實錄
Hsi Wang-mu 西王母
Hsi-yu chi 西遊記
Hsia 夏
Hsia-sheng pao-ching 下生寶經
Hsia-sheng t'an shih pao-chüan 下生嘆世寶卷
Hsia Yüan-chi 夏原吉
Hsiang-ch'eng hsien 項城縣
hsiang chün 香軍
Hsiang Hai-ming 向海明
Hsiang-shan pao-chüan 香山寶卷
hsiang t'ai-yang li-pai 向太陽禮拜
hsiang-yü 鄉愚
Hsiao Chüeh-kuei 蕭覺貴
Hsiao Mao 小茅
Hsiao ming-wang 小明王
hsiao-sheng 小乘
Hsiao-shih chen-k'ung pao-chüan 銷釋眞空寶卷

Hsiao-shih Chin-kang k'e-i 銷釋金剛科儀
Hsiao-shih shou-yüan hsing-chüeh pao-chüan 銷釋收源性覺寶卷
Hsiao-shih ta-hung chüeh-t'ung pao-chüan 銷釋大宏覺通寶卷
Hsiao-shih wu-hsing huan-yüan pao-chüan 銷釋悟性還源寶卷
hsiao tsui-an 消罪案
hsieh-chiao 邪教
"Hsieh-chiao shuo" 邪教說
Hsieh-chiao yin-pao lu 邪教陰報錄
hsieh-ching 邪經
hsieh-hsiang 邪像
hsieh pu neng fan cheng 邪不能犯正
hsieh-shu 邪術
Hsien-t'ien tao 先天道
hsien-tsai chuan shih 現在轉世
Hsin-hsing 信行
hsin-ssu 辛巳
Hsin T'ang shu 新唐書
Hsing-ch'ang 省常
Hsing-hai 性海
hsiu lai-yin 修來因
Hsiu-shui 秀水
hsiu-ts'ai 秀才
Hsü Chen 徐貞
hsü er wu p'ing 虛而無憑
Hsü Hung-ju 徐鴻儒
Hsü Shou-hui 徐壽輝
Hsü T'ien-te 徐添德
Hsüan-han 宣漢
Hsüan-ku ch'iao 玄鼓教
hsüan-kuan 玄關
Hsüan-tsung 玄宗
Hsüan-wu 宣武
hsüeh-p'en 血盆
Hsün Tzu 荀子
hu-jan hsien hui-yen 忽然見慧眼
Hu-kuang 湖廣
Hu-kuo wei-ling Hsi Wang-mu pao-chüan 護國威靈西王母寶卷
Hu-kuo yu-min fu-mo pao-chüan 護國佑民伏魔寶卷

hua-ch'u 化出

Hua-le kung 化樂宮

hua-min ch'eng-su 化民成俗

hua-pen 話本

hua-su fa-shih 化俗法師

Hua-yen 華嚴

Huai-nan Tzu 淮南子

Huai-hsi 淮西

Huan Hsüan 桓玄

huan shih-chieh 換世界

Huang Ch'ao 黃巢

huang-chi 皇極

Huang-fu Sung 皇甫嵩

Huang-Lao 黃老

huang-t'ai 皇胎

Huang-ti 黃帝

Huang ying er 黃鶯兒

hui-chu 會主

Hui-ch'ang 會昌

Hui-neng 慧能

hui-shou 會首

Hui-ssu 慧思

Hui-tsung 徽宗

Hui-yüan 慧遠

hun-meng 混濛

hun-tun 混沌

Hun-yüan 渾源

Hun-yüan chih-chen lao-tsu 混元至真老祖

Hun-yüan hung-yang k'u-kung wu-tao ching 混元紅陽苦功悟道經

Hun-yüan hung-yang hsien-hsing chieh-kuo ching 混元紅陽顯性結果經

Hun-yüan hung-yang hsüeh-hu pao-ch'an 混元紅陽血湖寶懺

Hun-yüan hung-yang lin-fan P'iao Kao ching 混元紅陽臨凡飄高經

hun-yüan i-ch'i so hua 混元一氣所化

hun-yüan liao 混元了

Hun-yüan wu-shang p'u-hua tz'u-pei chen-ching 混元無上普化慈悲眞經

Hun-yüan wu-shang ta-tao yüan-miao chen-ching 混元無上大道元妙眞經

hung ("wide," "extensive") 弘，宏

hung chün 紅軍

Hung Mai 洪邁

hung-t'ou 紅頭

Hung-wu 洪武

Hung-yang chiao 紅陽教

Hung-yang chung-hua pao-ching 弘陽中華寶經

Hung yu lu 鴻猷錄

huo-chü 火居

i 億 (100,000,000)

I 夷 (tribe)

i 亦 (also)

I-cheng 儀徵

i-ch'ieh chu tsao-hua ling-shen 一切注造化靈神

I-ch'un hsien 宜春縣

i-chün 義軍

i fo-fa huo chung 以佛法惑眾

I-kuan tao 一貫道

I-kuan tao hsin chieh-shao 一貫道新介紹

i tso fo-shih 以作佛事

Jen-tsung 仁宗

Ju-chou 汝州

Ju-yang 汝陽

"K'ai-ching chieh" 開經偈

k'ai-ch'uang sheng-mu 開創聖母

k'ai-huang chen-piao 開荒眞表

k'ai-t'ang 開堂

K'ai-yüan 開元

k'an-shou 看守

K'ang-hsi 康熙

Kao Chün-te 高均德

Kao Tai 高岱

Kao-tsung 高宗

Kao Yang (sect founder) 高揚

Kao-yang 高陽

k'e-t'ou 磕頭

ken-chi ch'ien 根基錢

keng-sheng 更生

Ko Hung 葛洪

ko-i 格義

k'ou 寇

ku 故

Ku-fo t'ien-chen k'ao-cheng lung-hua pao-ching 古佛天眞考証龍華寶經
Ku-su 姑蘇
ku-tzu tiao 鼓子調
k'u-hai 苦海
K'u-kung wu-tao chüan 苦功悟道卷
kua-hao piao-ming 掛號表名
kuan-hsiang 觀想
Kuan-yin 觀音
Kuan Kung (Kuan Ti) 關公（關帝）
k'uang-k'ou 礦寇
kuei 鬼
kuei-chia 歸家
Kuei-chia pao-en pao-chüan 歸家報恩寶卷
kuei-chia wen-tan 歸家文單
kuei-wei 癸未
K'un-lun 崑崙
K'un-shan 崑山
Kung Ch'ang 弓長
kung-fu 功夫
kung-te shui 功德水
kung-yang 供養
K'ung Ch'ing-chüeh 孔清覺
Kuo P'u-sa 郭菩薩
Kuo-shan 崞山
Kuo Tzu-hsing 郭子興
Lai-chou 萊州
Lan-feng 蘭風
Lao-chün 老君
Lao fo-wang 老佛王
Lao-kuan chai 老官齋
Lao-kuan niang 老官娘
Lao-shan 牢山
Lao Tzu 老子
Lao Tzu hua-hu ching 老子化胡經
Leng T'ien-lu 冷添祿
li 禮
Li chi 禮記
Li Ching 李靖
Li Fu-ta 李福達
li hsien-t'ien 立先天
Li Hsin-ch'uan 李心傳
Li Hung 李弘

Li Kuei-po 李歸伯
"Li lü" 禮律
Li Mou 李某
li-pai 禮拜
Li Shih-min 李世民
Li Tao-ming 李道明
"Li-tsung pen-chi" 理宗本紀
Li Tzu-ch'eng 李自成
Li T'ung 李同
Li Wei 李衛
Li Wen-ch'eng 李文成
li-yung 利用
Li Yü-lien 李玉蓮
Liang 梁
Liang-shan-p'o 梁山泊
liang-t'ien-ch'ih 量天尺
Liao 遼
lien-she 蓮社
lien-t'ai 蓮台
Lien-tsung ch'an-t'ang 蓮宗懺堂
Lien-tsung ch'en-chao ch'an-i 蓮宗晨朝懺儀
"Lin-chung chen nien chüeh" 臨終正念訣
"Lin-chung wang-sheng cheng nien wen" 臨終往生正念文
Lin Ch'ing 林清
lin-fan 臨凡
Lin-ju 臨汝
ling-fu 靈符
Ling-shan 靈山
Ling-chiu shan 靈鷲山
Ling-yin 靈隱
Ling-ying T'ai-shan niang-niang pao-chüan 靈應泰山娘娘寶卷
Liu Chih 劉摯
Liu Chih-hsieh 劉之協
Liu Fu-t'ung 劉福通
Liu Hui-wang 劉惠汪
liu-k'ou 流寇
liu-min 流民
Liu Seng-shao 劉僧紹
Liu Ssu-er 劉四兒
Liu Sung 劉松

Liu T'ien-hsü 劉天叙
Liu Wen-ching 劉文靜
Liu Ying 劉英
Lo chiao 羅教
Lo Ching 羅靜
Lo Ch'ing 羅清
Lo hsiang 羅像
Lo Huai 羅懷
Lo Hui-neng 羅慧能
Lo Ming 羅明
Lo Tao 羅道
Lo-t'ien 羅田
Lo Tsu 羅祖
Lo Wei-ch'ün 羅蔚群
Lo Yin 羅殷
Lu Fa-he 陸法和
Lu-shan 盧山
Lu Ta 魯達
"Lu-yüan chuan" 盧淵傳
Luan-ch'eng 欒城
Luan-chou 灤州
Lung-ch'üan 龍泉
Lung-feng 龍鳳
Lung-hua hui 龍華會
Lung-men 龍門
Lü K'un 呂坤
Ma-ch'eng 麻城
Ma Kang 馬剛
Ma-tsu 媽祖
Man 蠻
Mao-shan 茅山
Mao Tzu-yüan 茅子元
mi 迷
Mi-le t'uan 彌勒團
Mi-t'o chieh-yao 彌陀節要
Mi-t'o chüan 彌陀卷
mi-tsei 米賊
Mi-yün hsien 密雲縣
Miao 苗
miao fa 妙法
Min-hou 閩侯
min-tsu chu-i 民族主義
Ming 明
Ming chiao chai-t'ang 明教齋堂

Ming chiao hui 明教會
Ming Hsia 明夏
Ming-ming shang-ti 明明上帝
Ming shan ts'ang 名山藏
Ming T'ai-tsu 明太祖
Ming-t'ang 明堂
Ming t'ung-chi 明通紀
Ming Yü-chen 明玉珍
mo (devil) 魔
Mo-mo ni 末摩尼
Mo-mo-ni kuang fo 末摩尼光佛
Mo-ni fo 摩尼佛
mo-nien 默念
Mo-t'ou 摩頭
Mo Tzu 墨子
Mu 穆
Mu-i 母乙
Mu-lien 目蓮
Mu-lien chiu-mu ch'u-li ti-yü sheng-
    t'ien pao-chüan 目蓮救母出離地獄
    升天寶卷
Mu-lien chüan 目蓮卷
Na-yen-ch'eng 邢彦成
Nan-ch'üan 南泉
Nan-kung shu-tu 南宮署牘
Nan-shan 南山
niang 娘
nien-chou 念咒
nien-fo 念佛
nien-fo wu wu-sheng 念佛悟無生
Nien-fo yüan 念佛苑
Niu-pa 牛八
No-cha 哪吒
Nü-kua 女媧
nü-wu 女巫
O-mi-t'o-fo 阿彌陀佛
O-mei 峨嵋
pa-huang chen-piao 拔鑛眞表
Pa-kua chiao 八卦教
pa-tzu chen-yen 八字眞言
Pai-i hui 白衣會
Pai-lien chiao 白蓮教
Pai-lien she 白蓮社
Pai-lien tao-shih 白蓮導師

Pai-lien ts'ai 白蓮菜
pai-wen 白文
Pai-wu 白鳥
Pai-yang 白陽
Pai-yün tsung 白雲宗
'P'ai wei" 排偽
p'an hsieh cheng chih fen 判邪正之分
pang fa 謗法
Pang Hu 棒胡
Pang-tzu ch'iang-hsi 梆子腔戲
Pao-ch'eng 褒城
Pao Ching-yen 鮑敬言
pao-chüan 寶卷
Pao-en t'ang 報恩堂
Pao-en wan-shou t'ang 報恩萬壽堂
Pao P'u Tzu 抱朴子
pao-tung 暴動
Pao-yen 寶嚴
Pao-ying 寶應
Pei Ch'an Fan Fa-chu 北禪梵法主
Pei-chou 貝州
Pen-jan 本然
Pen-ju 本如
P'eng-lai wu-chung lao-tsu 蓬萊無終
　　老祖
P'eng Ying-yü 彭瑩玉
P'iao Kao 飄高
"Pien fo-fa yin-ts'ang" 辨佛法隱藏
pien-wen 變文
Pin hsien 濱縣
P'ing-chiang 平江
P'ing-mo chün-ssu 平魔軍司
Po-chou 亳州
Po Chü-i 白居易
P'o-hsieh hsien-cheng yao-shih chüan
　　破邪顯證鑰匙卷
pu-chiao shih 布教師
pu ching 不經
pu chü ch'i jen chih kao-pi 不拘其人
　　之高卑
pu k'e hsin yeh 不可信也
pu seng pu su 不僧不俗
Pu-tai 布袋
pu-wen hsien-yü pu-fen shan-e 不問賢

愚不分善惡
p'u 普
P'u-chao 普照
*P'u-ching Ju-lai yao-shih t'ung-t'ien
　　pao-chüan* 普靜如來鑰匙通天寶卷
P'u Fa-e 普法惡
P'u-ming 普明
P'u-ming ju-lai wu-wei liao-i pao-chüan
　　普明如來無爲了義寶卷
P'u-ning 普寧
P'u-shan 普善
P'u-shao 普少
p'u-tu chung-sheng 普渡衆生
P'u-tu hsin-sheng chiu-k'u pao-chüan
　　普渡新聲救苦寶卷
P'u-tung 普棟
P'u-yüan 普緣
san-chiao he-i 三教合一
san-chiao i-chia 三教一家
San-chiao t'ang 三教堂
*San-chiao ying-chieh tsung-kuan t'ung-
　　shu* 三教應刼總觀通書
San-chieh chiao 三階教
San-hsü p'o-hsieh hsiang-pien 三續破邪
　　詳辯
San Kuan 三官
San-pao 三寶
San-shan 三山
San-sheng chiao 三乘教
San-shih yin-yu 三世因由
san-tsung 三宗
San-yang chiao 三陽教
San-yüan chiao 三元教
Sang-yüan 桑園
seng-jen 僧人
Seng-ming 僧明
'Seng wu tsa shu" 僧務雜術
Shan-hai ching 山海經
shan-shu 善書
Shan-tao 善導
Shang 商
Shang-he 商河
Shang-ku sheng-jen 上古聖人
shang-kung 上供

shang-sheng 上乘

shang-shang-sheng 上上乘

Shang-ti 上帝

Shang-ti shen-nü 上帝神女

shang-t'ien 上天

Shao Ch'ing 邵青

shao-hsiang huo chung 燒香惑衆

she-chai 設齋

she-fan 捨凡

she-li 舍利

she-seng 社僧

she-shou 僧首

shen 神

Shen-chao 神照

shen-chia 申甲

Shen Chih-yüan 沈智元

shen-hsiang 神像

'Shen-i'' 神異

shen-jen 神人

Shen Ming-jen 沈明仁

hen-tao 神道

sheng-piao 升表

sheng-ssu yung hsi 生死永息

Shensi 陝西

Shih-chieh hung-wan tzu hui 世界紅卍字會

Shih Chin-chou 石金州

Shih-chu p'u-sa 十住菩薩

shih er yu chü 實而有據

Shih-fo chuang (k'ou) 石佛莊（口）

shih-kung 師公

shih lou 事漏

shih-p'o 師婆

shih-pu hsiu-hsing 十步修行

"Shih-ti ke" 十地歌

"Shih-tsung chi" 世宗記

shou-yüan liao 收元了

Shu ching 書經

shui-lu fa-hui 水陸法會

Shui Yim Tse 謝瑞琰

Shun 舜

shuo-ch'ang pao-chüan 說唱寶卷

shuo fa tu jen 說法渡人

shuo-hua 說話

shuo-shu 說書

ssu 寺

ssu feng 私奉

Ssu-ming shan 四明山

Ssu-t'ien-wang 四天王

su-chiang 俗講

su-chiang seng 俗講僧

sui (year) 歲

Sui 隋 (dynasty)

sui lei hua hsing 隨類化形

Sun Lin 孫絑

Sun Ta-yu 孫大有

Sun Wei-chien 孫維儉

Sung 宋

Sung Chiang 宋江

Sung-chiang 松江 (county)

sung-ching 誦經

Sung hsing-chu 宋星主

"Sung shih shih mo" 宋事始末

Sung Tzu-hsien 宋子賢

Ta chiang-chün 大將軍

ta-chieh 大刦

Ta-ch'eng chiao 大成教

Ta ch'eng hsing-sheng yüan-nien 大成興勝元年

Ta Ch'in 大秦

Ta-hsiao ming-wang ch'u-shih ching 大小明王出世經

ta-k'ai chia-hsiang ts'ang-k'u 打開家鄉倉庫

ta-le 大樂

Ta-ming chiao 大明教

Ta Ming t'ien-shun 大明天順

Ta-ning 大寧

ta-sheng 大乘

Ta-sheng chih-kuan fa-men 大乘止觀法門

Ta-sheng Mi-le-fo hua-tu pao-chüan 大乘彌勒佛化渡寶卷

Ta-yün ching 大雲經

tai chieh chin 待刦盡

tai-t'ien hsing-shih 代天行事

t'ai-chi 太極

T'ai-hang 太行

T'ai-ho 太和

T'ai-p'ing ching 太平經

T'ai-p'ing tao 太平道

t'an-ch'ang yin-yüan 彈唱因緣

T'an-luan 曇鸞

T'an shih wu-wei chüan 嘆世無爲卷

tang-jen 當人

tang-lai chen-chün 當來眞君

Tang-yang huang chi fo 當陽皇極佛

T'ang 唐

T'ang Sai-er 唐賽兒

Tao-an 道安

Tao-ch'o 道綽

tao-jen 道人

Te-sheng 得聖

Tao-te ching 道德經

Te-tsung 德宗

ti-tzu 弟子

Ti-yü chüan 地獄卷

t'i t'ien hsing tao 替天行道

t'iao-t'ung 跳童

tien-ch'uan shih 點傳師

Tien-shan hu 澱山湖

T'ien-chen 天眞

T'ien-chen lao-tsu 天眞老祖

T'ien-ch'i 天啓

T'ien-chiang 天將

T'ien Chiu-ch'eng 田九成

T'ien-hsia ta-luan Mi-le fo hsia-sheng
   Ming-wang ch'u-shih 天下大亂彌
   勒佛下生明王出世

T'ien-hsiu 天繡

T'ien-jen 天人

T'ien-li chiao (hui) 天理教(會)

T'ien-ning 天寧

T'ien-shang Mi-le 天上彌勒

T'ien-t'ai 天台

t'ien-ti hsüan huang 天地玄黃

T'ien-ti hui 天地會

T'ien-wen t'u-shu 天文圖書

T'ien-yin chi 天因記

T'ien-yün 天運

T'ien yü chih 天與之

t'ing-fa 聽法

Ting T'ien hou 定天侯

Toba Wei 拓赦魏

Tou Chien-te 竇建德

tsai chia feng chiao 在家奉教

Ts'ai Mao-t'ang 蔡懋棠

ts'ai-yu 菜友

Ts'ang-chou 滄州

ts'ao-an 草庵

tso-kung 坐功

tso-luan 作亂

tso-tao i-tuan 左道異端

Tsun-shih 遵式

Tsung-li 宗利

tsung-ping 總兵

tsung-shuai 總帥

Tsung Wang-hua 宗王化

tu-chiang 都講

tu chung-sheng ch'ü yu ching-t'u 渡衆
   生取於淨土

tu-fei 渡費

tu-hua chung-sheng 渡化衆生

"Tu-tsung pen-chi" 度宗本紀

Tu Wan-i 杜萬一

t'u-tang 徒黨

Tuan An-chieh 段安節

T'ui-pei t'u 推背圖

Tung Chung-shu 董仲舒

Tung-hsiang 東鄉

Tung p'ing chün wang 東平君王

Tung-sheng 東勝

tung-t'u 東土

t'ung-chi 童乩

t'ung hsiu ching-yeh 同修淨業

Tzu-ch'ih chi 資持記

tzu-hsing 自性

Tzu-mu 字母

Tzu-wei hsing 紫微星

Tz'u-hui t'ang 慈惠堂

Tz'u-chao tsung-chu 慈照宗主

*Tz'u-chao tsung-chu shih nien-fo fa-yüan
   chieh* 慈照宗主示念佛發願偈

tz'u-hua 詞話

Tz'u-yün 慈雲

wai-tao 外道 (non Buddhist)

Wan-li 萬曆

Wan-nien shih-hsien 萬年時限

Wan-shih hsiu 萬事休

Wang Ch'ang-sheng 汪長生

wang-ch'i hei-jan 王氣黑然

Wang Chung 王衷

Wang Chung-shun 王忠順

Wang Chüeh-i 王覺一

Wang Fo-er 王佛兒

Wang Hao-hsien 王好賢

Wang Hsiao-po 王小波

Wang Hsien-chih 王仙芝

Wang Huai-te 王懷德

Wang Huai-ku 王懷古

Wang Jih-hsiu 王日休

Wang K'e 王科

Wang Lun 王倫

Wang Pin 王斌

Wang P'u-shan 汪普善

Wang San-huai 王三槐

Wang Sen 王森

Wang Shuang-hsi 王雙喜

Wang Tien-k'uei 王殿魁

Wang Tse 王則

Wang Yang-ming 王陽明

wei 爲

Wei 魏 (dynasty)

wei-lai fo 未來佛

Wei-neng 韋能

Wei shu 魏書

Wei-t'o 韋陀

Wei-wei pu-tung T'ai-shan shen-ken chieh-kuo pao-chüan 巍巍不動太山深根結果寶卷

Wen-chou 溫州

Wen-ch'ang 文昌

Wen-ch'eng ti 文成帝

Wen-hsiang chiao 聞香教

Wen-hsü 文淑

Wen-ti 文帝

Wen-tsung 文宗

Wen Yen-po 文彥博

weng 翁

wu 巫 (shaman)

Wu 武

Wu-an shan 武安山

Wu-chen-ch'üan 悟眞全

Wu Ch'eng-en 吳承恩

wu-chi 無極

wu-chi ch'ing-yang chiao 無極青陽教

Wu-chi lao-tsu 無極老祖

Wu-chi sheng-tsu 無極聖祖

Wu-chiang 吳江

wu-chu 巫祝

Wu-chün 吳郡

Wu Tse-t'ien 武則天

wu-hsing 五行

Wu Kuang 吳廣

Wu-kung 五公

Wu-kung fu 五公符

Wu-k'ung 悟空

wu-lai 無賴

Wu-nien 無念

Wu-ning hsien 武寧縣

wu-p'ai 五派

wu-pu 五部

Wu-shang wang 無上王

Wu-sheng chi-le t'ien 無生極樂天

Wu-sheng ch'uan-ling 無生傳令

Wu-sheng lao-mu 無生老母

Wu-sheng sheng-mu 無生聖母

Wu-sheng pao-kuo 無生寶國

wu-shih 巫師

wu-su 悟俗

Wu-t'ai fo Mi-le 無台佛彌勒

Wu-ti 武帝

'Wu t'ien wu ti hun-tun hsü-k'ung p'in' 無天無地混沌虛空品

Wu-wei chiao 無爲教

Wu-wei chüan 無爲卷

Wu-wei ta-tao 無爲大道

Wu-ying kung fu 五營公符

Wu-ying-shan 無影山

yamen 衙門

yang 陽

yang (ocean) 洋

Yang Chu 楊朱

yang-ch'i 養氣
Yang Hsüan-kan 楊玄感
Yao 堯 (legendary ruler)
Yao 猺 (tribe)
Yao-ch'ih men 瑤池門
Yao-ch'ih chin-mu 瑤池金母
yao-seng 妖僧
Yao-shih ju-lai pao-chüan 藥師如來寶卷
Yao-shih pen-yüan kung-te pao-chüan 藥師本願功德寶卷
yao-tsei 妖賊
yao-tsei fu-che pu-shao 妖賊富者不少
Yao Wen-tzu 姚文字
yao-yen 妖言
Yen-nan 燕南
Yen-hsiang ssu 延祥寺
yin 寅
yin 陰 (female principle)
Yin Chi-nan 殷繼南
Yin hsien 鄞縣
Yin-hua lu 因話錄
Yin Ming-jen 尹明仁
yin-t'ou 印頭
Yin Tzu-yüan 尹資源
Ying-chieh ts'e 應刼冊
Ying-chou 潁州
ying-er 嬰兒
Ying-er chien niang 嬰兒見娘
"Ying-tsung pen-chi" 英宗本紀
yu fa seng 有髮僧
yu-hsia 遊俠
Yu-hsü p'o-hsieh hsiang-pien 又續破邪詳辯

yu-li ch'ien-k'un shih-chieh 又立乾坤世界
Yu-t'an P'u-tu 優曇普度
yu-wei 有爲
Yung-cheng 雍正
Yung-chia 永嘉
Yung-chia Hsüan-chüeh 永嘉玄覺
Yung-p'ing 永平
Yü 禹
Yü-hang 餘杭
Yü-lan Kuan-yin pao-chüan 魚籃觀音寶卷
Yü Sheng-kung 余聖功
Yüan 元
Yüan-chao 元照
Yüan chiao 圓教
yüan-ch'i 元氣
Yüan-chou 袁州
Yüan-chüeh ching 圓覺經
Yüan-jung ssu-t'u san-kuan hsüan fo t'u 圓融四土三觀選佛圖
Yüan-jung ssu-t'u t'u 圓融四土圖
yüan luan 元卵
yüan-shuai 元帥
Yüeh-fu tsa lu 樂府雜錄
Yüeh-kuang p'u-sa 月光菩薩
Yüeh-kuang t'ung-tzu ching 月光童子經
Yün-ch'eng 雲城
yün-ch'eng shou-chüan 雲程手卷
yün-ch'i 運氣
Yün-kang 雲岡

Index

Aboriginal mythology, 142-143,
    240n38-42
Aldebert, 169
Amitābha, 48, 141-142, 152, 156-
    157, 242n59
Anabaptists, 4, 69, 158
Aśoka, 68

Bodhisattva, 2, 48, 58, 89, 165-166
Böhm, Hans, 66, 71, 170
Burmese sects, 220, 244n83

Chai-t'ang, (vegetarian hall), 7, 107
Chan Hok-lam, 34
Chang Hsien-chung, 198
Ch'ang-sheng chiao, 7-11
Chen-k'ung chia-hsiang, wu-sheng
    fu-mu (native land of true empti-
    ness and the eternal parents), see
    Wu-sheng fu-mu
Ch'en Yu-liang, 100
Chia-ch'ing emperor, 38-40
Chih-p'an, 35
Chin-tan p'ai, 124
Ching-t'u, see Pure Land Buddhism
Chou Tzu-wang, vii
Chu-hung, 37, 236n9
Chu Yung-deh Richard, 47
Chu Yüan-chang (Ming T'ai-tsu),
    99-100, 147-148
Chüeh-lo Yung-te, 7

Confucius, 20
Cohn, Norman, 14
Creation myths, 135-136

DeGroot, J. J. M., 25, 49-50

Edkins, Joseph, 48
Eight Trigrams (sect, rebellion), 39,
    79
Eliade, Mircea, 15
Eschatology, 145-161
Eternal Mother, see Wu-sheng lao-
    mu
Eudo (Eudes de l'Etoile), 169-170

Fa-ch'ing, 82, 225n36
Fa-ch'üan, 82
Fatalism, 149-150, 242n58
Fate, 146-150
Feng-shen yen-i, 148
Five Pecks of Rice sect (Heavenly
    Master sect), 25, 73-75
Fo-shuo Mi-le hsia-sheng ching, 81-
    82, 150
Fu-hsi, 31-32, 135, 142-143

Han Lin-er, 99-101, 157
Han Shan-t'ung, 84, 98-100, 157
Heaven and Earth society, see T'ien-
    ti hui
Hobsbawn, E. J., 14

Index

Hsi Wang-mu, 128, 139-140,
 239nn24-28
Hsiang Hai-ming, 83
Hsiao-shih Chin-kang k'e-i (Liturgy
 explaining the Diamond Sūtra),
 182
Hsieh-chiao (heretical religion), 7
Hsien-t'ien tao, 107, 169
Hsü Hung-ju, 102, 173
Hsü-k'an p'o-hsieh hsiang-pien, 30,
 213n46
Hsü Shou-hui, 99, 230n81
Hsü T'ien-te, 248n28
Huang Ch'ao, 197-198
Huang Yü-p'ien, 29-32, 213n46
Hui-yüan, 34-35, 37, 214n67,
 227n46
Hutter, Jacob, 169-170

I-kuan tao, 2, 106-107, 201-202,
 231n95
Isis, cult of, 60

Kuan Ti (Kuan Kung), 10
Kuan-yin, 8-10, 139, 142, 165-166
Kung Ch'ang, 104, 166-168
K'ung Ch'ing-chüeh, 110-111
Kuo P'u-sa, 84
Kuo Tzu-hsing, 99, 173, 230n76

Lan-feng, 114
Lao-kuan chai, 119-120
Le-pang wen-lei, 86
Leadership, 64-66, 162-176, 248n28
Leff, Gordon, 16
Li-chi, 20, 22
Li Fu-ta, 101, 173
Li Shou-k'ung, 33
Li Tao-ming, 38
Li Tzu-ch'eng, 198
Li Wen-ch'eng, 105, 172, 175
Liang t'ien ch'ih, 84
Lin Ch'ing, 79, 105, 167, 249n28
Liu Chih-hsieh, 39, 105, 158, 172
Liu Fu-t'ung, 98-100, 157
Liu Sung, 105, 172
Lo Ch'ing (Lo Tsu, Lo Huai) 37,
 113-115, 167, 232n14, 247n16
Lo sect, (Lo chiao), 109, 113-129,

174, 232nn14-18, 233nn19-20
Lollards, 17
Lü K'un, 28, 102

Maitreya (Maitreyan eschatology),
 19, 40, 68-69, 97-99, 105-107,
 120-123, 150-161, 166-167,
 226n38, 233n30, 242n59, 245n86
Maitreya (sect) 2, 25-26, 80-85,
 226n40, 227nn41-43
Mandate of Heaven, 146-150
Manichaeism, 2, 75-80, 223nn6-11
Mao Tzu-yüan, 35-36, 66, 90-95,
 130-132
Marxist interpretations, 42-45
Meditation, 188-192
Membership rituals, 188-190
Mencius, 20
Ming Yü-chen, 29, 100
Mithra, cult of, 60
Mo-ni kuang fo chiao fa i lüeh, 78
Mu-lien, 181
Mystery societies, 58-62

Na-yen-ch'eng, 104, 149
Naquin, Susan, 39, 215n73
Nien-fo, 85-89
Nü-kua, 31-32, 135, 142-143

Official interpretations, 20-29
Orthodox Buddhist interpretations,
 34-37

Pai-yün tsung, *see* White Cloud sect
Pang Hu, 84
Pao-chüan, 31, 66, 176, 179-186,
 253nn62-64
Paradise, 144-146
Peasant rebellions, 69-70, 193-199
P'eng Ying-yü, *vii*
Phenomenology, 12
P'iao Kao, 125-126, 140, 143-144
Pien-wen, 178-179
Planchette, 185, 254n84
P'o-hsieh hsiang-pien, 29-32,
 213n46
Pu-tai, 151
P'u-tu, 91-93
Pure Land Buddhism, 85-89, 152

Puritans, 221n41

Red Swastika society, 192, 256n108
Republican Chinese interpretations,
  32-34, 41-42
Ritual, 186-192, 255n100
Russell, Jeffrey B., 17-18

Sākyamuni, 36, 83-84, 104, 136,
  159, 161, 166, 214n64, 245n86
San Kuan, 10
San-kuo yen-i, 243n64
Scriptures, 176-186
Secrecy, 5, 11, 199-203, 219n29
Secret societies, 5, 11, 49-50, 54-58,
  199-203, 259nn31-32
Sects, 62
Shamanism, 163-165
Shan-tao, 35
Shao Hsün-cheng, 44
Shigematsu Shunshō, 45-46
Shih-fo chuang (k'ou), 103-105
Shui-hu chuan, 156
Simons, Menno, 4, 72
Stone Buddha Village, *see* Shih-fo
  chuang
Sun Ta-yu, 71
Sun Tso-min, 43
Sun worship, 78-79, 224n20,
  225nn21-22
Sun Yat-sen, 41
Sung Chiang, 195
Sung Tzu-hsien, 83
Suzuki Chūsei, 45-47, 51

Tai Hsüan-chih, 33-34
T'ai-p'ing tao, *see* Yellow Turbans
Talmon, Yonina, 14-15
Tanchelm, 66, 169-170, 249n29
T'ang Sai-er, 38, 250n34
Tao-an, 82
T'ao Ch'eng-chang, 41
T'ao Hsi-sheng, 33
Taoist groups, 73-75, 222nn1-5
Three Religions (teachings), 133-
  134, 236nn9-10
Three Stages, Sect of the, 152

T'ien-t'ai, 61, 66, 68, 130-132
T'ien-ti hui 5, 55, 202-203, 218n10,
  259nn30-32
Triad society, *see* T'ien-ti hui
Tsukamoto Zenryū, 50
Tsung-chien, 35
Tsung-pen, 36
Tu Wan-i, 95
T'ui-pei t'u, 96, 229n69

Wai-tao (non-Buddhist), 233n19
Waldensians, 4, 158
Wang Chüeh-i, 106
Wang Huai-ku, 83
Wang Jih-hsiu, 88, 133, 154-155
Wang San-huai, 248n28
Wang Sen, 102
Wang Tse, 83-84
Weber, Max, 50, 215n73, 217n95
Wen-hsü, 177-178
Wen-ti (Sui dynasty), 153-154
White Cloud sect, 2, 109-113,
  232nn9-10
White Lotus (sect, society, religion),
  2, 27-28, 38-48, 54-55, 57, 72-73,
  84-85, 89-108
Williams, George H., 16
Wilson, Byron R., 14
Wu-chi sheng-tsu (Holy Patriarch of
  the Limitless), 121
Wu-shen fu-mu (Eternal Parents),
  66, 105, 156, 189, 238n20
Wu-sheng lao-mu, 31, 55-56, 105-
  107, 135-141, 239nn31-35
Wu-ti (Liang dynasty), 153
Wu Tse-t'ien, 226n38
Wu-wei chiao, *see* Lo sect (Lo chiao)

Yang, C. K. 6, 21, 51-52
Yang K'uan, 43-44
Yellow Turbans, 73-75, 222nn1-5,
  244n75
*Yüan-jung ssu-t'u san-kuan hsüan-
  fo t'u*, 92-93
Yüeh-kuang P'u-sa, 82

Zürcher, Erik, 23

HARVARD EAST ASIAN SERIES

1. *China's Early Industrialization: Sheng Hsuan-huai (1884-1916) and Mandarin Enterpise.* By Albert Feuerwerker.
2. *Intellectual Trends in the Ch'ing Period.* By Liang Ch'i-ch'ao. Translated by Immanuel C. Y. Hsü.
3. *Reform in Sung China: Wang An-shih (1021-1086) and His New Policies.* By James T. C. Liu.
4. *Studies on the Population of China, 1368-1953.* By Ping-ti Ho.
5. *China's Entrance into the Family of Nations: The Diplomatic Phase, 1858-1880.* By Immanuel C. Y. Hsü.
6. *The May Fourth Movement: Intellectual Revolution in Modern China.* By Chow Tse-tsung.
7. *Ch'ing Administrative Terms: A Translation of the Terminology of the Six Boards with Explanatory Notes.* Translated and edited by E-tu Zen Sun.
8. *Anglo-American Steamship Rivalry in China, 1862-1874.* By Kwang-Ching Liu.
9. *Local Government in China under the Ch'ing.* By T'ung-tsu Ch'ü.
10. *Communist China, 1955-1959: Policy Documents with Analysis.* With a foreword by Robert R. Bowie and John K. Fairbank. (Prepared at Harvard University under the joint auspices of the Center for International Affairs and the East Asian Research Center.)
11. *China and Christianity: The Missionary Movement and the Growth of Chinese Antiforeignisms, 1860-1870.* By Paul A. Cohen.
12. *China and the Helping Hand, 1937-1945.* By Arthur N. Young.
13. *Research Guide to the May Fourth Movement: Intellectual Revolution in Modern China, 1915-1924.* By Chow Tse-tsung.
14. *The United States and the Far Eastern Crisis of 1933-1938: From the Manchurian Incident through the Initial Stage of the Undeclared Sino-Japanese War.* By Dorothy Borg.
15. *China and the West, 1858-1861: The Origins of the Tsungli Yamen.* By Masataka Banno.
16. *In Search of Wealth and Power: Yen Fu and the West.* By Benjamin Schwartz.
17. *The Origins of Entrepreneurship in Meiji Japan.* By Johannes Hirschmeier, S.V.D.
18. *Commissioner Lin and the Opium War.* By Hsin-pao Chang.
19. *Money and Monetary Policy in China, 1845-1895.* By Frank H. H. King.
20. *China's Wartime Finance and Inflation, 1937-1945.* By Arthur N. Young.
21. *Foreign Investment and Economic Development in China, 1840-1937.* By Chi-ming Hou.

22. *After Imperialism: The Search for a New Order in the Far East, 1921-1931.* By Akira Iriye.
23. *Foundations of Constitutional Government in Modern Japan, 1868-1900.* By George Akita.
24. *Political Thought in Early Meiji Japan, 1868-1889.* By Joseph Pittau, S.J.
25. *China's Struggle for Naval Development, 1839-1895.* By John L. Rawlinson.
26. *The Practice of Buddhism in China, 1900-1950.* By Holmes Welch.
27. *Li Ta-chao and the Origins of Chinese Marxism.* By Maurice Meisner.
28. *Pa Chin and His Writings: Chinese Youth Between the Two Revolutions.* By Olga Lang.
29. *Literary Dissent in Communist China.* By Merle Goldman.
30. *Politics in the Tokugawa Bakufu, 1600-1843.* By Conrad Totman.
31. *Hara Kei in the Politics of Compromise, 1905-1915.* By Tetsuo Najita.
32. *The Chinese World Order: Traditional China's Foreign Relations.* Edited by John K. Fairbank.
33. *The Buddhist Revival in China.* By Holmes Welch.
34. *Traditional Medicine in Modern China: Science, Nationalism, and the Tensions of Cultural Change.* By Ralph C. Croizier.
35. *Party Rivalry and Political Change in Taishō Japan.* By Peter Duus.
36. *The Rhetoric of Empire: American China Policy, 1895-1901.* By Marilyn B. Young.
37. *Radical Nationalist in Japan: Kita Ikki, 1883-1937.* By George M. Wilson.
38. *While China Faced West: American Reformers in Nationalist China, 1928-1937.* By James C. Thomson, Jr.
39. *The Failure of Freedom: A Portrait of Modern Japanese Intellectuals.* By Tatsuo Arima.
40. *Asian Ideas of East and West: Tagore and His Critics in Japan, China, and India.* By Stephen N. Hay.
41. *Canton under Communism: Programs and Politics in a Provincial Capital, 1949-1968.* By Ezra F. Vogel.
42. *Ting Wen-chiang: Science and China's New Culture.* By Charlotte Furth.
43. *The Manchurian Frontier in Ch'ing History.* By Robert H. G. Lee.
44. *Motoori Norinaga, 1730-1801.* By Shigeru Matsumoto.
45. *The Comprador in Nineteenth Century China: Bridge between East and West.* By Yen-p'ing Hao.
46. *Hu Shih and the Chinese Renaissance: Liberalism in the Chinese Revolution, 1917-1937.* By Jerome B. Grieder.
47. *The Chinese Peasant Economy: Agricultural Development in Hopei and Shan-tung, 1890-1949.* By Ramon H. Myers.
48. *Japanese Tradition and Western Law: Emperor, State, and Law in the Thought of Hozumi Yatsuka.* By Richard H. Minear.

49. *Rebellion and Its Enemies in Late Imperial China: Militarization and Social Structure, 1796-1864.* By Philip A. Kuhn.

50. *Early Chinese Revolutionaries: Radical Intellectuals in Shanghai and Chekiang, 1902-1911.* By Mary Backus Rankin.

51. *Communications and Imperial Control in China: Evolution of the Palace Memorial System, 1693-1735.* By Silas H. L. Wu.

52. *Vietnam and the Chinese Model: A Comparative Study of Nguyễn and Ch'ing Civil Government in the First Half of the Nineteenth Century.* By Alexander Barton Woodside.

53. *The Modernization of the Chinese Salt Administration, 1900-1920.* By S. A. M. Adshead.

54. *Chang Chih-tung and Educational Reform in China.* By William Ayers.

55. *Kuo Mo-jo: The Early Years.* By David Tod Roy.

56. *Social Reformers in Urban China: The Chinese Y.M.C.A., 1895-1926.* By Shirley S. Garrett.

57. *Biographic Dictionary of Chinese Communism, 1921-1965.* By Donald W. Klein and Anne B. Clark.

58. *Imperialism and Chinese Nationalism: Germany in Shantung.* By John E. Shrecker.

59. *Monarchy in the Emperor's Eyes: Image and Reality in the Ch'ien-lung Reign.* By Harold L. Kahn.

60. *Yamagata Aritomo in the Rise of Modern Japan, 1838-1922.* By Roger F. Hackett.

61. *Russia and China: Their Diplomatic Relations to 1728.* By Mark Mancall.

62. *The Yenan Way in Revolutionary China.* By Mark Selden.

63. *The Mississippi Chinese: Between Black and White.* By James W. Loewen.

64. *Liang Ch'i-ch'ao and Intellectual Transition in China, 1890-1907.* By Hao Chang.

65. *A Korean Village: Between Farm and Sea.* By Vincent S. R. Brandt.

66. *Agricultural Change and the Peasant Economy of South China.* By Evelyn S. Rawski.

67. *The Peace Conspiracy: Wang Ching-wei and the China War, 1937-1941.* By Gerald Bunker.

68. *Mori Arinori.* By Ivan Hall.

69. *Buddhism under Mao.* By Holmes Welch.

70. *Student Radicals in Prewar Japan.* By Henry Dewitt Smith II.

71. *The Romantic Generation of Modern Chinese Writiers.* By Leo Ou-fan Lee.

72. *Deus Destroyed: The Image of Christianity in Early Modern Japan.* By George Elison.

73. *Land Taxation in Imperial China, 1750-1911.* By Yeh-chien Wang.

74. *Chinese Ways in Warfare.* Edited by Frank A. Kierman, Jr., and John K. Fairbank.

75. *Pepper, Guns, and Parleys: The Dutch East India Company and China, 1662-1681.* By John E. Wills, Jr.
76. *A Study of Samurai Income and Enrepreneurship: Quantitative Analyses of Economic and Social Aspects of the Samurai in Tokugawa and Meiji Japan.* By Kozo Yamamura.
77. *Between Tradition and Modernity: Wang T'ao and Reform in Late Ch'ing China.* By Paul. A. Cohen.
78. *The Abortive Revolution: China under Nationalist Rule, 1927-1937.* By Lloyd E. Eastman.
79. *Russia and the Roots of the Chinese Revolution, 1896-1911.* By Don C. Price.
80. *Toward Industrial Democracy: Management and Workers in Modern Japan.* By Kunio Odaka.
81. *China's Republican Revolution: The Case of Kwangtung, 1895-1913.* By Edward J. M. Rhoads.
82. *Politics and Policy in Traditional Korea.* By James B. Palais.
83. *Folk Buddhist Religion: Dissenting Sects in Late Traditional China.* By Daniel L. Overmyer.